Theories
of Counseling

Theories of Counseling

Third Edition

Herbert M. Burks, Jr.
Michigan State University

Buford Stefflre
Formerly of Michigan State University

McGraw-Hill Book Company

New York St. Louis San Francisco Auckland Bogotá Düsseldorf
Johannesburg London Madrid Mexico Montreal New Delhi
Panama Paris São Paulo Singapore Sydney Tokyo Toronto

THEORIES OF COUNSELING

1 2 3 4 5 6 7 8 9 0 FGRFGR 7 8 3 2 1 0 9

This book was set in Times Roman by Automated Composition Service, Inc.
The editors were William A. Talkington and James R. Belser;
the cover was designed by Pencils Portfolio, Inc.;
the production supervisor was Charles Hess.
Fairfield Graphics was printer and binder.

Library of Congress Cataloging in Publication Data

Main entry under title:

Theories of counseling.

    Second ed. by B. Stefflre and W. H. Grant.
    Includes indexes.
    1. Personnel service in education—Addresses,
essays, lectures. I. Burks, Herbert M.
II. Stefflre, Buford. III. Stefflre, Buford, ed.
Theories of counseling.
LB1027.5.S74 1979   371.4'08   78-23389
ISBN 0-07-009061-0

Contents

Preface

As counselors, all of us operate on the basis of theory. Our hypotheses and actions are based upon certain notions about the fundamental nature of people, the ways in which human behavior develops, and the ways in which it can be modified. Our theories may be largely implicit and unrecognized, or they may be highly formal and refined. Nevertheless, they are there, continually influencing our behavior as we attempt to help those who have sought our assistance. An assumption underlying this book is that one's efforts as a counselor are apt to be more sound and helpful if they are based upon a carefully developed personal theory rather than upon vaguely perceived assumptions and hypotheses. A second assumption of the book is that one's personal theory of counseling can best be developed—or modified—on the basis of a reasoned and critical examination of the best thinking, experience, and research by others who have faced counseling problems and have made their answers available for public scrutiny. Accordingly, we have presented those theories or approaches that, in our judgment, have the most relevance for the contemporary counselor. At the same time, we have attempted to help students in their quest for a personal theory by pointing out what good theories are like, what they are supposed to do, and how well the theories included in this volume have met those criteria. Students who are thus informed should be better equipped to find their own highly personal answers to the question, "How can I, as a counselor, best serve those who have placed their trust in me as a professional helper?"

This book is intended primarily for use as a text in courses with such titles as "Counseling Theories," "Theories of Counseling and Psychotherapy," "Introduction to Counseling," and "Counseling Practice." It may also be used as a supplementary text for a variety of courses in the general areas of counseling, counseling psychology, and pupil and student personnel services. It is suitable for use at either the master's or the doctoral level and for courses offered by departments of psychology as well as by colleges of education.

The organizational plan of the book proceeds from the general to the specific and back to the general. Chapter 1 describes the nature, origins, and functions of theory and establishes a set of criteria for evaluating theories; thus, it gives the student the necessary background and framework for reading and understanding the specific theory chapters that follow.

The eight theories are then presented in Chapters 2 through 7. Each of these chapters has largely the same format, in order to facilitate students' comparisons of the theories. The major headings in this format include Introduction, Philosophy and Major Concepts, Normal Development of the Individual, Development of Maladaptive Behavior, Goals of Counseling, Process and Techniques of Counseling, Illustrative Case Material, and Summary and Evaluation.

In Chapter 8, the theories are evaluated against the criteria that were established in Chapter 1, common elements are identified, and theory-related issues are discussed. This chapter helps students to see the relationship between what theories are supposed to do and what they have in fact done. Students are also helped to see that in many ways the various theories are more alike than different. This gives students a useful perspective from which to develop their own personal theories of counseling.

An examination of other current books about this subject suggests that this is the only book in which the theories are presented primarily by specialists, and independent evaluations of the theories are made by eclectics or generalists. Each separate theory chapter has been written by a person who is highly knowledgeable about that theory. Yet, Chapter 1 (in which criteria for evaluating the theories are established) and Chapter 8 (in which the theories are subsequently evaluated) are written by persons who are more eclectically oriented. This feature helps to ensure a high degree of familiarity and detail in presenting the content of a theory, yet preserves the objectivity and perspective needed in order to reach a balanced evaluation.

Many changes have taken place in the years that have elapsed since the earlier editions of this volume were published. In addition to broad social, economic, and political changes, a number of important developments have occurred that are directly related to counseling. One of the most prominent of these developments is that nontraditional theories of counseling have come to play an increasingly important role in the work of counselors. While most of these theories have been around for some time, it is only in recent years that they have caught on. Gestalt therapy, transactional analysis, and reality therapy are good examples of this trend. In a somewhat similar manner, Ellis's rational-emotive approach, although prominent in clinical settings for many years, has received increased attention from counselors.

A second major development has been a further broadening of the scope of counseling from the traditional educational setting—schools and colleges—to encompass a variety of community agencies and other institutional settings, including rehabilitation agencies, family service organizations, employment services, marriage counseling clinics, mental health clinics, drop-in centers, pregnancy counseling centers, correctional agencies, drug and alcohol abuse centers, and so on. While this has not been a sudden phenomenon, it has accelerated greatly in recent years. Interestingly, the shift has been reflected in the content of the two previous editions of this book. The first edition had two chapters about counseling in educational settings, while the second had only one such chapter.

A third development has to do with changes in the more traditional theories. For example, many adherents to the behavioral school have come to place increased importance upon thoughts and feelings, and such "internal behaviors" are now thought to be amenable to study and to self-control. This trend has been accompanied by a growing tendency on the part of some client-centered counselors to use highly directive techniques at times, such as information giving, confrontation, direct instruction, and overt behavior modification. Psychoanalytic theory likewise has been reexamined, with a greater degree of independence accorded the ego, while at the same time there has been a revival of interest in many of Freud's original formulations. Finally, trait-factor theory has developed an increased concern for the affective life of the client and now encourages the use of a broader scope of techniques.

Many additional developments in the field of counseling might be cited—changes in counselor role, including the conception of the counselor as a change agent; the use of paraprofessionals to handle certain counselor functions; a renewed emphasis upon in-service training; the sensitivity and encounter group movements; the increased attraction of counselors to private practice, with the attendant issues of licensure and certification; new research strategies, designs, and findings; and so on. Suffice it to say that in the last few years numerous changes have occurred which have a bearing upon the practice and theoretical underpinnings of counseling.

How, then, has this book been changed to meet more readily the needs of those who are counseling or who are preparing to become counselors? The major changes from previous editions are the following:

1 Four new theories have been added, which brings the total number of theories to eight. The Rational-Emotive Approach to Counseling has been added as the topic of Chapter 5. Gestalt Therapy, Transactional Analysis, and Reality Therapy have been added in a new Chapter 7 about Recent Approaches.

2 To make room for some of the new theories, and in recognition of the fact that the scope of counseling has expanded beyond strictly educational settings, the former chapter about counseling theory and practice in the school has been deleted. The number of pages allocated to the new edition has also been expanded in order to accommodate the new theories.

3 The previous chapters about Client-Centered Theory, Trait-Factor Theory, Psychoanalytic Theory, and Behavioral Views of Counseling have all been rewritten completely. This was necessary in order to update these chapters, since the second-edition versions of the chapters were largely unchanged from those in the first edition.

4 An organizational format that is basically the same has been used throughout the theory chapters. There was little commonality in the organization of such chapters in the previous editions.

5 More extended case examples have been included in all the theory chapters (Chapters 2 through 7).

6 The major content of the first and last chapters has been retained, since by its nature it is relatively timeless. However, important new material has been added to each of these chapters. In Chapter 1, new definitions of counseling have been included and discussed, and new material about the counselor's role has been added. The last chapter has been revised to incorporate an examination and evaluation of the four new theories in addition to the theories included originally. In addition, the sections dealing with supportive evidence and crucial determinants have been revised substantially.

As with any project of this magnitude, the efforts and sacrifices of many people were involved. I am especially indebted to Mrs. Leta Stefflre for allowing me to revise the work of her late husband, Buford Stefflre, and to share the editorship of this volume with him. In the editing process, I have reached an even deeper appreciation of his vision and depth of thinking. I would also like to thank Dr. Walter F. Johnson of Michigan State University, former Consulting Editor of the Guidance, Counseling, and Student Personnel in Education Series of the McGraw-Hill Book Company, for his guidance and support concerning the many problems with which an editor must deal.

The contributing authors must, of course, share much of the credit for the completion of this volume. My thanks to the "old" authors for their willingness to provide completely rewritten chapters; to the new authors for their willingness to undertake their challenging tasks; and to all—old and new—for their outstanding cooperation.

Finally, I wish to thank my wife and children, who have altered their plans unselfishly during so many evenings, weekends, and vacation periods to facilitate the completion of this book.

Herbert M. Burks, Jr.

About the Authors

Norman Abeles is professor of psychology and professor at the Counseling Center at Michigan State University. He received his bachelor's degree at New York University and his master's and doctorate are from the University of Texas at Austin. Professor Abeles is a diplomate of the American Board of Professional Psychology in counseling psychology and has served as a trustee of that Board. In 1968–1969 he was Fulbright Professor at the University of Utrecht in the Netherlands, and he served there again as a visiting professor in 1975. He is a fellow of the American Psychological Association and has served as the chairperson of its Policy and Planning Board. He has done research and writing in the fields of both counseling and clinical psychology and has served as consultant to the Peace Corps, the Social Security Administration, and various counseling and mental health agencies. Richard Levine, the editorial assistant on Professor Abeles' chapter, recently completed his doctorate in psychology at Michigan State University. His dissertation was entitled, "An Inquiry into Psychodynamic Correlates of High Romanticism in Males."

Donald A. Biggs is professor of Counseling Psychology and Student Development at the State University of New York at Albany. Formerly, he was professor of Educational Psychology, Director of Student Life Studies and Planning, and

Assistant to the Vice President for Student Affairs at the University of Minnesota. His master's degree is from Ball State University and his doctorate from the University of California, Los Angeles. From 1959 to the present he has been editor of *Counseling and Values*, and he has served on the Ethics Committee and the Research Awards Committee of the American Personnel and Guidance Association. As a visiting professor he has taught graduate courses in personnel work, counseling psychology, and tests and measurement at New York University, McGill University, and the University of Dayton, Ohio. During 1975–1976 he was a Fulbright Visiting Professor at the University of Aston, Birmingham, England. He is the author of numerous articles and research studies in the areas of evaluation of student personnel programs and studies of college student characteristics.

Herbert M. Burks, Jr. is a professor in the Department of Counseling, Personnel Services, and Educational Psychology at Michigan State University. He received his bachelor's degree summa cum laude from Roanoke College, his master's degree from the University of Virginia, and his doctorate in counseling psychology from the University of Minnesota. He served for six years in the public schools of Roanoke, Virginia as teacher, counselor, and guidance coordinator. He also served for five years as a full-time instructor in the Department of Educational Psychology at the University of Minnesota and for three years was a faculty member in the counseling department at the University of Virginia. Since 1969 he has been a member of the faculty of the College of Education at Michigan State University. Dr. Burks is coauthor of two books and author of a number of articles in the professional literature on counseling. He has served as a consulting editor to several professional journals and is a past president of the Counselor Educators of Michigan. He is a member of the American Psychological Association, the American Personnel and Guidance Association, and the American Educational Research Association.

Albert Ellis is executive director of the Institute for Rational-Emotive Therapy in New York City and adjunct professor of clinical psychology at Rutgers University and United States International University. He received his bachelor's degree from the City College of New York and his master's and doctorate in clinical psychology from Columbia University. Dr. Ellis is a diplomate of the American Board of Professional Psychology in clinical psychology and of the American Board of Psychological Hypnosis. He has been chief psychologist of the New Jersey State Diagnostic Center and of the New Jersey Department of Institutions and Agencies, and a consultant in clinical psychology to the Veterans Administration. He has received the Humanist Award of the Year in 1972 and awards for Distinguished Professional Psychology and for Research from the Society for the Scientific Study of Sex; the Association for Sex Educators, Counselors, and Therapists; and the Division of Psychotherapy of the American Psychological Association. He has held offices in several scientific and professional societies, having been president of the Division of Consulting Psychology of the American Psychological Association, president of the Society for the Scientific

Study of Sex, and vice president of the American Academy of Psychotherapists. He is the author of over 500 articles and 41 books and monographs.

Steven E. Elson is a staff psychologist at the Klingberg Family Centers in New Britain, Connecticut and a member of the adjunct faculty in the department of psychology at Central Connecticut State College. He received his bachelor's degree in psychology from Westmont College in Santa Barbara, California; his master's in experimental psychology from San Jose State University, also in California; and his doctorate from the Department of Counseling, Personnel Services, and Educational Psychology at Michigan State University. Dr. Elson previously served as a staff psychologist at the Ingham County Juvenile Court in Lansing, Michigan and as a personnel psychologist in the United States Army. He has published in the areas of counseling psychology and counselor education. He is licensed at the independent practice level of psychology in Connecticut and is listed in the National Register of Health Services Providers in Psychology.

Donald L. Grummon is professor of psychology at Michigan State University, where he serves as director of the clinical training program and has a joint appointment with the Counseling Center. He previously served as director of the Counseling Center. His bachelor's degree is from DePauw University, his master's from Ohio State University, and his doctorate from the University of Chicago. He served for two years as a psychologist at the Cheltenham School for Boys (a training school for court-committed delinquents) and then was at the University of Chicago where he was an assistant professor of psychology, a counselor, and administrative and research coordinator in the counseling center. He has written in the fields of both counseling and clinical psychology. While at Ohio State University and at the University of Chicago, Dr. Grummon worked closely with Carl Rogers.

N. Kenneth LaFleur is an associate professor in the counseling department at the University of Virginia. He formerly held positions as a secondary school teacher and counselor, a staff psychologist with the Battle Creek Veterans Administration Hospital, and a psychometrist consultant for the Michigan School for the Blind. His bachelor's degree is from Calvin College, and he has earned the Master's and Doctor of Philosophy degrees in counseling psychology from Michigan State University. He has published in the areas of behavioral counseling and research methods and holds memberships in the American Psychological Association (Division 17), the Association for the Advancement of Behavior Therapy, the American Educational Research Association (Division E), and the American Personnel and Guidance Association.

Buford Stefflre was a professor in the College of Education at Michigan State University at the time of his death. His bachelor's degree was in English from the University of California, and his graduate degrees in counseling were from the University of Southern California. He worked for fifteen years with the Los Angeles City Schools as a teacher, counselor, and supervisor of counseling. He had been at Michigan State University since 1955 in the Department of Guidance and Pupil Personnel Services. He served as editor of the *Personnel and Guidance Journal;* as issue chairman of the "Guidance and Pupil Personnel" issue of the *Review of Educational Research* which was published in April 1963; and as co-author of the section on "Counseling Theory" in the *Encyclopedia of Educational Research*, published in 1969. He was the author of numerous articles in professional psychological and educational journals and three books on guidance and counseling.

Edmund G. Williamson is professor emeritus of psychology and dean emeritus of students at the University of Minnesota. His bachelor's degree is from the University of Illinois and his doctorate from the University of Minnesota. Dean Williamson was the recipient of the research award in 1953 and the Nancy C. Wimmer Award in 1962 from the American Personnel and Guidance Association. He was a Fulbright visiting lecturer at Tokyo University in 1955. From 1950 to 1970 he was chairman of the Veterans Administration Advisory Committee on Counseling Services for Vocational Rehabilitation and Education. Dean Williamson is the author of numerous books and articles in the field of psychology and education and has been active in a number of organizations in these fields.

Theories
of Counseling

Chapter 1

Function of Theory in Counseling

Buford Stefflre and Herbert M. Burks, Jr.

As counseling becomes more recognized as a service of educational and other helping institutions, we must make an effort to conceptualize the counseling process so that its purposes and methods are more amenable to study and understanding. Experienced counselors may need to make a more systematic effort to look at what happens in the counseling interview, in order to understand it within a framework that utilizes their knowledge about human behavior. Inexperienced counselors, or counselors in training, may need to develop some guidelines about what to do during the counseling interview—guidelines that evolve logically from overarching theories. In this chapter, an attempt will be made to define theory and to show its values and limitations. A further attempt will be made to define counseling, and to distinguish it from psychotherapy on the one hand, and instruction on the other. Subsequent chapters will delineate eight of the most important theories that are currently in use.

WHAT IS A THEORY?

Scientists and philosophers have given us many definitions of *theory*. One philosopher has called it a human convention for keeping data in order (Pepper, 1957, p. 71). This philosopher points out that if human memories were better than they are, we should have no need for theory, since we could simply refer to raw data whenever we wanted to consider a problem. Because our memories are fallible, theories are not only convenient but necessary. They enable us to reduce complexities to manageable proportions, so that we can deal with an otherwise overwhelming amount of information. To perform this reducing function, a theory must consist of data plus an interrelating structure that tells us how one piece of information relates to another (Pepper, 1957, p. 72). Another definition says that a theory is a provisional systemization of events. Again, we are being told that a theory is a device that enables us to see relationships between one event or fact and another (McCabe, 1958, p. 49). Currently, it seems fashionable

1

to think of theories as models. A theory, then, may be called a *conceptual model*—for example, the id—which means that it is postulated to explain a process inferred from observed behavior. This definition says that we see certain happenings and that we strive to have them make sense. They make sense only if we are able to postulate some process that, if it were to operate, would result in the observed behavior (McCabe, 1958, p. 49). In a widely used discussion of theory in the field of psychology (Hall & Lindzey, 1970), the evolved definition indicates that "a theory is a set of conventions created by the theorist" (p. 10), and that a theory "should contain a cluster of relevant assumptions systematically related to each other and a set of empirical definitions" (p. 11). Here again are the elements of data—empirical definitions, postulates or conventions, and relevant assumptions—that have appeared in previous definitions. Finally, we come to a most usable and memorable definition which states merely that a theory is a possible world that can be checked against the real world (Pepinsky & Pepinsky, 1954, p. 18).

What these definitions have in common are the elements of reality and belief. *Reality* is the data or behavior that we see and strive to explain. *Belief* is the way that we try to make sense out of the data by relating what we see to conceivable explanations of it. Theory building, then, grows out of our need to make sense of life. A theory is a map on which a few points are known, and the road between points is inferred. Good maps can be filled in as we learn more about the world, and poor ones will need to be thrown away when we find that they are leading us astray.

DO WE NEED THEORY?

Often, experienced counselors and even trainees are scornful of theory, and question its value to them. Students frequently say that they want more practical courses and "not all this theory." A dichotomy between theory and practicality is often assumed. In reality, however, nothing is so practical as a good theory. Like a good map, it tells us what to look for, what to expect, and where to go. The use of theory can be analogous to the learning about life that helps newborn infants make sense out of the booming, buzzing confusion that is their world. The phenomena of nature are not in themselves necessarily ordered. But to operate, we must impose order on them, and this ordering is a function of theory.

Those who feel that they can operate entirely without theory, and even assume an antitheoretical position, are usually basing their behavior on vaguely defined but implicit theory. There is no other way in which they can decide what to do. Intuition, which is often advanced as a substitute for theory, is itself but a crude type of hypothesizing (McDaniel, Lallas, Saum, & Gilmore, 1959, p. 148). "The views of the 'practical men' are usually derived from assumptions and arguments no less complex than those on which theory is based; they are more and not less liable to error because they are less openly expressed" (Campbell, 1953, p. 289). The real question then is not whether we shall operate from theory, since we have no choice in the matter, but rather what theories we shall use and how we shall use them. Specifically, in a counseling situation where a client says to a male counselor, "I hate my mother," the counselor's reactions are limited only by his biological status. He can slap the client, he can run out of the room, he can jump up on his chair, he can reply, "It makes you bitter just thinking about her," or he can do any number of things. When he makes a choice among the responses that are open to him, he must act from theory. That is, he must act from some notion about what the client means by the statement, what that statement means in the life of the individual client, what the proper goals of counseling are, what the function of the counselor is, what techniques are successful in moving toward the determined goals, and the other elements that, taken together, constitute for him a theory of counseling.

WHAT UNDERLYING BASES DO THEORIES HAVE?

Just as the phenomena that we observe can be seen in many different ways, so countless possible theories can be constructed. To explain why we have the theories that we do, we must look at the bases of theory.

Personal Basis

One of the underlying sources of theory is the personal need structure of the theory builder or user. This dimension of theory has been pointed up by Shoben (1962, p. 619), who says that since there is little in the way of research evidence that points to one theory as being superior to another in the field of counseling, we must look within the counselors who use a given theory to determine why they are attracted to that particular one. Certainly this same personal element would seem to be present in theory building. The character, the genius, and the personality of the theory constructor are expressed in the theory developed by that individual.

Historical Basis

A good example of the influence of history on the possibility of theory building is given by Theobald:

> The stated aims of the physical and social sciences are indeed very similar. Their object is to reduce the overwhelming diversity and complexity of reality to simple theoretical regularities so that events can be understood, and, if possible, the future predicted on the basis of the laws discovered. Two steps are generally considered necessary in the evolution of a theory. First, observations of the facts of phenomena to be described, and, second, the formulation of a theory that will cover all the observed facts. It can then be tested by using it for the purposes of prediction: as long as it gives valid results, it remains useful. However, if exceptions are found, it should be modified so that it will cover all the observed facts (1961, p. 40).

Theobald goes on to point out that up to about 500 years ago, theory building in the physical sciences was bound by emotional attachment and belief. The examples of the difficulties of Copernicus are known to us. People could not build and believe in a theory that did not put the earth at the center of the universe.

The social sciences are today, and are perhaps forever, in the position of the physical sciences 500 years ago in terms of the limits placed upon them. It is impossible for us to be completely free of emotional and value elements as theory builders in the social sciences. The social sciences are such that we must always consider "ends." At least at this time in history, desirable ends, or goals, are apt to be "given," and so are not subject to investigation. We cannot escape ethical theory, which points toward what should be, even though it may limit the acceptance of psychological theories regarding what is or can be. Psychological theory may tell us the relative distance and the type of surface of several roads, but only ethical theory can tell us which one is worth taking. For example, we cannot construct theories meaningfully and freely to answer the question, "Which is more efficient, communism or free enterprise?" because we must first ask a prior ethical question, "Which is right?"

Still another limitation on theory building in social science is the fact that research itself, at least with our present techniques, may alter objective reality. In the physical sciences, this influence of researchers on their data is called *the principle of indeterminancy*. In the social sciences, it is quite clear that in many contexts, as soon as we begin to do research the situation we wanted to understand vanishes. A good example of this principle is shown by the placebo effect in counseling. If it may be assumed fairly that a client's behavior has changed as a result of counseling, it is difficult to determine whether the change is associated with the personality of the counselor, the technique of counseling, or the attention given to the client. This last factor—sympathetic attention—has been likened to the physician's placebo. An extension to another area is illustrated by some research on causes of leaving school, research that was conducted in a large school system. A group of potential dropouts was identified and randomized into two groups. One group—the experimental—got all kinds of special treatment and attention, and the other—the control group—did not. True, the experimental group began to behave in a more desirable fashion, but unfortunately for science, the control group began to respond in much the same way. In other words, as soon as research was being conducted in the school, it altered the reality of the situation. The classrooms were different, the halls were different, and objective reality was not what it was when the research began. We must conclude, then, that theories in the social sciences are bound by space and by time. The theories that explain behavior in 1850 may not explain it in the year 2000. The theory that seems reasonable in America may not be useful in the Middle East.

Sociological Basis

Theories are influenced not only by the personal context, but by the cultural context in which the theory builder and user lives. Americans are said to live in a world that is orderly, and so we are attracted to theory in general, and in particular to theories that attempt to make sense of natural phenomena. We believe that it is one's job to discover the order in the universe and to build models (theories) that reflect this order (Hall, 1959, p. 153). In such an orderly universe, we are apt to look for causality and to assume that it is present. The usual arguments against complete causality (*determinism*) include the belief that the individual is unique and complex, that causality may imply teleology, and finally, that the idea of behavior's being *caused* leaves us without the concept of guilt. On the other hand, those arguing for the acceptance of causality would reply that uniqueness is relative in psychology if not in etymology, and that in the history of science many previously complex problems now seem understandable. With regard to teleology, those assuming causality would say that perhaps it is the present expectation, and not the future goal, that motivates. Finally, those espousing causality would say that we may still punish antisocial behavior, but our motives would be to affect the future and not to correct the past. Regardless of the logic of the position, most counselors behave "as if" behavior were both caused, and to some extent, free. Logical contradictions notwithstanding, we believe that there is sufficient order in the psychological universe for us to understand and predict behavior to some extent, but sufficient individual freedom to give us some choices that are relatively free of genetics and of history. We do not ask, "Are people free?" but "How free are they?" The sociological base of theory in America, then, is an orderly one. We look for order in the world, and we find it.

Americans are also concerned with recent times rather than with remote history, and therefore our theories are apt to explain behavior in terms of relatively recent events. Because of this point of view, we may sometimes slip into the error of thinking that since B happened after A, B must have been caused by A. Instruction in formal logic will not always free us of this fallacy, since the culture within which we operate tends to value such causal explanations. A good example of the American concern with the present, as opposed to the concern of some other peoples with the past, was given recently by an American researcher who was working in Florence, Italy. The researcher was trying to discover the effects of university services on community life in small villages. His research designs always called for counting and analyzing the relationships among events that were happening or had just happened. His Italian colleagues, however, who were also interested in the problem, were more apt to approach the hypotheses through a discussion of what the Etruscans did and how this influenced the Romans, what the Romans did and how this influenced the Goths, and so on to the present. The theories built and held by Americans are apt to be time-bound in the sense that they look not very far into the past and not very far into the future, for Americans are most comfortable in "possible worlds" of this kind.

Still another sociological influence in American theory building and theory holding is the English language itself:

> The categories and types that we isolate from the world of phenomena we do not find there because they stare every observer in the face; on the contrary, the world is presented in a kaleidoscopic flux of impressions which has to be organized by our minds. . . . We cut nature up, organize it into concepts, and ascribe significance as we do, largely because we are parties to an agreement to organize it in this way— an agreement that holds throughout our speech community and is codified in the patterns of our language. . . . No individual is free to describe nature with absolute impartiality. . . . (From *The Silent Language*, by Edward T. Hall, pp. 146–147. Copy-

right 1959 by Edward T. Hall. Reprinted by permission of Doubleday & Company, Inc.)

Perhaps the best-known example of the influence of language on perception is the fact that some Eskimo dialects have as many as 20 different words for snow in its various forms and stages. A language like English, with its relative lack of concern for snow, would not lend itself to the same kinds of theory about snow that an Eskimo theorist might build. It has been suggested further that even such a seemingly objective phenomenon as the color spectrum itself is sliced up arbitrarily and differently by different languages. Therefore, there would be people who would be incapable of developing a theory involving, for example, "purple," for purple is not *seen* by the speakers of the language. Purple would not be seen because it could not be isolated and labeled. Our language too, by means of arbitrary designations, forbids us to see what others may see or to think thoughts that others might think.

Philosophical Basis

Although there would seem to be a logical connection between philosophy and practice, it may be questioned whether a given philosophical position will necessarily lead to a specific counseling theory. Wrenn (1959) made a notable attempt to relate philosophy to counseling. Essentially, however, Wrenn pointed to the several philosophical bases that could justify the various school personnel activities that have evolved, rather than starting from philosophical positions and drawing conclusions about the type of services they would suggest consistently. Curriculum theorists have largely given up trying to show necessary bonds between philosophical positions and classroom experiences. Rather, many of them postulate a series of principles between the philosophy and the practice. These principles might stem from a number of different philosophical positions, but they tend to narrow the field of practice if we assume them to be sound principles.

Perhaps the most ambitious effort to relate philosophy to counseling has been made by Barclay (1971), who arbitrarily divides counseling positions or theoretical approaches into two categories—those of the humanists and those of the environmentalists. *Humanistic* approaches are more subject-oriented, and emphasize the importance of self-understanding on the part of the client. By contrast, *environmentalist* approaches are object-oriented, and stress the force of external reality as applied through problem solving or manipulation of the client's environment. Barclay's excellent discussion of these approaches, including their philosophical roots and the corresponding implications for counseling goals, methods, and criteria of evaluation, is well worth the reader's attention.

Another source of guiding principles for counseling might come from the area of mental health. In other words, regardless of the basic philosophy that we hold, perhaps we can agree that mental health is a desirable goal, come to some conclusions as to what constitutes desirable mental health, and then construct a theory of counseling that we hope will lead toward desirable mental health. Unfortunately, however, there is no agreement about what constitutes mental health (Jahoda, 1958, p. 23). Jahoda summarizes current concepts of mental health, and says that there are six criteria that seem most fruitful in considering this concept. The six criteria that she lists are (1) attitudes of an individual toward oneself; (2) growth, development, or self-actualization; (3) integration; (4) autonomy; (5) perception of reality; and (6) environmental mastery. One or more of these criteria would probably be accepted by most theorists in the counseling field as a legitimate goal of their activity. If we accept the first criterion as the best indicator of mental health, certain counseling theories might be suggested, while the last criterion might suggest quite different ones. Our theory building and use are guided, if not by our philosophy, at least by our acceptance of basic principles that are near philosophy in sweep and depth. It is only after such a goal has been clarified and accepted, however, that a reasonable theory can be built. If we were to operate from other principles or philosophical bases, we should have to construct other theories.

In summary, then, theories do not appear at random. If we are to understand why certain theories are constructed and accepted, we need to know something about the philosophical assumptions from which the theory builders and the theory holders operate. We need to know something about the historical context in which the theory appears. We need to understand the sociocultural milieu in which the theory developed. In this milieu, we should want to pay particular attention to the language and to the life view that the inhabitant holds. Finally, we can understand the genesis of a theory only by knowing something about the personality, needs, strengths, and genius of the theory builder.

WHAT DO THEORIES DO?

Once theories have been constructed and accepted, they perform a variety of functions. A theory may lead us to observe relationships that we had overlooked previously. The germ theory pointed out relationships that had long been present, but had made no sense until a theory was built to relate one fact to another. The relationship between sleeping with the windows open in the malaria-ridden South and getting sick with malaria became apparent only after the theory regarding the disease was constructed.

Theories help us to incorporate our data, because theories predict laws just as laws predict events (Campbell, 1953, p. 300). From theories we may define operational truths, because theories involve assertions that lead to predictions which can be tested and verified (McCabe, 1958, p. 51). Theories focus our attention on relevant data by telling us what to look for, and they lead us to the use of consistent terminology. It was only after the construction and acceptance of self-theory that such matters as warmth and friendliness in the classroom received systematic attention from researchers. Theories may help us to construct new methods of behaving in a counseling situation, and may point to ways of evaluating the old ones (Brammer & Shostrom, 1977, p. 28). A doctoral student indicated that he was interested in studying the problem of college students who did not have a declared academic major. When he asked what he should look for in doing research on these students, there was obviously no way to give him an answer until there was some clarification as to what theory about them he was testing. Without a theory, he might have studied such diverse things as their intelligence, their blood types, the color of their hair, their height, or the names of their uncles. After the student had considered the problem, he decided that the most meaningful theory for his investigation was that developed by Super (1972), who suggests that a selection of an occupation constitutes the implementation of a self-concept. It would seem to follow from this theory that a student who was unable to make a tentative selection of occupation would have a very unclear self-concept. Starting from this theoretical basis, the doctoral student was able to proceed with his research. The theory told him what to look for. At the end of his investigation, the theory helped him to incorporate his findings and to make sense of them.

A special problem in the use of theory is its application to individual cases. Theories essentially lead to generalizations about averages, but when dealing with an individual, we often feel the need for principles that explain the unique personality. Yet, in dealing with an individual we need to remember that laws are probability statements, and that the more classes for which we have explanatory laws, the more effectively we can deal with an individual. It would seem that as we narrow the reference cases, we can become more explicit and helpful in explaining individual behavior (Phillips, 1956, p. 75; Pepinsky & Pepinsky, 1954, p. 20). The previously quoted article by Shoben (1962) refers to this problem and points out that the use of theory with an individual case both facilitates and inhibits our behavior. Theory facilitates by helping us to see sense and meaning in the client's behavior, but it may inhibit us by blinding us to the uniqueness of the client. We may force the client to fit on the Procrustean bed of a theory that is applicable to the many.

We need, then, not only theory to help us see what is happening within an individual, but skepticism stemming from the realization that present theories in social science will rarely, if ever, explain the behavior of a given individual completely. At the same time, theory builders should not be deterred in their efforts to develop better theories that will approximate that goal more closely (Allport, 1962a).

It should be noted also that while theories have generic uses, such as those described previously, they also have functions that are highly relevant to counseling per se. Stefflre and Matheny (1968) have presented a detailed discussion of theory in terms of its influence upon the client, the counselor, the counselor educator, and the counseling researcher. Counseling theory has both a direct and an indirect influence upon the client. It directly affects the client's expectations and manner of behaving during counseling; indirectly, the client is affected by the counselor's theory because the client must respond to theory-oriented behavior of the counselor. Theory affects the counselor's behavior insofar as the counselor's actions are based upon the explicit or implicit theories that he or she holds about the nature of counseling and the counseling process. The counselor educator, in turn, may reasonably be presumed to design the educational experiences of counselor candidates in accordance with a preferred model of how counselors should behave in their work. Finally, the researcher's view of the counseling process will help to determine the kind of research performed and the research strategies utilized.

HOW DO WE KNOW A GOOD THEORY?—FORMAL ATTRIBUTES

There are pigs and pigs; there are theories and theories. A good theory may be said to have five formal attributes:

1 *A good theory is clear*, in that there is agreement among its general principles (philosophy), and agreement of its consequences with observation (science). It is clear in that it is communicable, and those who read it will understand what is meant by it. It is an easily read map.

2 *A good theory is comprehensive*, in that it has scope and accounts for much behavior. It will explain what happens to many people in many situations. It approaches all-purpose utility.

3 *A good theory is explicit;* that is, it has precision. While it may make use of such evocative phrases as "psychological warmth" and "fully functioning," these concepts will be translatable into denotative statements so that they can be checked against clear referents in the real world (Frank, 1949, p. 27). It is not the mystical or obscure talk of the theorist that spoils a theory, but the failure to translate such poetry into science.

4 *A good theory is parsimonious* and does not overexplain phenomena. A theory that explains a given event in five different ways is apt not to explain it at all.

5 Finally, *a good theory generates useful research*. Some theories may stand untested for decades because they lack this formal attribute. Other theories that are more heuristic may be excellent theories simply because they stimulate much research that itself proves them false. For example, Ann Roe's theory of vocational development holds that certain kinds of parental treatment lead a person toward certain kinds of occupations. Yet, while the theory has generated numerous studies, in most of these investigations the theory has not been supported by the results (Osipow, 1973, pp. 36–37).

In summary, then, a theory is always a map that is in the process of being filled in with greater detail. We do not so much ask whether it is true, but whether it is helpful.

HOW DO WE USE THEORY?

Among counselors, we may find that attitudes toward the value of various types of theory are on a continuum from the dogmatically theoretical to the dogmatically antitheoretical. Six steps or gradations have been identified (Bone, 1959, p. 99). One person may see psychology as exactly the same as physical science in both goals and methods. Such a person would search for the most rigorous behavioristic theories, and would attempt to find them apart from the influence of society, history, and personality. A second person may believe that the above position is true in principle but not completely so in fact, and will therefore temper this "rigor" with the realization that what is good for physical science may not be good for counseling. A third person would value the idiographic but would press, insofar as possible, toward the nomothetic. Such a person would attempt to wed the values of the physical science with the peculiarities of the social science. A fourth person might use both approaches, yet really feel that the idiographic is the best for most purposes. A fifth might ordinarily make use of clinical insight when working with clients, but would try when possible to check such insight through an approximation of the scientific method. Such a person would have a basic commitment to the idiographic, but some sense of responsibility for using the nomothetic. Finally, there are counselors who would use the completely clinical method and would feel that attempts at theory building and rigorous research are inappropriate as well as impossible.

As we examine counseling theories, we may be appalled by the fact that they do not seem to be based very soundly upon empirical data, or that they are not always skillfully constructed to illuminate the relationships among the facts that we do have. Such a realization may tend to immobilize a new counselor, who may ask, "How can I act when our theories are so poorly supported?" It seems best to resolve this dilemma by making a distinction between action and belief. We may have to act on less evidence than we can demand for belief, since the basis of action is ethical and the basis of belief is cognitive. We cannot wait until theories are perfected, but must operate on the basis of the evidence we have. As we choose among the approaches that are open to us, we may have to take the best of what appears to be a very poor lot. We may have to act "as if" we know, when, in fact, we know we do not know (Allport, 1962b, p. 381).

Conflicting theories also may be somewhat traumatizing to the student. Closer examination, however, may in some cases indicate that theories complement rather than contradict one another (McCabe, 1958, p. 50). The use of more than one theory may point to the same facts, and may give clarity where previously we had confusion. The analogy might be made of the use of a variety of stage lights in a theatrical production. Sometimes the overhead light will give us the view we want; sometimes the red spotlight or blue will illuminate what we are looking for.

A philosopher has suggested that we strive for rational clarity in theory and reasonable eclecticism in practice (Pepper, 1957, p. 330). This advice would permit us to be as rigorous as we should like in a cognitive area, but as humane as we should be in action. "Rational clarity" demands that we hold our theory explicitly in order to make the best use of it, because it is only by doing this that we can correct for our biases in theory selection and valuation. It is the theory we use without knowing we are using it that is dangerous to us and to our clients. Just as the personality defects and emotional problems of the counselor need not preclude the possibility of effective work if they are taken into account and corrected for, so theory may be used better in counseling if we are aware that the theory is held, and if we acknowledge its limitations and some of the sources of its attraction to us.

Finally, it has been suggested that we make the best use of theories in social science by remembering that they will not long remain useful. Since they are bound by space, time, and the present level of our knowledge, even the best theories will not serve for long. If we accept this limitation, we should teach our students not only theories that are held presently, but ways of building new ones (Theobald, 1961, p. 100). Theory building will need to be a constant process for those who remain in counseling. It is for this reason that there may be value in examining—as we have—the structure, function, and genesis of theory.

WHAT IS COUNSELING?

Because we have considered the nature and function of theory, we must now discuss the activity to which it will be applied in this book—counseling. Defining counseling and distinguishing it from both psychotherapy and instruction are the next tasks to be performed to enable us to consider various theories of counseling.

In defining counseling, we are again faced with the fact that various authorities have seen it in different lights. These differences result not only from differences in point of view and in philosophy among the specialists in this field, but also from historical changes in more general perceptions of this art.

In 1945, the educational dictionary maker, Good, defined counseling as the "individualized and personalized assistance with personal, educational, vocational problems, in which all pertinent facts are studied and analyzed, and a solution is sought, often with the assistance of specialists, school and community resources, and personal interviews in which the counselee is taught to make his own decisions" (1945, p. 104). This older definition would now be seen as merely a statement supporting one point of view or theory of counseling. Its strong emphasis on cognitive material, immediate decision making, and use of external resources was characteristic of the views of counseling that were common at that time and are still held by certain proponents.

In a later edition of his dictionary, Good included several definitions of counseling. Of these, the primary definition states that counseling is "a relationship in which one or more persons with a problem or concern desire to discuss and work toward solving it with another person or persons attempting to help them reach their goals" (1973, p. 144). In contrast to the earlier (1945) definition, we see a shift away from specific techniques, an emphasis upon the "relationship," a recognition that counseling may involve more than two people, and an emphasis upon client-determined goals.

Another dictionary definition of counseling has been offered by English and English, who state that counseling is "a relationship in which one person endeavors to help another to understand and solve his adjustment problems. The area of adjustment is often indicated: educational counseling, vocational counseling, social counseling, etc." They go on to point out that "Counseling is a two-way affair involving both counselor and counselee. Unfortunately, both noun and verb *counsel* retain an older meaning of advice giving, which is now conceived as only part of the counseling process" (1958, p. 127).

Still another of the more psychologically oriented definitions is the one by Pepinsky and Pepinsky, who say that counseling is a process involving an interaction between a counselor and a client in a private setting, with the purpose of helping "the client change his behavior so that he may obtain a satisfactory resolution of his needs" (1954, p. 3). A middle-of-the-road definition is that given by Wrenn, when he says that "Counseling is a dynamic and purposeful relationship between two people in which procedures vary with the nature of the student's need, but in which there is always mutual participation by the counselor and the student with the focus upon self-clarification and self-determination by the student" (1951, p. 60). It will be seen that Wrenn's definition is sufficiently broad to encompass both the activities of the earlier proponents of counseling and those of the more modern practitioners. Hahn (1953, p. 234) points out that the reason for these different perceptions in the counseling process is that counseling itself seems to have three different bodies of supporters. He identifies the social welfare advocates, who have primarily an idiographic interest. Typical of these would be A. W. Combs and the others in the phenomenological school. A second group would be those who are more medically oriented and more nomothetic in their position. Foremost among these would be such people as F. C. Thorne. The final and third movement identified by Hahn would be those people who are concerned primarily with student personnel administration, and who have great interest in measurement. Typical of this group would be E. K. Strong, W. V. Bingham, and probably E. G. Williamson (Hahn, 1953, p. 234). Because counseling practitioners approach the process from a variety of directions and backgrounds, it should not seem unusual that they view and define counseling in a variety of ways. Although each may be patting the same elephant, they are all getting quite different notions of what the beast is like.

A common element in many definitions of counseling is the notion that counseling is aimed at helping people make choices and act on them—helping them answer the question, "What shall I do?" Perhaps the clearest advocate of this point of view is Tyler: "The purpose of counseling is to facilitate wise choices of the sort on which the person's later development depends" (1969, p. 13). Others have agreed that this element of choice is the key factor in counseling. Moore (1961, p. 63), in making the point that high school counselors should not do psychotherapy, defines counseling in the high school setting as help with choice making. Katz (1969, p. 244), in reviewing various counselor role statements by professional associations, notes an emphasis on decision making as a primary aspect of the counselor's role. Shostrom and Brammer quote a definition that tells us that counseling is "a purposeful, reciprocal relationship between two people in which one, a trained person, helps the other to change himself or his environment" (1952, p. 1). And finally, Wolberg tells us that counseling is "a form of interviewing in which the client is helped to understand himself more completely, in order that he may correct an environmental or adjustment difficulty" (1967, p. 41). Thus, an important element in any understanding of counseling is a recognition that many people see it as an aid in choice making prior to acting.

Learning is another element that is often used in defining counseling. Gustad, who reviewed a number of published definitions of counseling, has proposed the following composite definition:

> Counseling is a learning-oriented process, carried on in a simple, one-to-one social environment, in which a counselor, professionally competent in relevant psychological skills and knowledge, seeks to assist the client by methods appropriate to the latter's

needs and within the context of the total personnel program, to learn more about himself, to learn how to put such understanding into effect in relation to more clearly perceived, realistically defined goals to the end that the client may become a happier and more productive member of his society (1953, p. 17).

This concern with learning, which we have seen was an element in earlier definitions of counseling, has again come to the fore with research and study on the behavioral aspects of the counseling process. Krumboltz and Thoresen, for example, have defined "behavioral" counseling as "a process of helping people to learn how to solve certain interpersonal, emotional, and decision problems" (1976, p. 2). Indeed, most theorists now in the field would agree that counseling is a learning process, although they might have some sharp differences as to what facilitates learning and how learning occurs.

Still another element that is found frequently in definitions of counseling is that of personality development. Bordin says that the psychological counselor interacts with another person where the counselor "has taken the responsibility for making his role in the interaction process contribute positively to the other person's personality development" (1968, p. 10). Again, although almost all theorists might agree that counseling involves personality development, there might be relatively little agreement as to how personality development is furthered best.

One of the conceptions of counseling involves its effect on role clarification. An authoritative report by the American Psychological Association's Division of Counseling Psychology (1961) defines counseling as being involved primarily with role problems. This report points out that three trends merge in counseling psychology—vocational guidance, psychometrics, and personality development. The fact that these three streams have different sources may indicate some of the reasons for differences of opinion regarding what counseling is or should be. The report goes on to say that the present emphasis in counseling embraces such goals for the client as clear self-perception and harmony with environment, and such goals for society as the recognition of individual differences and the encouragement of the full development of all people. This report would suggest that there will remain some differences in the specifics of what counseling should be, but that there might be general agreement that one of the purposes of counseling is to help an individual understand one of his or her role commitments, and then carry it out more successfully.

One of the most novel and thought-provoking definitions of counseling has been offered by Krumboltz (1965, p. 384), who states that "Counseling consists of whatever ethical activities a counselor undertakes in an effort to help the client engage in those types of behavior which will lead to a resolution of the client's problems." Here, the emphasis is clearly upon what the counselor is trying to accomplish—the attainment of client goals—rather than the methods to be used. Krumboltz points out, however, that the counselor's willingness to work with a client on a particular problem should be based upon a consideration of the counselor's interests, competencies, and ethical standards.

Most of the attempts at definitions that are quoted here have had in common the primarily instrumental character of counseling. Although some definitions would suggest that counseling is basically concerned with dynamic problems, the bulk of counseling theorists seem to believe that counseling deals with such problems as choice, action, and role definition. It has been seen that many writers have attempted to define counseling without, on the one hand, succeeding to everyone's satisfaction, or, on the other hand, damaging themselves or the profession seriously. The following definition is therefore offered for the reader's consideration: "Counseling denotes a professional relationship between a trained counselor and a client. This relationship is usually person-to-person, although it may sometimes involve more than two people. It is designed to help clients to understand and clarify their views of their life space, and to learn to reach their self-determined goals through meaningful, well-informed choices and through resolution of problems of an emotional or interpersonal nature." This definition, like many quoted above, indicates that counseling is a relationship, that it is a process, that it is designed to help people make choices and resolve other kinds of problems, and that underlying the choice making and problem resolution are such matters as learning, personality development, and self-knowledge, which can be translated into better role perception and more effective role behavior.

DISTINCTIONS BETWEEN COUNSELING AND PSYCHOTHERAPY

Efforts to distinguish counseling from psychotherapy have not met with universal approval. Some people think that such a distinction should not be made and that the two terms should be used synonymously. However, others, particularly those who are preparing school counselors, are of the opinion that such a distinction *must* be made. If it is not present in nature, it must be invented. If no distinction is possible, then certainly all master's-level counselor education programs should stop at once, and 40,000 secondary school counselors who are presently employed to do "counseling" should be dismissed, for few would hold that such people are properly trained psychotherapists. A distinction, then, must be found, even though the edges of the distinction may blur and agreement on all particulars is unlikely. The problem is clearly posed by Hahn, who writes:

> I know of few counselors or psychologists who are completely satisfied that clear distinctions [between counseling and psychotherapy] have been made. . . . Perhaps the most complete agreements are: 1—that counseling and psychotherapy cannot be distinguished clearly, 2—that counselors practice what psychotherapists consider psychotherapy, 3—that psychotherapists practice what counselors consider to be counseling, and 4—that despite the above they are different (1953, p. 232).

The difficulty of distinction is also recognized by Eysenck, Arnold, and Meili, who state that "Counseling differs from psychotherapy in that it is usually applied to help 'normals' rather than patients, although the two processes merge imperceptibly on many occasions . . ." (1972, p. 226).

Before trying to make a distinction between counseling and psychotherapy, we might find it helpful to pause and define psychotherapy itself. Wolberg defines psychotherapy as "The treatment, by psychological means, of problems of an emotional nature in which a trained person deliberately establishes a professional relationship with the patient with the object (1) of removing, modifying or retarding existing symptoms, (2) of mediating disturbed patterns of behavior, and (3) of promoting positive personality growth and development" (1967, p. 3). Eysenck quotes an amusing definition that says that psychotherapy is "an unidentified technique applied to unspecified problems with unpredictable outcomes. For this technique we recommend rigorous training" (1961, p. 698). Eysenck then defines psychotherapy more seriously as containing such elements as (1) a prolonged interpersonal relationship, (2) the involvement of trained personnel, (3) a self-dissatisfaction with emotional and/or interpersonal adjustment on the part of the client, (4) the use of psychological methods, (5) an activity based on a theory of mental disorders, and (6) an aim through this relationship of ameliorating self-dissatisfaction.

To see some of the differences between counseling and psychotherapy, we shall look at their respective goals, clients, practitioners, settings, and methods. Although we shall examine these differences, no completely satisfactory, defensible, and clear distinctions are expected. It seems more likely that a continuum may exist from one activity to the other in regard to each of these elements. Just as first aid may shade into the practice of medicine, so counseling may shade into psychotherapy, but no one thinks that it is impossible to distinguish the application of a Band-Aid from brain surgery. Or as Goldman writes, "True, there are times, around dusk, when one is uncertain about turning on the lights. . . . Do these borderline decisions mean that there is no value in differentiating between day and night . . . ?" (1964, p. 418).

This notion of a continuum from counseling to psychotherapy has been expressed well by Brammer and Shostrom, who indicate that the two activities may overlap, but that in general counseling would be characterized by such terms as "educational, vocational, supportive, situational, problem-solving, conscious awareness, normal, present time, and short term," whereas therapy would be characterized by such terms as "supportive (in a crisis setting), reconstructive, depth emphasis, analytical, focus on the past, emphasis on 'neurotics' or other severe emotional problems, and long term" (1977, pp. 6–7). Patterson, in reviewing the literature on counseling, indicates that the counseling end of a counseling-psychotherapy continuum would be characterized by such elements as "normal, preventive, developmental, not severe, area versus total, reality oriented, positive, non-imbedded" (1959, p. 4). This emphasis on distinction by relative position on several continua provides a useful framework from which to attempt more specific differences with regard to goals, clients, practitioners, settings, and methods.

Goals

In looking at the goals of counseling as distinguished from the goals of psychotherapy, it would seem that a frequent goal of counseling is to help an individual deal with the developmental tasks that are appropriate to his or her age. The adolescent who is being helped with the problems of sexual definition, emotional independence from parents, preparation for an occupation, and the other tasks typical of that age and our culture would be receiving counseling. On the other hand, a middle-aged person who is grappling with these same problems might be closer to the appropriate concern of a psychotherapist.

The previously cited report of the American Psychological Association Division of Counseling Psychology says:

> When we consider these discussions and look at the contribution counseling psychologists are making and can make to society, we can summarize what is important about the specialty by saying that it focuses on *plans* individuals must make to play productive *roles* in their social environments. Whether the person being helped with such planning is sick or well, abnormal or normal, is really irrelevant. The focus is on assets, skills, strengths, possibilities for further development. Personality difficulties are dealt with only when they constitute obstacles to the individual's forward progress (1961, p. 6).

Another suggested distinction regarding goals has been made by Hahn and MacLean (1955, p. 31), who indicate that the counselor would give heavy emphasis to prevention of disruptive deviations, whereas the psychotherapist might give primary emphasis to present deviations with secondary attention to prevention. They make another distinction with regard to reality testing, and indicate that a goal of counseling is to permit reality testing in a somewhat sheltered situation, whereas in psychotherapy testing is permitted in an almost completely sheltered situation. Finally, they say that counseling has as a goal long-range educational and vocational planning. Hahn and MacLean's total emphasis seems to involve distinguishing counseling as being concerned with preventive mental health, and psychotherapy with remediation.

Another distinction is sometimes made with regard to the goals of these two activities, in that counseling is more concerned with narrowly situational matters, while psychotherapy is more concerned with changing the organism so that the client can handle not only the present but future problems. In other words, counseling sometimes is defined as being more peripheral and psychotherapy more central.

Shaw (1957, p. 357) indicates that counseling should be more concerned with creative help, while psychotherapy is more concerned with mental illness. That is, counseling is not so much involved with curing or treating as with pointing out new vistas of opportunity. Mowrer (1953, p. 70) has indicated the possibility of distinguishing the goals of counseling and psychotherapy on the basis of two kinds of anxiety. Normal anxiety is the proper business of counseling, whereas psychotherapy might more appropriately deal with neurotic anxiety.

Tyler (1969, p. 20) suggests that the counseling profession should define itself as a service concerned mainly with helping normal persons to make choices in order to further their development, and implies that the function of producing personality change and overcoming adjustment difficulties should be left to psychotherapy.

Vance and Volsky (1962, pp. 565–570) suggest that a common goal in much psychotherapy and counseling is the reduction of psychological discordance. When this discordance is accompanied by considerable psychopathology, it falls more appropriately into the domain of the psychotherapist, but when it is reality-based, as for example with a client whose goals call for abilities he or she lacks, it requires counseling skills. However, these authors contend that the dimensions of discordance and psychopathology are correlated, and they therefore believe that all psychologists who offer personalized treatment services will do both psychotherapy and psychological discordance reduction.

The most ambitious attempt to distinguish counseling from psychotherapy has been made by Wolberg (1967, pp. 71–320). Wolberg distinguishes three kinds of approaches to problems in this area: supportive, reeducative, and reconstructive. *Supportive psychotherapy* has as its object emotional equilibrium with a minimization of symptoms, so that the individual can function near his or her norm. Examples of treatment in this area would be directive guidance, environmental manipulation, externalization of interests, and persuasion. These and other supportive treatments might appropriately be given by a counselor. In passing, he suggests that indications for the appropriateness of this goal would include (1) a strong ego beset by temporary problems or (2) an ego so weak that even psychotherapy would not be useful. Contraindicators would include great authority problems and therefore a tendency to resist persuasion or to succumb to it.

Reeducative psychotherapy, according to Wolberg, attempts to modify attitudes or behavior to more adaptive life integration. The goal of such psychotherapy would be further insight into conscious processes, so that behavior or goals might be changed. Wolberg would include both counseling and social casework in this area. By implication, this treatment is indicated for those relatively slight problems or for problems within a circumscribed area.

Finally, Wolberg writes of *reconstructive therapy*. In this kind of psychotherapy, the practitioner works toward an awareness of unconscious conflicts and hopes to make extensive alterations in the character structure of the client. Wolberg points out that, although supportive therapy and reeducative psychotherapy may lead to reconstructive psychotherapy, it is important to make distinctions among these three approaches in terms of their goals. Reconstructive therapy, particularly in the form of psychoanalysis, is indicated for those who have neuroses that are sufficiently severe to justify the considerable expenditure of time and money, and who are, at the same time, bright and neither too young to be "reasonable" nor too old to be "flexible." Contraindicators include severe symptoms that demand rapid attention, psychosis, irremediable life situations provoking neurotic defenses, and great secondary gains that accrue to the neurosis. If we accept Wolberg's distinction, the psychotherapist would be concerned with reconstructive goals, and the counselor with reeducative and supportive goals. Obviously, however, there might be occasions when a psychotherapist would properly work toward supportive or reeducative goals, and there also would be times when the counselor might be doing reconstructive psychotherapy.

In summary, the goals of psychotherapy usually involve quite a complete change of basic character structure. The goals of counseling are apt to be more limited, more concerned with aiding growth, more concerned with the immediate situation, and more concerned with helping the individual function adequately in appropriate roles.

Clients

Some attempts have been made to distinguish counseling from psychotherapy on the basis of the clients each serves. Traditionally, it has been said that the counselor deals with normal people, and the psychotherapist with the neurotic or psychotic. The most systematic delineation of this kind has been made by Hahn and MacLean (1955, p. 31), who indicate that the normal person is a major type of client for the counselor and a secondary type for the psychotherapist. The neurotic would be seen by the counselor only on an emergency basis, or when the counselor is acting as a consultant to other specialists, whereas the neurotic would be the usual type of client for the psychotherapist. Finally, a psychotic would be seen by a counselor only in an emergency or on a consultative basis, whereas such an individual might be treated by a psychotherapist who was working in collaboration with a medical doctor.

These distinctions, though once widely accepted, now seem to be under some attack. Tyler (1969, pp. 186–187) specifically rejects a distinction between counseling and psychotherapy that is based upon clients or settings. Others, too, have complained that while the distinction between normal and neurotic is easy to make clear, it may be difficult to make practical. Still, many would say that one useful distinction between counseling and psychotherapy is that the counselor is primarily trained to deal with normal people, and that the psychotherapist is primarily trained to deal with disturbed people.

Practitioners

Distinctions between counseling and psychotherapy necessarily involve some consideration of the practitioner. Black says that "a major share of therapy done today is performed by people who are not even called therapists" (1952, p. 302). The previously discussed report (American Psychological Association, 1961) points out that there is considerable overlap in the memberships of Division 17 (Counseling Psychology) and Division 12 (Clinical Psychology) in their association. There is some indication, however, that this overlap is less prevalent among new members.

It should be remembered that although this report indicates that psychological therapists and counseling psychologists are very similar in their training and professional identification, we are speaking here only of the more highly trained counselors. It is estimated that there are between 55,000 and 60,000 counselors operating in the American schools. The average training for these people would probably be that which is represented by a master's degree in guidance and counseling from a college of education. Most counseling is done by people with considerably less training than that of psychotherapists, even if we should agree that some psychotherapy is done by those with training at the master's degree level.

Perhaps it could be said that the better-trained counselor is scarcely distinguishable from the better-trained psychotherapist. Both will have basic training in personality theory and in interviewing and research methods, as well as considerable background in biological and physical sciences, in sociology, in mathematics, and in community organization. Both will have a formal internship of two or more years, and will be apt to hold a doctor's degree. The relatively untrained psychotherapist, however, would be most apt to have a master's degree either in social work or in clinical psychology, whereas the relatively untrained counselor might have almost any kind of background, but generally a teaching credential plus a few guidance courses. Some will have a master's degree in counseling, but many will have not even this much preparation. The difference in practitioners, then, may be great or minimal. It may be true on occasion, but certainly not always, that one can tell whether counseling or psychotherapy is going on by looking at who is doing it. Thompson and Super (1964, pp. 31–32) report the conclusions of an important conference on the training of counseling psychologists and point out that degrees may be granted either by departments of psychology or departments of education.

Settings

Some attempt has been made to distinguish between counseling and psychotherapy in terms of where it is happening. It is observed that psychotherapists are more apt to work in hospital settings or in private practice; counselors are more apt to be working in educational settings. While this is true to some extent, it is less a distinguishing feature than it once was. Counselors are now employed in a wide range of settings, including Veterans Administration hospitals, rehabilitation centers, mental health agencies, substance abuse centers, correctional institutions, probate courts, juvenile homes, family counseling agencies, crisis intervention centers, and so on. On the other hand, school systems and colleges are now hiring clinical psychologists and other therapeutically oriented practitioners. Thus, it can be said that while counseling may occur more often in educational institutions and psychotherapy more often in medical settings, we cannot always determine which activity is going on by noting where it is happening.

Methods

In attempting to distinguish counseling from psychotherapy on the basis of difference of methods, we would run counter to the advice of Patterson (1973, pp. xii–xiv), who sees no essential differences between them. Of course, this would be the general position of most client-centered counselors. Certainly, commonality of method is widespread. Where universals or essentials of method have been listed for psychotherapy and for counseling, the lists evidence a great deal of overlap. Black (1952, p. 305) believes that all psychotherapists would have in common the building of rapport between patient and therapist, the acceptance and appreciation of the basic human worth of the individual (although not necessarily the complete negation of any possibility of evaluation), the supportive relationship of the psychotherapist to the patient, the status—implicit or explicit—of the psychotherapist, and the provision of controls and limits in the relationship. These universals of psychotherapy would be equally applicable to counseling. Counseling, too, involves rapport, acceptance, support, status, control, and limits.

Tyler lists what she feels are the essentials of any counseling relationship, and again they would seem to apply to psychotherapy (1969, pp. 13–16): interest of the counselor in the client, confidence in the counselor by the client, limits on their relationship, the use of information as a resource when appropriate, and a relationship that has as a goal facilitating the development of the client. Black and Tyler seem to say that the methods of psychotherapy are so varied, and the methods of counseling are so varied, that sometimes there are more differences within the several approaches to therapy than there are between therapy and counseling, and more differences within the several approaches to counseling than there are between counseling and psychotherapy.

Wolberg (1967, pp. 285–290) believes that concern with the conscious level is more characteristic of counselors and that concern with the unconscious level is more characteristic of therapists. Other distinctions between counseling (re-educative psychotherapy) and therapy (reconstructive psychotherapy) are these: (1) counseling is usually of less duration than therapy, (2) the sessions are apt to occur less frequently, (3) more case history taking and more psychological examination are typical and characteristic of counseling, and (4) more advice giving and less transference are characteristic of counseling. Whereas a therapist is more apt to make an individual assessment or diagnosis chiefly through a clinical interview, the counselor may frequently make use of psychometric tools.

Method has been discussed by Bordin, who feels that the distinction should be primarily quantitative rather than qualitative. He believes that both counseling and psychotherapy should be preceded by a medical examination. Counseling would deal with less emotionally intense matters, and would generally be more positive than therapy (1968, pp. 18–19). Counseling is more likely than therapy to deal with cognition, and therapy is more likely than counseling to deal with conative aspects. A major contribution of Bordin to the problem of definition is the way in which he deals with the concept of ambiguity (1968, p. 150). Statements can be ambiguous with regard to the topic to be discussed, the relationship between the counselor and the client, and the goals of counseling. To the extent that counselors move toward a more ambiguous structure in their counseling, they are moving toward therapy. Ambiguity leads to anxiety, and the forcing of anxiety leads to a more therapeutic relationship. The method of counseling, then, would be to limit the ambiguity, and the method of therapy to maximize it.

To review some differences in method between counseling and psychotherapy, we can say that counseling is characterized by shorter duration of treatment, less frequent visits, more use of psychological examination, more concern with the client's present daily problems, more focus on the client's conscious activities, more advice giving, less concern with transference, more emphasis on the reality situation, more cognition and less emotional intensity, and more clarity and less ambiguity.

Summary

The distinction between counseling and psychotherapy cannot be made with complete clarity and satisfaction. At the same time, an attempt must be made to at least distinguish the master's-level school counselor from the psychoanalyst, and to distinguish many intermediate positions. The total length of training for school counselors is presently averaging about one year of graduate work, and of that probably less than half is psychological in nature. Can we not make it clear to these counselors that they are not trained as therapists? The position of this chapter is that at least the extremes of differences between counseling and psychotherapy can be identified. While it is true that "tall" cannot be distinguished from "short" when men are roughly five-feet-nine, it is equally clear that five-feet-two is different from six-feet-five. An attempt to distinguish between these two activities— counseling and psychotherapy—is made particularly difficult by the prestige structure in American academic circles. In general, education is less valued than psychology as a discipline. Since education departments train most counselors, counseling does not have the prestige of psychotherapy. As a consequence, master's-level school counselors like to think of themselves as counseling psychologists, counseling psychologists sometimes like to think of themselves as clinical psychologists, and clinical psychologists like to muddy the distinction with psychiatry. Although snobbery—as well as professional psychopathy— makes these distinctions difficult, the distinctions themselves are not without value.

In attempting to point to some differences between counseling and psychotherapy, we can now look at the several elements that we have considered, and compare the two activities with regard to their position on various continua:

1 Counseling tends to be concerned with instrumental behavior, with role problems, with situations, with choices that must be made, and with actions that must be taken. Goals of counseling are more limited than those of psychotherapy, but this does not mean that these limited goals are unimportant, or that changes in immediate behavior may not have lasting global effects.

2 Counselors deal primarily with normal individuals (the distinction between "normal" and "neurotic" is as fraught with difficulties, of course, as the distinction between counseling and psychotherapy).

3 The practitioner of counseling may be trained at the doctoral level with a two-year internship, as would be his or her counterpart in clinical psychology. Many counselors, however, are trained at less than a doctoral level, or at the doctoral level but with relatively little psychology and little or no formal supervised internship. These people, because of the prestige rank of psychology and because of their own confused role concepts, may quickly come to think of themselves as psychotherapists. Although they have difficulty making the distinction, there is no reason why more objective observers should.

4 The setting in which counseling takes place is most apt to be an educa-

tional setting or a community agency, although counselors may work in a medical setting or in private practice.

    5 The methods used will indicate that counseling, unlike psychotherapy, shows more concern with present events than with those of the past, more concern with cognition than with affect, and more concern with clarity than with ambiguity.

There seems to be no litmus paper that will distinguish counseling from psychotherapy as it changes from blue to red. Combinations of clues, however, may be helpful in distinguishing the two activities. Assume that we observe an interview relationship between Mr. Jones, the professional helper, and Mr. Smith, the client. If Mr. Jones is trained at less than the doctoral level (or at the doctoral level without a formal two-year internship), if Mr. Smith is a normal client, if Mr. Jones is dealing with him in an educational setting, if he is primarily concerned with conscious processes, if his goals are to help Mr. Smith play one of his life roles more effectively by making better choices, then we can say that counseling is going on. On the other hand, if Mr. Smith seems to be a very disturbed client, if they are working in a medical setting, if the goals are to reconstruct Mr. Smith's personality, and if Mr. Jones' methods are characterized by ambiguity, intense emotion, and concern for unconscious processes, then we may appropriately label the activity as psychotherapy.

COUNSELING DISTINGUISHED FROM INSTRUCTION

If to a counseling practitioner the thunder on the left is representative of psychotherapy, the thunder on the right is representative of instruction. There are educational theorists who see little distinction between counseling and teaching. Certainly in a broad sense, the goals of both may be much the same, since both are concerned with helping an individual develop to the point where one can assume responsibilities for oneself and live a satisfying life. More narrowly, however, the goals of counseling are determined more by the needs of the individual as they are viewed by the individual, whereas the goals of instruction are more apt to be determined societally. The most permissive and student-centered teacher of an algebra class has some views as to what should be covered in an instructional situation, because society has, to some extent, defined such goals, but in the counseling situation the counselor has less preconception about what will be needed to help the individual.

    With regard to the client (or student), instruction is thought to be for all. With regard to counseling, there are those who think counseling should be given to everyone, but frequently it happens that counseling is given only to those who request it voluntarily, or perhaps to those who are seen as "needing" it.

    The practitioner of teaching has been trained in specific instructional techniques and subject matter, while hopefully the counselor has had additional training in interviewing, psychometrics, occupational information, and other competencies required by the specialized counseling role. It would seem to be true, however, that often teachers do counseling and sometimes counselors do teaching. The wisdom of having the same person play both roles can be questioned, because the teacher is required to be judgmental and to operate as a representative of an educational institution with certain responsibilities determined by the function of that institution, whereas the counselor has primary responsibility to the individual and so can be less judgmental. Part of this confusion stems from the fact that educational institutions in America have two purposes, the developmental and the screening. They have the job of helping a student grow, but they also have the job of acting as gatekeeper to certain occupations and roles. This screening function, which is now being performed by the educational institution, would seem to inhibit the kind of relationship that is thought to be most helpful in counseling. Counseling, then, may be difficult to distinguish from instruction, particularly if it concerns individual educational problems.

The methods of teaching are more apt to be group methods, and the methods of counseling are more apt to be individual methods. However, teachers may teach one student at a time, and this tutoring function has long been recognized and valued, while more and more counselors are experimenting with group procedures.

If we see that an individual in a group is being dealt with by a teacher who has some societally determined preconception as to the goals of the interaction, we are apt to call this activity instruction rather than counseling.

SUBSTANTIVE ELEMENTS IN THEORIES OF COUNSELING

Now that we have considered the activity of counseling, let us return to our discussion of theory.

We have previously considered the nature of theory and the formal attributes of a theory. Since we are concerned with a special kind of theory—one dealing with counseling—we need to look now at the substantive elements that would characterize such a theory. Substantive elements are determined by what the theory is about, what it deals with. Substantive elements in learning theory might involve such matters as environmentalism versus nativism and historical versus contemporary causation, while in administrative theory such matters as direction, staffing, and planning might be included. Substantive elements of a counseling theory would include (1) assumptions regarding the basic nature of people (2) beliefs regarding learning theory and changes in behavior, (3) a commitment to certain goals of counseling, (4) a definition of the role of the counselor, and (5) evidence supporting the theory.

While we have noted previously that counseling theory may not necessarily derive from a specific philosophy, some assumptions about the basic nature of people must be made in order to construct a theory about counseling them. As we examine specific theories, we should note, for example, whether the theorist is assuming such things as the innate goodness or evil of people, the problems attendant upon the human condition, and the pliability of people—that is, whether they are sufficiently plastic in nature that they can be shaped in one way or another by the interaction of genetic elements and environment.

Counseling theories also include beliefs about how people change or learn. In examining such theories, we will want to note hypotheses that tell us which behaviors of the individual are determined biologically and are therefore less likely to change, and which behaviors develop as a result of experience or learning and may therefore be changed by a process of unlearning or relearning (Ford & Urban, 1963, p. 76). While there is some agreement that counseling constitutes a learning process, theorists may disagree about how this learning takes place. For example, is learning furthered by a general atmosphere or by specific stimulus-response situations? Change would seem to be a goal of counseling, but there may be great differences among theorists in their theories of how change comes about.

The goals of counseling will differ for different theories. We have indicated previously that even if we assume that mental health is the goal we are aiming at, there are various definitions of mental health. For example, most school counselors seem to assume that mental health can be equated with a mastery of environment, particularly as exemplified by grades in school or the ability to get along in an educational institution and meet the expectations of the teachers. Glad (1959), at least by inference, suggests that the goals of various therapeutic approaches are so different that one person could be considered to have been treated successfully by advocates of one theory, and at the same time be seen as in need of therapy by advocates of another theory. A good counseling theory will be explicit and clear regarding its goals.

The role of the counselor and the ways in which that role is implemented through the process and techniques of counseling will also be different for different theories. This role will differ with regard to the place and importance of diagnosis, for example, and some theories may make much use of tests, case histories, and screening interviews, while others will not. Other elements that would constitute differences would be the extent to which interpretation, advice, and persuasion are thought to be proper behavior for the counselor. We may find differences in the extent to which theories permit and support the intrusion of the counselor's values into the counseling situation. Differences may also be found in terms of whether the counselor attempts to function as the sole helping person in the relationship versus the use of group counseling or the use of significant others in the client's everyday environment to monitor client behavior and to reward progress. Above all, the basic counseling style and its clarification regarding such matters as acceptance as opposed to interpretation, advice as opposed to clarification, use of authority as opposed to denial of authority, and encouragement of transference versus denial of transference will typify a theory. Finally, there may be differences with regard to such special problems as dependency of a client, the communication problem, and other elements that may appear to help define the role of the counselor.

The different theories may lend themselves to illustrative case material which will tell us in more specific terms how the theory functions for a given case.

It is only by examining such material that we can see the relationship between logical constructs and the events of the counseling interview. Since a theory deals not only with logical structure but with specific data, we shall want to look for research evidence and support with regard to the theories that we are considering. A theory that is completely abstract is a poor theory, not because it is wrong, but because it does not help us to understand the facts that are available already.

In summary, a theory of counseling must not only meet certain formal criteria, but must make explicit its position regarding certain substantive elements that seem appropriate to the judgment of a theory in this field.

BIBLIOGRAPHY

Allport, G. W. The general and the unique in psychological science. *Journal of Personality*, 1962, *30*, 405–422. (a)

Allport, G. W. Psychological models for guidance. *Harvard Educational Review*, 1962, *32*, 373–381. (b)

American Psychological Association, Division of Counseling Psychology, Special Committee. The current status of counseling psychology. Washington, D.C.: Author, 1961. (Multilithed)

Barclay, J. R. *Foundations of counseling strategies.* New York: Wiley, 1971.

Black, J. D. Common factors in patient-therapist relationship in diverse psychotherapies. *Journal of Clinical Psychology*, 1952, *8*, 302–306.

Bone, H. Personality theory. In S. Arieti (Ed.), *American handbook of psychiatry.* New York: Basic Books, 1959.

Bordin, E. S. *Psychological counseling* (2nd ed.). New York: Appleton-Century-Crofts, 1968.

Brammer, L. M., & Shostrom, E. L. *Therapeutic psychology: Fundamentals of counseling and psychotherapy* (3rd ed.). Englewood Cliffs, N.J.: Prentice-Hall, 1977.

Campbell, N. R. The structure of theories. In H. Feigl & M. Brodbeck (Eds.), *Readings in the philosophy of science.* New York: Appleton-Century-Crofts, 1953.

English, H. B., & English, A. C. *A comprehensive dictionary of psychological and psychoanalytical terms.* New York: McKay, 1958.

Eysenck, H. J. The effects of psychotherapy. In H. J. Eysenck (Ed.), *Handbook of abnormal psychology.* New York: Basic Books, 1961.

Eysenck, H. J., Arnold, W., & Meili, R. *Encyclopedia of psychology* (Vol. 1). New York: Herder & Herder, 1972.

Ford, D. H., & Urban, H. B. *Systems of psychotherapy: A comparative study.* New York: Wiley, 1963.

Frank, P. *Modern science and its philosophy.* Cambridge, Mass.: Harvard University Press, 1949.

Glad, D. D. *Operational values in psychotherapy: A conceptual framework of interpersonality.* New York: Oxford University Press, 1959.

Goldman, L. Another log. *American Psychologist*, 1964, *19*, 418–419.

Good, C. V. (Ed.) *Dictionary of education.* New York: McGraw-Hill, 1945.

Good, C. V. (Ed.) *Dictionary of education* (3rd ed.). New York: McGraw-Hill, 1973.

Gustad, J. W. The definition of counseling. In R. F. Berdie (Ed.), *Roles and relationships in counseling.* Minneapolis: University of Minnesota Press, 1953.

Hahn, M. E. Conceptual trends in counseling. *Personnel and Guidance Journal*, 1953, *31*, 231–235.

Hahn, M. E., & MacLean, M. S. *Counseling psychology* (2nd ed.). New York: McGraw-Hill, 1955.

Hall, C. S., & Lindzey, G. *Theories of personality* (2nd ed.). New York: Wiley, 1970.

Hall, E. T. *The silent language*. Garden City, N.Y.: Doubleday, 1959.

Jahoda, M. *Current concepts of positive mental health*. New York: Basic Books, 1958.

Katz, M. Counseling—secondary schools. In R. L. Ebel (Ed.), *Encyclopedia of educational research* (4th ed.). New York: Macmillan, 1969.

Krumboltz, J. D. Behavioral counseling: Rationale and research. *Personnel and Guidance Journal*, 1965, *44*, 383–387.

Krumboltz, J. D., & Thoresen, C. E. (Eds.) *Counseling methods*. New York: Holt, Rinehart & Winston, 1976.

McCabe, G. E. When is a good theory practical? *Personnel and Guidance Journal*, 1958, *37*, 47–52.

McDaniel, H. B., Lallas, J. E., Saum, J. A., & Gilmore, J. L. *Readings in guidance*. New York: Holt, 1959.

Moore, G. D. A negative view toward therapeutic counseling in the public school. *Counselor Education and Supervision*, 1961, *1*, 60–68.

Mowrer, O. H. *Psychotherapy: Theory and research*. New York: Ronald Press, 1953.

Osipow, S. H. *Theories of career development* (2nd ed.). New York: Appleton-Century-Crofts, 1973.

Patterson, C. H. *Counseling and psychotherapy: Theory and practice*. New York: Harper & Row, 1959.

Patterson, C. H. *Theories of counseling and psychotherapy* (2nd ed.). New York: Harper & Row, 1973.

Pepinsky, H. B., & Pepinsky, P. *Counseling: Theory and practice*. New York: Ronald Press, 1954.

Pepper, S. C. *World hypotheses: A study in evidence*. Berkeley, Calif.: University of California Press, 1957.

Phillips, E. L. *Psychotherapy: A modern theory and practice*. Englewood Cliffs, N.J.: Prentice-Hall, 1956.

Shaw, F. J. Counseling. *Annual Review of Psychology*, 1957, *8*, 357–376.

Shoben, E. J., Jr. The counselor's theory as a personal trait. *Personnel and Guidance Journal*, 1962, *40*, 617–621.

Shostrom, E. L., & Brammer, L. M. *The dynamics of the counseling process*. New York: McGraw-Hill, 1952.

Stefflre, B., & Matheny, K. B. The function of counseling theory. In S. C. Stone & B. Shertzer (Eds.), *Guidance Monograph Series II: Counseling*. Boston: Houghton Mifflin, 1968.

Super, D. E. Vocational development theory: Persons, positions, and processes. In J. M. Whiteley & A. Resnikoff (Eds.), *Perspectives on vocational development*. Washington, D.C.: American Personnel and Guidance Association, 1972.

Theobald, R. *The challenge of abundance*. New York: New American Library, 1961.

Thompson, A. S., & Super, D. E. (Eds.) *The professional preparation of counseling psychologists. Report of the 1964 Greyston Conference*. New York: Bureau of Publications, Teachers College, Columbia University, 1964.

Tyler, L. E. *The work of the counselor* (3rd ed.). New York: Appleton-Century-Crofts, 1969.

Vance, F. L., & Volsky, T. C., Jr. Counseling and psychotherapy: Split personalities or Siamese twins. *American Psychologist*, 1962, *17*, 565–570.

Wolberg, L. R. *The technique of psychotherapy* (2nd ed.). New York: Grune & Stratton, 1967.

Wrenn, C. G. *Student personnel work in college.* New York: Ronald Press, 1951.

Wrenn, C. G. Philosophical and psychological bases of personnel services in education. *Personnel services in education* (1958 Yearbook of the National Society for the Study of Education, Part II). Chicago: University of Chicago Press, 1959.

Chapter 2

Client-Centered Theory

Donald L. Grummon

BIOGRAPHICAL DATA

Client-centered theory derives from the work of many men and women, but Carl R. Rogers is its undisputed founder and major proponent.

Rogers was born in 1902 in the Chicago suburb of Oak Park, Illinois. In his autobiography, Rogers (1967) described his well-to-do Protestant family as close-knit, loving, practical, and dedicated—even overly dedicated—to Christian principles and to the virtues of hard work. Rogers, who was an intellectually precocious child, loved to read but reports feeling guilty during the times that his reading interfered with his chores. When Rogers was 12, his family purchased a large farm 30 miles west of Chicago that his father, a successful contractor, ran through a manager on a modern, scientific basis. Through his readings in scientific agriculture and through activities on the farm, young Carl developed a lasting interest in and respect for the essential elements of science and the experimental method before he was 16 years of age.

At the University of Wisconsin, Rogers majored in history and became deeply involved with student religious groups. During his junior year, he was selected as one of 10 American students to attend a World Student Christian Federation Conference in Peking, China. For more than six months away from his family, he encountered a wide range of cultures and enjoyed intensive study and discussions with a highly gifted, cultured, and well-informed group of fellow students and senior advisors. The result was an intellectual renaissance out of which Rogers became more independent and liberal in his political and religious beliefs—but without realizing, in part because of the slowness of the mail, the consternation this was causing his family. In his autobiography, Rogers reports this experience as a significant developmental milestone in which he broke the psychological and religious ties with his family: "I had been able to freely, with no sense of defiance or guilt, to think my own thoughts, come to my own conclusions, and to take stands I believed in" (1967, p. 351).

However, Rogers maintained his interest in religion for a time, and after graduating from the University of Wisconsin spent two years at the Union Theological Seminary before transferring to Columbia University's Teachers College to complete a Ph.D. in clinical and educational psychology. At Teachers College, he was exposed to the quantitative tradition in American psychology, to the views of John Dewey on the value of experiential learning, and to the "warmly human and commonsense approach" to clinical work of Leta Hollingsworth. During a year of internship at the Institute for Child Guidance, Rogers learned much about the Freudian orientation and engaged in his first regular therapy with clients.

For the next twelve years in Rochester, New York, Rogers immersed himself in practical clinical work in a child-guidance-clinic setting. These were years of relative professional isolation, in which he focused on his own experiences of what did or did not work as he attempted to be helpful to children and to their parents. Through social workers on the staff, he became acquainted with the work of Otto Rank, Jessie Taft, and Frederick Allen—writers whose ideas were germinal to Rogers' later views about counseling and psychotherapy. Otto Rank, for example, emphasizes reliance on the client's will to health, the therapeutic value of the present relationship between therapist and client, and the therapist's role in gently guiding the client to individual self-understanding and self-acceptance. Rogers' first book, *The Clinical Treatment of the Problem Child*, written in 1937 and published in 1939, was devoted mostly to general clinical issues and procedures, but two chapters surveyed existing points of view about treatment interviews. In retrospect, Rogers' leanings toward relationship therapy can be discerned in these chapters.

In January 1940, Rogers accepted a professorship in clinical psychology at Ohio State University. The public birth of client-centered therapy should perhaps be dated about a year later, with a paper Rogers delivered at the University of Minnesota, which became Chapter 2 in his book, *Counseling and Psychotherapy*, published in 1942. Client-centered theory and practice evolved considerably in the next two and one-half decades, but *Counseling and Psychotherapy* described in preliminary form the distinctive features of the Rogerian approach. Still, it was a heavily technique-oriented book that emphasized many activities that the therapist should avoid, as opposed to the theory's later emphasis on more positive and active goals for the therapist. A chapter contrasting "directive" versus "nondirective" counselor activities helped earn this new approach the name "*nondirective counseling*," a label that Rogers later rejected as seriously misleading. This book included some features that were new to the field and came to characterize Rogers' later work, such as the use of verbatim electrical recordings of counseling cases, an attempt to discern the underlying order in the counseling process, and research to confirm or disconfirm this underlying order.

Rogers accepted an appointment at the University of Chicago in 1945 and moved on to the University of Wisconsin in 1957. During his nearly two decades in Chicago and Madison, the client-centered approach was developed as a systematic theory of psychotherapy and personality change. Well over 100 research and theoretical papers, plus several books, were published by Rogers and his colleagues during this period. These included Rogers' most comprehensive theoretical statement, which appeared in 1959 under the title, "A Theory of Therapy, Personality and Interpersonal Relationships as Developed in the Client-Centered Framework." At the University of Wisconsin, the client-centered approach was extended to relatively chronic, hospitalized schizophrenic patients. Working with withdrawn and often nonverbal schizophrenics consolidated a new emphasis in client-centered therapy that had been slowly evolving for several years. Client-centered therapists became more active in relating to their clients. Very often this activity consisted in the therapist's attending to her[1] own self-experiencing in the relationship, and in the therapist's attempt to reach out and to communicate this self-experiencing to the client. The therapist, as well as the client, was freed to trust and to act on her own "organismic experience" in the helping relationship.

In 1964, Rogers left Wisconsin for California to become a Resident Fellow, first at the Western Behavioral Sciences Institute and then at the Center for the Studies of the Person, which he helped found in 1968. His writings and professional practice since leaving Wisconsin have focused mainly on encounter groups, on interpersonal relationships generally, and on extending the client-centered approach to various social concerns, especially to the philosophy of science, to education, and to issues of alienation and powerlessness in today's society. He continues to rethink parts of client-centered theory, and at 76 years of age Rogers is still active in both professional work and writing.

Carl R. Rogers is without question one of the most controversial, but also one of the most distinguished and influential, psychologists of the modern era. He has influenced the development of clinical and counseling psychology profoundly, even though many of his ideas have been questioned or rejected. His influence extends beyond psychology to other helping professions and to other disciplines, such as education, religion, and business and industry. His writings appear on the required reading lists of diverse undergraduate and graduate courses. He is widely read by the general public, paperback copies of his books can be found in most book stores, and his recent books are reviewed in such outlets as *The New York Times Book Review*. His works have been translated into more than a half-dozen foreign languages, and students from all over the world come to study with him.

This influence has been accompanied by distinguished awards and honors. In 1944 he was elected president of the now disbanded American Association of Applied Psychology, and in 1947 he became president of the American Psychological Association. In 1956 he received, along with Wolfgang Kohler and Kenneth Spence, the first American Psychological Association Distinguished Scientific Contribution Award, in 1968 the American Board of Professional Psychology Award for Outstanding Contributions to Professional Psychology,

---

[1]The publisher's request for sex-fair language is fitting and proper, but this writer and many others are distracted by the frequent use of "he or she," "her or his," etc. A reasonable solution to this dilemma adopted by Rogers in his latest book is to alternate masculine and feminine forms. In this chapter when the reference is to males and females collectively, I will use feminine pronouns where these fit and masculine forms for such expressions as "mankind" or "the nature of man."

and in 1972 the first American Psychological Association Distinguished Professional Contribution Award.

It is doubtful that this influence and acclaim result solely from Rogers' having developed and researched a relatively distinct system of counseling and psychotherapy; very probably it also results from the not-fully-understood appeal of Rogerian thought to problems of living in our industrial mass society.

INTRODUCTION

Client-centered theory, which was once known as nondirective theory and now sometimes is known as person-centered theory, developed originally as a distinctive approach to individual counseling and psychotherapy, and included major concepts about personality and the nature of man. The theory has been extended, although on a less systematic basis, to all helping relationships, and even further as a psychological-philosophical value system for some of the major social issues of our time.

This chapter will focus primarily on individual counseling and psychotherapy, an emphasis that fits the subject matter of this book. Because of this focus the term "client-centered" will be retained. The reader should know, however, that Rogers now prefers the term "person-centered" because of his interest in the wider applications of the client-centered approach. These extensions of Rogerian theory to other areas have not materially changed those parts of the theory that deal with individual psychotherapy as presented originally by Rogers.[2]

In this chapter, client-centered theory will be presented on the intellectual or conceptual level—an approach that, of necessity, largely ignores the subjective nature of the interview. While the theory can be understood on the conceptual level, one cannot learn to use it effectively in the counseling situation without attending to one's own subjective experience. The very nature of the theory prohibits learning a set of rules and procedures and then applying them mechanically and objectively in the counseling interview. Rogers believes that the subjective nature of the client-therapist interaction is one of the fundamental characteristics of the interview, and that no theory can capture its meaning fully:

> I let myself go into the immediacy of the relationship where it is my total organism which takes over and is sensitive to the relationship, not simply my consciousness. I am not consciously responding in a planful or analytic way, but simply react in an unreflective way to the other individual, my reaction being based (but not consciously) on my total organismic sensitivity to this other person. I live the relationship on this basis.
>
> The essence of some of the deepest parts of therapy seems to be a unity of experiencing. . . . In these moments there is, to borrow Buber's phrase, a real and 'I-thou' relationship, a timeless living in the experience which is *between* the client and me. It is the opposite pole from seeing the client, or myself, as an object. It is the height of personal subjectivity (Rogers, 1955, pp. 267–268).

[2]Personal communication, August, 1977.

Learning to use client-centered theory, or any therapeutic theory for that matter, involves discovering for oneself what the theory builder originally discovered for himself. The theory can serve as a map on the route to discovery, but it cannot by itself teach anyone to become an effective counselor. Thus, the application of therapeutic theory is quite different from the application of physical theory, which can be applied with little regard to human interaction. Therapeutic theory, because it is applied in the subjectively oriented give-and-take between two persons, must be integrated into the therapist's personality. To apply it as we customarily apply theory in physics and chemistry would be to view the client and oneself as objects and would thereby result in the loss of the subjective element that Rogers and many others see as essential. It is in this sense, perhaps, that counseling and psychotherapy will always remain an art, no matter how refined and sophisticated our theories become.

For the sake of clarity and simplicity, Rogers' theory will be presented in a declarative style that will tend to give the reader the impression that Rogers views his theory as established fact. Nothing could be further from the truth. Rogers has emphasized repeatedly that his theory cannot be taken as dogma and can best be used as an impetus to new discovery. He welcomes and fully expects new research evidence and new clinical insights to change his and other theories of counseling and psychotherapy. Rogers (1959a) noted that even mature theories contain unknown amounts of error and mistaken inference, and therapeutic theory, which has advanced little beyond the stage of hypothesis development and crude discovery, is especially vulnerable to change.

Rogers (1959a) also pointed out that any theory is a more dependable guide when applied to the events out of which the theory grew, because less inference is needed to apply it to such events, and unknown errors are apt to be less consequential. A theory becomes a less dependable guide as it is used to explain more remote events; that is, more inference is required and slight errors may be magnified. Client-centered theory developed primarily from therapeutic interviews where personality growth and change were either the explicit or the implied goal. This goal may be more or less salient in each specific counseling situation. When it is less salient, client-centered theory can be a useful guide, but some of the specific counseling procedures discussed in this chapter may require adaptation.

The presentation to follow draws heavily from Rogers' (1959a) most comprehensive theoretical statement although earlier and later writings will be considered. Some more recent neo-Rogerian theorizing will also be presented but in less depth. Because of space limitations, the theory will be abbreviated and at times stated tersely. For a fuller view, the reader is referred to Rogers' main books (1951, 1961b, 1967), and to his statement of formal theory (1959a).

PHILOSOPHY AND MAJOR CONCEPTS

Philosophically, Rogerian theory is usually seen in contrast with the more dominant traditions both of Freudian and of experimental-behavioristic psychology; and it is seen as being closely allied with phenomenology, existentialism, and humanistic psychology.

This characterization is not wholly correct. Midway through his career, Rogers did discover common ground with parts of existential philosophy, especially the writings of Søren Kierkegaard; he also joined the humanistic psychologists in condemning the mechanistic view of human beings that is often associated with behaviorism and Freudian psychology; and clearly he embraces phenomenology that uses personal, subjective knowledge as the foundation for an abstract, scientific psychology of human beings (see Snygg & Combs, 1949; Shlien, 1963).

But especially regarding his views of science, the humanistic, existential, phenomenological description of Rogers is misleading. Rogers is an empiricist who insists upon returning again and again to the raw data. He believes in the importance of subjective experience, but he does not reject the objective methods of science. Instead, he believes that rigorous thinking and research validation are needed to avoid self-deception. Science begins with choices and intuitions that occur in persons who have aims, values, and purposes imbued with personal and subjective meanings; but science is incomplete unless it also includes operational definitions, experimental methods, control groups, and mathematical proofs.

Nor is the contrast between Freudian and Rogerian personality theory completely correct in this writer's view, even though Rogers often encourages this contrast. Their systems of therapy are quite different, but both present psychodynamic theories of personality with an unconscious (Rogers: "unavailable to awareness") and a superego (Rogers: "conditions of worth"). Of course, important differences also exist: Freud's id and Rogers' actualizing tendency (see below) are miles apart.

The Rogerian system is not just a theoretical position about personality and psychotherapy; it is also an approach, an orientation, or a point of view about life. In this sense, it is fair to speak of a Rogerian psychology, and the recent introduction of the term "person-centered" to replace "client-centered" seems intended to highlight this development.

Before elaborating this point further, we should note that the more circumscribed client-centered theory of counseling and psychotherapy can stand on its own merit and does not necessarily require agreement with all aspects of the Rogerian system. Of course, Rogers' "philosophy of life" influenced his formulations about counseling and psychotherapy, and in turn his observations about successful clients influenced what has become a more general Rogerian psychology. But the client-centered theory of counseling and psychotherapy can, and to a large extent does, rest upon research and the direct observation of the actual events of psychotherapy. The client-centered theory of therapy follows an "if-then" model and states that if certain conditions exist, then a predictable process that has certain characteristic outcomes is set in motion. In this form, client-centered theory is less than satisfying because most of us want an "explanation" of why a particular sequence of events should occur. In the present instance, Rogers' conceptions about personality and the nature of human beings help to satisfy our need for a more complete explanation, but other explanations are possible and in fact have been put forth.

Let us return briefly to the Rogerian system as an approach to life. Rogers has consistently been suspicious of almost anything that interferes with the person's freedom and own inner sense of direction. Not only is this theme present in his theory of therapy and personality, but over the years it has appeared in his writings about groups, education, student personnel work, leadership, business, science, and our society generally. From the beginning, client-centered counseling and psychotherapy had something of the quality of the protest movement. Rogers continually raised perceptive and often needling questions about the "approach of the expert," in which a therapist, an administrator, a scientific theory, or a social institution functions in such a way as to prescribe the goals and the appropriate behavior of the individual. Rogers questions almost anything that interferes with human freedom and individuality.

But the reverse side of the Rogerian coin is a positive psychology of becoming. He sees great possibilities for a rich and fulfilling life when human beings are freed to live according to their own inherent organismic natures. Human nature is "good," it is trustworthy, it is exquisitely rational. For the person who is living in terms of her inherent nature, Rogers paints a picture of the good life that is characterized by such adjectives as enriching, exciting, rewarding, challenging, and meaningful. A corollary is that society's needs are best met when individuals are free to live as independent and self-directing persons. Rogers is not explicit about the contents of the good life, for he sees it as a process, as something continually in flux and changing. It is not a state or a particular end point to be sought after. Such words as happiness, contentment, adjustment or tension reduction can distort its meaning. These qualities will exist in the person who is living the good life, but so will qualities of anger, anxiety, and pain. All of these will be experienced more vividly and richly, but more important, all will be experienced as acceptable parts of oneself. The person who accepts and lives nondefensively in terms of her inherent organismic nature becomes engaged creatively with the process of life.

The tragedy for Rogers is that most of us live not according to our own organismic valuing process but by values introjected from others, and thereby we become untrue to ourselves. The Rogerian orientation, both as a system of counseling and psychotherapy and as a philosophical-psychological approach to life, should free us to be ourselves, and this state of being will be both meaningful personally and constructive socially. This emphasis upon personal autonomy does not, as some persons assume, lead to a rejection of social norms; rather, Rogers believes that living by one's organismic valuing process is both uniquely personal for each individual and at the same time deeply social. In a short but thoughtful essay, Peter Homans (1974) notes that Rogerian psychology "presupposes a collective or universal form of sociality" that is grounded in our inherent nature and in the character of the experiencing self. "On the one hand Rogerian therapy releases the individual from social restraint . . . ; on the other hand it returns the individual to a deeper, more organic, more universal form of sociality" (pp. 324–325).

Thus, Rogers offers us a possible solution to the social and personal alienation so rampant in today's mass society, and herein may lie his appeal to psychologist and nonpsychologist alike. In the preface to *On Becoming a Person*, Rogers (1961b) tells us that his purpose in writing this book is to communicate what he has learned "in the jungles of modern life, in the largely unmapped territory of personal relationships." His recent interest in encounter groups (Rogers, 1970) continues this theme. Personality changes that are similar to those seen in individual counseling may occur in encounter group participants, and Rogers values this result when it occurs; but he writes about encounter groups within a much broader context. He expresses concern about the impersonal milieu of this culture, which is associated with scientific and industrial technology, big cities and "multiversities," and computerization in education and even medicine. He sees encounter groups as a "growing counterforce to the dehumanization of our culture," and as a way "to overcome the isolation and alienation of the individual in contemporary life." Encounter groups are further "an avenue to personal fulfillment and growth," an "instrument of institutional change," a way of "exploring new solutions to the problem of the man-woman relationship" and of "relations between parents and children." Rogers expands this theme still further in his most recent book, *Carl Rogers on Personal Power* (1977), where he states in the introduction that "Our work has 'gone to the root' of many of the concepts and values of our culture and has brought about 'a complete or marked change' in many principles and procedures. Most notably it has altered the thinking about power and control in relationships between persons. That is what this book is about" (p. xii). Some of the chapter titles in this book include "The Politics of Administration," "Resolving Intercultural Tensions," and "The Emerging Person: Spearhead of the Quiet Revolution."

While we should note the recent development of person-centered theory as a philosophical-psychological system, a further elaboration is beyond the scope of this chapter. We continue now with Rogers' ideas about human nature, which were formulated when he was focused more centrally on individual counseling and psychotherapy.

Conception of Human Beings

1   *Humans are experiencing beings.*   We are first and foremost *experiencing* (feeling, thinking, willing, inquiring) *beings*. Rogers believes that an adequate science of man must take this characteristic into account. He also believes that the valued core of human life resides in this experiencing, inner person.

2   *Life exists in the moment; life is lived now.*   This is an existentialist concept by which Rogers means to emphasize that life is more than automatic behavior determined by past events, and that the value of life resides in the present rather than in the past or in some desired future. "It has been part of my own therapeutic experience that living fully in this moment is the only way of building constructively on one's past without being owned by it, that living fully in the moment is the only effective way of living for all time" (Rogers, 1974, p. 11).

3   *Fundamental predominance of the subjective.*   The significance of the subjective elements in a client-counselor interaction has already been mentioned, but Rogers' belief in the fundamental predominance of the subjective extends beyond the practice of counseling to most of human behavior. "Man lives essen-

tially in his own personal and subjective world, and even his most objective functioning, in science, mathematics, and the like, is the result of subjective purpose and subjective choice" (Rogers, 1959a, p. 191). Rogers would say that the reader's act of reading this chapter can ultimately be traced to a subjective choice.

Rogers believes that developments in the behavioral sciences will someday enable us to understand human behavior objectively, much as we now understand events in the physical world. However, he also holds

> . . . a very different view, a paradox which does not deny the objective view, but which exists as co-equal with it.
>
> No matter how completely man comes to understand himself as a determined phenomenon, the products of past elements and forces, and the determined cause of future events and behaviors, he can never *live* as an object. He can only live subjectively. . . .
>
> The person who is developing his full potential is able to accept the subjective aspect of himself, and to *live* subjectively. When he is angry he is *angry*, not merely an exhibition of the effects of adrenalin. When he loves he is loving, not merely "cathected towards a love object." He moves in self-selected directions, he chooses responsibly, he is a person who thinks and feels and experiences; he is not merely an object in whom these events occur. He plays a part in a universe which may be determined, but he lives himself subjectively, thus fulfilling his own need to be a person (Rogers, 1961c, pp. 20–21).

4 *"A deep human relationship is one of man's most crying needs."* Rogers has early writings about the significance of what Martin Buber terms the "I-thou relationship," but he has given increased emphasis to this theme in recent years. He now stresses that every individual has a need for a free, spontaneous, mutual and deeply communicative relationship with others, and he sees this need as often frustrated in today's mass society. This newer emphasis is consistent with Rogers' encounter group work and with client-centered theory's recent stress upon the therapist's being genuine and expressing feeling in the therapeutic relationship. Rogers also believes that the furtherance of deep, interpersonal relationships in families, in schools, on the job and the like, has enormous potential as a "mental health resource that will help prevent many, if not most, of the psychological disturbances that plague our culture" (Rogers, 1974, p. 11).

5 *Tendency toward actualization.* Rogers' early writings emphasized that the client's natural capacity for growth and development is an important human characteristic upon which counseling and psychotherapeutic procedures should rely. Over the years, his conviction has grown stronger that the *inherent* tendency of human beings is to move in directions that can be roughly described as growth, health, adjustment, socialization, self-realization, independence, and autonomy. This directional tendency is now labeled the *actualizing tendency*, and is defined as "the inherent tendency of the organism to develop all its capacities in ways which serve to maintain and enhance the organism" (Rogers, 1959a, p. 196).

This conception is simple and all-inclusive. In fact, it is the fundamental characteristic of all life, and applies not only to humans but also to a protozoan, a starfish, a daisy, and a lion. The essential nature of life is that it is an active and not a passive process, in which the organism interacts with its environment in ways that are designed to maintain, to enhance, and to reproduce itself. The actualizing tendency is expressed differently in different species. An acorn develops into an oak tree, tall and sturdy in favorable soil and climate, scrubby and gnarled under unfavorable conditions, but a live oak tree nonetheless, maintaining, enhancing, and reproducing itself as its environment allows.

In humans, the actualizing tendency expresses itself in varied ways. Consider, for example, the child who is learning to walk. Because of the forward direction of growth and development that is inherent in the child's nature, she learns to walk if only the proper conditions are present. She need not be taught to walk. This directional process is not, of course, smooth and unfaltering. The child takes a few steps, falls, and experiences pain. For a time she may revert to crawling. But in spite of the bumps and the pain and even though walking at first is a less efficient means of locomotion than crawling, the child tries again and again. The process is a painful struggle, but because of her nature, the child continues her efforts until she learns to walk and eventually to run and to skip and to jump.

This life-force can be observed in many areas. At the physiological level, the organism's tendency to maintain itself is revealed in the assimilation of food, the maintenance of body heat, and the regulation of body chemistry. At another level, the child strives to feed herself rather than to be fed, to dress herself rather than to be dressed, and to read to herself rather than to be read to. Studies show that humans share with other animals a spontaneous curiosity, a tendency to explore and to produce changes in the stimulus field. Human beings tend to actualize themselves by learning to use tools and verbal concepts, and to maintain themselves by building a shelter against heat and cold. We build theories to improve our understanding and our control of the world. We also tend to strive for meaningful interpersonal contacts and toward socialization, broadly defined.

Rogers' thinking has been influenced by many theorists who have observed and emphasized different aspects of this forward-moving characteristic of the organism. Maslow (1954) spoke of a hierarchy of motives and needs. As the organism satisfies the needs lower in the hierarchy, such as the need for food, water, and safety, it is motivated then by higher needs, such as those for belonging and love and self-actualization. Goldstein (1940) also used the term self-actualization for this basic striving. Mowrer and Kluckhohn spoke of "the basic propensity of living things to preserve and increase integration" (1944, p. 74). Rogers was particularly influenced by Angyal, who stressed that a fundamental characteristic of life is to move in the direction of increasing independence, self-regulation, and autonomy, and away from external control. Angyal said, "Life is an autonomous dynamic event which takes place between the organism and the environment. Life processes do not merely tend to preserve life but transcend the momentary status-quo of the organism, expanding itself continually and imposing its autonomous determination upon an ever increasing realm of events" (1941, p. 48).[3]

[3]Butler and Rice (1963) theorized that self-actualization and drive-reduction theories do not necessarily conflict with one another. They marshal evidence that stimulus hunger or adient motivation is a primary drive, which serves as the basis for self-actualization behavior.

In stressing this actualizing tendency, Rogers wishes to emphasize several ideas:

a The actualizing tendency is the primary motivating force of the human organism.

b It is a function of the whole organism, not just some part of it. Needs and motives can be, and characteristically have been, thought of as more specific. While human beings do seek such specific things as food, sex, and self-esteem, Rogers believes that these more specific conceptions of motivation may obscure more truth than they encourage. In any event, he wishes to emphasize that the organism responds as a whole. Even though at one moment in time the organism may seek food or sex, it characteristically seeks them in ways that enhance rather than diminish its self-esteem and other strivings.

c The actualizing tendency is a broad conception of motivation that includes the usual needs and motives, such as physiological needs for food and water, those aspects of motivation that are often termed tension reduction or need reduction, curiosity, and the seeking of pleasurable activity. However, more than some other theorists of motivation, Rogers emphasizes the human tendency to physical growth, maturation (as illustrated by the infant's learning to walk), the need for close interpersonal relationships ("man is incurably social"), and the human tendency to impose oneself on one's environment—to move toward autonomy and away from external control.

d Life is an active, not a passive, process. Rogers sees the organism as an "active, directional initiator," and he rejects the "empty organism" concept of life, in which nothing intervenes between stimulus and response. He rejects Freud's thinking that the nervous system would, if it could, maintain itself in an altogether unstimulated condition.

e Human beings have the capacity as well as the tendency or motivation to actualize themselves. These capacities, which often are more latent than evident, are released under the proper conditions. Counseling is aimed not at doing something *to* or *for* the individual, but at freeing the individual's capacities for normal growth and development. Counseling theory attempts to specify the conditions that allow growth and development to occur.

6 *Human beings are trustworthy.* Closely related to these ideas is Rogers' confident view of human beings as basically good and trustworthy. Words such as "trustworthy," "reliable," "constructive," and "good" describe characteristics that seem inherent in humans.

Rogers, of course, is fully aware that human beings frequently behave in untrustworthy, even "evil" ways. They are certainly capable of deceit, hate, cruelty, and stupidity. But Rogers views these unsavory characteristics as arising out of a defensiveness that alienates us from our own natures. As defensiveness diminishes and we become more sensitively open to all our experiences, human beings tend to move in ways we think of as socialized and trustworthy. We strive for meaningful and constructive relationships with other beings in ways that enhance our own development and also that of the species.

Rogers' conception contrasts sharply with the view of many psychoanalysts, who see human beings as innately destructive and antisocial: humans are said to be born with instinctual urges that must be controlled if healthy personality development is to occur. To this Rogers answers:

> I have little sympathy with the rather prevalent concept that man is basically irrational, and that his impulses, if not controlled, will lead to destruction of others and self. Man's behavior is exquisitely rational, moving with subtle and ordered complexity toward the goals his organism is endeavoring to achieve. The tragedy for most of us is that our defenses keep us from being aware of this rationality, so that consciously we are moving in one direction, while organismically we are moving in another. But in the person who is living the process of the good life, there would be a decreasing number of such barriers, and he would be increasingly a participant in the rationality of his organism. The only control of impulses which would exist, or which would prove necessary, is the natural and internal balancing of one need against another, and the discovery of behaviors which follow the vector most closely approximating the satisfaction of all needs. The experience of extreme satisfaction of one need (for aggression or sex, etc.) in such a way as to do violence to the satisfaction of other needs (for companionship, tender relationships, etc.)—an experience very common in the defensively organized person—would be greatly decreased. He would participate in the vastly complex self-regulatory activities of his organism—the psychological as well as physiological thermostatic controls—in such a fashion as to live in increasing harmony with himself and with others (1961b, pp. 194–195).

    7 *Human beings are wiser than their intellects.* Closely related to the foregoing is Rogers' belief that human beings are wiser than their intellects, wiser than their conscious thoughts. When humans are functioning nondefensively and well, they trust their total organismic reaction, which often results in better (although more intuitive) judgments than conscious thinking alone.

    Rogers has puzzled about the function of consciousness or awareness. He has written about awareness as one of the latest evolutionary developments, as a "tiny peak of awareness, of symbolizing capacity, based upon a vast pyramid of nonconscious organismic functioning" (1963, p. 17). When the organism functions freely and effectively, awareness is only a small part of the total activity and "tends to be reflexive rather than the sharp spotlight of focused attention" (1963, p. 17). Awareness is sharpened and focused when the organism encounters some difficulty in functioning. Rogers was stimulated by Whyte, who says: "The main purpose of conscious thought, its neobiological function, may be first to identify, and then to eliminate, the factors which evoke it" (1960, p. 37). If Rogers' and Whyte's views about how humans function best are correct, why are the conscious thinking and functioning of human beings so often at odds with their organismic functioning? This problem is considered in the next section on personality theory.

PERSONALITY THEORY: NORMAL AND MALADAPTIVE DEVELOPMENT

Although still tentative and little more than an outline, client-centered personality theory has been elaborated into a series of interlocking formal propositions (Rogers, 1951, 1959a). Others have contributed to the theory: Raimy (1943, 1948) to the self-theory, Snygg and Combs (1949) to its phenomenological emphasis, and Standal (1954) to the theory of childhood development. The account below is considerably abbreviated.

1 *Every individual exists in a continually changing world of experience of which she is the center* (Rogers, 1951, p. 483).

This is the private world of each individual's experience, and is sometimes called the "phenomenal field" or the "experiential field." It includes all that goes on within the organism that might reach consciousness, although only a small part of the organism's experiences are ever conscious at any given time. For example, I can be deeply engrossed in a game or in a conversation and not be consciously aware of the physiological accompaniments of hunger that are being experienced by my organism.

Rogers wishes to emphasize in this proposition that only the individual herself can know this world of experience in any genuine and complete way. We can never know the full experience of another as she fails an examination or goes to a job interview. We can observe another individual, measure her reactions to various stimuli, have her record her thoughts and reactions on psychometric tests, etc., but we can never know fully and vividly how she experiences and perceives any given situation.

Of course, many of the individual's experiences are not readily available to her awareness and thus are not a part of her phenomenal field. If she becomes aware of them, she will do so only under certain conditions, which are discussed more fully in a later section.

2 *"The organism reacts to the field as it is experienced and perceived. This perceptual field is, for the individual, 'reality'"* (Rogers, 1951, p. 484).

3 *"Behavior is basically the goal-directed attempt of the organism to satisfy its needs as experienced, in the field as perceived"* (Rogers, 1951, p. 491).

These two propositions emphasize that we do not react to some absolute reality but to our perceptions of that reality. Rogers has observed that a man who is dying of thirst in a desert will struggle as hard toward a mirage as he would to reach a real body of water. Snygg and Combs (1949) cite a personal example to emphasize this point. One of the authors was riding as a passenger in a friend's automobile on a lonely Western highway at night. Suddenly the headlights illuminated a large object in the middle of the road. The driver appeared unconcerned, but the passenger feared a serious accident. Finally the passenger grabbed the steering wheel and guided the car around the object. The driver, a native of the West, had seen the object as a harmless tumbleweed, whereas the passenger, who lived in a landslide area of the East, had seen it as a boulder. Each reacted according to his own perceptual reality. By knowing the "perceptual reality" of each, we can understand and even predict the behavior of both persons without knowing the objective reality of whether the object was actually a rock or a tumbleweed.

Rogers notes that individuals are continually checking their perceptions against each other to make them a more reliable guide to reality. Each perception is like an hypothesis to be checked against further perceptions: A substance that is first seen as salt is found to taste sweet, and the perception changes to regard it as sugar. While human perceptions tend to become accurate representations of reality as we interact with our environment in attempts to satisfy our needs, many perceptions remain unconfirmed or only partially confirmed. The important psychological fact to remember is that reality for any given individual is her perceptions of reality, regardless of whether those perceptions have been tested and confirmed.

4   *"The best vantage point for understanding behavior is from the internal frame of reference of the individual himself"* (Rogers, 1951, p. 494).

Rogers defines the internal frame of reference as "all of the realm of experience which is available to the awareness of the individual at a given moment. It includes the full range of sensations, perceptions, meanings, and memories, which are available to consciousness" (1959a, p. 210). Understanding another individual from the internal frame of reference involves concentrating on the subjective reality that exists in that individual's experience at any given time. *Empathy is required to achieve this understanding.* By contrast, to understand another individual from the *external frame of reference* is to view her, without empathy, as an object, usually with the intent of emphasizing *objective reality.* Objects such as a stone or an electron have no experience with which we can empathize. Persons become objects in this sense when we make no empathic inferences about their subjective experiences.

Rogers sees the internal and external frames of reference as two different ways of knowing, each of which has its usefulness. His theory of therapy is built on understanding the client's internal frame of reference, but hypotheses of that theory can be verified only by adopting the external frame of reference. Nevertheless, understanding another person from the external frame of reference involves viewing her from our own internal frame of reference. The counselor's internal frame of reference may or may not approximate objective reality more closely than the client's, but it is still only the counselor's *perception* of objective reality and it tends to ignore the client's subjective experience of reality.

5   *"Most of the ways of behaving adopted by the organism are consistent with the concept of self"* (Rogers, 1951, p. 507).

The *self-concept* or *self-structure* is an important construct in the client-centered theoretical system. For Rogers, it is an organized conceptual gestalt consisting of the individual's perception of herself alone and of herself in relation to other persons and objects in her environment, together with the values attached to these perceptions. The self-concept is not always in awareness, but it is always available to awareness. That is, the self-concept by definition excludes unconscious self-attitudes that are not available to consciousness. The self-concept is considered fluid, a process rather than an entity, but at any given moment it is a fixed entity.

Stated more informally, the self-concept is the picture an individual has of herself, along with her evaluation of this picture. For example, a client may perceive of herself as above average in intelligence, as a good student except in mathematics, as unattractive to members of the opposite sex, as liking to work with her hands, as loving her parents, as afraid of the future, etc. And she may value any of these characteristics either positively or negatively.

The importance of the self as a regulator of behavior was one of the earliest ideas emphasized by the client-centered group, and it assumed considerable importance in their counseling long before most other parts of the personality theory were developed. Of course, many theorists have been interested in the self, but attention was drawn to the importance of the self in client-centered counseling because clients continually talked about their "selves" once they became deeply involved in counseling. Expressions such as the following were common: "I just cannot see myself as capable of directing a bunch of unruly kids in a classroom"; "I am good at jokes and making small talk, but I am really a very shy person underneath"; "I have always been a loving and dutiful son, and I owe it to my father to consider carefully his wishes about my schooling"; "I am capable of doing good work when I study, but I am really more the socializing type"; "I try to hide the real me"; and "I'm just no good underneath this false front."

Over the years clinical observation and considerable research made it apparent that attitudes toward the self were important determinants of behavior. Changes in the client's behavior and attitudes toward others seemed to follow changes in attitudes about self. As the evidence accumulated, the self-concept evolved into a central construct of client-centered theory.

Of course, needs are also important determinants of behavior. But needs can usually be satisfied in a wide variety of ways, and the particular behavior selected to meet a need is usually consistent with the self-concept. For example, the need for food or physical activity is satisfied by behaviors that are consistent with the person's self-concept: "I need food, but I also consider myself an honest person and therefore do not steal from the local supermarket." Similarly, a person who does not view herself as aggressive does not react with anger and violence when some need is frustrated by another person. Instead, she may cajole or flatter or withdraw, in an attempt to meet her need in ways that are more consistent with her self-concept.

The reader should note that this part of client-centered theory states that most of the behavior adopted by a person is consistent with the self-concept. However, maintaining this consistency is often difficult, particularly, for example, if the satisfaction of a strong need necessitates behavior that, objectively, would be contrary to the individual's self-concept. In such situations, the individual can employ various defensive maneuvers in an attempt to keep her perception of her behavior consistent with her self-concept. This kind of situation forms the basis for Rogers' view of maladjustment and will be considered in the next sections, which present the client-centered theory of childhood development and the theory of threat and defense.

6 *Early childhood development and the basic estrangement of human beings.* How does it happen that individuals are so often at war with themselves? Rogers calls this the problem of incongruence or dissociation, which is a problem encountered repeatedly by those who study the dynamics of human behavior. A clarifying example would be that of the student who wishes consciously to succeed in school, but who engages repeatedly in behavior that diverts her from her studies and ensures her failure.

In general terms, Rogers' answer is that an incongruence or rift develops between the individual's self-concept and her organismic experience, because love from her parents and significant others is made conditional upon her introjecting certain constructs and values as if they were her own. The constructs and values that are incorporated into her self-concept are often rigid and static and prevent the child's normal process of evaluating her experiences. Therefore, the child develops and attempts to actualize a self that is contradictory or incongruent with organismic processes based on the actualizing tendency.

a *The organismic valuing process.* As the human infant begins life, she evaluates her experiences against the criterion of her basic actualizing tendency, which as noted earlier is the only motive postulated by the theoretical system. The infant values and seeks those activities that further the aim of the actualizing tendency; those that negate this aim she values negatively and avoids. This way of regulating behavior is known as the *organismic valuing process.* It involves a feedback mechanism that ensures that the infant's behavior will meet her motivational needs.

b *The development of the self-concept.* Some of the infant's experiences are differentiated and symbolized crudely as an awareness of being. They are termed "self-experiences" and eventually become elaborated into the *self-concept.* A part of the actualizing tendency becomes differentiated as a tendency toward self-actualization.

c *The development of the need for positive regard.* As her awareness of self is emerging, the infant is also developing a need for positive regard, which can be viewed roughly as the need for warmth and love from her mother. According to Rogers, this is a persistent and pervasive need, and is present universally in all human beings.

The infant must infer from her mother's tone of voice, gestures, and other ambiguous stimuli whether or not she is receiving positive regard. Partly because of this ambiguity, the child develops a total gestalt about how her mother regards her, and she tends to generalize each new experience of approval or disapproval within the context of her total experience of being loved or unloved. In addition, because of the strength of the need for love, the infant can at times become more responsive to her mother's approval than to experiences that actualize the organism.

d *The development of the need for positive self-regard.* The experiences of being loved or not loved become attached to self-experiences, and thus to the developing self-concept. The result is the development of a learned need for *positive self-regard.*

e *The development of the conditions of worth.* This is a key Rogerian concept. The development of the need for positive regard sets the stage for the child to seek experiences, not because they satisfy her actualizing tendency, but because they satisfy her need for her mother's love. When these sought-after experiences are self-experiences, they also satisfy her learned need for positive self-regard. In this way, the need for positive self-regard also becomes selective.

We now come to an important characteristic of the need for positive self-regard, namely, that it can be satisfied or frustrated in the absence of interaction with the mother or other significant persons in the child's life. In time, therefore, the child comes to seek (or avoid) self-experiences solely because they satisfy (or frustrate) the need for positive self-regard. In other words, the child learns to discriminate the conditions under which her need for mother's love and her own self-esteem are more apt to be satisfied than frustrated. When the infant seeks or avoids self-experiences on this basis, she is, in Rogers' terminology, living by the conditions of worth or, in Rogers' older terminology, by values introjected from others. Thus, a secondary regulatory system of behavior comes into existence, and it can conflict with the organismic valuing process, where the actualizing tendency is the criterion.

f *The development of incongruence between self and experience.* Incongruence, or inconsistency, between the self-concept and experience is also a key concept in client-centered theory. A state of *incongruence* exists when an individual's self-concept is different from the actual experience of her organism. A child is incongruent if she thinks of herself as loving and wishing to take care of her younger sister, when she is organismically experiencing anger and jealousy over having to share her mother's love and attention.

We can now return to our account of childhood development and explain how an incongruence between self and experience is brought about. As noted earlier, self-experiences are the raw material out of which the self-concept develops. Self-experiences that are consistent with both the organismic valuing process and the conditions of worth present no problems, of course. They are perceived accurately and symbolized in awareness, and become incorporated into the self-concept. However, self-experiences that contradict the conditions of worth would, if perceived and assimilated accurately, frustrate the child's need for positive self-regard. Thus, they tend to be perceived selectively and distorted in awareness, or even completely denied to awareness, in an attempt to make them consistent with the conditions of worth. This maneuver allows the child to act in terms of her actualizing tendency, and still meet her need for self-esteem. These denied or distortedly perceived self-experiences cannot, however, be integrated into the developing self-concept accurately. It is in this manner that the self-concept becomes partially incongruent with organismic experiences based upon the actualizing tendency.

g *The basic estrangement of man.* In short, the child learns to need love and to avoid the behavior that she anticipates might bring disapproval. Soon she learns to view herself and her behavior as she thinks her mother views her, even though her mother is absent. In this way, she seeks some behaviors that are not satisfying organismically, and when these are also self-experiences, they may become incorporated into the developing self-concept. Other behaviors that are organismically satisfying are distorted in awareness in an attempt to maintain her mother's love and her own self-esteem. Nor can these experiences be integrated satisfactorily into the developing self-concept. The result is an incongruence between self and experience.

The basic tendency of the organism is to fulfill itself according to the actualizing tendency; however, as the self-concept develops, this same inherent characteristic is also expressed as a tendency to actualize the self. As long as the self-concept and organismic experience are congruent, the individual remains whole and integrated. But when incongruence between self and experience develops, the individual is in conflict, torn between the basic actualizing tendency and the actualization of self. She is now vulnerable to psychological maladjustment. She can no longer live as a whole, integrated person. She becomes a person divided against herself, with one part of her true to the actualizing tendency and one part of her true to the inaccurate self-structure and its incorporated conditions of worth.

Rogers (1963, 1964a) sees this situation as the basic estrangement in human beings. Because of the common but tragic developments in early life, which result in specific types of social learning, human beings have become untrue to themselves. This conception is central to all of Rogers' thinking. Individuals avoid this war within themselves when their self-concepts are changing gestalts based upon their organismic experiences. People need to be more open to their experiences, rather than trying to defend a rigidly organized self-concept based upon the conditions of worth—i.e., the values introjected from others. The self must be organized loosely and viewed as a continuing process of becoming. Instead of being rigidly defended as a static entity, the self-concept needs to become a process of continual change and expansion, as the individual is open to each new experience.

Rogers' main theoretical interests about personality and psychotherapy are centered in this process of change and becoming. This interest helps to explain why the developmental aspect of personality theory has expanded so little. Rogers is interested primarily in how people change and become, not in how they got the way they are. Nonetheless, the theory of childhood development is important logically to Rogers' main interest, and it has implications for child-rearing practices.

    h *Illustration and application to child rearing.* Consider the young child who has just discovered her mother's china tea cups. Young children are naturally interested in the world around them, and the child will use all her senses to examine the tea cups. She notices their shape and color; she feels them to see whether they are rough or smooth; she puts them in her mouth to taste them; she swings them in the air to experience their weight; and she bangs them against something to hear how they sound. Only the unusual mother is not upset emotionally to discover the child among the wreckage. She roughly grabs the remaining cups away, plunks her daughter (not too gently or lovingly) into her playpen, and calls her a naughty, bad child. In short, an experience that was organismically satisfying is now associated with loss of love and diminished self-esteem.

The child experiences an almost endless repetition of this general situation. The child experiences loss of love if she touches this or that, if she asks too persistently for help when her parents are engaged in other activities, if she fights with her brother over a toy, if she hits her sister when she is jealous and angry with her, if she wanders away from home and frightens her mother about her safety, if she shows too much interest in her sexual organs, if she urinates outdoors, and so on. It is small wonder that the child develops a self-concept that is incongruent with many organismic experiences based upon her actualizing tendency.

In theory, the incongruence between self and experience would not develop if the child were unable to discriminate any of her self-experiences as being more or less worthy of love than any other self-experience. In practice, this seldom happens. However, less incongruence will develop as more of her self-experiences are met with love and acceptance.

In practice, the mother values her tea cups and naturally is frustrated and angry when they are broken. The more this anger violates a rigidly held self-image of what she thinks a good mother should be (her conditions of worth), the more likely she is to externalize the cause of the anger as her child's "bad" behavior. The more the mother is open to her experience, the more she can own the anger *as hers* and assume responsibility for it *as hers*. She might feel, for example, "I love my child, but I like my tea cups too, and I am hurt and angry that they are broken." If these feelings can be owned and communicated as *her* feelings because she values both the tea cups and the child, then a somewhat different learning situation is possible. The potential is present for the child to discriminate between her experience and her mother's experience: "I enjoy playing with the tea cups" (versus, "I am a bad girl, unworthy of mother's love if I play with the tea cups"), "but mother is hurt and angry when her tea cups are broken." This learning helps to socialize the child without establishing, at least so strongly and rigidly, the conditions of worth. Haim Ginott (1965) and Thomas Gordon (1970) make excellent use of this principle in their books about parent-child interactions.

The essence of the matter as seen by this writer is simply this. If parents can be *open* and *nondefensive* to both their own and their child's experience, can *value* both their own and their child's experience, can *differentiate* between the two, and can *communicate* this valuing and understanding to the child, then the child is less likely to grow into an adult who is at war within herself. In the language of the theory, the conditions of worth are less likely to develop.

7 *Threat and the process of defense.* "The essential nature of threat is that if the experience (which is incongruent with the self-concept) were accurately symbolized in awareness, the self-concept would no longer be a consistent gestalt, the conditions of worth (incorporated within the self) would be violated, and the need for self-regard would be frustrated. A state of anxiety would exist" (Rogers, 1959a, p. 227).

When an individual is incongruent, she is also *vulnerable;* an accurate perception of her organismic experience would threaten a disruption of her self-concept. If, in addition, she is even dimly aware of this threat, a state of tension or *anxiety* exists. The threat need not be perceived clearly. It is sufficient that it be *subceived*, a term Rogers borrows from experimental studies of perception. To be subceived means to be discriminated just below the level of conscious awareness. *Anxiety* is thus the response of the organism when a discrepancy between the self-concept and experience threatens to enter awareness, thus forcing a possible disruption of the self-concept.

The individual defends herself against threat and the accompanying anxiety by denying the experience, or more frequently by misperceiving the experience to make it more consistent with the self-concept. By means of this maneuver, the individual maintains the consistency of her self-structure, and reduces both the awareness of threat and the anxiety. The actual threat, of course, remains (she is still vulnerable), but the person has defended herself against it. She pays the price for this gain, however, in a rigidity of perception and in a distortion of reality.

In response to strong and unsatisfied needs of the organism, behavior sometimes occurs that is inconsistent with the self-concept, within a context where it cannot be denied or distorted easily. In such instances, the person typically disowns the behavior with reactions like, "I didn't know what I was doing," "I was very upset and not myself," or "If the evidence weren't right in front of me, I wouldn't believe it; it's just not like me at all."

The probability of this kind of reaction increases with the severity of emotional disturbance. Neurotic behavior is often incomprehensible to the individual since "it is at variance with what he consciously 'wants' to do, which is to actualize a self no longer congruent with experience" (Rogers, 1959a, p. 203). Statements like the following are frequent in the counseling interviews of neurotic clients: "I didn't want to do it, but I did. I just can't understand why," or "I just have no control over this feeling. It doesn't even seem a part of me but is like some intruder."

The usual defensive behaviors that are discussed so frequently in the literature (such as projection, rationalization, wish-fulfilling fantasy, and the like) can, according to Rogers, be fitted into the client-centered scheme of threat and defense, but we shall not take the time to illustrate this here.[4]

8 *The process of change.*   To change the process of threat and defense, the self-concept must become more congruent with the individual's actual organismic experiences. But changes in the self-structure are resisted, because these tend to violate the conditions of worth and the learned need for positive self-regard. The avenue to change, therefore, involves creating the conditions where there is less threat and less need to resist. According to the theory, this calls for a corrective relationship with another person, which will decrease the necessity to act upon the conditions of worth and will increase the individual's positive self-regard. That is, there must be a reversal of the conditions described in the section on infant development. The theory of therapy, to be presented shortly, describes the conditions that make this possible. The aim is to relax the boundaries of the client's self-concept, so that it may assimilate denied and distorted experiences. In this way, the self becomes more congruent with experience.

9 *Optimal adjustment or the fully functioning person.*   The ideally adjusted person is completely open to all her experiences. Her experiences are not, of course, always in awareness, but they are always available to awareness in

---

[4]Psychotic behavior is accounted for by a different part of the theory, and results when a failure of the defenses is accompanied by a serious disorganization and a breaking down of the self-structure.

accurately symbolized form. That is, she exhibits no defensiveness. There are no conditions of worth, and she experiences unconditional positive self-regard. Her self-concept is congruent with her experience, and she acts in terms of her basic actualizing tendency, which also actualizes the self. Since her experiences change as she meets different life situations, her self-structure becomes a fluid gestalt that is always in the process of assimilating new experiences. The individual experiences herself not as a static being, but as a process of becoming. This hypothetical, fully functioning person would be:

> . . . fully open to his experience (and) would have access to all of the available data in the situation, on which to base his behavior: The social demands; his own complex and possibly conflicting needs; his memories of similar situations; his perception of the uniqueness of this situation. The data would be very complex indeed. But he could permit his total organism, his consciousness participating, to consider each stimulus, need and demand, its relative intensity and importance, and out of this complex weighing and balancing, discover that course of action which would come closest to satisfying all his needs in the situation. An analogy which might come close to a description would be to compare this person to a giant electronic computing machine. Since he is open to his experience, all of the data from his sense impressions, from his memory, from previous learning, from his visceral and internal states, are fed into the machine. The machine takes all of these multitudinous pulls and forces which are fed in as data, and quickly computes the course of action which would be the most economical vector of need satisfaction in this existential situation. This is the behavior of our hypothetical person.
>
> The defects that make this process untrustworthy in most of us are the inclusion of information that does *not* belong to this present situation, or the exclusion of information that *does*. It is when memories and previous learning are fed into the computations as if they were *this* reality, and not memories and learning, that erroneous behavioral answers arise. Or when certain threatening experiences are inhibited from awareness, and hence are withheld from the computation or fed into it in distorted form, this too produces error. But our hypothetical person would find his organism thoroughly trustworthy, because all the available data would be used, and it would be present in accurate rather than in distorted form. Hence his behavior would come as close as possible to satisfying all his needs—for enhancement, for affiliation with others, and the like.
>
> In this weighing, balancing, and computation, his organism would not by any means be infallible. It would always give the best possible answer for the available data, but sometimes data would be missing. Because of the element of openness to experience, however, any errors, any following of behavior that was not satisfying, would be corrected quickly. The computations, as it were, would always be in the process of being corrected, because they would be checked continually against their consequences[5] (Rogers, 1961b, pp. 190–191).

GOALS OF COUNSELING

The goal of all counseling and psychotherapy can usefully be divided into two broad categories, namely, personality-growth-type goals and cure-type or prob-

---

[5]Rogers' theory of creativity is closely related to his theory of the fully functioning person.

lem-solving-type goals. Growth-type goals are illustrated by such phrases as "developing a positive life-style," "increasing personality integration," or "decreasing intrapsychic conflicts." The common theme in growth-type goals is broadly based personality changes that help the client to develop a sense of personal progress in living life. Cure-type or problem-solving-type goals have more specific objectives, and are illustrated by such phrases as "reduction of symptomatic pain," "becoming more assertive," or "making an effective vocational choice." These two types of goals have profoundly different implications for the work of the counselor, even though they are not completely disparate. Solving a specific problem or relieving a specific symptom may well occur in growth-type counseling, but it is incidental to the larger enterprise; conversely, broader personality changes may be subsidiary, but not directly sought after, benefits in "treat-and-cure-therapies."

Before pursuing the discussion further, I wish to note and then set aside an important theoretical issue that the behavior modification adherents have placed center stage. This group rejects categorically the contention that change in underlying personality is ever the appropriate goal of counseling. They advocate the position that counselors should help clients to specify their problems in concrete, behavioral terms, and that all counseling should aim *directly* at altering the troublesome behavior. They view psychodynamic theories of personality and behavior, of whatever variety, as simply misguided and false, and thus as irrelevant to the work of the counselor. The central issue here, of course, is the relative validities of competing families of theories, and this chapter is not the appropriate place to consider this dispute. Counselors who view all psychodynamic theories of behavior as mistaken will not be interested in the application of client-centered theory to the work of the counselor.

Client-centered counseling and psychotherapy clearly advocate growth-type goals. The aim is reorganization of the self. The theory states that successful counseling will dissolve the conditions of worth, increase openness to organismic experience, and thereby increase the degree of congruence between the self-concept and experience. In this way, the client becomes a more fully functioning person. Client-centered counselors do not ask how they can solve particular problems, or promote this or that specific behavior change. They ask how they can provide a relationship that the client can use for personal growth. Within this emphasis there is, of course, the expectation that clients will discover better ways of coping with troublesome aspects of life, and that they will solve specific problems; but the counselor does not set a specific problem solution or a specific behavior change as the goal of counseling. Nor does the client-centered counselor seek to adjust the client to society.

An important caveat must be noted. Practical limitations of time and setting frequently mean that the personal growth goal of the client-centered theory sets a direction rather than an end state. Limitations of time and of setting or other factors may well mean that the client will not move very far toward Rogers' ideal of the fully functioning person. Rogers would accept such practical limitations as reality, and still emphasize the necessity of providing a therapeutic relationship in which the client can move as far as time and circumstances permit. An encounter group can extend for two hours, a weekend, or ten full days—as can individual counseling. When the counseling is less extensive, less movement toward the goal of personal growth is to be both expected and accepted.

Many work settings impose limits on the time a counselor may spend with any one client. All systems, but especially growth-type systems of counseling and psychotherapy, have difficulty coping with this reality limitation. Three general approaches to this problem have been explored within the client-centered framework as well as within other frameworks. The first approach, more typical of client-centered therapy than other therapies, is *time-limited psychotherapy*, in which the total number of interviews is specified in the first client contact. Research indicates that this approach can be effective (Lewis, Rogers, & Shlien, 1959; Shlien, 1957). This writer has told clients, with some success, that because of the waiting list, they could have only a limited number of appointments. A client may be disappointed, but can still use the available time constructively.

Group therapy is a second approach, even though its aims often address other issues as well. Like other theories, client-centered theory has been adapted to group procedures (Beck, 1974; Gorlow, Hoch, & Telschow, 1952; Hobbs, 1951; Rogers, 1970; Truax, 1961).

A third approach, which again is not unique to client-centered therapy, may be the wave of the future, and takes various forms that cannot be described adequately in a few words. Its central characteristic is a deemphasis of the direct therapeutic role of the professionally trained counselor or therapist, in favor of other ways of assisting. It includes, but is broader than, the approach of community psychology. It embraces activities as diverse as the use of paraprofessionals and nonprofessionals, hot-line services, milieu therapy, therapeutic communities, parent effectiveness training, leaderless encounter groups, companionship therapy, and organizational functioning and systems change, all of which are humanly and personally beneficial to the individuals involved. The general principles of human growth and change that are derived from client-centered therapy have been applied, often in combination with other ideas, to most of the areas just mentioned. A discussion of these diverse applications of client-centered theory is beyond the scope of this chapter, but several sources of information about these applications are available to the interested reader (Batten & Batten, 1967; Barrett-Lennard, 1977; Berzon, Solomon & Riesel, 1972; Carkhuff, 1969, 1972; Carkhuff & Bierman, 1970; Farson, 1972; Gendlin, 1967b, 1970; Gendlin & Beebe, 1968; Gendlin & Hendricks, 1972; Goodman, 1972; Gordon, 1955, 1970; Guerney, 1964; Guerney, et al., 1972; Rogers, 1977; W. Rogers, 1974).

Although the growth-type goals of client-centered therapy can be implemented in any of the three approaches just outlined, they remain growth-type goals, and a weakness of client-centered theory is that growth-type goals are not necessarily appropriate to all the presenting problems that clients bring to the counselor. This writer at least believes that cure-type or problem-solving type goals are sometimes more salient, and that the happy resolution of many client problems does not require the reorganization of the self or any other broad personality changes. This belief might be most applicable to uncomplicated educational and vocational problems, sexual problems, or problems of conditioned responding, such as many phobic behaviors. Again, this is not an issue for client-centered theory alone, since other theories that emphasize growth-type goals encounter similar difficulties. In any event, this writer believes that it is unwise to proceed in all counseling situations as if the reorganization of self should be the main goal for all clients and for all presenting problems. Frequently, more conservative objectives will suffice, and will meet the client's needs and expectations better. Very probably this is one of the reasons why most counselors and psychotherapists, including client-centered counselors, have become more eclectic in recent years. This writer, for example, offers assistance to persons with sexual dysfunctions, such as erectile failure or anorgasmia, where direct symptomatic treatment of roughly the Masters and Johnson variety is often the treatment of choice for reasons both of effectiveness and of economy. Sometimes simple information alone, which can be provided in one or two sessions, is sufficient.

Even when the presenting problem suggests a problem-solving-type goal, it is not always easy to know with certainty whether a problem-solving-type approach is appropriate. Not infrequently, sexual dysfunctions or educational and vocational problems are deeply intertwined with other aspects of the client's personality. Values and attitudes, personal identity issues, and intrapsychic conflicts may need attention before clients can resolve their presenting concerns effectively. In such instances, growth-type goals may not only be appropriate but necessary. At other times both approaches may be needed. For example, suppose a growth-type therapy is needed to deal effectively with a particular client's sexual problem. In such an instance, it is commonly reported that a successful growth-type therapy experience may still not alleviate the client's sexual dysfunction, whereas a growth-type approach that is followed by direct symptomatic treatment may succeed where either alone would have failed.

Rogers' theoretical statements are not necessarily inconsistent with the above view. One of his necessary conditions for therapy, to be presented shortly, is that the client should be "incongruent," and preferably anxious as well. For some counseling situations, we can modify this proposition to state that the client should be incongruent in those areas of personality that are significantly related to the presenting problem. If this condition does not hold, client-centered theory is only partially relevant. To illustrate, many students seek counseling assistance before deciding on their educational and/or vocational goals. The fact that such students may have marked incongruence in the sexual area of their lives or in their relationship with their parents may be essentially irrelevant to solving the immediate problem. If we assume no incongruence of consequence in areas relating to, say, their vocational choice (an assumption that seems justified in many instances), then counseling as conceived by Rogers would not get underway with the immediate problem at hand. Of course, counseling might get underway in those areas where the student is incongruent, but desirable as this might be, it still leaves both student and counselor with the issue of selecting an appropriate major.

It should be added that even when client-centered growth goals may not be the best choice for a particular presenting problem, the client-centered view of the effective interpersonal relationship between counselor and client (to be presented in the next section) can still be useful. The counselor's genuineness, the counselor's empathic understanding of the student and of the situation, and the counselor's liking and respect for the student as a person help to create an effective working relationship that is beneficial for most counseling objectives.

Alan Bergin (1971) discusses another aspect of counseling goals that merits attention: as we learn more and more about which therapeutic procedures produce given kinds of client change, how do we decide which changes are desirable? Perry London (1964) argues that therapists tend to promote what they value personally, and they thus become "secular moralists." In this vein, Bergin notes that counselors or therapists who advocate cure-type or problem-solving-type goals tend to advocate values that are shared widely in the society: it is better, for example, to have a harmonious marriage or to not be phobic or to not have an erectile problem. "Treat-and-cure" therapists follow closely the current societal view that the role of counselors and therapists is to help individuals function effectively in the mainstream of society. Growth-type therapists, on the other hand, may promote less widely shared value systems, and they often do this without society's (or the client's) assent or knowledge. Worse yet, therapists themselves are frequently unaware of this role.

It is to Rogers' credit that he is explicit about what he values. Inherent in his system is the view that ultimate moral authority derives from one's own organismic experience, and not from society or from some higher power. His values and his therapeutic goals are spelled out in his concept of the fully functioning person (see Chapters 8 and 9 in Rogers, 1961b). He states clearly that his fully functioning person would *not* necessarily be adjusted to society, would *not* be conformist, would *not* fit the Menninger Clinic's concept of the "normal" personality, would *not* form a self-concept around the goal of trying to please others. He states clearly that his *is* a value position. He thus confronts society with a conflicting value system, and becomes an agent of social ferment and change that has implications beyond the consulting room.

In this sense, Rogers is anything but nondirective. Specificity about the valued goal of counseling and psychotherapy constitutes advocacy of a moral system and a view of the desired relationship between the individual and society. Paradoxically, Rogers has in one sense conscientiously avoided counselors' imposing their values on clients, but in another sense he advocates a controversial moral position. However, Rogers would undoubtedly argue that while he does have an explicit value position about the nature of the healthy personality, he does not impose his value system on clients; rather, because of the inherent nature of human beings, his fully functioning person emerges naturally out of a counseling system or out of a social system that permits this emergence. Others might argue that because the fully functioning person is itself a product of Rogerian therapy, his value system *is* thereby imposed on the client.

However these knotty issues are resolved, it does seem evident that our values do influence our work as counselors and psychotherapists. Bergin (1971) points out that this fact should compel us "to argue more explicitly our views for and against the values of the social milieu in which we live." Again to his credit, this is precisely what Rogers has done.

PROCESS AND PROCEDURES OF COUNSELING

Rogers' (1959a) formal theory of therapy and personality change follows an "if-then" model, and consists of three main parts: conditions, process, and outcome. *If* certain *conditions* exist, then a definable *process* is set in motion, which leads to certain *outcomes* or changes in the client's personality and behavior. Alongside this formal theory, the current description stresses the *concept of experiencing* as formulated by Gendlin, by Rogers, and by others. Gendlin's view, which is accepted by Rogers, is that a flow of self-experiencing goes on in the human organism at all times, a flow to which clients can turn again and again as a reference to discover significant personal meanings. Both the formal theory and the concept of experiencing will be presented in this section.

The Conditions of Therapy

Most schools of therapy emphasize technical psychotherapeutic skills and the specialized training needed to acquire them. Consequently, much has been written about such topics as dream interpretation, free imagery, handling transference, manipulating ambiguity, or the subtle use of positive and negative reinforcement. In contrast, a concern with such topics is conspicuously absent from Rogers' theory of therapy. He does not believe that the therapist's technical skills and training account for success. Instead, Rogers has long believed that certain attitudes that are held and communicated by the therapist are the important ingredients that promote change in the client. These therapist attitudes have come to be known as the "therapist condition variables," or simply as the "facilitative conditions."

In 1957, Rogers presented a formal theory of the conditions that are both *necessary* and *sufficient* to get the process of therapeutic personality change underway; that is, the process will begin only if the stated conditions are present, and will not begin unless they are present. Other conditions that might help to get the process underway were not included in the formal theory. Since then Rogers (1967) has agreed that it is difficult, if not impossible, to establish the necessary and sufficient conditions of therapy, but he still believes that therapist attitudes can account for much of the constructive change that occurs in counseling and psychotherapy. The fact that the more precise formulation of the therapist conditions variables had heuristic value has been demonstrated clearly by the flood of research that followed Rogers' 1957 paper.

As paraphrased from Rogers (1957, 1959a) and Rogers, Gendlin, Kiesler, & Truax (1967) the theory states that the amount of process movement and the amount of constructive personality change that occur in therapy are dependent upon the degree to which:

   1   The therapist is *congruent* or *genuine* in the relationship.
   2   The therapist experiences *unconditional positive regard* or *warm acceptance* for the client.
   3   The therapist exhibits *accurate, empathic understanding* of the client's *internal frame of reference.*

Three other condition variables that do not deal with therapist attitudes are added for the sake of completeness and of clarity.

4 The client and the therapist are in *contact* with each other.

5 The client is in a state of *incongruence*, and is *vulnerable* and preferably *anxious.*

6 The client perceives, at least to a minimal degree, the therapist's *genuineness, unconditional positive regard,* and *empathic understanding.*

The fourth proposition merely calls attention to the logical necessity that there must be at least a minimal relationship between client and counselor. Two persons are in contact if each makes a difference in the experience of the other. This condition will certainly be met in most counseling situations, although Rogers points out that it often appears necessary for the contact to be of some duration before the therapeutic process begins. The condition might be very difficult to meet in working with extremely withdrawn psychotics. See Gendlin (Chapter 16) in Rogers, Gendlin, Kiesler, & Truax (1967) for a fascinating account of the client-centered approach with withdrawn schizophrenics.

The reader will recall from the section on personality theory that clients are incongruent, and therefore are vulnerable when their self-concepts are different from the actual experiences of their organisms. Although Rogers theorizes that the process can get underway if the client is merely *vulnerable,* he believes that the process is more likely to begin if the client is also *anxious* and aware of the threat to the self-concept.

The first three propositions—dealing with genuineness, warm acceptance, and accurate empathy—are the important part of the theory. The therapist who is holding and acting in terms of these attitudes builds a therapeutic climate that results in what Rogers sometimes refers to as the client's experience of being accepted fully or received fully. This climate enables the client to attend more fully to inward meanings, and to perceive new aspects of self that become the first step toward significant change.

Client-centered therapy has frequently been misconstrued and even parodied. It is sometimes described as "um-hm" counseling; the counselor is seen as passive and withholding, and the counselor's job is seen to be repeating what the client has said last. To some extent these distortions may have been encouraged by early client-centered formulations that understood only dimly the full meaning of empathy and of warm acceptance, and that spoke about such techniques as structuring the interview, silence, simple acceptance, and reflection of feelings versus responding to the intellectual content. But long ago Rogers deemphasized techniques in favor of attitudes that facilitate the therapeutic relationship. Many persons who have only a superficial understanding of the client-centered approach fail to comprehend this shift in emphasis. Not only do they see client-centered therapy as a set of special interview techniques, but frequently they have used so-called "nondirective" techniques to implement attitudes that are quite different from those advocated by Rogerian theory. In his reaction against technique-oriented counselors, Rogers goes so far as to declare reflection of feelings a misnomer that contributes to misunderstanding. "When it plays a real function, this kind of response is not a reflection of feeling, but an honest, groping attempt on the part of the therapist to understand fully, sensitively, and accurately the internal feeling of his client" (Rogers, Gendlin, Kiesler, & Truax, 1967, p. 515). Another misconception is that client-centered responding is easy and not very challenging to the therapist. In actuality, enormous sensitivity and skill are required to apply it deftly and without woodenness.

The current view is that the essence of the facilitative conditions resides in the moment-to-moment living of the relationship *between* counselor and client. The facilitative conditions describe a special way of *being with* another person, in which the counselor tries to *experience* the client's inward feelings and personal meaning or, in Gendlin's terms, the flow of the client's inner experiences. The newer formulation stresses the active involvement of the counselor as a person, an involvement in which the counselor's experience is sometimes attended to and expressed, but not imposed upon the client. The counselor's self, feelings, images, and fantasies may at times become a part of the interaction, and this may result in a basic human encounter that is fulfilling and growth-producing for both client and counselor. The modern formulation also speaks less about prohibitions on the counselor, such as avoiding answering questions. Differences in personal style among therapists are recognized, and the emphasis is upon creating a living relationship in which the client feels fully received, no matter how this may be achieved by a particular counselor.

The three facilitative conditions are not distinct states, but are interdependent and related logically. An empathic sensitivity to the inward experience of another person can hardly be achieved without, at least to some degree, caring for that person. And neither empathic understanding nor nonpossessive caring can mean much to the client unless these are real or genuine elements in the counselor's own experience. In 1967, Rogers wrote that congruence or genuineness was of first importance, for without genuineness, warm acceptance and empathic understanding lost much of their significance. In 1975, however, he wrote that empathic understanding is probably most salient when the other person is anxious, hurt, confused, or the like; that congruence is probably more important in "ordinary interactions of life," such as marriage or employer-employee relationships; and that caring or prizing may be more significant in special situations, such as the relationship between mother and infant or therapist and mute psychotic. Be that as it may, the overriding consideration is that the three conditions are intertwined.

Congruence or Genuineness In the formal language of personality theory, *congruence* means that all aspects of the counselor's organismic experience during the interview are freely admissible to awareness, and that the self-concept is congruent with that experience. The counselor trusts that experience and is free to act in terms of it. In more familiar language, the counselor is a genuine, integrated person in the counseling relationship. She is freely and deeply herself, with no front or facade, even an unknowing one. In everyday life, we sense this quality in a person readily. And we tend to trust such persons, because we sense they are being what they are in an open, transparent way. We also sense when a person plays a role and relates to us from behind a facade, and we tend to be cautious about revealing ourselves to such persons. The genuine counselor is spontaneous and expresses the feelings and attitudes that flow in her openly. She is open to both pleasant and hurtful feelings. If negative feelings are present, the counselor can employ these constructively, not destructively, to facilitate honest communication between self and client. The genuine counselor comes into direct personal encounter with the client.

Since counselors are human beings and cannot achieve the ideal of perfect adjustment, let us note immediately that the theory does not say that the counselor must be a completely congruent person. It states that if the counselor is congruent in this relationship with this client, then the process of therapy will get underway. It is sufficient that the counselor be herself accurately during the counseling hour. In addition, this proposition, like the others, should be understood as existing on a continuum rather than on an all-or-none basis.

This aim of counseling is not, of course, for the counselor to discuss her own feelings with her client continually. At one level, this part of the theory stresses the therapeutic value of a nonexploitive, authentic interpersonal encounter; the potential value of open, honest feedback when meaningful exploration or communication is being blocked; and the facilitative encouragement to nondefensive self-exploration that genuineness provides. At another level, the theory stresses that counseling will be inhibited if the counselor feels one way about the interview and the client but acts, even though subtly, in a different way.

Genuineness sometimes means that the counselor will have feelings that inhibit the other facilitative conditions. For example, if I experience boredom or irritation with my client, I will at least to some degree be less empathic and less warmly accepting. Although as stated above the aim is not for the counselor to continually impose her own thoughts and feelings on the client, the counselor does bring her feelings into the interview openly when these are persistent feelings that interfere with the therapeutic relationship. This helps the counselor to be genuine in the relationship, and even where the counselor's feelings pose a problem for the client, the difficulty is now at least out in the open, where the client has the opportunity to deal with it. As noted previously in the section about personality theory, it is important that the counselor both recognize and express the feeling as her own, and not as something for which the client is to blame. It is after all the counselor's and not the client's feeling. To be sure, the feeling arose in the client-counselor interaction, but another counselor might have reacted quite differently.

In his work with encounter groups, Rogers (1970, Chapter 3) extends the concept of congruence by expressing his own feelings more frequently and by using more of his conscious self. He trusts and acts on "the feelings, words, impulses, fantasies, that emerge in me." Such activity is extended to confrontation and feedback, as when he might say, "I don't like the way you chatter on," or "I have the feeling that I never want to see you again." Note how these are expressed as his feelings. Rogers adds that to attack a person's defenses seems to him judgmental, and that he would not say, for example, "You are hiding a lot of hostility," or "You are afraid of your own feelings." It is this writer's understanding that such confrontation and feedback would be infrequent in individual counseling and psychotherapy, not because they are "prohibited," but because the counselor's focus and therefore her experiences are different. In encounter groups, on the other hand, Rogers, as facilitator, strives to become an active participant in the group, especially in the later stages, in which he shares his feelings and even his own personal concerns with the group.

Unconditional Positive Regard or Warm Acceptance   The essence of this facilitative condition is that the therapist experiences a deep and genuine, but non-possessive, caring for the client as a person, and that this caring is uncontaminated by evaluation of the client's feelings, thoughts, and behavior as being good or bad. The therapist values and warmly accepts the client, but this concept goes still further and states that no conditions are placed upon this valuing and warm acceptance. Rogers began using the technical, although more awkward, term *unconditional positive regard* to emphasize this absence of conditionality. The therapist genuinely accepts and cares for the client and experiences none of the client's self-experiences as being more or less worthy of positive regard. The new term also places more emphasis than did earlier conceptions upon liking or caring for the client, which clinical evidence and some research evidence indicate accompanies successful therapy. Rogers carefully points out, however, that this is not a possessive caring that arises out of the counselor's own needs.

Butler (1952) resurrected Dewey's terms *prizing* and *appraising* to help define this concept. To prize another person means to value or esteem her. Appraising, on the other hand, implies an ongoing discriminating, comparing, and selecting process, in which different values are assigned to the various aspects of the person thus discriminated. Thus, the concept of unconditional positive regard implies that the counselor is not appraising the client but rather is prizing her no matter what feelings and motivations the client experiences during the interview. The client is prized as much when she experiences "bad" feelings such as hate, selfish desire, confusion, or self-pity, as when she experiences "good" feelings such as friendliness, accomplishment, mature self-confidence, or tender affection.

Some persons become disturbed and think that this concept implies approval of all the client's behavior. It does not. None of the client's behaviors is judged as making the client more or less worthy of being prized as a person.

The term unconditional positive regard is an unfortunate choice in that it implies an absolute, all-or-none characteristic, whereas it should be thought of as a matter of degree. The counselor can experience more or less unconditional positive regard for the client, but the complete experience of this, as the term seems to make mandatory, is seldom a practical possibility (although Rogers does think that there are brief periods in counseling when the counselor experiences a complete and unconditional positive regard for the client).

It should be noted that the theory states that the counselor must *experience* unconditional positive regard for the client. The word "experience" means that the counselor actually *feels* a prizing for the client. It is not enough that the counselor holds abstract attitudes of respect and acceptance of the dignity and worth of other persons. This abstract or intellectual attitude may help the counselor to develop feelings of unconditional positive regard for her client, but the crucial condition is that the counselor experience such feelings as she relates to her client. Obviously, this experience cannot exist until there is a basis for it in the client-counselor interaction. In this sense, there is always an element of uncertainty and risk in each new counseling case.

Although client-centered counselors have written much about unconditional positive regard and the related concepts of acceptance, respect for the client's separateness, prizing, and even love for the client, it is difficult to convey the precise meaning of the concept. It is a deep and pervasive experience on the part of the counselor; yet it is not blind, maudlin, intense, or possessive. Perhaps it involves basically a deep respect for life, for what *is,* for *being,* and a willingness to experience this life fully, without reservation, as it is revealed through the client.

Most theories have concepts that are similar to the client-centered concept of positive regard, and so many people believe that Rogers offers nothing unique. Yet client-centered theory goes further than other theories. Rogers has defined the concept more precisely, has articulated theories about the influence of positive regard on the process and outcome of therapy, and has stimulated research to test these propositions. Also, client-centered counselors think that other theoretical orientations employ additional concepts that contradict at least to a degree the full meaning of unconditional positive regard. For example, counseling approaches that call for considerable diagnostic activity on the part of the counselor must introduce situations in which the client will experience the feeling that some of her self-experiences are being more or less prized by the counselor.

Accurate Empathy Rogers believed that the empathic way of being with another person is a powerful and usually underrated route both to understanding personality dynamics and to effecting changes in personality and behavior. Accurate empathy is the "main work" of the counselor. Accurate empathy means striving to understand sensitively and accurately the client's experiences and feelings, and their meanings to the client as these are revealed during the moment-by-moment interaction of the therapy hour. It means becoming thoroughly at home in the client's private perceptual world. It means being sensitive in the here-and-now to the ever changing flow of self-meanings that are a part of the client's experiencing process. It means that the counselor is inwardly secure enough to lay aside, temporarily, all personal views, values, and concerns, and to enter the private world of the client. On the negative side, it means not trying to uncover feelings of which the client is totally unaware. It means trying not to divert the client's own inner experience. The purpose of accurate empathy is to help the client to get closer to her own experience, which in turn becomes the reference that guides her behavior and self-understanding. In the language of formal theory, accurate empathy encourages recognition and resolution of the incongruences between self and organismic experiences.

Like the other facilitative conditions, the concept of accurate empathy has evolved toward freeing the counselor to be a more active participant in the therapeutic relationship. High levels of accurate empathy go beyond recognition of obvious feelings to a sensing of the less obvious and less clearly experienced feelings and personal meanings of the client. The client's apparent feelings are, of course, recognized and understood, but the therapist also strives to understand those aspects of feeling that are present but that the client perceives and communicates less clearly. The therapist helps the client to expand awareness of these feelings. High levels of accurate empathy often involve using subtle cues to help the client get closer to implicitly meaningful aspects of her experience that are still preconceptual, and thus are difficult to understand and express. This sensing of implicit meanings is partly intellectual, but it also relies on the counselor's organismic experience of what it would be like to live the experiences of the client. For example, the counselor's images and fantasies can be used as an aid to understanding (Butler, 1974). These images and fantasies are not imposed on the client but are expressed in a sensitive way. And the counselor checks continually with the client about how well the counselor's self-sensings fit the client's actual experience.

In his formal theory, Rogers defines the state of being empathic as perceiving

> . . . the internal frame of reference of another with accuracy, and with the emotional components and meanings which pertain thereto, as if one were the other person, but without ever losing the "as if" condition. Thus it means to sense the hurt or pleasure of another as he senses it, and to perceive the causes thereof as he perceives them, but without ever losing the recognition that it is as if I were hurt or pleased, etc. If this "as if" quality is lost, then the state is one of identification (1959a, pp. 210–211).

This passage still provides a good description of accurate empathy, but Rogers (1957b) now prefers to describe empathy as a process rather than as a state. By emphasizing process, I think he is attempting to highlight the counselor's sometimes intuitive attempts to sense the felt meanings of the client's experience. Empathy is a way of being with the client.

From the section about personality theory, the reader will recall that to concentrate on the client's internal frame of reference is to concentrate on the client's *experience* of reality as contrasted with objective reality. One of the difficulties in mastering the client-centered approach to counseling is that in the main we are not accustomed to concentrating on the internal frame of reference of another individual but instead view that individual and her situation from our own internal frame of reference, that is, from our own view of what objective reality is for the individual and for her situation. The client-centered approach thus requires that the counselor unlearn familiar ways of relating to others.

Communication of the Facilitative Conditions The final condition listed by Rogers in his formal theory is that the client herself must perceive the counselor's genuineness, unconditional positive regard, and empathic understanding. Obviously, the client will not perceive these things unless the counselor communicates her experiences successfully to the client. The counselor, therefore, strives to relate to the client in such a way that her basic attitudes are implicit in everything she says and does. Body posture, facial expression, tone of voice, comments made, comments not made, etc., are all important. When these arise naturally and spontaneously out of the counselor's experience of unconditional positive regard and empathic understanding of the client's internal frame of reference, much of the problem of communication is solved.

The Process of Counseling and Psychotherapy

The client-centered group has approached questions about the process of counseling and psychotherapy in several different ways. At times the search has emphasized naturalistic descriptions of a sequence of events that tend to occur regularly in successful counseling, and at other times it has emphasized an attempt to specify the essential change-producing variables. As a result, there is no one client-centered theory about the process of therapy.

   1 *Early formulation.* In his earliest formulation, Rogers (1942) described the counseling and psychotherapy process as proceeding through successive but overlapping stages of release and exploration of feeling, through the stage of seeing relationships and achieving insight, followed by decision making and positive action. This description was confirmed when Snyder (1945) and later Seeman (1949) studied case protocols and found that the release of negative feelings was followed by the expression of positive feelings, and that successful counseling tended to move from statements of problems, to insight, to discussion and planning of activity.
   2 *Characteristic changes in the self.* Another approach has been to describe the process in terms of changes in the self-concept and in attitudes toward the self. Many studies that examine electrically recorded and transcribed cases have shown that there is a movement from negative to positive feelings about the self during successful client-centered counseling, and that this movement fails to occur or is much less pronounced in unsuccessful cases (Raimy, 1948; Seeman, 1949; Sheerer, 1949; Stock, 1949).
   These shifts in self-attitudes are seen as an important part of the process that may account for other kinds of changes taking place in the client. For example, Sheerer (1949) has shown that increased acceptance of self is accompanied by an increased acceptance of other persons. Another example is Raskin's (1952) study, which confirmed a shift in the source or locus of evaluations from others to self during successful therapy.
   3 *The formal theory of process.* Rogers developed a formal theory of therapeutic process in 1953, although it was not published until six years later (Rogers, 1959a). This theory spelled out a series of propositions that are abbreviated and are summarized below. Following the if-then model, the theory states that if the conditions of therapy presented earlier are established and maintained over a period of time, then the following process is set into motion:
   a The client gradually becomes freer in expressing feelings in verbal and motor channels, and these feelings refer increasingly to the self rather than to the nonself.
   b "He increasingly differentiates and discriminates the objects of his feelings and perceptions, including his environment, other persons, his self, his experiences, and the interrelationships of these" (Rogers, 1959a, p. 216). In so

doing, the client's experiences become symbolized more accurately in awareness, and she gradually becomes aware of experiences that she had denied or
distorted previously.

   c "His expressed feelings increasingly have reference to the incongruity
between certain of his experiences and his concept of self" (Rogers, 1959a, p. 216).
Because of this, the client experiences threat and anxiety. The defensive process
presented in the theory of personality would prevent this overt experience of
threat were it not for the "continued unconditional positive regard of the therapist which is extended to incongruence as much as to congruence, to anxiety as
much as to the absence of anxiety" (Rogers, 1959a, p. 216).

   d The self-concept becomes reorganized gradually to include experience that has previously been denied or distorted in awareness. Thus, there is an
increasing congruence between self and experience with less need for defensiveness.

   e The client feels positive self-regard increasingly, and reacts to
experiences less in terms of the conditions of worth that are based on the values
introjected from others, and more in terms of the organismic valuing process that
is based on the actualizing tendency.

   4 *The role of immediate experience in psychotherapy.* It should be
noted that the formal theory of process outlined above restricts itself to describing the sequence of events that occurs once the appropriate therapeutic conditions
are established and maintained. A somewhat different view of process attempts to
specify the events of therapy by which changes in personality and behavior are
achieved; during the late 1950s and early 1960s, Rogers and others probed this
question.

   A first step was taken by Gendlin and Zimring (1955) and was later expanded
by Gendlin (1961), who proposed that the concrete, ongoing feeling process
itself was the crucial change-producing element in psychotherapy. Gendlin and
Zimring introduced the term "experiencing" to convey their views that the personality is not made up of contents ("experiences"), but is an ever-changing *experiencing* process that, if attended to, is always implicitly meaningful to the
person. From a philosophical perspective, Gendlin (1962b) treated the concept of
experiencing systematically and attempted to show its explanatory power for
many concepts in personality and psychotherapy (see also Gendlin, 1967a).

   Gendlin's concept of experiencing, although not entirely new, is difficult to
convey in words because it is a contentless ongoing process and not an entity.
It always occurs in the immediate present. If attended to, it is always implicitly
meaningful to the person and can be referred to directly by the individual as a
sensed datum in her own phenomenal field (Gendlin, 1962b). The experiencing
process may or may not be conceptualized in words by the individual, but experiencing is always something different from, and more than, the conceptualization.
Experiencing consists of many elements, but these separate elements are part of
a larger whole that can be sensed in a physically felt way. Much of the client's
experiencing in successful therapy may be preconceptual. It is a common occurrence in interviews for clients to refer to their experiential meanings without being

able to label them or even to describe them very adequately. Instead, the client may point to experiencing with phrases like "this all-tied-up feeling," or "this thing I sense . . . I don't know, but it is really something." Not infrequently, client and counselor will communicate meaningfully about the experience for some considerable time, and yet each has only the vaguest idea in logical and conceptual terms what the experience actually is. It is implicitly meaningful but still preconceptual.

To illustrate that experiencing is always implicitly meaningful, even when it cannot be conceptualized in words, Gendlin cites an everyday experience. Suppose you are listening to a discussion and are now about to say something that you feel is relevant and important. But as you wait your turn to speak, you are distracted and lose the sense of what you are about to say. You had never conceptualized your thoughts in words. You had a "felt sense" of what you wanted to say, and that felt sense was meaningful to you. You search for that sense again, and the experience of recapturing it, if indeed you do, is distinct and unambiguous. There is a physically felt release, a change in bodily felt condition, and you now "know" what you are about to say even though you do not yet "know" it in words. In this illustration, Gendlin notes that a person can have, lose, and regain "a felt meaning" that never was conceptualized in the form of words.

Gendlin gives the term *direct referent* to this felt meaning in experience. Experiential *focusing* (Gendlin, 1969) is the directing of one's attention to these felt meanings. When the client guides verbalizations and interactions with the therapist by these direct referents, there is a carrying forward of experience that Gendlin calls *referent movement*. The direct referent changes, different facets of it emerge into prominence, and different meanings are felt. The direct referent in experience always consists of many things that are potentially separable but are not really separate. They function together in "this" feeling in a physically felt ongoing process. If the client allows the "wholeness" of such meanings to guide verbalizations, rather than some imposed logic or value system, Gendlin believes that referent movement will occur. There will be an unfolding that has its own organismic sense and value direction. The experiencing process is underway and produces change in the client. Gendlin sees no individual as being made of preset "contents," of ideas or emotions that can be manipulated by logic; rather, there is an experiencing process that changes as human beings respond to it in words or in actions. The client's attempts to verbalize experience, as well as her interactions with the therapist, carry the process forward in ways that were blocked or constricted previously. A sensed fear of the boss becomes more a feeling of hurt when she disapproves of me, which turns out to involve feelings of helplessness, which involve feelings of deprivation and loneliness, and so on.

Oversimplifying, the essence of therapy for Gendlin is the unfolding of the experiencing process with client and therapist groping to conceptualize its implicitly felt meanings without at the same time intellectualizing and diverting the process. He sees a direct interpersonal encounter between client and therapist, the empathic reflection of feeling that is traditionally associated with the client-centered method, or the properly timed interpretations of other approaches as capable of achieving this objective.

Following a similar line of thought, Rogers (1958, 1961a, 1961b, Chapter 7) presented his "process equation" of psychotherapy and a scale for measuring that process (Rogers & Rablen, 1958; Rogers, 1959c; Gendlin & Tomlinson, 1967). Rogers defines seven parallel variables that become more of a unity as therapy proceeds: (1) feelings and personal meanings, (2) manner of experiencing, (3) degree of incongruence, (4) communication of self, (5) manner in which experience is construed, (6) the relationship to problems, and (7) the manner of relating to others. Each variable was rated along a continuum that ranged from rigidity and fixity of perceptions, feelings, and experience at one end to "flowingness" and "changingness" at the other end. A brief summary of one part of the process scale should give the reader an idea of how Rogers attempted to conceptualize and study the essential nature of personality change:

> The process involves a change in the manner of experiencing. The continuum begins with a fixity in which the individual is very remote from his experiencing and unable to draw upon or symbolize its implicit meaning. Experiencing must be safely in the past before a meaning can be drawn from it and the present is interpreted in terms of these past meanings. From this remoteness in relation to his experiencing, the individual moves toward the recognition of experiencing as a troubling process going on within him. Experiencing gradually becomes a more accepted inner referent to which he can turn for increasingly accurate meanings. Finally he becomes able to live freely and acceptingly in a fluid process of experiencing, using it comfortably as a major reference for his behavior (1961b, pp. 156–157).

Rogers cites the following example as illustrating what he calls a "molecule of change."

> In the thirty-first interview she is trying to discover what it is that she is experiencing. It is a strong emotion. She thinks it is not guilt. She weeps for a time, then:
> Client: It's just being terribly hurt! . . . and then of course I've come to see and to feel that over this . . . see, I've covered it up.
> A moment later she puts it slightly differently.
> Client: You know, it's almost a physical thing. It's . . . It's sort of as though I were looking at myself at all kinds of . . . nerve endings and bits of . . . things that have been sort of mashed. (Weeping)
> Therapist: As though some of the most delicate aspects of you—physically almost—have been crushed or hurt.
> Client: Yes. And you know, I do get the feeling, Oh, you poor thing. (Pause)
> Therapist: You just can't help but feel very deeply sorry for the person that is you (Rogers, 1959b, p. 52).

Rogers thinks that repeated experiences such as these are the essence of psychotherapy and have the following characteristics:

a. It occurs in the existential moment. It is not "thinking about" but "an experience of something in this instant."
b. There are no barriers to the experiencing, no holding back.
c. The experience is complete in that all elements are freely present in awareness.

Often the experience is not really new; it may have been experienced before but not experienced completely. It has a new intensity.

d.   It has a quality of being acceptable to the client. The feeling *is*, it exists, and it is found acceptable on this basis. The client in the example above "*is* the self-pity she feels—entering fully and acceptingly into it—and this is integration at that moment" (Rogers, 1959b).

Outcomes of Counseling and Psychotherapy

It is difficult to distinguish clearly between process and outcome. When we study outcomes directly, we examine the differences between two sets of observations that are made at the beginning and at the end of the interview series. Many process studies make successive observations over a series of counseling interviews and, in a sense, are miniature outcome measures that establish a trend line for the case. Consider, for example, a study cited earlier, which shows an increase in acceptance of self and of others between the beginning and the end of counseling.[6]

Nor does Rogers' formal theory make a distinction between process and outcomes. The main proposition in Rogers' theoretical statement about outcomes is, "The client is more congruent, more open to his experience, less defensive" (1959a, p. 218), but we note that the formal theory of process has already stated that the same conditions are developing gradually throughout the interviews. The outcome theory, then, goes on to spell out more specific dimensions of personality and of behavior that are associated with this main outcome. For example, the theory states that the client's psychological adjustment improves, that she experiences more acceptance of others, that she becomes more realistic and objective, that her self-ideal becomes more realistic, and that her behavior is seen by others as being more socialized and mature. I will list some of the empirically observed outcomes of client-centered counseling and psychotherapy in the next section, which is about research.

Research on the Theory of Therapy

A distinctive feature of client-centered counseling and psychotherapy has been a strong research orientation. Probably it is more extensively researched than any other method of therapy in existence, except perhaps behavior therapy. Cartwright's (1957) annotated bibliography of client-centered research contains well over 100 titles, and a voluminous literature has accumulated since then, with much of it examining new applications of the client-centered system. Several factors contribute to this research emphasis. One factor is Rogers' predilection for scientific understanding combined with his insistence on examining the raw data of psychotherapy. His typical approach has been to start with the actual events of psychotherapy, and then to conceptualize more general propositions about these events that can be tested empirically with crude measuring instruments. Scales for rating therapist empathy or client "experiencing" are examples. Another factor that contributes to the research orientation is that client-centered therapy,

---

[6]Process studies that attempt to isolate the change-producing events of therapy are in a somewhat different category.

unlike most approaches, has developed in university settings that encouraged research productivity.

Research on client-centered theory cannot be reviewed systematically in this chapter for two reasons: the literature is too extensive, and the research issues so complex, that findings are subject to differing interpretations. See Korchin (1976, Chapter 16) for a useful introduction to the research issues, and Shlien and Zimring (1970) for a general overview of client-centered research. We can, however, outline a few significant findings briefly in this chapter.

The therapist-offered condition variables have been researched extensively, and the findings provide strong support for this part of Rogerian theory. At least in client-centered counseling and in psychotherapy, empathy, genuineness, and nonpossessive caring do seem causally related to many process variables, such as depth of self-exploration, and to successful outcomes. See, for example, Barrett-Lennard (1962), Truax and Carkuff (1967), Truax and Mitchell (1971), and Rogers, Gendlin, Kiesler, and Truax (1967). Some evidence suggests that low levels of the therapist condition variables may be associated with a worsening of the client's situation (Truax & Carkuff, 1967, especially Chapters 1 and 3; Bergin, 1963, 1966). It appears that psychotherapy can be for better or for worse (Carkuff, 1967). In spite of these positive findings, many questions remain. It is not precisely clear in these studies what the scales, such as the accurate empathy scale, are actually measuring (Kurtz & Grummon, 1972). Also, much of the outcome variance is not accounted for by the therapist-offered conditions. Carkuff and Berenson (1967) estimate that we can account for about 20 percent of the variance of typical outcome indices, and 33 to 50 percent of quasi-outcome indices, such as insight scales. Thus, other factors besides just the therapist-offered condition variables are influencing the outcome of counseling and of psychotherapy.

Rogers hypothesizes that genuineness, empathy, and nonpossessive caring are important growth-facilitating conditions in all psychotherapy, not just in client-centered psychotherapy, and in interpersonal relationships generally. This hypothesis was confirmed in a collaborative study by Truax and the Johns Hopkins group (Truax, Wargo, Frank, Imber, Battle, Hoehn-Savic, Nash, & Stone, 1966). The Kurtz and Grummon (1972) data on accurate empathy are also consistent with Rogers' hypothesis. However, Garfield and Bergin (1971) were unable to replicate these findings, and suggested that the Rogerian constructs may be valid only for client-centered counseling and psychotherapy.

A few studies showing that facilitative conditions may be important in other-than-counseling situations are summarized by Truax and Carkuff (1967, especially Chapter 2) and by Carkuff (1967). Aspy (1967) found that teachers who scored high on the facilitative conditions were able to elicit, over the period of a school year, significantly higher gains on four of five achievement tests, as compared with low-level-functioning teachers. Only the spelling test revealed nonsignificant differences. In another study, Aspy and Hadlock (1967) found that students of the highest-level-functioning teacher gained an average of two and one-half academic years during the school year, while students with the lowest-level teachers gained only six achievement months.

Several samples of process research were reported in a previous section of this chapter. However, the process research that utilizes the Experiencing Scales developed by Gendlin, Rogers, and others for the Wisconsin research project with schizophrenics deserves fuller discussion. By rating samples of the client's behavior throughout a series of interviews, it is possible to relate process level and movement during therapy to condition and outcome variables. Rogers and Gendlin both theorize that process movement should be greater in successful than in unsuccessful cases, and some preliminary research indicated that this was in fact true (Rogers, 1961b, Chapter 7). However, further research with counseling center clients at the University of Chicago and schizophrenics at the University of Wisconsin produced some unexpected findings (see Gendlin, Beebe, Cassens, & Oberlander, 1968 for a summary, and Rogers, Gendlin, Kiesler, & Truax, 1967).

The research findings show that higher levels on the experiencing scale and on the other closely related process scales do in fact differentiate successful from unsuccessful cases; however, the successful cases are high on the experiencing variables even at the start of therapy. Clients who enter therapy with the ability to engage in experiential focusing become the success cases, while those low in this ability become the failure cases. This was true for both the neurotic and schizophrenic subjects. It appears that experiential focusing is an important behavior leading to change, and thus process level is a good index of ongoing effective therapy. In this sense, Rogers' and Gendlin's theorizing was confirmed. But it was also predicted that this mode of behavior would increase over the course of therapy; that is, the therapist could create the conditions that would encourage the growth and development of this behavior. Some studies found upward movement on the process scales, but others did not. And even where the upward movement was significant statistically (which it was for all cases combined), the increase was so small for most cases that it could hardly account for the difference between success and failure. Very few cases increased by more than half a scale point.

Thus, process level on the experiencing scale rather than process movement is associated with success, and the client-centered counselor was doing little, in most cases at least, to improve the client's experiential focusing ability. Nor is openness to one's ongoing experiential process equivalent to psychological health, because many clients scored high on this ability when they entered therapy, even though they were also quite maladjusted.[7] Instead of defining psychological health, experiencing variables and the other process scale variables seem to measure behaviors that enable a person to profit from psychotherapy.

Many research studies deal with the outcomes of client-centered counseling and psychotherapy. As suggested in an earlier section of this chapter, "Goals of Counseling," the question of what constitutes successful counseling and psychotherapy is a perplexing one that is complicated by our value judgments and by unresolved questions in the area of personality theory. Very probably, different outcomes result from different types of therapy with different types of clients. Ideally, we would like to know what specific outcomes might be expected from

---

[7]The schizophrenics did, however, score considerably lower on the process scale variables than did the neurotics.

each type of therapy with particular kinds of clients. Then the therapeutic approach of choice could be selected according to the client's, the therapist's, and/or the society's valued outcome. In the meantime, we live in an imperfect world. It will help to note a sample of the outcomes that seem, on the basis of the available research evidence, to be associated with client-centered counseling and psychotherapy:

1   There is an improvement in psychological adjustment as shown on the Rorschach, the Thematic Apperception Test, and personality inventories of the self-report type (Dymond, 1954a; Dymond, 1954b; Grummon & John, 1954; Haimowitz & Haimowitz, 1952; Mosak, 1950; Muench, 1947).

2   There is less physiological tension and greater adaptive capacity in response to frustration, as evidenced by autonomic nervous system reactivity (Thetford, 1952).

3   There is a decrease in psychological tension (or an increase in personal comfort), as measured by the Discomfort-Relief Quotient (Assum & Levy, 1948; Cofer & Chance, 1950; N. Rogers, 1948).

4   There is a decrease in defensiveness (Grummon & John, 1954).

5   There is a greater degree of correspondence between the client's description of her self-picture and her description of her wanted or ideal self. Among other things, this is sometimes viewed as an index of self-esteem (Butler & Haigh, 1954; Hartley, 1951).

6   Friends tend to rate the client's behavior as more emotionally mature (Rogers & Dymond, Chapter 13).

7   There is an improvement in overall adjustment in the vocational training setting (Bartlett, 1949; Seeman & Raskin, 1953). This study is perhaps of special interest to the educational-vocational counselor, since the outcome measure was training officers' observations over a six-month period of such things as interpersonal factors, academic achievement, efficiency in study and work habits, tendency to worry, and commitment to goals.

8   Axline's (1947) research suggests that client-centered play methods with elementary school children may result in accelerated reading improvement, even though no special reading instruction has been given.

9   Successful clients evidence strong gains in creativeness (Gaylin, 1966).

10   That part of the Wisconsin study (Rogers, Gendlin, Kiesler, & Truax, 1967) that examines the outcome of client-centered therapy with hospitalized schizophrenics reveals ambiguous findings. The results varied somewhat with the specific outcome measure under investigation, but in many respects the therapy group as a whole showed no greater evidence of positive change than did the matched control group of patients. This result is qualified by the finding that both groups improved and that, with the exception of individual therapy, the control group received all the best treatment a modern hospital can afford, including in some instances group therapy. The therapy group did show some advantages over the control groups, such as a slightly better rate of release from the hospital and statistically significant improvements in personal and interpersonal functioning, as judged from Thematic Apperception Test records.

11   Other research found that some clients fail to respond to the client-centered approach. Kirtner and Cartwright (1958) found a lower incidence of success among clients who accept little self-responsibility for their problems,

and who see the source of their problems as residing outside themselves. This finding was replicated by Farkas (1969).

To the best of this writer's knowledge, no studies exist that evaluate the success or failure of client-centered therapy with specific symptoms such as phobias; sexual dysfunction; or psychosomatic problems, such as high blood pressure.

ILLUSTRATIVE CASE MATERIAL: A SILENT YOUNG MAN— BY CARL ROGERS

The following case material, which was originally published as Chapter 17 in the report on the Wisconsin schizophrenia project (Rogers, Gendlin, Kiesler, & Truax, 1967), illustrates Rogers' way of working with clients. It is reproduced here by permission of Carl Rogers and the University of Wisconsin Press.

It would surely be desirable, if it were possible, to give the reader some experience of the process of therapy as it was lived by each therapist in his interaction with his schizophrenic clients. Yet long descriptions of therapy in a variety of cases tend to be unconsciously distorted; the transcription of a whole case would be much too long for presentation (and misleading in its omission of voice qualities); and consequently some other solution must be found.

What I propose to do in this chapter is to present, in transcribed form, two significant and I believe crucial interviews in the therapy with James Brown (pseudonym, of course) together with my comments as therapist on this experience. This seems to be a doubly valuable approach since the two interviews presented here are available in tape recorded form to any professional worker through the Tape Library of the American Academy of Psychotherapists.[1] Also, in a subsequent chapter of this book there are presented fifteen segments of the tape-recorded interviews with Mr. Brown, taken at spaced intervals throughout the therapy. These segments are commented on by six experienced therapists who have listened to these recorded samples. Thus the person who is seriously interested in the interaction in this case can read and study these two interviews and my presentation of the meanings I see in them; can listen to the two interviews in order to judge the quality of the interaction for himself; can read and study an unbiased sampling of the whole therapy experience for this man; and can compare his own judgments and impressions with those of six other therapists who, like himself, have no personal investment in the research.

Let me give a few of the facts which will introduce James Brown. He was twenty-eight years old when I first began to see him as a part of the research. A coin toss had selected him as the member of a matched pair to receive therapy. He had been hospitalized three times, the first time for a period of three months when he was twenty-five. He had been hospitalized for a total of nineteen months when I first began to see him, and for two and one-half years at the time of these interviews. He is a person of some intellectual capacity, having completed high school and taken a little college work. The hospital diagnosis was "schizophrenic reaction, simple type."

[1]I am very grateful to Mr. Brown for his permission to make professional use of this material. The current address of the Tape Library of the American Academy of Psychotherapists is 6420 City Line Avenue, Philadelphia, Pennsylvania. In their listing this is "The Case of Mr. VAC."

Editor's Note: The address of the Tape Library of the American Academy of Psychotherapists has subsequently been changed to 1040 Woodcock Road, Orlando, Florida 32803.

Some readers will be disappointed that I am not presenting any of the facts from his case history. A superficial reason for this is that it might be identifying of this individual. A deeper reason is that I myself, as his therapist, have never seen his case history and do not know its contents. I should like to state briefly my reasons for this.

If I were trying to select the most promising candidates for psychotherapy from a large group, then an examination of the case histories by me—or by someone else—might be helpful in making such a selection. But in this instance Brown had been selected by the impersonal criteria of our research as a person to whom a relationship was to be offered. I preferred to endeavor to relate to him as he was in the relationship, as he was as a person at this moment, not as a configuration of past historical events. It is my conviction that therapy (if it takes place at all) takes place in the immediate moment-by-moment inter-action in the relationship. This is the way in which I encountered Mr. Brown, and I am asking the reader to encounter him in the same way.

At the time of these two interviews, I had been seeing Mr. Brown on a twice a week basis (with the exception of some vacation periods) for a period of eleven months. Unlike many of the clients in this research the relationship had, almost from the first, seemed to have some meaning to him. He had ground privileges, so he was able to come to his appoint-ments, and he was almost always on time, and rather rarely forgot them. The relationship between us was good. I liked him and I feel sure that he liked me. Rather early in our inter-views he muttered to his ward physician that he had finally found someone who understood him. He was never articulate, and the silences were often prolonged, although when he was expressing bitterness and anger he could talk a bit more freely. He had, previous to these two interviews, worked through a number of his problems, the most important being his facing of the fact that he was entirely rejected by his stepmother, relatives, and, worst of all, by his father. During a few interviews preceding these two he had been even more silent than usual, and I had no clue to the meaning of this silence. As will be evident from the transcript his silences in these two interviews were monumental. I believe that a word count would show that he uttered little more than 50 words in the first of these interviews! (In the tape recording mentioned above, each of the silences has been reduced to 15 seconds, no matter what its actual length.)

In the two interviews presented here I was endeavoring to understand all that I pos-sibly could of his feelings. I had little hesitancy in doing a good deal of empathic guessing, for I had learned that though he might not respond in any discernible way when I was right in my inferences, he would usually let me know by a negative shake of his head if I was wrong. Mostly, however, I was simply trying to be my feelings in relationship to him, and in these particular interviews my feelings I think were largely those of interest, gentleness, compassion, desire to understand, desire to share something of myself, eagerness to stand with him in his despairing experiences.

To me any further introduction would be superfluous. I hope and believe that the interaction of the two hours speaks for itself of many convictions, operationally expressed, about psychotherapy.

The Interviews

Tuesday

T: I see there are some cigarettes here in the drawer. Hm? Yeah, it is hot out.
[*Silence of 25 seconds*]

T: Do you look kind of angry this morning, or is that my imagination? [*Client shakes his head slightly.*] Not angry, huh?
[*Silence of 1 minute, 26 seconds*]

T: Feel like letting me in on whatever is going on?

[*Silence of 12 minutes, 52 seconds*]

T: [*softly*] I kind of feel like saying that "If it would be of any help at all I'd like to come in." On the other hand if it's something you'd rather—if you just feel more like being within yourself, feeling whatever you're feeling within yourself, why that's O.K. too—I guess another thing I'm saying, really, in saying that is, "I do care. I'm not just sitting here like a stick."

[*Silence of 1 minute, 11 seconds*]

T: And I guess your silence is saying to me that either you don't want to or can't come out right now and that's O.K. So I won't pester you but I just want you to know, I'm here.

[*Silence of 17 minutes, 41 seconds*]

T: I see I'm going to have to stop in a few minutes.[2]

[*Silence of 20 seconds*]

T: It's hard for me to know how you've been feeling, but it looks as though part of the time maybe you'd rather I didn't know how you were feeling. Anyway it looks as though part of the time it just feels very good to let down and—relax the tension. But as I say I don't really know—how you feel. It's just the way it looks to me. Have things been pretty bad lately?

[*Silence of 45 seconds*]

T: Maybe this morning you just wish I'd shut up—and maybe I should, but I just keep feeling I'd like to—I don't know, be in touch with you in some way.

[*Silence of 2 minutes, 21 seconds*] [*Jim yawns.*]

T: Sounds discouraged or tired.

[*Silence of 41 seconds*]

C: No. Just lousy.

T: Everything's lousy, huh? You feel lousy?

[*Silence of 39 seconds*]

T: Want to come in Friday at 12 at the usual time?

C: [*Yawns and mutters something unintelligible.*]

[*Silence of 48 seconds*]

T: Just kind of feel sunk way down deep in these lousy, lousy feelings, hm?—Is that something like it?

C: No.

T: No?

[*Silence of 20 seconds*]

C: No. I just ain't no good to nobody, never was, and never will be.

T: Feeling that now, hm? That you're just no good to yourself, no good to anybody. Never will be any good to anybody. Just that you're completely worthless, huh?—Those really are lousy feelings. Just feel that you're no good at *all*, hm?

C: Yeah. [*muttering in low, discouraged voice*] That's what this guy I went to town with just the other day told me.

T: This guy that you went to town with really told you that you were no good? Is that what you're saying? Did I get that right?

C: M-hm.

T: I guess the meaning of that if I get it right is that here's somebody that—meant something to you and what does he think of you? Why, he's told you that he thinks you're no

---

[2]Long experience had shown me that it was very difficult for Jim to leave. Hence I had gradually adopted the practice of letting him know, ten or twelve minutes before the conclusion of the hour, that "our time is nearly up." This enabled us to work through the leaving process without my feeling hurried.

good at all. And that just really knocks the props out from under you. [*Jim weeps quietly.*] It just brings the tears.

[*Silence of 20 seconds*]

C: [*rather defiantly*] I don't care though.

T: You tell yourself you don't care at all, but somehow I guess some part of you cares because some part of you weeps over it.

[*Silence of 19 seconds*]

T: I guess some part of you just feels, "Here I am hit with another blow, as if I hadn't had enough blows like this during my life when I feel that people don't like me. Here's someone I've begun to feel attached to and now *he* doesn't like me. And I'll say I don't care. I won't let it make any difference to me—But just the same the tears run down my cheeks."

C: [*muttering*] I guess I always knew it.

T: Hm?

C: I guess I always knew it.

T: If I'm getting that right, it is that what makes it hurt worst of all is that when he tells you you're no good, well shucks, that's what you've always felt about yourself. Is that— the meaning of what you're saying? [*Jim nods slightly, indicating agreement.*]—M-hm. So you feel as though he's just confirming what—you've already known. He's confirming what you've already felt in some way.

[*Silence of 23 seconds*]

T: So that between his saying so and your perhaps feeling it underneath, you just feel about as no good as anybody could feel.

[*Silence of 2 minutes, 1 second*]

T: [*thoughtfully*] As I sort of let it soak in and try to feel what you must be feeling—It comes up sorta this way in me and I don't know—but as though here was someone you'd made a contact with, someone you'd really done things for and done things with. Somebody that had some meaning to you. Now, wow! He slaps you in the face by telling you you're just no good. And this really cuts *so* deep, you can hardly stand it.

[*Silence of 30 seconds*]

T: I've got to call it quits for today, Jim.

[*Silence of 1 minute, 18 seconds*]

T: It really hurts, doesn't it? [*This is in response to his quiet tears.*]

[*Silence of 26 seconds*]

T: I guess if the feelings came out you'd just weep and weep and weep.

[*Silence of 1 minute, 3 seconds*]

T: Help yourself to some Kleenex if you'd like—Can you go now?

[*Silence of 23 seconds*]

T: I guess you really hate to, but I've got to see somebody else.

[*Silence of 20 seconds*]

T: It's really bad, isn't it?

[*Silence of 22 seconds*]

T: Let me ask you one question and say one thing. Do you still have that piece of paper with my phone numbers on it and instructions, and so on? [*Jim nods.*] O.K. And if things get bad, so that you feel real down, you have them call me. 'Cause that's what I'm here for, to try to be of some help when you need it. If you need it, you have them call me.[3]

---

[3]Two words of explanation are needed here. He seemed so depressed that I was concerned that he might be feeling suicidal. I wanted to be available to him if he felt desperate. Since no patient was allowed to phone without permission, I had given him a note which would permit a staff member or Jim himself to phone me at any time he wished to contact me, and with both my office and home phone numbers.

C: I think I'm beyond help.

T: Huh? Feel as though you're beyond help. I know. You feel just completely hopeless about yourself. I can understand that. I don't feel hopeless, but I can realize that you do.[4] Just feel as though nobody can help *you* and you're really beyond help.

[*Silence of 2 minutes, 1 second*]

T: I guess you just feel so, so down that—it's awful.

[*Silence of 2 minutes*]

T: I guess there's one other thing too. I, I'm going to be busy here this afternoon 'til four o'clock and maybe a little after. But if you should want to see me again this afternoon, you can drop around about four o'clock. O.K.?—Otherwise, I'll see you Friday noon. Unless I get a call from you. If you—If you're kind of concerned for fear anybody would see that you've been weeping a little, you can go out and sit for a while where you waited for me. Do just as you wish on that. Or go down and sit in the waiting room there and read magazines—I guess you'll really have to go.

C: Don't want to go back to work.

T: You don't want to go back to work, hm?

This is the end of the interview. Later in the day the therapist saw Mr. Brown on the hospital grounds. He seemed much more cheerful and said that he thought he could get a ride into town that afternoon.

The next time the therapist saw Mr. Brown was three days later, on Friday. This interview follows.

Friday

T: I brought a few magazines you can take with you if you want.[5]

[*Silence of 47 seconds*]

T: I didn't hear from you since last time. Were you able to go to town that day?

C: Yeah. I went in with a kid driving the truck.

T: M-hm. [*Voices from next office are heard in background.*]

[*Silence of 2 minutes*]

T: Excuse me just a minute. [*Goes to stop noise.*]

[*Silence of 2 minutes, 20 seconds*]

T: I don't know why, but I realize that somehow it makes me feel good that today you don't have your hand up to your face so that I can somehow kind of see you more. I was wondering why I felt as though you were a little more here than you are sometimes and then I realized well, it's because—I don't feel as though you're hiding behind your hand, or something.

[*Silence of 50 seconds*]

T: And I think I sense, though I could be mistaken, I think I do sense that today just like some other days when you come in here, it's just as though you let yourself sink down into feelings that run very deep in you. Sometimes they're very bad feelings like the last time and sometimes probably they're not so bad, though they're sort of—I think I understand that somehow when you come in here it's as though you do let yourself down into those feelings. And now—

C: I'm gonna take off.

[4]This is an example of the greater willingness I have developed to express my own feelings of the moment, at the same time accepting the client's right to possess *his* feelings, no matter how different from mine.

[5]I had, on several occasions, given magazines and small amounts of money to Mr. Brown and loaned him books. There was no special rationale behind this. The hospital environment was impoverished for a man of Brown's sort, and I felt like giving him things which would relieve the monotony.

T: Huh?

C: I'm gonna take off.[6]

T: You're going to take off? Really run away from here? Is that what you mean? Must be some—what's the—what's the background of that? Can you tell me? Or I guess what I mean more accurately is I know you don't like the place but it must be that something special came up or something?

C: I just want to run away and die.

T: M-hm, m-hm, m-hm. It isn't even that you want to get away from here *to* something. You just want to leave here and go away and die in a corner, hm?
[*Silence of 30 seconds*]

T: I guess as I let that soak in I really do sense how, how deep that feeling sounds, that you—I guess the image that comes to my mind is sort of a, a wounded animal that wants to crawl away and die. It sounds as though that's kind of the way you feel that you just want to get away from here and, and vanish. Perish. Not exist.
[*Silence of 1 minute*]

C: [*almost inaudibly*] All day yesterday and all morning I wished I were dead. I even prayed last night that I could die.

T: I think I caught all of that, that—for a couple of days now you've just *wished* you could be dead and you've even prayed for that—I guess that—One way this strikes me is that to live is such an awful thing to you, you just wish you could die, and not live.
[*Silence of 1 minute, 12 seconds*]

T: So that you've been just wishing and wishing that you were not living. You wish that life would pass away from you.
[*Silence of 30 seconds*]

C: I wish it more'n anything else I've ever wished around here.

T: M-hm, m-hm, m-hm. I guess you've wished for lots of things but boy! It seems as though this wish to not live is deeper and stronger than anything you ever wished before.
[*Silence of 1 minute, 36 seconds*]

T: Can't help but wonder whether it's still true that some things this friend said to you—are those still part of the thing that makes you feel so awful?

C: In general, yes.

T: M-hm.
[*Silence of 47 seconds*]

T: The way I'm understanding that is that in a general way the fact that he felt you were no good has just set off a whole flood of feeling in you that makes you really wish, *wish* you weren't alive. Is that—somewhat near it?

C: I ain't no good to nobody, or I ain't no good for nothin', so what's the use of living?

T: M-hm. You feel, "I'm not any good to another living person, so—why should I go on living?"
[*Silence of 21 seconds*]

T: And I guess a part of that is that—here I'm kind of guessing and you can set me straight, I guess a part of that is that you felt, "I tried to *be* good for something as far as he was concerned. I really tried. And now—if I'm no good to him, if he feels I'm no good, then that proves I'm just no good to anybody." Is that, uh—anywhere near it?

C: Oh, well, other people have told me that too.

T: Yeah. M-hm. I see. So you feel if, if you go by what others—what several others have said, then, then you are *no good.* No good to anybody.
[*Silence of 3 minutes, 40 seconds*]

---

[6]Clearly my empathic guessing in the two previous responses was completely erroneous. This was not troublesome to me, nor, I believe, to him. There is no doubt, however, that my surprise shows.

T: I don't know whether this will help or not, but I would just like to say that—I think I can understand pretty well—what it's like to feel that you're just *no damn good* to anybody, because there was a time when—I felt that way about *myself*. And I know it can be *really rough*.[7]

[*Silence of 13 minutes*]

T: I see we've only got a few more minutes left.

[*Silence of 2 minutes, 51 seconds*]

T: Shall we make it next Tuesday at eleven, the usual time?

[*Silence of 1 minute, 35 seconds*]

T: If you gave me any answer, I really didn't get it. Do you want to see me next Tuesday at eleven?

C: Don't know.

T: "I just don't know."

[*Silence of 34 seconds*]

T: Right at this point you just don't know—whether you want to say "yes" to that or not, hm?—I guess you feel so down and so—awful that you just don't know whether you can—can see that far ahead. Hm?

[*Silence of 1 minute, 5 seconds*]

T: I'm going to give you an appointment at that time because *I'd* sure like to see *you* then. [*Writing out appointment slip.*]

[*Silence of 50 seconds*]

T: And another thing I would say is that—if things continue to stay so rough for you, don't hesitate to have them call me. And if you should decide to take off, I would very much appreciate it if you would have them call me and—so I could see you first. I wouldn't try to dissuade you. I'd just want to see you.

C: I might go today. Where, I don't know, but I don't care.

T: Just feel that your mind is made up and that you're going to leave. You're not going *to* anywhere. You're just—just going to leave, hm?

[*Silence of 53 seconds*]

C: [*muttering in discouraged tone*] That's why I want to go, 'cause I don't care what happens.

T: Huh?

C: That's why I want to go, 'cause I don't care what happens.

T: M-hm, m-hm. That's why you want to go, because you really don't care about yourself. You just don't care *what* happens. And I guess I'd just like to say—*I* care about you. And *I* care what happens.[8]

[*Silence of 30 seconds*] [*Jim bursts into tears and unintelligible sobs.*]

T: [*tenderly*] Somehow that just—makes all the feelings pour out.

[*Silence of 35 seconds*]

T: And you just weep and weep and weep. And feel so badly. [*Jim continues to sob, then blows nose and breathes in great gasps.*]

T: I do get some sense of how awful you feel inside—You just sob and sob. [*He puts his head on desk, bursting out in great gulping, gasping sobs.*]

T: I guess all the pent-up feelings you've been feeling the last few days just—just come rolling out.

[*Silence of 32 seconds, while sobbing continues*]

T: There's some Kleenex there, if you'd like it—Hmm. [*sympathetically*] You just feel kind of torn to pieces inside.

---

[7]This is a most unusual kind of response for me to make. I simply felt that I wanted to share my experience with him—to let him know he was not alone.

[8]This was the spontaneous feeling which welled up in me, and which I expressed. It was certainly not planned, and I had no idea it would bring such an explosive response.

[*Silence of 1 minute, 56 seconds*]

C: I wish I could die. [*sobbing*]

T: You just wish you could die, don't you? M-hm. You just feel so awful, you wish you could perish.

[*Therapist laid his hand gently on Jim's arm during this period. Jim showed no definite response. However, the storm subsides somewhat. Very heavy breathing.*] [*Silence of 1 minute, 10 seconds*]

T: You just feel so awful and so torn apart inside that, that it just makes you wish you could pass out.

[*Silence of 3 minutes, 29 seconds*]

T: I guess life is so tough, isn't it? You just feel you could weep and sob your heart away and wish you could die.[9]

[*Heavy breathing continues.*] [*Silence of 6 minutes, 14 seconds*]

T: I don't want to rush you, and I'll stay as long as you really need me, but I do have another appointment, that I'm already late for.

C: Yeah.

[*Silence of 17 minutes*]

T: Certainly been through something, haven't you?

[*Silence of 1 minute, 18 seconds*]

T: May I see you Tuesday?

C: [*Inaudible response.*]

T: Hm?

C: Don't know. [*almost unintelligible*]

T: "I just don't know." M-hm. You know all the things I said before, I mean very much. I want to see you Tuesday and I want to see you before then if you want to see me. So, if you need me, don't hesitate to call me.

[*Silence of 1 minute*]

T: It's really rough, isn't it?

[*Silence of 24 seconds*]

C: Yes.

T: Sure is. [*Jim slowly gets up to go.*]

[*Silence of 29 seconds*]

T: Want to take that too? [*Jim takes appointment slip.*]

[*Silence of 20 seconds*]

T: There's a washroom right down the hall where you can wash your face. [*Jim opens door; noise and voices are heard from corridor.*]

[*Silence of 18 seconds*] [*Jim turns back into the room.*]

C: You don't have a cigarette, do you? [*Therapist finds one.*]

T: There's just one. I looked in the package but—I don't know. I haven't any idea how old it is, but it looks sort of old.

C: I'll see you. [*hardly audible*]

T: O.K. I'll be looking for you Tuesday, Jim.

Commentary

What has happened here? I am sure there will be many interpretations of this material. I would like to make it plain that what follows is my own perception of it, a perception which is perhaps biased by the fact that I was a deeply involved participant.

[9]As I have listened to the recording of this interview, I wish I had responded to the relief he must have been experiencing in letting his despair pour out, as well as to the despair itself.

Here is a young man who has been a troublesome person in the institution. He has been quick to feel mistreated, quick to take offense, often involved in fights with the staff. He has, by his own account, no tender feelings, only bitter ones against others. In these two interviews he has experienced the depth of his own feelings of worthlessness, of having no excuse for living. He has been unsupported by his frequently felt feelings of anger, and has experienced only his deep, deep despair. In this situation something happens. What is it, and why does it occur?

In my estimation, I was functioning well as a therapist in this interaction. I felt a warm and spontaneous caring for him as a person, which found expression in several ways—but most deeply at the moment when he was despairing. I was continuously desirous of understanding his feelings, even though he gave very few clues. I believe that my erroneous guesses were unimportant as compared to my willingness to go with him in his feelings of worthlessness and despair when he was able to voice these. I think we were relating as two real and genuine persons. In the moments of real encounter the differences in education, in status, in degree of psychological disturbance, had no importance—we were two persons in a relationship.

In this relationship there was a moment of real, and I believe irreversible, change. Jim Brown, who sees himself as stubborn, bitter, mistreated, worthless, useless, hopeless, unloved, unlovable, *experiences* my caring. In that moment his defensive shell cracks wide open, and can never again be quite the same. When someone *cares* for him, and when he feels and experiences this caring, he becomes a softer person whose years of stored up hurt come pouring out in anguished sobs. He is not the shell of hardness and bitterness, the stranger to tenderness. He is a person hurt beyond words, and aching for the love and caring which alone can make him human. This is evident in his sobs. It is evident too in his returning to the office, partly for a cigarette, partly to say spontaneously that he will return.

In my judgment what we have here is a "moment of change" in therapy. Many events are necessary to lead up to such a moment. Many later events will flow from it. But in this moment something is experienced openly which has never been experienced before. Once it had been experienced openly, and the emotions surrounding it flow to their natural expression, the person can never be quite the same. He can never completely deny these feelings when they recur again. He can never quite maintain the concept of self which he had before that moment. Here is an instance of the heart and essence of therapeutic change.

An Objective Look at the Process

If we look at the few client expressions in these interviews in terms of the hypotheses of this research, we can see that being deeply in therapy does not necessarily involve a ready flow of words. Let us take some of the feeling themes Brown expresses and look at them in terms of the process continuum we have conceptualized.

My feelings are lousy.

I ain't no good to nobody.

I think I'm beyond help.

I don't want to go back to work.

I just want to run away and die.

I ain't no good, so what's the use of living?

I don't care what happens.

I wish I could die.

Compare these themes with brief descriptions of the process continuum at stages 3, 4, 5, and 6 of the seven stages of the original Process Scale.

Stage 3. "There is much description of feelings and personal meanings which are not now present." "The experiencing of situations is largely described in terms of the past." "Personal constructs are rigid but may at times be thought of as constructs."

Clearly Mr. Brown's manner of expression does not fit this stage in any respect except that his concept of himself as no good is held in rigid fashion.

Stage 4. "Feelings and personal meanings are freely described as present objects owned by the self. . . . Occasionally feelings are expressed in the present but this occurs as if against the individual's wishes." "There is an unwilling fearful recognition that one is experiencing things—a vague realization that a disturbing type of inner referent does exist." "The individual is willing to risk relating himself occasionally to others on a feeling basis."

It is evident that this matches more closely Mr. Brown's experience in these hours.

Stage 5. "In this stage we find many feelings freely expressed in the moment of their occurrence and thus experienced in the immediate present." "This tends to be a frightening and disturbing thing because it involves being in process." There is a desire to be these feelings, to be 'the real me.'"

This stage seems to catch even more of the quality of the experiencing in these interviews.

Stage 6. "Feelings which have previously been denied to awareness are now experienced with immediacy and acceptance . . . not something to be denied, feared, or struggled against." "In the moments of movement which occur at this stage there is a dissolving of significant personal constructs in a vivid experiencing of a feeling which runs counter to the constructs.'"

While some aspects of Jim's experiencing in these interviews come close to this description, it is clear that he is not acceptant of the feelings which well up in him. It appears that ratings of the stage he has reached in these interviews would probably cluster modally around stage 5, with some elements rated 4 or 6.
Perhaps this will give the reader some feeling for both the strengths and inadequacies of our conceptualizing of the process continuum and our attempts to capture it in an objective rating scale. It is relevant to what has occurred in these interviews, yet Brown's unique expression of his feelings is certainly not fully contained in the descriptions supplied by the original Process Scale, or the further separate scales developed from it.
This examination of the process aspect of these interviews may help to explain something which has mystified colleagues who have listened to the interviews. They often marvel at the patience I displayed in sitting through a silence of, say, seventeen minutes. The major reason I was able to do so was that when Jim said something it was usually worth listening to, showed real involvement in a therapeutic process. After all, most therapists can listen to talk, even when the talk is saying very little and indicates that very little that is therapeutic is going on. I can listen to silence, when I think that the silence is likely to end with significant feelings. I should add, however, that when I ceased to be patient, or ceased to be acceptant of the silence, I felt free to express my own feelings as they were occurring in me at the moment. There are various examples of this in these interviews. I do recognize, however,

that it is easier for me to be patient than it is for a number of my colleagues. I have my style, and they have theirs.

Later Events

If one expects some quick and miraculous change from such a moment of change as we saw in the Friday interview, he will be disappointed. I was, myself, somewhat surprised that in the next interview it was as though these two had never happened—Jim was inarticulate, silent, uncommunicative, and made no reference to his sobbing or to any other portion of the interviews. But over the next months the change showed. Little by little he became willing to risk himself in a positive approach to life. Yet even in this respect he would often revert to self-defeating behaviors. Several times he managed to make all the necessary arrangements for leaving the hospital to attend school. Always at the last moment he would become involved in violent altercations (completely the fault of the other person, naturally!) which caused the hospital staff to confine him and which thus destroyed all the carefully laid arrangements. Finally, however, he was able to admit that he himself was terrified of going out—afraid he couldn't make good. When I told him that this was something to decide within himself—that I would see him if he chose to stay in the hospital, and that I would continue to see him if he chose to leave—he tentatively and fearfully moved out toward the world. First he attended school, living at the hospital. Then he worked through many realistic problems regarding a suitable room, finally found a place for himself in the community, and fully moved out.

As he could permit others to care for him, he was able to care for others. He accepted friendly gestures from members of the research staff, and it meant much to him to be treated as a person by them. He moved out to make friends of his own. He found a part-time job on his own. He began to live his own life, apart from any hospital or therapy influence.

The best evidence of the change is in a letter to me, a little more than two years after these interviews. At the time I was away for an academic year. I was seeing him very infrequently at the time I left, but I made arrangements for him to see another therapist (whom he knew slightly) if at any time he wished to do so. A few months after I left, I received the following letter from him:

Hi Doc,
    I suppose you thought I had died, but I'm still here.
    I've often thought of you and have been wanting to write but I'll use the old excuse that I've been busy.
    Things are moving along pretty fast. I'm back in school, but things have changed slightly there. Mr. B. decided to quit teaching, so everything I had planned with him fell through.

(There follow three paragraphs about the courses he is taking and his pleasure at having been given—through the rehabilitation officer—an expensive tool of his trade. He also speaks of his part-time job which is continuing. Unfortunately, this material is too identifying to quote. He continues on a more personal note):

    . . . I had a wonderful summer. Probably the best in years. I sure hate to see it come to an end.
    I've met lots of people and made lots of friends. I hardly saw any of the kids from school all summer, and I didn't go out to hospital all summer.

Now, when I look back, it was like going down a different road. A very enjoyable one at that.

Also I haven't seen G. S. [substitute therapist in therapist's absence] at all this summer so far. As far as I could see it was good not seeing anybody, nor having to think about hospitals, doctors, and being out there. It was more or less like being free as a bird.

In fact, Doc, I was suppose to have gone up to the university and write those tests again. Some Mrs. N. has been calling and it irritates me because *I* think I did good and all that going up there will do is spoil the effect more or less. I don't mind seeing you, Doc. That's not the point. I still want to see you when you get back, but it is a good feeling not having to have to see anybody.

I can't really explain it, so I won't try.

I sure wish I was out there at this time. It's been down in the low 40's every night here lately and it's starting to rain a lot.

By the way, I finally went home. That was last Wednesday. I got there at noon and I could hardly wait to get back. Back to Madison, back to my room, back to my friends and civilization.

Well, Doc, I guess I've talked enough about myself and I guess about half way back, I'd have let you do all of it. Right?

All in all things couldn't be too much better for me, compared to what they have been. It sure feels good to be able to say, "To hell with it," when things bother me.

I'll write later when I have "time," Doc. Maybe I'll be mean and won't write until you do, because I did wonder how come I never heard from you before I did.

> Bye for now, Doc.
> Sincerely,
> JIM.

It is amusing that in his new-found independence he is refusing to take the final tests for the research project—amusing, but thought-provoking too. Perhaps when people accept themselves as persons, they refuse to be the objects of an investigation such as this one. It is a challenging, and in some deep sense a positive, thought.[10]

Concluding Comment

In the case of Jim Brown, the progress he made appeared to grow primarily out of the qualities of the relationship. It appeared to have very little to do with fresh insights, or new and conscious self-perceptions. He *became* a new person in many ways, but he talked about it very little. Perhaps it is more accurate to say that he lived himself, used himself, in many new ways. In some fundamental characteristics he is still very much the same person. As of this writing he is completely on his own, functioning well, with friends of both sexes, entirely out of touch with the personnel of the hospital or the research group.

---

[10]Perhaps this will cast a revealing light on one bit of dry statistics. If one looks at Table 11.1 one finds that the last battery of tests for this client (listed as VAC) was given more than 300 days before actual termination of therapy. This would appear to be an unforgivable lapse and discrepancy. It means that VAC was ruled out of the statistical consideration of outcomes, measured from pre- to post-therapy. This is unfortunate from the point of view of the findings, since the changes in him were unquestionably positive. But from a human point of view, his refusal to take the final test battery may well point to one of the best measures of his growth as a separate and self-directed person. In any event, many of the numbers in many of the tables have behind them stories as unique as this one.

CRITIQUE AND RECENT DEVELOPMENTS

This section begins with some of the typical criticisms made of client-centered theory. Many of these criticisms note what Rogers fails to include, and while essentially correct and useful, they are partly unfair in the sense that Rogers makes no claim to presenting a comprehensive theory of personality and behavior. Clearly his conceptions fail to specify and synthesize all factors that influence behavior. Instead, Rogers has focused on such subjective responses as thoughts, feelings, and attitudes, and has insisted that these are important to understanding personality and psychotherapy. Conceptual clarity and scientific rigor in the area of the subjective are sufficiently difficult for many psychologists to have bypassed the problem altogether. Rogers accepts the challenge and thereby becomes an inviting target.

One weakness of client-centered theory is that it says little about how antecedent conditions and external events influence behavior, or, in the language of the theory, how antecedent conditions and external events influence self-actualization. There is much value to Rogers' reminding us that reality for the individual is that person's perception of reality, and that we react not just to some absolute reality but to reality as we perceive it. In psychology generally, and in counseling specifically, we often slide over this truth too quickly. Clients often fail to perceive the counselor's intended input. It is also useful to call attention to the role of the self and of the defensive process as determinants of what is actually perceived. However, it is equally useful and valid to recognize how perception is influenced by antecedent conditions and by the current stimulus situation. And client-centered theory's failure to elaborate these influences is a significant omission that has special relevance for many counseling situations. Of course, this statement also applies in varying ways to other psychodynamic theories.

Take as a specific instance the role of information giving in counseling. Information can influence perception and behavior, and it is appropriate that information giving is a time honored tool of the counselor.

The writer has elaborated client-centered theory previously to include providing information to the client. To be maximally useful, information must be assimilated accurately and then used by the client in an integrative manner. We can infer from client-centered theory that if the information is threatening to the self, it will be distorted and resisted in some way. Under these circumstances, the counselor can profitably play down the need for information and concentrate instead on creating the conditions that reduce the threat and allow the self to change. On the other hand, if the information is not threatening and can be perceived by the client as providing ways to maintain and enhance the self, then the information should be provided. Appropriate information can be assimilated when it helps the client to meet her perceived needs and to achieve or to formulate her goals. Sometimes information is also given to change a perceived goal to a more suitable goal, but this is apt to be effective only when the information is perceived as nonthreatening to the self and when it points to a new goal that is perceived as self-enhancing.

Of course, this is but one limited attempt to incorporate within client-centered theory the more general problem of how antecedent conditions and the stimulus situation influence personality and behavior. Further attempts of a similar kind could make client-centered theory more useful in many counseling situations.

Another criticism is that many Rogerian concepts, while intuitively appealing, are so global and so abstract that their precise meanings in actual counseling situations are difficult to grasp. Consider such key ideas as the actualizing tendency and the organismic valuing process. The actualizing tendency includes almost everything that is related to needs and motivations in one global concept, and the organismic valuing process involves the workings of such diverse things as perceptions, muscle sensations, past memories, feelings, the need for intimate relationships, and the pleasures of sex—without specifying the interrelationships among these things. Of course, global concepts can have a valued place in theory, for they can call our attention to important directional tendencies of the organism. But their usefulness is limited and their evaluation difficult, unless the theoretical system also specifies the interrelationships among the global concepts and lower order concepts, and eventually their concrete workings in the observable behaviors. Client-centered theory, especially the personality theory, has not yet progressed to this stage.

Another broad criticism is that Rogerian theory does not make use of and articulate well with other observed phenomena, concepts, and theories in psychology. For example, client-centered theory makes little use of cognitive theory, of learning theory, or of the influence of neurotransmitters and hormones on behavior. Not that there is an inherent requirement that new conceptions must be related to existing theory. In fact, insisting on this is often counterproductive of new insights. Nonetheless, many of the phenomena that are of interest to client-centered theory have been studied in other contexts and have generated knowledge that potentially could enrich client-centered theory. Avoidance learning, with its resistance to extinction, is one possible example.

Another criticism has already been implied in the earlier section on "The Goals of Counseling," namely, that if taken literally client-centered theory seems to say that living by the conditions of worth rather than by the organismic valuing process is the primary source of all psychopathology and all problems of living. Stated somewhat differently, the client-centered group has made little effort to determine how its conceptions of personality and the therapeutic process relate to such specific problems as delinquency, sexual dysfunctions, phobias, impulse disorders, depression, or the like. Without an intensive study of well-defined problem areas, the client-centered group risks overgeneralizing from a limited sample of clients. To be fair, this criticism applies to most systems of counseling and psychotherapy.

From these criticisms, let me turn to comments about the current status of client-centered therapy.

For several reasons, client-centered counseling and psychotherapy is a less distinct school or system than it was 20 to 30 years ago. This is true primarily because many of its once unique features have been absorbed. Whether independently or because of Rogers' influence, many systems of counseling and psychotherapy have incorporated Rogerian ideas in varying ways. For example, compared to 30 years ago, it is now commonplace to find an emphasis upon empathic understanding, a deemphasis upon formal diagnosis as a prerequisite to therapy, a reliance upon the client's inherent motivations and capacity for help, a view of people as being more proactive than reactive, a focus on the here-and-now more than on the client's past, increased respect for the integrity and individuality of the client, an emphasis upon the importance of the relationship between therapist and client, the counselor's attending more to feelings than to intellectual content, a process view of psychotherapy, and so on. This is not to say that most counselors and therapists have become Rogerian, but Rogers clearly did succeed in raising a number of questions about psychotherapy that have helped alter the field.

Client-centered therapists have also been influenced by other schools of thought. It is perhaps fair to state that the field generally is in a state of healthy eclecticism. Few practicing psychotherapists, including most client-centered therapists, seem to believe that a single technique or theory can encompass the full range of problems and situations that they encounter in clinical work. Perhaps Roger is the only true Rogerian, and even he is suspect, since he has revised his theories several times since 1942.

Client-centered therapy is moving into what might be called a postschool period that consists of greater diversity in (a) areas of application (see the section on "The Goals of Counseling"), (b) therapeutic procedures, and (c) theoretical concepts. These trends are too diverse to cover adequately here, but edited books by Hart and Tomlinson (1970) and Wexler and Rice (1974) provide a good sampling of these developments.

One trend is for therapists to become more active and to diversify their interview procedures. More information giving, direct teaching, and helping the client to cope with difficult current life situations are evident. Carkhuff and Berenson (1967) retain empathy, warm acceptance, and genuineness as primary core dimensions of the helping relationship, but expand the model considerably with other procedures such as confrontation, interpretation, behavior modification, and information giving. Carkhuff (1969) offers, among other modifications, the direct teaching of client-centered interpersonal behaviors as the preferred mode of treatment. Cochrane and Holloway (1974) attempt a merger between client-centered and Gestalt therapy. Laura Rice (1974) writes about the evocative function of the therapist. Raskin and van der Veen (1970) adapt client-centered principles to family therapy.

These and other contributions, while geared primarily to therapeutic practice, contain theoretical developments as well. Other significant papers aim more directly at theory modifications, often by making use of concepts from cognitive and information-processing psychology (Zimring, 1974; Anderson, 1974). And Butler (1974) writes about "The Iconic Mode in Psychotherapy."

The question of whether these developments constitute extensions of client-centered theory or establish new schools entirely is not altogether clear. The Rogerian influence is readily apparent, but the theoretical orientations are taking a different form, and the therapist's operations vary with different clients or with different phases of the therapy. A process view of therapeutic change is still apt to be emphasized. For example, in deciding what to do at a given moment, the therapist is guided typically by the "stylistic and structural aspects of the client's participation in the therapy process," and not by "underlying personality dynamics or focal conflicts," such as the expression of hostility, or by the therapist's view that the client needs to focus on a particular personal relationship (Wexler & Rice, 1974, p. 208).

By way of illustrating recent developments, let me conclude by outlining briefly the views of two neo-Rogerians.

Gendlin's concept of experiencing, which was presented earlier, is now expanded into what he calls "experiential psychotherapy" (1969, 1974). Gendlin's concept, the reader will recall, is that a concretely felt flow of experiencing goes on in the organism at all times, and that this experiencing is rich in implicit meanings that are never equatable with words or concepts. The essence of therapy for Gendlin is focusing on this directly felt experiencing to discover and clarify its implicit meanings, and in so doing there occurs a further experiencing (experiential or referent movement) *that is change itself.*

The basic principle of experiential psychotherapy is that whatever is said or done must be checked against the concretely felt experiencing of the client, with the aim of carrying the experiencing process forward. Gendlin sees the essence of the client-centered approach as empathic responding or "responding in a listening way," and he advocates that all therapist responding "should take off from, and return to, client-centered responding." But experiential psychotherapy also calls for much additional therapist activity. Clients are instructed specifically always to "check inside" and, as new meanings emerge, to check again. Numerous therapist activities are suggested to help the client with this subjective process of inner referring. Gendlin believes that most clients and therapists spend most of their time talking *about* experiences rather than getting into experiencing, and he advocates any therapist activity that will carry the experiencing process forward. For example, interpretative guessing, Gestalt therapy procedures, role playing, and daydreams may all be employed usefully—so long as therapist and client allow the felt sense of experiencing to form and to move. Gendlin believes further that his experiential therapy can employ any concept or theory, from psychoanalysis to behavior therapy, and that each may have its usefulness on specific occasions. Except for its emphasis upon empathic responding, client-centered therapy is no more related to experiential therapy than is any other approach.

Gendlin believes that his approach is not mere eclecticism; rather, concepts from any theoretical position can be employed either in experiential or in contrary ways. Most concepts and therapeutic procedures can be productive when they are aimed at the client's sensed concrete experiencing, and all can be equally empty when they fail to relate to this. Gendlin also believes that his approach is a "method of methods," and gets us beyond questions of which abstractions, including Rogerian concepts, describe the nature of human beings best. Human experience is always richer and different from these abstractions, but each abstraction can be a useful guide for trying out different distinctions and ways of articulating the experiencing process. Gendlin's therapist is both active and adventuresome, but she continually starts from and returns to client-centered responding as the way to stay in close touch with the client's inner experience.

David Wexler (1974) builds on Rogerian ideas, but in the process he criticizes and then reformulates important parts of client-centered theory.

Wexler finds many faults with such key concepts as self-actualization, experiencing, openness to experience, organismic trusting, and the conditions of worth. These concepts are too molar and too ambiguous to operationalize and investigate empirically. Thus, these concepts as presently formulated inhibit a better understanding of how clients change and how therapists facilitate this change. Furthermore, some of these concepts fit badly with other known facts in psychology. For example, Rogers' fully functioning person is defined as being open to all his experience; every internal and external stimulus is relayed freely through the nervous system without inhibition or defensiveness. But Wexler notes that a known characteristic of the organism is its ability to select relevant stimuli for processing while ignoring other stimuli, and that this characteristic is not only adaptive but is essential for survival. The issues are more complex than just being "open." Wexler also finds problems with Gendlin's and Rogers' concepts of experiencing. He dislikes the idea of a person who is *passively* open to inner experience, and he rejects the *duality* between experience and awareness that is implied when Rogers speaks of the defensive process in which experience is denied to awareness.

Wexler's aim is not just to be critical, but to reformulate in more useful ways the key concepts of self-actualization and experiencing. To do this, he makes extensive use of concepts that are taken from cognitive and information processing as developed by experimental psychology.

In Wexler's view, individuals are the creators of their own experience. Experience does not exist as something to be "open to," but is created by the functioning of the cognitive process. Neither are feelings "things" that can exist outside the client's awareness, as in the Rogerian and Gendlin views; feelings are affects that are generated in the process of organizing substantive information.

Wexler then describes different modes of experiencing as defined by different ways of processing information cognitively. And self-actualization, instead of being defined globally as a fulfillment of the potentials inherent in the actualizing tendency, is seen as reflecting the optimal mode of experiencing as defined by cognitive operations. The therapist, while still relying heavily on empathy, becomes a "surrogate information processor." In Wexler's scheme, empathic responding is no longer defined as an attitude, as it is for Rogers, but becomes a specific set of behaviors with specific functions. Different aspects of empathic behavior are to be emphasized at different times in the therapy process.

SUMMARY STATEMENT

The central hypothesis of client-centered counseling and psychotherapy is that the growth potential inherent in all individuals tends to be released in a relationship in which the helping person experiences and communicates genuineness, caring, and a sensitive nonjudgmental understanding of the client's inner flow of experiencing. Developed originally as a distinctive approach to individual counseling and psychotherapy, client-centered theory has been extended to all interpersonal relationships and even further, as a psychological-philosophical value system about living in today's society.

Much that was once unique to Rogerian thought has now been absorbed in various ways by other systems, and client-centered theory seems to be evolving to a neo-Rogerian stage that incorporates therapeutic procedures and theoretical conceptions from other sources.

Client-centered counseling speaks to the processes of helping relationships in which healthy psychological growth is the goal, rather than to ways of solving specific problems or of curing specific symptoms. When client and counselor wish to emphasize problem solving rather than growth-type goals, the counselor may need to supplement the client-centered approach with other theories and with other counseling procedures. However, whatever the goal, all counseling takes place in an interpersonal relationship, and since the nature of the helping relationship is a central concern of client-centered theory, it is applicable to any counseling or therapeutic situation.

BIBLIOGRAPHY

Anderson, W. Personal growth and client-centered therapy: An information-processing view. In D. Wexler & L. Rice (Eds.), *Innovations in client-centered therapy*. New York: Wiley, 1974.

Angyal, A. *Foundations for a science of personality*. New York: Commonwealth Fund, 1941.

Aspy, D. The differential effect of high and low functioning teachers upon student achievement (abstract). In R. R. Carkhuff & B. G. Berenson (Eds.), *Beyond counseling and psychotherapy*. New York: Holt, Rinehart & Winston, 1967.

Aspy, D., & Hadlock, W. The effects of high and low functioning teachers upon student performance (abstract). In R. R. Carkhuff & B. G. Berenson (Eds.), *Beyond counseling and psychotherapy*. New York: Holt, Rinehart & Winston, 1967.

Assum, A. L. & Levy, S. J. Analysis of a nondirective case with follow-up interview. *Journal of Abnormal and Social Psychology*, 1948, *43*, 78–79.

Axline, V. M. Nondirective therapy for poor readers. *Journal of Consulting Psychology*, 1947, *11*, 61–69.

Barrett-Lennard, G. T. Dimensions of therapist response as causal factors in therapeutic change. *Psychological Monographs*, 1962, *76* (43, Whole No. 562).

Barrett-Lennard, G. T. Toward a person-centered theory of community. Paper delivered at the Convention of the American Psychological Association, San Francisco, August, 1977.

Bartlett, M. R. et al. Data on the personal adjustment counseling program for veterans (Personal Adjustment Counseling Division, Advisement and Guidance Service). Washington, D.C.: Office of Vocational Rehabilitation and Education, 1949.

Batten, T., & Batten, M. *Nondirective approach in group and community work*. New York: Oxford University Press, 1967.

Beck, A. P. Phases in the development of structure in therapy and encounter groups. In D. Wexler & L. Rice (Eds.), *Innovations in client-centered therapy*. New York: Wiley, 1974.

Bergin, A. E. The effects of psychotherapy: Negative results revisited. *Journal of Counseling Psychology*, 1963, *10*, 244–255.

Bergin, A. E. Some implications of psychotherapy research for therapeutic practice. *Journal of Abnormal Psychology*, 1966, *71*, 235–246.

Bergin, A. E. Carl Rogers' contribution to a fully functioning psychology. In A. R. Mahrer & L. Pearson (Eds.), *Creative developments in psychotherapy* (Vol. I). Cleveland: Case Western Reserve University Press, 1971.

Berzon, B., Solomon, L., & Riesel, R. Audio-tape programs for the self-directed groups. In L. N. Solomon & B. Berzon (Eds.), *New perspectives on encounter groups*. San Francisco: Jossey-Bass, 1972.

Butler, J. M. The evaluative attitude of the client-centered counselor: A linguistic-behavioral formulation. Dittoed paper, Counseling Center, University of Chicago, about 1952.

Butler, J. M. The iconic mode in psychotherapy. In D. Wexler & L. Rice (Eds.), *Innovations in client-centered therapy*. New York: Wiley, 1974.

Butler, J. M., & Haigh, G. V. Changes in the relation between self-concepts and ideal concepts consequent upon client-centered counseling. In C. R. Rogers & R. F. Dymond (Eds.), *Psychotherapy and personality change*. Chicago: University of Chicago Press, 1954.

Butler, J. M. & Rice, L. Adience, self-actualization, and drive theory. In J. M. Wepman & R. W. Heine (Eds.), *Concepts of personality*. Chicago: Aldine, 1963.

Carkhuff, R. R. An integration of practice and training. In G. Berenson & R. Carkhuff (Eds.), *Sources of gain in counseling and psychotherapy*. New York: Holt, Rinehart & Winston, 1967.

Carkhuff, R. R. *Helping and human relations* (Vols. I and II). New York: Holt, Rinehart & Winston, 1969.

Carkhuff, R. R. Toward a new technology for human and community resource development. *The Counseling Psychologist*, 1972, *3*, 12–30.

Carkhuff, R. R., & Berenson, B. G. *Beyond counseling and psychotherapy*. New York: Holt, Rinehart & Winston, 1967.

Carkhuff, R. R., & Bierman, R. Training as the preferred mode of treatment of parents of emotionally disturbed children. *Journal of Counseling Psychology*, 1970, *17*, 157–161.

Cartwright, D. Annotated bibliography of research and theory construction in client-centered therapy. *Journal of Counseling Psychology*, 1957, *4*, 82–100.

Cochrane, C., & Holloway, A. Client-centered therapy and gestalt therapy: In search of a merger. In D. Wexler & L. Rice (Eds.), *Innovations in client-centered therapy*. New York: Wiley, 1974.

Cofer, C. N., & Chance, J. The discomfort-relief quotient in published cases of counseling and psychotherapy. *Journal of Psychology*, 1950, *29*, 219–224.

Dymond, R. F. Adjustment changes over therapy from Thematic Appreciation Test ratings. In C. R. Rogers & R. F. Dymond (Eds.), *Psychotherapy and personality change*. Chicago: University of Chicago Press, 1954. (a)

Dymond, R. F. Adjustment changes over therapy from self sorts. In C. R. Rogers & R. F. Dymond (Eds.), *Psychotherapy and personality change*. Chicago: University of Chicago Press, 1954. (b)

Farkas, A. The internal-external dimension of experience in relation to procss and outcome of psychotherapy. Unpublished master's thesis, Michigan State University, 1969.

Farson, R. Self-directed groups and community mental health. In L. N. Solomon & B. Berzon (Eds.), *New perspectives on encounter groups*. San Francisco: Jossey-Bass, 1972.

Garfield, S., & Bergin, A. E. Personal therapy, outcome and some therapist variables. *Psychotherapy: Theory, Research and Practice*, 1971, *8*, 251–253.

Gaylin, N. L. Psychotherapy and psychological health: A Rorschach function and structure analysis. *Journal of Consulting Psychology*, 1966, *30*, 494–500.

Gendlin, E. T. Experiencing: A variable in the process of therapeutic change. *American Journal of Psychotherapy*, 1961, *15*, 233–245.

Gendlin, E. T. Client-centered developments and work with schizophrenics. *Journal of Counseling Psychology*, 1962, *9*, 205–212. (a)

Gendlin, E. T. Experiencing and the creation of meaning. New York: Free Press, 1962. (b)

Gendlin, E. T. Values and the process of experiencing. In A. R. Mahrer (Ed.), *The goals of psychotherapy*. New York: Appleton-Century-Crofts, 1967. (a)

Gendlin, E. T. The social significance of the research. In C. R. Rogers et al. (Eds.), *The therapeutic relationship and its impact*. Madison: University of Wisconsin Press, 1967. (b)

Gendlin, E. T. Focusing. *Psychotherapy: Theory, Research and Practice*, 1969, *6*, 4–15.

Gendlin, E. T. A short summary and some long predictions. In J. T. Hart & T. M. Tomlinson (Eds.), *New directions in client-centered therapy*. Boston: Houghton Mifflin, 1970.

Gendlin, E. T. Client-centered and experiential psychotherapy. In D. Wexler & L. Rice (Eds.), *Innovations in client-centered therapy*. New York: Wiley, 1974.

Gendlin, E. T., & Beebe, J. Experiential groups: Instructions for groups. In G. M. Gazda (Ed.), *Innovations to group psychotherapy*. Springfield, Ill.: Charles C Thomas, 1968.

Gendlin, E. T., Beebe, J., Cassens, M., & Oberlander, M. Focusing ability in psychotherapy, personality and creativity. In J. M. Shlien (Ed.), *Research in psychotherapy* (Vol. III). Washington, D.C.: American Psychological Association, 1968.

Gendlin, E. T., & Hendricks, M. Rap manual. Chicago, Ill.: *Changes*. Mimeographed document, 1972.

Gendlin, E. T., & Tomlinson, T. M. The process conception and its measurement. In C. R. Rogers et al. (Eds.), *The therapeutic relationship and its impact*. Madison: University of Wisconsin Press, 1967.

Gendlin, E. T., & Zimring, F. The qualities or dimensions of experiencing and their change. *Discussion papers* (Vol 1, No. 3). Counseling Center, University of Chicago, 1955.

Ginott, H. G. *Between parent and child*. New York: Macmillan, 1965.

Goldstein, J. *Human nature in the light of psychopathology*. Cambridge, Mass.: Harvard University Press, 1940.

Goodman, G. Companionship as therapy: The use of nonprofessional talent. In L. N. Solomon & B. Berzon (Eds.), *New perspectives on encounter groups*. San Francisco: Jossey-Bass, 1972.

Gordon, T. A. *Group-centered leadership*. Boston: Houghton Mifflin, 1955.

Gordon, T. A. *Parent effectiveness training*. New York: Peter Wyden, 1970.

Gorlow, L., Hoch, E. L., & Telschow, E. F. *The nature of nondirective group therapy*. New York: Bureau of Publications, Teachers College, Columbia University, 1952.

Grummon, D. L., & John, E. S. Changes over client-centered therapy evaluated on psychoanalytically based Thematic Apperception Test scales. In C. R. Rogers & R. F. Dymond (Eds.), *Psychotherapy and personality change*. Chicago: University of Chicago Press, 1954.

Guerney, B. Filial therapy: Description and rationale. *Journal of Consulting Psychology*, 1964, *23*, 304–310.

Guerney, B., Guerney, L., & Andronico, M. Filial therapy. In L. N. Solomon & B. Berzon (Eds.), *New directions in encounter groups*. San Francisco: Jossey-Bass, 1972.

Haimowitz, N. R., & Haimowitz, M. L. Personality changes in client-centered therapy. In W. Wolff (Ed.), *Success in psychotherapy.* New York: Grune & Stratton, 1952.

Hart, J. T., & Tomlinson, T. M. (Eds.) *New developments in client-centered therapy.* Boston: Houghton Mifflin, 1970.

Hartley, M. Changes in the self-concept during psychotherapy. Unpublished doctoral dissertation, University of Chicago, 1951.

Hobbs, W. Group-centered psychotherapy. In C. R. Rogers (Ed.), *Client-centered therapy.* Boston: Houghton Mifflin, 1951.

Homans, P. Carl Rogers' psychology and the theory of mass society. In D. Wexler & L. Rice (Eds.), *Innovations in client-centered therapy.* New York: Wiley, 1974.

Kirtner, W. L., & Cartwright, D. S. Success and failure in client-centered therapy as a function of initial in-therapy behavior. *Journal of Consulting Psychology,* 1958, *22,* 239–333.

Korchin, S. J. *Modern clinical psychology.* New York: Basic Books, 1976.

Kurtz, R. R., & Grummon, D. L. Different approaches to the measurement of therapist empathy and their relationship to therapy outcomes. *Journal of Consulting and Clinical Psychology,* 1972, *39,* 106–115.

Lewis, M., Rogers, C. R., & Shlien, J. M. Time-limited, client-centered psychotherapy: Two cases. In A. Burton (Ed.), *Case studies in counseling and psychotherapy.* Englewood Cliffs, N. J.: Prentice-Hall, 1959.

London, P. *The modes and morals of psychotherapy.* New York: Holt, Rinehart & Winston, 1964.

Maslow, A. H. Motivation and personality. New York: Harper, 1954.

Mosak, H. Evaluation in psychotherapy: A study of some current measures. Unpublished doctoral dissertation, University of Chicago, 1950.

Mowrer, O. H., & Kluckhohn, C. A. A dynamic theory of personality. In J. McV. Hunt, *Personality and the behavior disorders.* New York: Ronald Press, 1944.

Muench, G. A. An evaluation of nondirective psychotherapy by the means of Rorschach and other tests. *Psychological Monographs,* 1947 (13) 1–163.

Raimy, V. C. The self-concept as a factor in counseling and personality organization. Doctoral dissertation, Ohio State University, 1943.

Raimy, V. C. Self references in counseling interviews. *Journal of Applied Psychology,* 1948, *12,* 153–163.

Raskin, N. J. An objective study of the locus of evaluation factor in psychotherapy. In W. Wolff (Ed.), *Success in psychotherapy.* New York: Grune & Stratton, 1952.

Raskin, N. J., and van der Veen, F. Client-centered family therapy: Some clinical and research perspectives. In J. T. Hart & T. M. Tomlinson, *New directions in client-centered therapy.* Boston: Houghton Mifflin, 1970.

Rice, L. The evocative function of the therapist. In D. Wexler & L. Rice (Eds.), *Innovations in client-centered therapy.* New York: Wiley, 1974.

Rogers, C. R. *Counseling and psychotherapy.* Boston: Houghton Mifflin, 1942.

Rogers, C. R. *Client-centered therapy.* Boston: Houghton Mifflin, 1951.

Rogers, C. R. Changes in the maturity of behavior as related to therapy. In C. R. Rogers & R. F. Dymond (Eds.), *Psychotherapy and personality change.* Chicago: University of Chicago Press, 1954

Rogers, C. R. Persons or science? A philosophical question. *American Psychologist,* 1955, *10,* 267–278.

Rogers, C. R. The necessary and sufficient conditions of therapeutic personality change. *Journal of Consulting Psychology,* 1957, *21,* 95–103.

Rogers, C. R. A process conception of psychotherapy. *American Psychologist,* 1958, *13,* 142–149.

Rogers, C. R. A theory of therapy, personality, and interpersonal relationships, as developed in the client-centered framework. In S. Koch (Ed.), *Psychology: A study of a science* (Vol. III, *Formulations of the person and the social context*). New York: McGraw-Hill, 1959. (a)

Rogers, C. R. The essence of psychotherapy: A client-centered view. *Annals of Psychotherapy,* 1959, *1,* 51–57. (b)

Rogers, C. R. A tentative scale for the measurement of process in psychotherapy. In E. A. Rubinstein & M. B. Parloff (Eds.), *Research in psychotherapy.* Washington, D.C.: American Psychological Association, 1959. (c)

Rogers, C. R. The process equation of psychotherapy. *American Journal of Psychotherapy,* 1961, *15,* 27–45. (a)

Rogers, C. R. *On becoming a person.* Boston: Houghton Mifflin, 1961. (b)

Rogers, C. R. The potential of the human individual: The capacity for becoming fully functioning. Mimeographed paper, Madison, Wis.: University of Wisconsin, 1961. (c)

Rogers, C. R. Toward becoming a fully functioning person. In *Perceiving, behaving, becoming* (1962 Yearbook Association for Supervision and Curriculum Development). Washington, D.C.: National Education Association.

Rogers, C. R. The actualizing tendency in relation to "motives" and to consciousness. *Nebraska symposium on motivation.* Lincoln: University of Nebraska Press, 1963.

Rogers, C. R. Toward a modern approach to values: The valuing process in the mature person. *Journal of Abnormal and Social Psychology,* 1964, *68,* 160–167. (a)

Rogers, C. R. Toward a science of the person. In T. W. Wann (Ed.), *Behaviorism and phenomenology.* Chicago: University of Chicago Press, 1964. (b)

Rogers, C. R. Autobiography. In E. Boring & G. Lindzey (Eds.), *A history of psychology in autobiography* (Vol. V). New York: Appleton-Century-Crofts, 1967.

Rogers, C. R. Some thoughts regarding the current presuppositions of the behavioral sciences. In C. R. Rogers & W. R. Coulson (Eds.), *Man and the science of man.* Columbus, Ohio: Merrill, 1968.

Rogers, C. R. *Freedom to learn: A view of what education might become.* Columbus, Ohio: Merrill, 1969.

Rogers, C. R. *Carl Rogers on encounter groups.* New York: Harper & Row, 1970.

Rogers, C. R. *Becoming partners: Marriage and its alternatives.* New York: Delacorte, 1972.

Rogers, C. R. Remarks on the future of client-centered therapy. In D. Wexler & L. Rice (Eds.), *Innovations in client-centered therapy.* New York: Wiley, 1974.

Rogers, C. R. Client-centered psychotherapy. In A. Freedman, H. Kaplan, & B. Sadock, (Eds.), *Comprehensive textbook of psychiatry.* Baltimore: Williams & Wilkins, 1975. (a)

Rogers, C. R. Empathic: An unappreciated way of being. *The Counseling Psychologist,* 1975, *5,* (2), 2–10. (b)

Rogers, C. R. *Carl Rogers on personal power.* New York: Delacorte, 1977.

Rogers, C. R., & Dymond, R. F. (Eds.), *Psychotherapy and personality change.* Chicago: University of Chicago Press, 1954.

Rogers, C. R., Gendlin, E. T., Kiesler, D. J., & Truax, C. B. (Eds.), *The therapeutic relationship and its impact.* Madison: University of Wisconsin Press, 1967.

Rogers, C. R., & Rablen, R. A. *A scale of process in psychotherapy.* Mimeographed manual, University of Wisconsin, 1958.

Rogers, N. Measuring psychological tension in nondirective counseling. *Personal Counselor,* 1948, *3,* 237–264.

Rogers, W. R. Client-centered and symbolic perspectives on social change. In D. Wexler & L. Rice (Eds.), *Innovations in client-centered therapy.* New York: Wiley, 1974.

Seeman, J. A study of the process of nondirective therapy. *Journal of Consulting Psychology,* 1949, *13,* 157–168.

Seeman, J. Client-centered therapy. In D. Brower & L. E. Abt (Eds.),Progress in clinical psychology (Vol. V). New York: Grune & Stratton, 1956.

Seeman, J., & Raskin, N. J. Research perspective in client-centered therapy. In O. H. Mowrer (Ed.), *Psychotherapy theory and research.* New York: Ronald Press, 1953.

Sheerer, E. T. The relationship between acceptance of self and acceptance of others. *Journal of Consulting Psychology,* 1949, *13,* 169–175.

Shlien, J. M. Time-limited psychotherapy: An experimental investigation of practical values and theoretical implications. *Journal of Counseling Psychology,* 1957, *4,* 318–322.

Shlien, J. Phenomenology and personality. In J. Wepman & R. Heine (Eds.), *Conceptions of personality.* Chicago: Aldine, 1963.

Shlien, J., & Zimring, F. M. Research directives and methods in client-centered therapy. In J. T. Hart & T. M. Tomlinson (Eds.), *New directions in client-centered therapy.* Boston: Houghton Mifflin, 1970.

Snyder, W. U. An investigation of the nature of nondirective psychotherapy. *Journal of General Psychology,* 1945, *33,* 193–223.

Snygg, D., & Combs, A. W. *Individual behavior: A new frame of reference for psychology.* New York: Harper, 1949 (now Combs and Snygg, 1959).

Standal, S. The need for positive regard: A contribution to client-centered theory. Unpublished doctoral dissertation, University of Chicago, 1954.

Stock, D. The self-concept and feelings toward others. *Journal of Consulting Psychology,* 1949, *13,* 176–180.

Thetford, W. N. An objective measure of frustration tolerance in evaluating psychotherapy. In W. Wolff (Ed.), *Success in psychotherapy.* New York: Grune & Stratton, 1952.

Truax, C. B. The process of group psychotherapy: Relationships between hypothesized therapeutic conditions and intrapersonal exploration. *Psychological Monographs,* 1961, *75,* (7).

Truax, C. B., & Carkhuff, R. R. *Toward effective counseling and psychotherapy.* Chicago: Aldine, 1967.

Truax, C. B., & Mitchell, K. M. Research on certain therapist interpersonal skills in relation to process and outcomes. In A. E. Bergin & S. L. Garfield (Eds.), *Handbook of psychotherapy and behavior change.* New York: Wiley, 1971.

Truax, C. B., Wargo, D. G., Frank, J. D., Imber, S. D., Battle, C. C., Hoehn-Savic, R., Nash, E. H., & Stone, A. R. Therapist empathy, genuineness, warmth and patient therapeutic outcome. *Journal of Consulting Psychology,* 1966, *30,* 395–401.

Wexler, D. A cognitive theory of experiencing, self-actualization, and therapeutic process. In D. Wexler & L. Rice (Eds.), *Innovations in client-centered therapy.* New York: Wiley, 1974.

Wexler, D., & Rice, L. N. (Eds.), *Innovations in client-centered therapy.* New York: Wiley, 1974.

Whyte, L. L. *The unconscious before Freud.* London: Tavistock Publications, 1960.

Zimring, F. Theory and practice of client-centered therapy: A cognitive view. In D. Wexler & L. Rice (Eds.), *Innovations in client-centered therapy.* New York: Wiley, 1974.

Chapter 3

Trait-Factor Theory and Individual Differences

E. G. Williamson
Donald A. Biggs

INTRODUCTION

The definitive history of trait-factor counseling has yet to be written. Pepinsky and Pepinsky (1954) identified three stages in the development of the trait-and-factor approach to counseling.

The first stage was characterized by a concern with developing ways to measure the attributes of clients, such as aptitudes, abilities, interests, attitudes, and personality, that would be predictors of educational and vocational success. The aim was to use these tools in scientific programs of selection and guidance that would match clients with appropriate educational and vocational alternatives by objective methods. This period, which began at about the turn of the century and ended at about the time World War II started, involved numerous attempts to apply testing methods to counseling and personnel problems.

An early pioneer, Hugo Munsterberg, experimented with workers in the transportation industry, by using available psychological tests of capabilities to identify those workers who would prove to be satisfactory in their work performance. This effort preceded the development of the World War I Army Alpha and Beta Tests. A corps of Army psychologists used these tests to assign recruits to various types of military occupations. After the war, some of these psychologists were employed in universities to develop similar tests for the guidance and classification of students who flocked to the universities.

Quite independently of the pioneering work being done in individual differences and measurement, Parsons in Boston originated the idea of vocational guidance for the underprivileged youth of Boston, which involved using "common sense" appraisal of students' interests and aptitudes and some psychological tests of the sensory-motor type. He also utilized available general information about vocations and the supposed qualifications required for success in them. When he died in 1908, his successor abandoned tests on the grounds that they were less than perfect predictors of success in work, and instead turned to vocational information as the basis for a student's choice of career.

About the time of World War I, many people publicly favored testing in both educational and industrial settings. However, this was also a time of controversy about mental testing. Cronbach (1975) describes the major figures in a national debate about ethnicity and mental age. The story of how World War I test data on draftees were used in racist attacks against immigrants from Southern and Eastern Europe is a sad commentary on those times.

One recalls W. D. Scott of Northwestern University and D. G. Paterson at Minnesota, who were prominent as early differential psychologists. Indeed, Scott and many others turned from the Army to industry with their methods of work force classification and utilization, and brought to the universities industrial management experience as well as Army techniques. The research and theories of the early differential psychologists later fused with Parsons' vocational guidance, thus forming the foundations for a trait-and-factor approach to counseling.

Paterson and his colleagues at the Minnesota Employment Stabilization Research Institute utilized psychological tests and measures to analyze the vocational abilities of out-of-school and out-of-work youth and adults. D. G. Paterson (1949) described the variety of techniques used in this early vocational counseling service: (a) case histories of unemployed individuals; (b) staff conferences that pooled the judgments of staff members to arrive at a vocational diagnosis, a prognosis, and an outline of steps to be taken in occupational rehabilitation of each case; (c) the provision of educational and training opportunities to assist individuals in preparing themselves for an appropriate occupation; and (d) utilization of placement agencies, chiefly the public employment service, in securing appropriate employment opportunities. Moreover, he cautioned his readers that "the approach was comprehensive and was not confined, as many personnel workers have erroneously assumed, to the administration and interpretation of psychological tests alone" (p. 81). The purpose of counseling was defined broadly and entailed the total development of the individual client. As Paterson, Schneidler, and Williamson (1938) said:

> Guidance counselors are concerned with students as individuals in the process of adjusting to life. In this capacity, the counselor steps out of the role of a mere teacher in order to consider the student as an integrated human being (p. 1).

A student of Donald Paterson, Edmund G. Williamson, was appointed Director of the University of Minnesota Testing Bureau in 1932. The bureau was to apply guidance procedures to educational and vocational problems. Students were helped to decide on their vocational and educational goals, and to plan appropriate courses.

In the second stage of the development of the trait-and-factor approach to counseling, models for the counseling process were developed, and the concept of differential diagnosis was broadened to include a variety of client adjustment problems beyond educational and vocational ones. Williamson (1939) urged clinical counselors to diagnose both normal and problem students and to diagnose in all areas of each student's life. The counselor was to perceive "the dynamic and multidimensional character of personality and thus seek an understanding of its unique pattern or individuality" (p. 103). Bordin (1946) developed a fairly elaborate system of diagnostic categories, and Pepinsky (1948) refined them with the headings: (a) lack of assurance, (b) lack of information, (c) lack of skill, (d) dependence, (e) self-conflict, and (f) choice anxiety.

Williamson and Darley (1937) and Williamson (1939) outlined a model for a trait-and-factor approach to counseling. Counseling was viewed as involving six steps: analysis, synthesis, diagnosis, prognosis, counseling (treatment), and follow-up. A major emphasis of this model was on differential diagnosis. However, the sequence of steps was not to be rigid, and there could be overlaps and reversals. The whole process was viewed as counseling, and one phase in the sequence, the interview, was labeled specifically as counseling or treatment.

The third stage in the development of the trait-and-factor approach to counseling, which culminated in the years following World War II, was described as the age of factorization studies (Pepinsky & Pepinsky, 1954). In his work with the Primary Mental Abilities Test, L. L. Thurstone was a leader in applying factor analytic methods to differential psychology. Both test data and criterion data were subjected to factor analyses. Many assumptions about traits and criteria were brought into question. Traits that were once viewed as homogeneous had to be redefined in light of the results of factor-analytic studies. Also, counselors learned to question the objectivity of factor analysis.

We would like to add a fourth stage in the development of the trait-and-factor approach to counseling, which might be described as a philosophical and theoretical stage. After World War II and the development of the client-centered approach to counseling, trait-and-factor counselors found themselves often labeled as Directivists, who supposedly were forcing their wills upon hapless clients. They were also criticized in some areas for their lack of value neutrality. In a series of articles (1958, 1961, 1966), Williamson discussed the role of values in the counseling process. He proposed that counselors should not hesitate to influence students to commit themselves to a value system in which an intellectual life is dominant. However, he cautioned that there was to be no single criterion for the good life, but a diversity of options for rational choice.

This was also a time when efforts were made to develop systematic descriptions of the trait-and-factor approach to counseling. Williamson's *Counseling Adolescents* (1950) and Hahn and MacLean's *Counseling Psychology* (1955) provided more sophisticated models for the counseling process and outlined a variety of techniques. Williamson (1950) argued that techniques should be specific to individuals and to problems. He identified five techniques of counseling: (1) establishing rapport, (2) cultivating self-understanding, (3) advising or planning a program of action, (4) assisting directly in the implementation of plans, and (5) making referrals to other personnel workers.

Somewhat later, Williamson (1961) suggested that a cognitive purpose of the counseling interview was to help students to modify their subjective and often error-ridden skills in self-appraisal of potentialities, aspirations, and self-concept with the aid of the scientific method. He goes on to say:

> In a real sense, I see a parallel between methods of self-appraisal and the use of the counseling interview as a means of teaching students. . . . Dewey's major emphasis on teaching the scientific method (not facts of science) of separating fact from non-fact via the subject matter of classrooms (p. 33).

Sorenson (1967) has described an instructional model for counseling that is quite compatible with this approach to counseling. The interview is described as a set of instructional procedures that have predetermined order; (a) identification of goals, (b) identification of obstacles, and (c) development of strategies. In this approach, the counselor is to help a client deal with an immediate problem situation in which a client is motivated toward a goal but is unable to attain it.

Measuring Traits

From time immemorial, people have appraised or estimated traits in one another. Linden and Linden (1968) provide a historical perspective for modern mental measurement. They argue that Juan Huarte (1530–1589) may have been the first person to suggest formal mental testing. This Spanish physician wrote a book entitled *The Trial of Wit, Discovering the Great Difference of Wits among Men and What Sorts of Learning Suit Best with Each Genius.*

Much later in history, Sir Francis Galton (1822–1911), a cousin of Charles Darwin, was to lay the foundation for the study of individual differences and for the development of modern mental measurements. He measured individual differences in people systematically, by means of replicable devices with a known degree of accuracy. At first these were physical characteristics, such as strength of hand grip, lung capacity, and the like. True, German psychologists early in the 1850s invented instruments that made it possible to measure such characteristics as reaction time and sensations. But it remained for J. M. Cattell (1890) to publish the early experiences in the measurement of mental or psychological traits in terms of individual differences. G. T. Fechner, Wilhelm Wundt, and other German psychologists preceded Cattell and other Americans and Britons in measuring human capabilities, but they centered on human beings in general rather than on individuals. James Cattell was one of the Americans who began the study of individuals as well as of people in general. Subsequently, Cattell and Farrand (1896) published the famous paper that contained many of the research studies that had used students of Columbia University as subjects. Wissler (1901) later reported that Cattell's psychophysical measures were not related to measures of school achievement.

The principles of mental measurement were greatly advanced when in 1904 Edward Lee Thorndike published *Introduction to the Theory of Mental and Social Measurements*. This book was a major impetus to the modern measurement movement in psychology because it described how Galton and Pearson statistics might be useful in measurement.

The measurement of general intelligence was one of the first major measurement problems. The translation and restandardization of the Binet-Simon intelligence test for children and adolescents at Stanford University provided a significant tool for the child guidance movement. Lewis Terman's student, A. S. Otis, led in the development of paper-and-pencil general intelligence measures, which were employed in a variety of guidance settings. The Army Alpha and Beta tests were used for the screening of recruits during World War I. In 1917, the University of Minnesota began using the Army Alpha for testing incoming freshmen.

In 1939, David Wechsler published the Wechsler-Bellevue Intelligence Scale, which dropped the traditional and controversial concepts of mental age and intelligence quotient in favor of standard score definitions. With the publication of the Wechsler, trait-and-factor counselors had a significant mental measurement tool for working with adults.

Edward Lee Thorndike vigorously opposed the general intelligence theory and approach to measuring intelligence, and he argued that there were different kinds of intelligences. Later, L. L. Thurstone published the Primary Mental Abilities Test, a systematic differential approach to measuring intelligence. Present-day examples of differential abilities measures that are useful in counseling include the Differential Aptitude Tests and the General Aptitude Test Battery (Super, 1957).

The development of the formal achievement test is also credited to E. L. Thorndike (Levine, 1976). Levine recounts the history and social functions of achievement tests, and tells the story of how achievement test results were used to provide evidence in a number of turn-of-the-century political debates about schools. J. M. Rice, an advocate of progressive education and a critic of the schools, administered a standardized list of spelling words to school children and found that the amount of time spent in teaching spelling was unrelated to the number of words on his list spelled correctly. In contrast, S. A. Courtis administered an arithmetic test to students in the New York public schools, and his results showed grade-by-grade increments.

Personality tests developed along two major paths. A Swiss psychiatrist, Herman Rorschach, used inkblots as stimuli for the systematic study of personality. He formulated the projective hypothesis, which holds that a subject's responses to random forms are a reflection of wishes, attitudes, and beliefs about the world. Henry Murray later developed a highly popular projective instrument, the Thematic Apperception Test, in which a subject's style of handling a problem was the focus of attention.

A second major form of personality tests is the structured personality inventory. During World War I, Robert Woodworth developed a "personality data questionnaire," the ancestor of present-day structured personality inventories, schedules, and questionnaires. Woodworth's questionnaire was to assist in discovering recruits who were especially susceptible to psychoneurosis, and was to be a substitute for a psychiatric interview. The assumption was that the items had face validity. Later, after psychologists became aware of the effects of test-taking attitudes on responses to personality inventories, an empirical approach to test construction was taken. Test behavior was considered significant behavior in itself, and was not assumed to be an accurate reflection of social reality. One of the most successful of the structured personality inventories that are based on the empirical approach is the Minnesota Multiphasic Personality Inventory (Hathaway & McKinley, 1951).

The development of interest inventories can be traced back to work done in 1919 by L. S. Yoakum at the Carnegie Institute of Technology (Campbell, 1971). Yoakum conducted a seminar for graduate students in which a pool of 1000 interest items was developed. An early attempt at interest measurement was made by Bruce Moore, who developed a 20-item inventory to differentiate between sales and design engineers. Later, K. M. Cowdery tried to differentiate physicians and lawyers. By building on the work of earlier researchers, E. K. Strong developed one of the most useful interest inventories, the Strong Vocational Interest Blank. He used a people-in-general group as a common point of reference, and differentiated between this group and each of 18 occupational groups. Another pioneer in interest research is G. Frederick Kuder, who developed a highly popular interest inventory based on a rational rather than an empirical approach to test construction. Scales were assembled from items that were similar in content, were intercorrelated significantly, and were reflective of some particular area of interest. Kuder, in contrast to Strong, was trying to develop an interest inventory that would be useful in school guidance programs. Over the years, there was healthy debate between those espousing Kuder's approach and those espousing Strong's approach. However, more recently, Kuder has developed an interest inventory that uses an empirical approach that is quite similar to the one espoused by Strong.

MAJOR CONCEPTS

Hall and Lindzey (1957) have defined trait-factor theory as follows:

> The essence of such theories is customarily a set of carefully specified variables or factors that are seen as underlying and accounting for the broad complexity of behavior (p. 378).

> Proponents of such systems [of personality organization] propose that a rational and largely objective procedure be substituted for the intuitive and usually unspecified manner in which most variables within the domain of personality have been formulated (p. 378). One particularly important function of factor analytic studies is to provide a completely independent means of confirming or denying the variables that have been inferred or intuited out of experimental and clinical observation (p. 415).

A major assumption in the trait-and-factor centered approach is that human behavior can be ordered and measured along continua of defined traits or factors (Pepinsky & Pepinsky, 1954). The traditional emphasis in this approach has been on differential diagnosis in the treatment of clients. Measurement has been and continues to be a major element in trait-and-factor counseling.

The trait-and-factor approach is based upon several assumptions that are taken from the tradition of differential psychology (Berdie, 1972): (a) To some extent, individuals differ from one another in every behavioral respect, and individual differences are all-pervasive; (b) Within broad limits that are imposed genetically, behavior is modifiable, and can be modified within limits that are a function of the organism and of the environment; (c) Enough consistency of behavior characterizes individuals to allow for generalizations in describing behavior over time; (d) The individual's behavior is a product of current status, experiences, and present physical and social setting; (e) Human behavior can be conceptualized conveniently in terms of ability, general personality, and temperament and motivation; and (f) Social and intrapersonal conflicts are inevitable, necessary, and can be constructive or destructive.

The trait-factor approach also assumes that individual differences can be identified objectively, that present human differences are related to future significant social behaviors, and that comparisons with defined social groups have relevance for understanding and improving the self-evaluation process (Berdie, 1972).

Two major concepts in this approach to counseling are *trait* and *factor*. We believe that traits are categories that are used for describing individual differences in behaviors. We differ with Allport (1966), who views traits as having more than a nominal existence—as being dynamic or at least determinative in behavior. We caution the reader that there is no general agreement among psychologists in their definitions of traits.

Factor analysis was developed as a means of ascertaining how many basic traits are sufficient to account for similarities and differences in individual test scores. We consider factor analysis to be an aid in improving definitions of human characteristics.

Trait-and-factor psychology uses external observations of behavior to make inferences about traits. For example, inferences are derived from observations of the interrelationships of behaviors. If a student performs consistently well or poorly on several verbal tests, such as vocabulary, analogies, and sentence completion, and if performance on these tests shows little or no relationship to performance on other tests that measure different kinds of behaviors, a verbal score may then be used to make inferences about a verbal trait that is considered to be an abstract category or dimension (Berdie, 1972).

Inferences about traits are derived from four kinds of external observations of behavior. The first observation concerns two kinds of individual differences. *Interindividual variability* has to do with differences among people in similar patterns of behavior. For example, individuals differ among themselves in their ability to solve arithmetic problems, and these differences are consistent across situations. *Intraindividual variability* has to do with differences in an individual's own patterns of behavior.

Interindividual distributions of differences in patterns of behavior are often described by a normal bell-shaped curve. Quetelet (1796–1874) is credited with being the first to apply the "normal law of error" to distributions of human data. He found that certain human measurements were distributed in approximation to the normal law and could be depicted graphically in the form of a symmetrical bell-shaped curve (Linden & Linden, 1968). Trait psychology assumes that interindividual differences are continuous across situations and will approximate the normal curve. Most trait psychologists seem to think that a particular trait is applicable to many people, varies in amount, and can be inferred by measuring differences in behaviors across situations. However, distributions of traits will vary, depending upon the sample of individuals being observed and the methods used to make observations. Methods used in observing behaviors need to be appropriate for a particular sample of individuals. If test questions are "too easy" or "too difficult" for a sample of people, the distribution of responses will be skewed. Distributions may also be discontinuous if these behaviors are specific to situations.

The second observation about human behavior that is used for making inferences about traits is that individual behaviors covary and form clusters. Covariance of behaviors can be observed, and inferences concerning the implications of these clusters of behaviors can be made. For example, when a person completes the Strong-Campbell Interest Blank, he or she makes a large number of simple behavioral responses to test items. Because of the instructions and the format of the items, we infer that these responses have to do with likes and dislikes. Responses on the inventory form patterns at various levels.

Although there is considerable research to indicate that behavior patterns do cluster, Berdie (1969) cautioned counselors not to overgeneralize about how human behaviors cluster. He said that trait theory requires us to assume that small behavior patterns can be grouped rather consistently into some larger patterns, but not into others. The theory assumes a certain amount of independence of one larger pattern from other patterns and some dependence among the smaller behaviors within a given pattern. The idea in trait theory is to group certain behaviors together and call them "aptitudes," to group other behaviors together and call them "interests," and so on. Within the broad category of aptitude, some behaviors are classified as mechanical aptitude, some as clerical aptitude, and some as academic aptitude. However, Berdie cautions that counselors should realize the inferential nature of these trait categories because, empirically, some categories of behaviors that we define as aptitudes in one area are predictive of behaviors in other areas. Counselors should be wary of the extent to which generalizations about specific behavior clusters can be made, and they should be cognizant of the fact that the extent to which specific behaviors cluster varies from individual to individual, from behavior to behavior, and even from time to time.

The third observation about behavior that is used to define traits is that behaviors are consistent over time, and are predictable. A number of factors, such as the age of an individual, his or her training, experiences, and expectations can influence the consistency of behavior patterns across time. Also, the consistency or predictability of behavior depends upon the methods used for measuring present and future behaviors. Biographical information about 10-year-olds may be more predictive of their adult interests than statements regarding their likes and dislikes would be. The predictability of behaviors also varies with the traits being considered. Examples are the MMPI Mood scales and the Character scales; scores on Mood scales are more apt to change over time than scores on the Character scales are.

A fourth observation about behavior that is used in defining traits is that different patterns of behavior can be related to important social, vocational, educational, and mental health criteria. In other words, traits represent important differences in behaviors. A test author who has developed a new verbal aptitude test would want to provide evidence that scores on this test are related to certain educational and vocational criteria. For example, individuals who have completed more years of advanced education should obtain higher scores on the test than those individuals who have completed fewer years; individuals who are employed in professional occupations should get higher scores than those who are employed in unskilled job. Furthermore, scores on the new verbal aptitude test should be related to other measures of verbal characteristics, but not to measures of nonverbal characteristics.

The trait-and-factor approach argues that counselors must go beyond common-sense criteria and must attempt to establish the validity and reliability of their counseling data. Tests are helpful in counseling when they allow the client to make meaningful inferences about personal characteristics or attributes. In this way, tests promote self-knowledge.

Validity and reliability are critical processes in determining the usefulness of psychological tests. Three types of validity are: (1) *content validity*, (2) *criterion-related validity*, and (3) *construct validity* (Betz & Weiss, 1975). Validity is specific to populations and to the purpose associated with the use of a test. Content validity refers to how well a particular sample of behavior or items used to measure a trait reflect performance on the whole domain of behaviors that constitute the trait. Evidence in support of content validity is the subjective judgment of those who construct the test or of other "experts" who are familiar with the subject area or trait definition. Criterion-related validity concerns the extent to which a measure of a trait shows a relationship with some independent measure of the same trait. Test scores are used to predict status or performance on the criterion. Two kinds of criterion-related validity are *predictive* and *concurrent validity*. Construct validity has to do with whether a test measures the construct it purports to measure. Evidence for construct validity comes about through demonstrating that the interrelationships of the measure follow the hypothesized interrelationships of the relevant construct. This form of validity is based upon empirical evidence that relates a test to other relevant vairables.

Validity is concerned with the usefulness of test information, while *reliability* has to do with the accuracy of the data. Random errors of measurement, which vary from time to time or from situation to situation, influence reliability. Three basic test-retest designs have been utilized to estimate reliability. In the *stability model*, a test is administered to the same representative sample of individuals on two separate occasions, with a sufficient time interval between them. In the *equivalence model*, two equivalent forms of a test are administered to the same representative sample of individuals. In the *stability-equivalence model*, two equivalent forms of a test are administered on two separate occasions with an appropriate time interval between them. Reliability is also estimated by using a variety of split-half procedures. These procedures use data that are internal to a test and can be classified as *internal consistency methods*. Reliability is a property of a total set of scores, while standard error of measurement is used to assess the accuracy of an individual score.

It should be noted that the use of statistical data permits the determination of degree of accuracy or precision that has been achieved in identifying important variables or traits. For example, the standard error is determined for each measure, thus revealing the degree of accuracy of that score. It is evident that such data are seldom, if ever, available to appraise the precision of many other kinds of counselor judgments, impressions, or intuitions.

Goldman (1972) has made the important point that tests still yield only low or moderate correlations with any criterion, and even with themselves. He seems to argue that tests are not useful to counselors, because of their low-to-moderate validity correlations. But the history of measurement of human characteristics is one of successive approximation, moving toward increased accuracy. Compared with the unknown accuracy of many human judgments, psychological tests and actuarial procedures are usually notably superior in accuracy. Research by both Meehl (1957) and Watley (1966) seems generally to indicate the superiority of actuarial over clinical prediction of a large number of social, psychological, and educational criteria. Nevertheless, in the case of many important traits and factors, no tests are available presently, and we must depend upon and use subjective judgments of unknown accuracy as the only data at hand, while keeping constantly in mind their unknown or roughly approximate accuracy.

We ask, what are the alternatives to the use of tests in counseling: Kitson's self-analysis (1931), human judgment, estimation or appraisal (Hollingworth, 1922), or what? We note that Holland and Nichols (1964), Crites (1962), and Super (1955) have devised assessment booklets that enable students to analyze their vocational preferences in a more structured and accurate manner than that advocated earlier by Kitson and still practiced—regrettably—by many students and even by counselors.

We are by no means asserting or even implying that in the trait-and-factor mode of counseling about choice of career, only objective test data are used in aiding clients to ascertain their vocational interests and to choose a career goal. As is true of all modes of counseling, both counselor and clients use "subjective" impressions, estimations, and judgments about factors that are not measured or as yet measurable. The very act of appraising self or others in any respect must rely upon data that are of unknown and even less-than-full accuracy. When using subjective data, the counselor and client should be fully aware of the unknown reliability and validity of the data, and should try both to make comparisons with similar and repeated appraisals and to use judgments from other sources— teachers, parents, and peers. By such means, the counselor and client "reduce" the possible errors in case data about the client. To be sure, such procedures require that interpretations and judgments be made tentatively, subject to later checks with relevant data from other sources. In this way, hasty interpretations and judgments are avoided, and counselor and client learn to live day by day with "tentative" interpretations.

With respect to the use of reference or criterion groups for validation of data about an individual who is seeking counseling assistance in the choice of a career objective, this procedure is usually termed the matching of the client with the requirements of a vocation, a procedure employed long ago by Munsterberg (1913). Holland (1974) deplores the tendency of some advocates of the newer career development pattern of counseling to characterize this matching procedure as "static and outmoded." In rebuttal, he asserts that "the facts seem clear—nearly all of our most useful vocational assessment devices, classifications, and simulations rely upon well-established matching models" (p. 6).

DEVELOPMENT OF THE INDIVIDUAL

Our position is that development is not simply the unfolding of "positive potentials." History shows that individuals are capable of both positive and negative behaviors. For us, self-actualization is too often equated with unbridled independence, which is good neither for individuals nor for society as a whole. Because human development is not independent of forces in society, the "bud cannot merely unfold." Social criteria are a part of development.

A major problem in personal development is to forge interdependent relationships that promote a developing society. We hold that the nature of the "good life" may very well prove to be a striving to attain the teleological goal of *areté*, or excellence, as formulated jointly by the individual and by society. Striving for *areté* yields a richness of being, and counselors are fortunate to have the task of assisting others to strive for the "good life." Along the way, counselors also help their clients to formulate merged internal and external criteria for evaluating their striving.

We use the ancient Greek concept of *areté* to indicate the kind of development that individuals should strive to achieve. Castle (1961) tells us:

> Homer's heroes were endowed with *areté*, a word which defies easy translation. It is often translated by the English word 'virtue', but this is misleading because *areté* can mean less than virtue as we understand it, with its overtones of moral goodness, and also more, because it can mean excellence of many kinds not implied by the English word. To the Greeks *areté* was that peculiar excellence that makes a thing, or a horse, or a soldier, or a hero, the best, the most effective, of their kind. Consequently the meaning given to the word depended on what contemporary views of excellence happened to be (pp. 11–12).

He goes on to elaborate his point:

> Steadily men's conception of *areté* changed to higher and more complex views of human capacity. When Hector gently turned aside the appeal of Andromache and his little son to face certain death, and when, centuries later, Socrates preferred hemlock to silence when truth must be spoken, each was obedient to his *areté* (p. 13).

For us, the concept of *areté* serves as a guideline and an external criterion for personal development.

Still, we reiterate that individuals do not attain a state of full personal development, but instead they "strive" for personal development. Although the goal of personal development is experiential, not all experiences are equally valuable forms of development. For instance, those experiences that lead to more experiences are better than those experiences that are terminal or those that inhibit the individual from seeking new experiences. A criterion for evaluating experiences is the effect that a particular experience has on future experiences. Experiences that restrict or block future experiences are obviously not developmental.

We recognize that students in school and in college are judged properly by their teachers, in part, in terms of their performance on scholarship examinations. Similarly, workers are judged by employers and supervisors in terms of their performance at assigned work. But no counselor of the trait-and-factor persuasion is limited to such criteria in judging the satisfactory development of clients. Throughout the counseling interviews, both parties will find themselves expressing evaluative comments about other aspects of the individual's development of full potentialities. These comments may refer to overt expressions or to other behaviors, to expressed or to indicated aspirations, to frustrations and disappointments, or even to failures in certain undertakings. In the highly personalized relationship of counseling, both parties are engaged in the task of ferreting out the many possible expressions and behaviors that are involved in full development. And the task is never completed during the "last" interview with a particular counselor. The task of full development continues over the years, even though a certain counselor may complete his or her role in the development of a client.

It is regrettable that some counselors who are operating in a restricted situation must "close" their part of the counseling process prematurely by writing a phrase, such as one naming the client's presently chosen vocational goal. Unfortunately, in too many cases that action "closes" the case for the counselor, as though the client's "tentative" choice of a vocational goal were final for all time. Far too few counselors are motivated to "open" the case at a later date to evaluate, or to aid the client to evaluate, the effect of a new experience on the tentative choice of a vocational goal. But the few long-range studies that are reported in the literature indicate that subsequent tryout experiences of tentative vocational and educational choices are frequently and sometimes repeatedly reconsidered in light of subsequent experiences.

It is to be expected that subsequent experiences will have some bearing on one's original vocational choices, and will often cause an individual to make an entirely new choice. Although some vocational and educational choices have an aura of finality and certainty about them, one may well change objectives many times, even after formal retirement. And sometimes years later, inquiry will reveal that the original choice proved to be unsatisfactory for one of many reasons. The "pop psychology" described by Sheehy (1974) in *Passages* illustrates case after case of adult changes in vocational choice. The author argues rather persuasively that adult development involves a series of crises that offer the potential for dramatic personal changes in one's life.

Career planning programs for adults are more evident today than they were five years ago. Tichenor (1977) provides some research evidence regarding the impact of one such program on adults. He reported that a small-group career planning program had a significant impact on the self-actualizing attitudes of the participants. Obviously, more research of this type is needed, and outcomes other than attitudes also need to be assessed.

An illustrative case is found in the comparison of clients' long-range evaluative reactions to the results of counseling. Williamson and Bordin (1941) described a one-year follow-up study of the reported satisfaction of counseled students, compared with that of a matched control group. After one year, approximately 90 percent of counseled students reported satisfaction with the choice of vocational-educational goal that resulted from the counseling. The counseled students were more successful academically, as indicated by higher average grades.

Twenty-five years later, David Campbell (1963) made a similar inquiry about these same individuals. The counseled students were superior in all phases of academic achievement: degrees earned, honors won, percentage elected to Phi Beta Kappa, and so on. After twenty-five years, two-thirds of the counseled students remembered seeing a counselor, and three-fourths had favorable recollections. Twenty-eight percent recalled counseling as an "important influence on their educational and occupational planning while four percent felt it had been definitely harmful" (Campbell, 1963–1965, pp. 2–3).

Counseling and Interruptions in the Development Process

Often an individual changes plans and aspirations as a result of failure or of less-than-acceptable performance in school or on the job. Individual case histories reveal many instances of such situations. At times, the cause lies in the less-than-full effort made by the individual because of lack of basic desire to succeed at the level expected by teacher or employer. After all, in few instances and circumstances do individuals set their own levels of acceptable performance, though their motivations and aspirations will influence their level of success. In the best of working conditions, individuals are deeply involved in setting their own goals and expectations. But criteria of success in school or on the job are established largely by forces that are external to the individuals themselves, and they must expect to be judged by those in authority as to the acceptability of their performance.

Counselors deal with failures or less-than-acceptable performance in a number of ways. Mutual reappraisal of aptitudes and interests in achieving a particular objective quite frequently becomes one or more stages of adequate counseling. At times, a major or minor change in objectives results from such reappraisal. In other cases, a hard-headed review of study habits produces desired success in school. In many instances, counseling is directed to some emotional, familial, or interpersonal stress or conflict that has intervened to divert the counselee's efforts to achieve. Every counselor soon learns that many individuals encounter unforeseen obstacles to the achievement of a well-conceived plan of self-development.

Individuals can be taught to think rationally about failures and obstacles. Berger (1974) presents an analysis of irrational, negative self-evaluation as seen in clients at a university counseling service, and includes suggestions for a program of psychological education. He describes how a student who said that he was a failure because he had not completed a difficult electronics project as quickly as he thought he should, apparently profited from being told by a counselor that excellence does not require perfection and that mistakes or difficulties are not the same as failure. In a later interview, the same client said that he had "had difficulty" hooking up a computer, after beginning to say that he had been "a failure" in doing that job. A program of psychological education that is designed to deal with irrational negative self-evaluation would, for the most part, involve teaching students directly to understand how either-or thinking and negative attributions lead to irrational negative self-evaluation. Such teaching would involve discussions about the roles of language and logic in such self-defeating thinking.

GOALS OF COUNSELING

The overall purpose of the trait-and-factor mode of counseling is to teach clients effective decision-making skills by aiding them to evaluate their characteristics more effectively and to relate those self-evaluations to significant social and psychological criteria. We believe that the purposes of counseling are specified differently for each client. Even though counselors teach decision-making skills, the substance of counseling is concerned with clients' particular needs. This means that counselors' techniques are adapted to the individuality of each client. The goals of the trait-and-factor counselor are very similar to those described by Krumboltz (1966) as "learning the decision-making process." Krumboltz also thinks that the central purpose of counseling is to help clients resolve those problems for which they seek help, and that the criteria for evaluation should be tailored to particular clients' problems.

In the trait-and-factor approach, a counselor may provide a variety of social comparison data that clients can use for improving their self-evaluations. However, sometimes the counselor may not provide new social data, but instead may help clients to organize their present self-evaluations of their characteristics and to identify the implications of these self-appraisals. Trait-and-factor counselors use test data in order to improve self-understanding. Both self-appraisals and actuarial data that are based on tests and background information are used in counseling. Sometimes self-appraisals may be more accurate than test data. Two recent research reports bear on this topic. Norris and Cochran (1977) found that in an actual career guidance setting, nontest variables that include clients' self-ratings and informed self-estimates of performance do provide satisfactory validities and appear to be more valid predictors of college grades than are test scores. Similarly, Dolliver (1969) compared the relative merits of the Strong Vocational Interest Blank with clients' direct expressions of vocational interests. His review of the literature does not support the position of the counselor who fails to use the information that is available from clients' expressions of vocational interests. Yet, here again we want to introduce a note of caution about the use of self-estimates in counseling. Hodgson and Cramer (1977), in a preliminary study of the accuracy of the self-rated abilities of high school students, found little support for the idea of relying solely on self-estimates of ability. They found that realistic self-estimates vary greatly. Self-estimates and test data provide complementary information.

Trait-and-factor counselors assume that improved decision-making skills are a function of both affective and cognitive information. We cite several ways by which counselors help clients to develop effective decision-making skills.

First, counselors help their clients to describe their characteristics more fully. Clients may compare their behaviors to those of new social comparison groups, or they may compare their behaviors to new points of reference. Clients may also consider which methods they want to use to describe their characteristics and, hopefully, they will discover new ways of measuring and labeling their traits.

Second, counselors help their clients to explore their decision-making philosophies or strategies. Clients examine the ways in which their personal values, as well as their attitudes about risk taking, will affect the outcomes of their decisions. Clients speculate about those outcomes that are most probable and determine whether they consider them to be desirable also.

Third, counselors help their clients to compare their characteristics to the "distinctive" characteristics of individuals who are involved in various educational and occupational alternatives. Alternatives are differentiated and are related to clients' descriptions of their traits. Clients learn to label vocational and educational alternatives in new ways, as they distinguish among their similarities and differences.

Fourth, counselors help their clients to assess the individual probabilities of certain outcomes if they choose different alternatives. Very often, actuarial information is presented so that clients may determine how groups of individuals who are similar to themselves on certain predictor measures have performed on criterion measures. Clients consider the relevance of certain statistical data for making personal predictions and decide whether they may be an "exception to the rule."

It must be recognized that tests are not the only data of significance in counseling. Other information, much of it nonquantitative, is also an integral part of the case history of the client. These data vary both in their relevancy and in their accuracy. We have referred to the Munsterberg concept of comparing an individual to a norm group as one means of interpreting test data to counselees. But we do not contend that only by reference to an external norm group can the counselor gain relevant information about the client. Norm groups are one way of understanding how a client compares with other relevant individuals. Although such comparisons are quantitative, they can be of questionable validity for particular individuals. Normative comparisons are affected by a number of social and cultural factors.

Counselors should refer frequently to *Standards for Educational and Psychological Tests and Manuals* (1966) for guidelines in learning to use test data. Some of the points covered in this manual have significance and meaning for data other than the quantitative test kind. Counselors must learn to identify accurate and relevant data if they are to achieve a helpful relationship with each client. But especially important is the practice of verifying one piece of clinical data by reference to similar data that go to make up the complete case history of the individual.

It is especially important that nonquantitative clinical information be collected to make a complete picture of the individual who is being counseled. We hold that, before visiting a counselor, clients have learned much about their own characteristics by comparing their behaviors with the behaviors of other individuals. Clients may have compared their behaviors previously to the typical behaviors of different groups of people; or they may have compared their behaviors to some objective and measurable criteria; or they may have compared their behaviors to personalistic and subjective criteria. Their present self-knowledge is to a great extent a reflection of these comparisons. Thus, a counselor needs to help clients to understand how their social comparison history is related to their past and present self-evaluations.

In the process of counseling, the counselor must remember that the client has final responsibility for judging the meaning of evaluation information (Berdie, 1969). The counselor and client consider the implications of test information, its accuracy, and the ways in which it can be interpreted, but the client is free to accept or reject the many meanings of the information. Far too frequently, counselors who use tests seem to lose sight of this basic point.

Clients are aided to make their own self-evaluations of their personal characteristics. The process is often a time-consuming one, since individuals must often appraise relevant data about themselves by comparing themselves with others who are enrolled in particular school courses or employed in various jobs. Obviously, this process can extend over time with additional conferences in which new experiences or alternative choices are the subject of further counseling relationships. This process is *not* to be completed in one short interview!

PROCESSES AND TECHNIQUES

In this mode of counseling, the processes and techniques that are employed involve cognitive and rational problem solving, as well as relationship techniques. Still, as with other forms of counseling, the major process is the decision-making interview, which may include interpretation of psychological tests of aptitude, vocational interests, and personality, as well as observations or appraisals from other counselors, from teachers, from employers, from family, and from associates. These data are all included in the case history or record of each counselee, and the record is reopened frequently to include new and current relevant information about the counselee.

The case study is an important part of the counseling interview and one of the most valuable means for developing an understanding of the client. There are many models for doing case studies, and we urge counselors to develop their own individual approaches. Six recommended steps in performing a case study are: (1) organization of the case record data into a systematic framework, (2) collection of additional data if necessary for diagnosis, (3) interpretation and weighting of the data, (4) diagnosis, (5) treatment planning, and (6) evaluation (Tollefson, 1968). Of course, all these steps are not necessary in every case study, and the steps may not necessarily follow in this sequence each and every time.

The counseling interview has four important uses: collecting necessary information about counselees, appraising potentiality, remediating problems, and facilitating the development of full potentiality. The interview involves cognitive and affective processes. The counselor uses the interview to assist the client in considering how these factors play roles in effective decision making. We again cite Sorenson's (1967) instructional model as a useful approach to the interview process. For him, the interview is a set of instructional procedures for dealing with the client's immediate problem.

The counseling interview also involves interpersonal influence processes (Strong, 1968). During counseling interviews, the counselor increases his or her influence over the client by enhancing perceived counselor credibility and attractiveness, and during this time the counselor also increases the client's persuadability by enhancing the client's involvement in counseling. In the counseling interviews, the counselor uses his or her influence power to achieve desired changes in the client's cognitive framework and behaviors.

While we will stress the decision-making interview as the principal process in counseling, counselors in many schools and colleges have also acted as teachers of classes and of workshops. For a number of years, counselors have supplemented their individual counseling tasks with occupational information classes. These classes have usually included organized field trips to nearby industries, class visits by specialists in various occupations, and opportunities to interview adults who are actively engaged in various occupations. Students are often asked to report, both to the counselor and to the class, about the information that they have acquired from these sources.

Another promising group technique, which is called *Deliberate Psychological Education*, is a curriculum or set of educational experiences that is designed to affect personal, ethical, aesthetic, and philosophical development in adolescents and in young adults (Mosher & Sprinthall, 1971). In this process, counselors are to act as developmental instructors (Widich, Knefelkamp, & Parker, 1975) or as psychological educators (Sprinthall & Ojemann, in press). Erickson (1975) provides a description of a course that was designed to promote psychological growth in young women. The course, which was entitled "A Study of Women through Literature," involved field interviews, seminars, and value clarification activities. Play readings and short stories were used to get a representative view about stages of ego and of moral maturity.

External Criteria and Social Comparison Groups

Festinger (1954) is credited as the first to describe a comprehensive theory of social comparison processes. He argued that the human organism has a drive to evaluate opinions and abilities; and that to the extent that objective, nonsocial means are not available, people evaluate their opinions and abilities by comparing them with those of others. Strong and Gray (1972), building on the work of Festinger, state that the purpose of much counseling is to provide social comparison data or normative information to influence self-evaluations of clients. In a well-designed study, these authors found that social comparison activities in counseling result in changes in self-evaluation that are consistent with relative performances. Indeed, a test interpretation interview produced dramatic effects on the subjects' self-evaluations.

One special feature of the trait-and-factor mode of counseling is the use of social comparison groups for estimating the probabilities of "successful" performance of students in given types of vocational and educational tasks. For example, a student who is being counseled may be given a scholastic aptitude test, and the score may be compared with those of a group of students who have been admitted to a given college and who have completed the first semester of class work successfully. Such comparisons should be made for a number of colleges, since grading standards are not universal among college classes, but instead vary widely.

One obvious but often overlooked point is that social comparison groups must be relevant to an individual's specific decision. Norms are often too heterogeneous to make useful social comparisons. For example, a comparison group might consist of all "admitted" students who have completed one quarter or one semester of college studies. Adults who are seeking employment might be compared with a group of employed adults who have X years of work of the type that the applicant has indicated as being of possible interest. Obviously, to compare a student who is being counseled with adults who are engaged in a type of work for which the student reveals little interest or inclination will yield few valuable results. That is, comparison groups that are composed of highly dissimilar individuals with respect to traits of major importance for the task involved would yield inadequate descriptions of characteristics and questionable predictions about future performance.

But we cite a case in point, which reveals further complexities about predicting scholastic achievement of students. Festinger (1954) points out that most real-life instances present situations that are a mixture of opinion and of ability evaluation. Abilities are manifested only through performance, which is assumed to depend upon the particular ability. However, the clarity of the performance can vary from instances where the performance that reflects the ability can be clearly ordered, to instances where there is no clear ordering criterion for the ability. Real-life criteria for ability usually reflect both comparisons of performance for individuals and opinions about their performance. This means that, in some cases, counselors must try to influence the clarity with which certain ability criteria are ordered.

Cartwright and Taylor (1971) have stated this problem as follows:

> It has been noted by the writers that a tendency of faculty frequently is to retain the same grade distribution even though the performance of the class on some other basis may improve. In an attempt to break down certain of these barriers, the Dean's office in recent years has circulated to faculty data regarding the quality of the students admitted—high school rank distribution, comparison with other colleges at the University and other colleges in the state and comparison of grading patterns. All this was done with the hope that perhaps the faculty would develop an enlightened attitude on the matter of grading patterns. This has indeed been accomplished but it should be stated parenthetically that grading patterns are changing in colleges and universities all over the country (p. 6).

This example demonstrates a criterion-measure problem that will influence the accuracy with which students can make self-evaluations of their abilities. Hood (1968) reported data from a study of Minnesota colleges that bears on this topic. He found that the grade-point average achieved by a student in a given college is greatly affected by the overall distribution of grades in that college. Counselors need to take note of the fact that there was little relationship between the ability of students in a particular college and the mean grade-point averages they received at that college. For instance, students at the University of Minnesota College of Liberal Arts and Institute of Technology ranked among students from the top Minnesota colleges on ability but ranked near the bottom on mean grade-point average. Given this situation one might ask, What should be the nature of the counseling program in a college like the University of Minnesota Institute of Technology?

Individualized Counseling and Tutoring

We would argue that the trait-and-factor approach to counseling should try to influence both predictor and criterion variables in academic achievement. Counselors try to improve the "odds for success" of their clients, and this involves both individual and organizational interventions. For example, Cartwright and Taylor organized a number of programs that were designed to influence those student characteristics that were found to be related to grades at the University of Minnesota Institute of Technology:

   1   Beginning in 1966, special faculty advisors were available to students who wished to change, or had considered changing, curricula during the first two years of college (Cartwright & Taylor, 1971).
   2   One hundred seniors were selected to serve as "big brother" advisors to about 300 freshmen.
   3   Broad-spectrum tutoring was provided with respect to mathematics, physics, and chemistry. These programs were available five days a week. Teaching assistants were available to aid students seeking assistance. Most of those who utilized this form of assistance were commuters.
   4   The most "successful" program involved Institute of Technology (IT) students who were living in a specially designated University residence hall. "Studies made in 1965 indicated that for groups of comparable ability levels the groups living in dormitories performed better academically than the group consisting of commuter students" (Cartwright & Taylor, 1971, p. 9). This finding led to programs of tutoring for residence hall students. Honors students served as tutors for particular houses of resident IT students. The program was expanded to include six residence hall houses, involving a total of about 300 students. Additional "tutors-at-large" were provided for students who were not participating in the program (Taylor, Cartwright, & Hanson, 1970).
   5   Tutorial assistance was made available for other students who were not living in dormitories, and was usually scheduled during the evening before examinations. In addition to the advanced student tutors, some faculty members were usually present at such meetings. Unfortunately, few commuting students took advantage of such assistance. A teaching assistant was available for tutorial assistance in the college office from 3 to 5 P.M., four days each week. A commuter tutoring program was organized, first in one of the suburban high schools, and then in one of the neighboring junior colleges.
   6   A counseling psychologist was available personally for special counseling services. About 300 students sought such counseling services yearly.
   7   As part of the orientation program, a refresher course in mathematics

was offered for students. A study (Taylor & Hanson, 1969) indicated that participating students earned significantly better mathematics grades than did nonparticipants.

The general results of the several programs may be summarized as follows:

The more a student used tutorial services, the more extensive the improvement in grades (Taylor, 1969).

Tutored students' grades improved, and nontutored students' grades dropped.

First-year students in a math workshop obtained higher mathematics grades than did controls.

First-year students in a math workshop obtained higher-than-predicted grades, and a control group received lower grades than were predicted (Taylor & Hanson, 1970).

In the one-year tutoring program, 51 percent of the tutored group achieved above a C average over one year, as contrasted with two control groups with 43 percent and 22 percent receiving above a C average (Taylor, Cartwright, & Hanson, 1970).

The authors summarize the results as follows: "While the academic ability, high school achievement and interest patterns of IT freshmen have not markedly changed in recent years, the enrollment, academic achievement and persistence have all increased substantially" (Cartwright & Taylor, 1971, p. 20).

The program described by Cartwright and Taylor, which offered greatly increased tutorial assistance, counseling, and encouragement of students by faculty, assistants, and fellow students, especially in the close relationships of residence halls, had an impact on the grades that were received by students. And one must not ignore the probably facilitating effect on students' motivation of the fact that the tutorial programs were seen as a sign of the faculty's concern for the welfare of individual students. This might well be the equivalent of the placebo effect.

One of the significant generalizations to be derived from this study of students is the evident fact that certain kinds of personalized and individualized assistance will help even capable students to exceed the normal expectations of scholastic performance. No doubt other valuable outcomes were achieved, such as personal pride and satisfaction and confirmation of the soundness of the students' original choice of career. Thus, increased morale and self-confidence can also be expected, as well as improvement in grades earned.

We reemphasize our point about criteria of "success." One must never take it for granted that empirical criteria, such as teachers' grades or employers' ratings of work, are infallible and unchangeable under any and all conditions that influence these judgments, ratings, or grades.

The Achievement Problems of Students

Frequently, a student who is seeking counseling is found to be performing scholastically either above or below the expected grades for someone with that particular level of scholastic aptitude. Such students present fascinating possibilities for unusual efforts. We may illustrate these cases with the following diagram.

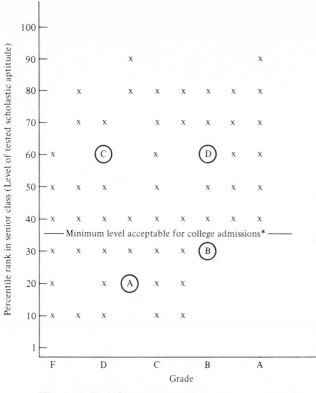

Figure 3-1   Achievement of students.

*The threshold of 30 is an arbitrary selection because colleges differ
widely in admissions standards.

Students in sectors (A) and (D) are performing as expected from their scores on scholastic aptitude tests. It is the students in categories (C) and (B), as well as those who are functioning at the minimum level acceptable for college admission, who present challenging problems to the alert counselor. Academic achievement of students presents exciting challenges to the innovative counselor. A wide variety of personality and skill variables is related to achievement, and it is no small task for counselors to try to help their clients sort them out, prioritize them, and develop action plans to meet achievement needs effectively. Goldman (1971) states two very important cautions about underachievement and overachievement. First, there are many ways to judge whether underachievement or overachievement is present in an individual case, and these ways are not highly correlated with one another. Second, under- and overachievement obviously are merely symptoms, not syndromes; each can be caused by many different factors—emotional, social, motivational, etc.

The research evidence suggests that the following personality traits are related to academic achievement:

   1   ability to handle anxiety

2 sense of self-worth
3 ability to conform and/or accept authority demands
4 acceptance among peers in school
5 minimal conflict over independence-dependence relationships
6 activities that are centered about academic interests
7 realistic goals (Taylor, 1964)

Berger (1961) uses a concept called "willingness to accept limitations" to describe a pattern of attitudes that is found in certain cases of underachievement. His research has provided some support for the hypothesis that, with all other things being equal, those high-ability college students who are willing to accept limitations will achieve at higher levels in college. Students with a "healthy" willingness to accept limitations deny that they have extremely high standards for themselves, admit wholeheartedness in their efforts to achieve, admit willingness to try their best despite a risk of not doing well, and acknowledge the credibility of hard work in achievement.

McClelland (1965) presents an excellent theoretical description of achievement motivation and makes some practical suggestions about how to increase the desire to achieve. He found that achievers like situations where there is moderate risk, concrete feedback, and the opportunity to take responsibility. Counselors must not just say "be an achiever"; they must get students to associate achievement with more and more events in their lives. This may mean teaching students to talk about their real, everyday tasks in terms of achievement. Achievement needs to be seen as a way of improving the student's self-image.

It seems reasonable to believe that underachieving students might be helped by some form of encouragement. However, in one study (Biggs, 1970), it was found that students who received academic encouragement either by letter or through interviews did not receive higher grades than a control group. Although the results from the study were not significant, the research did succeed in operationally defining the rather "vague" concept of academic encouragement and in assessing the relative utility of providing academic encouragement by means of counseling letters and interviews. More needs to be done in developing operational definitions of academic encouragement that are based on different theoretical perspectives. Counselors can use encouragement as a simplistic treatment for academic underachievement. Yet we all know that sometimes a "word of encouragement" may be useless or even detrimental.

As for the overachiever, the counselor may learn that an intensity of desire and motivation have been coupled with a degree of concentration well beyond that found in some of the students who possess higher aptitude. After all, not all students work up to the limit of their capabilities most of the time. In such cases the counselor will wish to encourage the student. However, in time, the counselor may well seek to suggest an objective that is more in keeping with capabilities—after having retested the level of scholastic aptitude attained.

In the past several years, there has been an increase in the number of students entering colleges and universities who have marginal skills for achieving academic success. In response to this problem, some institutions have developed educational support programs. Jones and Osborne (1977) describe one such program, which included diagnostic and counseling services, English and mathematics study laboratories, developmental programs in reading and study skills, and tutorial programs. A unique aspect of this particular program was that it was a cooperative venture of student personnel services staff and faculty from relevant departments. An evaluation of this program yielded very promising results:

    1 Students who participated in the reading/study skills component of the program made highly significant improvements.

    2 A significant relationship existed between students' attendance at the English component of the program and their final grade in English composition.

    3 There was a significant difference between mathematics test scores obtained before and those obtained after the hours spent in the mathematics laboratory.

Overall, the results from this research suggest that this particular counseling/remedial program was fairly successful in enhancing the academic success of marginal students.

Another kind of successful counseling/remedial program that is designed to improve the academic success of marginal students is the peer-tutoring program. Although peer-tutoring programs are not new, the development of such programs for students with marginal academic skills is a fairly recent occurrence. Reed (1974) concluded from his survey of peer-tutoring programs in higher education that most of them appear to be successful for both tutors and tutees. However, he points out that the reasons for their success have been elusive. One suggested hypothesis is that the individualized instructional arrangement and the personal pride both tutor and tutee seek to maintain are prominent parts of the success of peer-tutoring programs.

Brown (1974) reviewed the research evaluating the effectiveness of paraprofessionals in academic settings. He concluded:

> The consistent research results led to the conclusion that paraprofessional counseling was an effective, acceptable, practical, and adaptable counseling procedure, whether the counseling effort was aimed at the prevention or the correction of academic difficulties, whether the counselees were from affluent or poverty backgrounds, and whether the language spoken was English or Spanish (p. 260).

Varenhorst (1974) provides some specific suggestions for training high school students as peer counselors. Her recommended curriculum includes (a) communication skills, (b) decision making as applied to working on common problems, and (c) ethics and strategies of counseling.

Career Counseling with Adults

Two theories of career development for adults have had a major impact on the trait-factor approach to counseling adults. The first is the Theory of Work Adjustment (Dawis, Lofquist, & Weiss, 1968), and the second is the model of vocational maturity described by Super (1977). The Theory of Work Adjustment was developed by the Work Adjustment Project Team at the University of Minnesota. The basic assumption of the Work Adjustment Theory is that individuals seek to achieve and maintain correspondence with their environment, home, work, and school. Work adjustment is the dynamic process by means of which individuals seek to achieve correspondence with the requirements of their job. The stability of that process is called "tenure." The length of a person's tenure on a job indicates the degree of congruence between the needs and abilities of the person and the rewards and demands of the job. Satisfaction and satisfactoriness are twin indicators of the extent to which an individual adjusts to the requirements of a job. Estimations of the degree of correspondence between individuals and their work environment are used to predict satisfaction and satisfactoriness in the work adjustment process.

A number of assessment devices have been developed, based upon the Theory of Work Adjustment. By means of such instruments, clients may predict their satisfactoriness and satisfaction before they actually enter a work or job situation. Such a system of vocational counseling is clearly based upon traits of the individual's personality and his or her relationship to the requirements of a particular type of work.

On the basis of this theory of work adjustment, Dawis and Lofquist (1975) developed a taxonomy of homogeneous groups of occupations. In another article (1976), these authors described the work personality styles of flexibility, activeness, reactiveness, and impulsive behavior. Value dimensions that were derived by factor analysis of the Minnesota Importance Questionnaire were safety, comfort, aggrandizement, altruism, achievement, and autonomy.

The Theory of Work Adjustment has been used as a basis for developing a self-directed counseling unit (Vandergoot & Engelkes, 1977). First, a rationale for participating in counseling was presented. Then the concepts of the theory were presented in a programmed learning format, followed by a series of activities that helped clients to operationalize the concepts. Self-assessment procedures were used to assess needs and abilities, and the results were coded to enable the client to enter a series of tables containing listings of jobs. A knowledge check was included, along with instructions for counselor follow-up to verify the accuracy of self-estimates. Although counselors rated the utility of the unit quite positively, the unit had little impact or utility beyond that of traditional counseling. An interesting finding was that both the self-directed unit and traditional counseling were successful in helping clients to develop job goals and relevant job information. However, neither counseling nor the experimental unit had much impact on the direct job-seeking behavior of clients.

Super (1977) makes a distinction between vocational maturity and vocational adjustment. *Vocational maturity* is the ability to cope with the vocational or career development tasks with which an individual is confronted. *Vocational adjustment* is defined as an outcome of behavior, such as satisfaction or success. Vocationally adjusted people are those who are doing what they like to do and are successful at doing; vocationally mature people are those who are coping with tasks that are appropriate to their life-stage in ways that are likely to produce desired outcomes.

The model of vocational maturity in mid-career has the same basic dimensions as those listed for adolescence: Planfulness or Time Perspective, Exploration, Information, Decision Making, and Reality Orientation. However, the tasks, the topics to be explored, and the kinds of information that are needed by mid-career adults are different. The difference between vocational maturity in adolescence and mid-adult life is primarily that, in adulthood, the required awareness and information are more particular.

Super and his colleagues have developed an adult form of the Career Development Inventory, which focuses on planfulness. The items cover career development tasks from (a) the exploratory stage, (b) the establishment stage, (c) the maintenance stage, and (d) the stage of decline, including preparation for retirement. Responses are on a five-point scale ranging from "I have already done this" to "I have not yet thought much about it." This measure helps to identify those types of developmental tasks that the individual has completed, those with which he or she is coping actively, those that are of some concern, and those that are not yet being faced.

As with students, the career counseling of adults is *personal* counseling. Career changes in adults often are a reflection of deeper changes in an individual's personal life, including goals, values, and life-style. For most adults, their career is an important component of their life structure, which includes both an external aspect—an overall pattern of roles, memberships, and goals—and an internal aspect consisting of inner identities and core values (Thomas, 1977).

The relationship between career changes and life structures is only approximate. For instance, there can be a considerable life-structure change for an adult who remains in the same job. Thomas (1977) presents the following typology based on career change and life-structure change:

1   Changers—Adults who change both their careers and their life structures.
2   Pseudochangers—Adults who make career changes without any change in their life structures.
3   Crypto-changers—Adults who remain in the same careers and make significant life-structure changes.
4   Persisters—Adults who change neither their life structures nor their careers.

This typology highlights the point that "career change by itself is only a rough indicator of what is going on in an individual's life during the mid-life period, much as divorce is a very gross indicator of the quality of the family life" (Thomas, 1977, p. 326).

Career counseling of adults will also have elements of the unexpected. Career development is a part of adult development, an area about which we know relatively little. Erikson (1968), one of the foremost writers about ego development, treats adult development in terms of stages; (a) Intimacy versus Self-Absorption, (b) Generativity versus Stagnation, and (c) Integrity versus Despair. These stages in adult development often involve crises or "turning points," which may lead to unexpected and sometimes surprising career changes in adults.

Another important aspect of career counseling with adults is that career thinking and career choice often reflect nonrational or quasi-rational processes. Baumgardner (1977) argues that counselors can help students with the inevitable conflicts and dilemmas that individuals must face in our society. He goes on to make a point with which we agree strongly:

> Certainty over making a right career choice should not be a goal of career counseling. What should be a desired outcome is students' recognition of the irreducible uncertainty in the career process, the likely sources of career confict and the inadequacy of the conventional career wisdom (p. 21).

ILLUSTRATIVE CASE HISTORIES[1]

The following case histories illustrate a trait-and-factor approach to counseling. In each of the cases the counselor, after establishing a relationship with the client, employs social comparison data—for example, tests—to help the client evaluate personal characteristics. The assumption is that the major way in which clients obtain knowledge of their characteristics is to compare their behaviors to those of others. However, sometimes clients have not had adequate social groups to compare themselves to, or their past social comparisons have been distorted because of the influence of other factors. This is the reason why trait-and-factor counselors almost always review the client's self-evaluation history before they introduce any new social comparison information.

Although counselors may often provide systematic social comparison data as a means of improving client self-evaluation, the contemporary trait-and-factor counselor realizes that self-knowledge is only one part of counseling. He or she must also be concerned with increased self-acceptance and the affective life of the client. Self-knowledge and self-acceptance are of one cloth. The trait-and-factor counselor is also aware that one of the pitfalls of using test data in counseling is that clients may reify their definitions of their traits. Instead, we hold that trait-and-factor counselors should use test data or any other social comparison to help clients generate or evaluate hypotheses about self. Since these hypotheses can never be proved completely, counseling always contains a flavor of tentativeness.

A final point about the trait-and-factor approach to counseling is that it has a limited realm of effectiveness. We do not hold that counselors who employ mainly a trait-and-factor approach should not employ other counseling approaches when they may seem appropriate. No one approach to counseling is effective with all types of problems, clients, or counselors.

As is obvious, the five case histories are not "typical" by any criteria of comparison. We hold that there are no "typical" cases, but rather that counseling aims to help clients understand the meaning and significance of their individualities. For us, differences among clients are important and not to be stereotyped.

[1]These five cases are presented by counselors: John and Sally by Professor Ellen Betz, counselor, Student Counseling Bureau, University of Minnesota; and Anne, Barbara, and Charles by Dr. Lloyd Lofquist, Chairman, and Dr. René Dawis, Professor, Department of Psychology, University of Minnesota. Professors Lofquist and Dawis are responsible for a vocational counseling service for adults. We are grateful for their assistance in depicting the trait-and-factor approach to counseling.

However, these cases highlight some of the often neglected aspects of adequate case histories.

The case of John illustrates one major point of importance in counseling of all patterns or modes. Students do not come to a counselor neatly catalogued and packaged as to a single type or pattern of problem. For instance, it is clear that John's vocational choice problem was complicated, if not caused, by his relationships with his father. He therefore presented not only a problem of vocational goal choice, but also one of emotional blocking of a rational solution to that problem. The counselor wisely saw the possible relationship between these two areas in John's life, and indirectly used affective-rational means of aiding John to understand his situation, and thus to deal with both aspects of the problem in an interrelated manner. Such subtle approaches to dealing with interrelated aspects of one's life adjustment are necessary steps in maturing.

John

John was an 18-year-old freshman in his third quarter at the University when he first came to the Student Counseling Bureau. The younger of two children of aging parents, both currently in their fifties, John was the first in the family to attempt college. His father had managed a small family business for many years; his mother had never been employed outside the home; his only sister, age 20, was working in their home town, which was a community of 25,000.

According to test data presented with John's application to the University, his high school rank had been at the 70th percentile for entering first-year students at this University (the rank was standardized for the size of graduating class). His score on the Minnesota Scholastic Aptitude Test (MSAT)[2] was at the 79th percentile for the normative group of entering University first-year students.

During the first interview, John said that he was enjoying the University so far, but was apprehensive because his grades were not as high as he wanted them to be. He planned to become a lawyer, he said, and he wanted help in evaluating his chances of being accepted for law school. When I suggested that we could also investigate other career alternatives, he seemed to tense up somewhat, so I dropped this line of thinking and moved on to other topics.

John said that he currently was working for 15 hours or more a week as a clerk in the furniture department of a local department store. When asked to evaluate this experience, he said he liked it most of the time, especially the chance to talk with people and help them find what they needed in the store. He was not very happy with the pay, however, and he had some ideas about how the department should be improved. He said that he was thinking about changing jobs in order to increase his paycheck, but had not yet done anything about it.

When he was not at work, John said, he preferred to be outdoors. This interest had developed through camping experiences with his church youth group, although he had also gone on some hikes and short trips with one or two friends. In high school, he had participated in football and basketball, and also in debate.

---

[2]The Minnesota Scholastic Aptitude Test is given to all Minnesota high school seniors in all schools and is reported to all Minnesota colleges and universities.

He said he was never outstanding at any of these pursuits, but was always able to make the school team anyway. John's grades in high school had been mostly B's and C's, but he felt that he had never worked very hard on his classwork. His University grades included B's in "Man and Society" and public speaking; C's in freshman composition courses, biology, and introduction to political science; and a D in German. John was not really enthusiastic about any of the courses he had taken so far. In fact, he said school work was never really very interesting to him. He thought he should go to law school, however, because it would give him a good, secure career future.

Meanwhile, John was anxious to find out more about his chances of getting into law school. He wanted to take the Strong-Campbell Interest Inventory (SCII) and the Minnesota Multiphasic Personality Inventory (MMPI), because he had heard that some schools require these tests with the application. I also assigned the Allport-Vernon-Lindzey Study of Values (AVL), since I thought that it might help John give more thought to his values as they related to his career goals.

A few days later John was back, and was eager to find out about his test scores. Accordingly, I began the process of showing him his scores, interpreting their possible meanings, and helping him to clarify his self-knowledge and his career possibilities.

We started with the Strong-Campbell Interest Inventory (1974). On the Basic Interest Scales, John obtained high scores on the Nature, Adventure, Athletics, Public Speaking, Law-Politics, and Business Management scales. Similarly, John had a number of Occupational Scale scores of 40 or higher, the highest among them being Public Administrator, Guidance Counselor, Social Scientist, Personnel Director, Advertising Executive, Recreation Leader, Chamber of Commerce Executive, and Credit Manager. His General Occupational Theme scores were highest on the Social, Economic, and Conventional Themes (SEC). His Academic Orientation (AOR) score was 35. I pointed out the similarity of this score with the AOR scores of people who go into business, an occupational choice that was also supported by many of John's other scores. John had little to say in response to this interpretation; he was looking at his score on the Occupational Scale for lawyer, which was in the average range. He said he thought that the lawyer score was low because he had not yet had a chance to do many of the things that lawyers do.

We moved on to the Minnesota Multiphasic Personality Inventory (MMPI). John's scores here were quite typical of many male college students. His T score (72) on the K scale was a bit high, which suggested some defensiveness in taking the inventory. This might have been the result of a desire to "look good," the kind of desire that people often experience when a school or job application is involved. John agreed that he had been very "up tight" when he took the test. On the clinical scales, John's only T score above 70 was his Scale 4 score of 71, a result that suggested some rebelliousness, and perhaps occasional problems with family or with other authority figures. This tentative interpretation seemed quite acceptable to John. He said that he had had problems getting along with his father, and did not like the way in which his father tried to control him. His father wanted him to go into business, John pointed out, and he thought that his father's decisions had been too conservative.

John's scores on the Allport-Vernon-Lindzey Study of Values (1960) were highest on the Economic (56), Social (50), and Political (48) scales. These were interpreted as being generally consistent with John's interest scores, and leaning toward occupations in the business world, which actually could include law and politics as well as, perhaps, sales and administration. As we talked about his scores, John said that he had been quite successful so far in his sales job, and he told of a project he had initiated recently to attract more buyers from the customers passing through his area.

John agreed to continue exploring his skills, interests, and values. He had already begun reading materials in the University's career library. I also suggested that he make an appointment with the undergraduate advisor for prelaw students. We developed a list of questions regarding law school requirements and the law school curriculum.

In the weeks that followed, John did contact the law school advisor. He was quite discouraged by the results of that interview, but again decided to stay with his law school goal, even though his chances of being admitted would depend upon his improving his grade-point average markedly. Meanwhile, we talked further about John's hopes for the near and more distant future, and the kind of life he would like to lead. We also developed a plan for further experiences that he would try out to test his possibilities and goals. At this point, counseling was discontinued to give John time for further thinking and exploring.

John returned to the Student Counseling Bureau the following winter. His grade-point average was about the same as before, despite the fact that he had taken a "How to Study" course during the fall quarter and had been working hard to make the necessary grades for law school entrance. We spent some time talking about how he had originally decided he wanted to be a lawyer, and we worked through his discouragement, as he was now realizing that he should at least consider other career alternatives. This led to a discussion of how important it was to John to be different from his father, a concern that John was now willing to talk about fully. Gradually, this process seemed to relieve some of John's tension about his own worth and identity. Eventually we returned to his Interest Inventory and Values scores, and developed some specific alternatives to the law school choice.

After another trial period, John decided to go into Business Administration, with a major in sales or in marketing. He decided that he would try to combine his love for the outdoors with eventual employment in an organization or business involved with outdoor equipment and/or activities. In the following year, he had a hard time getting through the accounting course sequence in the School of Business Administration, and I saw him briefly during this crisis. Apparently, the rest of his undergraduate career went by satisfactorily. He stopped by once during his last quarter and said that he was feeling good about his decision to go into Business Administration and was now getting ready to tackle the job market.

Sally

Sally was a first-year student when she first came to the Counseling Bureau. She had grown up in a family of educators, with two older brothers and an older sister who had followed a variety of careers in high school and college teaching. Sally's academic record to date was excellent. Her high school rank was at the 91st percentile in a normative group of entering University freshmen. On the Minnesota Scholastic Aptitude Test, her raw score was 62, which fell at the 98th percentile for entering students. Sally's concern was the fact that she had no idea what she wanted to major in, and had found no career that really intrigued her.

During our first interview, Sally reviewed some of her thoughts about careers: that she did not want to be a teacher, that she would like to get married some day but was not in a hurry, and that she planned to work outside the home all her life and wanted to do something interesting. Activities that she liked during her high school years included sports, music, student government, travel, and camping. She had played the cello in the high school orchestra and had held several offices in high school groups. During high school she had also held part-time jobs as a counter girl in a restaurant and as a camp counselor. She had liked both jobs, particularly because of the contact with people. She had given some thought to the possibility of becoming a camp director or working for a youth organization. She said she had decided against this, however, mostly because she wanted a career with more long-range options. Also, she said, she enjoyed learning and liked to study, and hoped to include these interests in her career planning. Her grades so far had been split between A's and B's, with A's in geology, English composition, and psychology. Sally said that she had considered a geology major but had decided she wasn't really interested in the content of that field.

Sally's highest scores on the Strong-Campbell Interest Inventory Basic Interest Scales were Nature, Medical Science, Music/Dramatics, Art, Writing, and Social Service. Her highest scores on the Occupational Scales included Occupational Therapist, Psychologist, College Professor, and Musician; her next highest scores were Dentist, Physician, Speech Pathologist, Recreation Leader, Social Worker, YMCA Secretary, Artist, Art Teacher, and English Teacher.

Sally's highest scores on the Occupational Themes were Artistic, Investigative, and Social. Her Academic Orientation score was 64, which indicated a great deal of similarity with people who complete graduate or professional training. Her Introversion/Extroversion score was 44, falling in the average range but in the direction of occupational extroversion.

In the next interview, we reviewed and talked about Sally's scores on the Edwards Personal Preference Schedule (EPPS). Scores above the 75th percentile included Achievement, Autonomy, Affiliation, Nurturance, and Endurance; scores below the 25th percentile included Deference, Exhibition, and Change. All others fell in the middle range. As Sally considered the preferences or needs that she desired from her life, she agreed with most of the test results and saw them as being validated by her typical orientation toward helping people and her desire to be an achieving, autonomous person. Combining these preferences, she said, had often seemed impossible, but she hoped to have a career that would allow both aspects of herself, the achieving and the nurturing, to be expressed.

Sally agreed to do some reading in the Occupational Library, to search for occupations that might meet her career needs and also to follow up on some of the job titles suggested by the Strong-Campbell Interest Inventory.

To my surprise, two months passed before Sally returned for another interview, and even then she had not yet done any reading in the Occupational

Library. She had, however, been thinking. She had decided that she did not want to do graduate work in any area that would restrict her to employment in a college or university; she wanted to get into the "real world," doing something worthwhile. Without my knowing what dynamics might have discouraged her explorations in the Occupational Library, Sally and I started making a list of the various careers that had come up in our past conversations, including careers suggested by the Strong-Campbell Interest Inventory and other resources. From the list, I asked Sally to choose two or three career possibilities that she would like to investigate. After much hesitation, she finally decided that she would like to learn more about being a dentist or physician. There was support for these possibilities in Sally's Strong-Campbell Interest Inventory Occupational Scale scores; her scores for these and for some of the other medical sciences were fairly high. I went to the Occupational Library with Sally, and together we found some materials on medicine, which Sally immediately began to devour. Later, she said that she had been afraid to read about these topics because she had always thought that she would not have the ability to enter a profession. As we talked, Sally remembered an old desire to be a doctor, an idea that she had discarded in her early teens as being unrealistic—a child's goal.

After this interview, Sally continued the career exploration on her own. The next time I saw her she had made contacts in the Medical School and also in the Psychology Department and had come up with two alternatives—being a pediatrician or a child psychologist. She had also developed a plan of courses to take as a means of investigating the alternatives. We talked about various work experiences that might also help her test her goals.

This was the last interview with Sally. Two years later I talked to her one day when our paths crossed on campus. She was then a junior, eagerly involved in psychology courses and pretty well decided on the child psychologist goal.

Anne

Anne, age 21, was an excellent student in high school but decided against going to college after graduation because she had no idea what she really wanted to study. She thought that some practical job experience would help her to decide, while enabling her to earn the money she would need to pay tuition. After she had worked as a computer operator for three years, her motivation to return to school was strong, but she still did not know what career to pursue. Her parents thought that she should consider nursing, while a high school art teacher had encouraged her earlier to pursue a design career. Anne herself wondered about the possibility of a career in computer programming. Anne came to the Vocational Assessment Clinic at the University of Minnesota to evaluate these alternatives and to find out about other career possibilities that she might not have considered. She also wanted help in choosing educational programs that would prepare her for a suitable career.

Anne and her counselor began by examining her vocational abilities. They considered what she had done well in school, what she did well in her present job, and what she might learn to do well in the future. Ability testing revealed that she had many outstanding abilities and particularly strong numerical and spatial aptitudes. Anne had known that she had some ability, but the high scores surprised her.

Next, Anne and her counselor assessed her work-related needs. Anne preferred jobs that would allow her to use her special talents, to express herself creatively and, especially, to be able to see the results of her work. Anne had always derived much satisfaction from figuring out better ways to do things, but she needed to see how things turned out.

Finally, they focused on her vocational interests. The results of the interest inventory showed three interest patterns—social, artistic, and scientific—that stood out. They discussed Anne's concern for the environment and her desire to learn more about the world around her so that she could help to make it a better place for people to live in.

Anne's work personality—abilities, needs, and interests—was examined in relation to a wide variety of occupations. Each occupation was considered in terms of what had been learned about her work personality. Anne agreed that occupations in such areas as engineering, architecture, and commercial art seemed to capitalize on her best aptitudes, to offer opportunities that would meet her needs, and to involve activities that were in line with her interests. The counselor suggested that she look more closely into these areas. After some research, Anne became particularly enthusiastic about engineering specialties, such as bio-engineering and environmental engineering. She learned about the University's engineering programs in these areas and decided to apply for admission.

On the services evaluation form that each Clinic client is requested to complete a short time after the conclusion of assessment, Anne informed the Clinic that she had been accepted into a program in environmental engineering.

Barbara

Barbara, age 27, was married and the mother of two school-aged children. She had grown up in a small farming community where most women married and began raising families shortly after high school graduation.

Barbara had taken a commercial course in high school, which qualified her for entry-level clerical positions. After high school graduation, she decided that she did not want to remain in a small town all her life and moved to a big city, where she took a secretarial job with a large insurance company. She had met her husband at work, and after their marriage they had begun to raise a family.

Barbara continued to work for two or three days a week on a temporary-help basis while her children were small. Working as a temporary clerk-typist gave her a chance to become acquainted with a number of businesses.

Now that her children were in school full-time, Barbara wanted to resume a full-time career. However, secretarial work had lost its appeal for her. She felt that she would be too confined with a desk job. She preferred to be active for at least part of the day.

At the time she came to the Vocational Assessment Clinic, Barbara was thinking seriously of a career in nursing. During her first pregnancy, she had become interested in biology and had taken a course in human physiology through University extension classes. Barbara felt that she had the ability to master the required science courses. Nursing seemed like a good choice because there were more jobs available than there were in some other fields, she would be active on the job, and she would be of direct service to others. However, she was not completely sure—maybe there was some field she had overlooked.

At the Clinic, the results of ability testing showed that Barbara had college-level abilities. However, she decided that she was not ready to commit herself to a four-year degree program. The results of needs assessment (Table 3-1) revealed that Barbara should probably be in an occupation where she could help other people and use her abilities in a challenging and varied job that would keep her busy and provide her with steady employment. A good salary was important to her because she and her husband had developed many outdoor sports interests, such as camping, hunting, and skeet-shooting, and they had wanted to take flying lessons and join a parachuting club. However, such expensive activities would have to wait until Barbara was working full-time.

As a result of vocational assessment, Barbara decided to examine the following occupations in addition to her original choice of nursing: policewoman, physical therapist, x-ray technician, respiratory therapist, recreation leader, and physical education teacher. Initially, she eliminated physical education teacher and physical therapist because these would require a four-year program. Recreation leader was a strong possibility, but she would need a four-year degree to qualify for a position at the salary level she wanted. For the same reasons, she ruled out physical therapist. While x-ray technician and respiratory therapist looked good in terms of salary and training time, both occupations involved working indoors and might not provide the variety and activity Barbara wanted.

Table 3-1 Barbara's Vocational Need Scores, Minnesota Importance Questionnaire

	Need	Score	Significance
1	Ability utilization	1.7	Very important
2	Achievement	1.0	Important
3	Activity	1.3	Important
4	Advancement	0.7	
5	Authority	−0.9	Not important
6	Company policies and practices	0.9	
7	Compensation	1.4	Important
8	Coworkers	0.5	
9	Creativity	0.6	
10	Independence	−0.4	Not important
11	Moral values	0.9	
12	Recognition	0.4	
13	Responsibility	1.0	Important
14	Security	1.3	Important
15	Social service	1.2	Important
16	Social status	0.2	
17	Supervision–human relations	0.3	
18	Supervision–technical	0.9	
19	Variety	0.7	
20	Working conditions	0.0	Not important

After careful deliberation, Barbara finally decided to become a policewoman. She saw the field of police work as satisfying her interest in the medical and social service areas, as well as her need for adventure, physical activity, a good salary, and job security. She could begin work as a policewoman without a bachelor's degree, and could pursue one later on, or in stages, if she felt that this would be important to her advancement in the police force.

Charles

Charles, 42 years old, had had a successful career as a manufacturer's representative. He and his family had moved quite frequently early in his career, but three years ago, when he was promoted to the position of regional sales manager, Charles found that he would be spending more time in his new city and began to get involved in community activities. In addition to leading a Boy Scout troop, Charles joined a political organization and participated in a local hospital's community action efforts. As his spare time commitments increased, Charles began to feel vaguely dissatisfied with his work insofar as it did not command his commitment and interest as it once had.

At the Vocational Assessment Clinic, Charles found that he had high scores on the verbal, numerical, spatial, and perceptual aptitude parts of the General Aptitude Test Battery. With respect to his vocational needs, Charles showed a strong preference for work that would give him a feeling of accomplishment as well as moral rectitude—work that would make use of his abilities, allow him to make his own decisions, and provide him with the opportunity to help others. Charles' need scores are shown in Table 3-2.

Table 3-2   Charles' Vocational Need Scores, Minnesota Importance Questionnaire

	Need	Score	Significance
1	Ability utilization	1.6	Very important
2	Achievement	2.3	Very important
3	Activity	−0.4	Not important
4	Advancement	1.0	Important
5	Authority	0.4	
6	Company policies and practices	1.0	Important
7	Compensation	0.7	
8	Coworkers	0.8	
9	Creativity	1.2	Important
10	Independence	−0.7	Not important
11	Moral values	2.1	Very important
12	Recognition	0.7	
13	Responsibility	1.5	Very important
14	Security	0.9	
15	Social service	1.5	Very important
16	Social status	0.6	
17	Supervision—human relations	0.0	Not important
18	Supervision—technical	−0.3	Not important
19	Variety	0.3	
20	Working conditions	0.5	

Through vocational assessment and counseling, Charles recognized the strength of his social service interests and his preference for work that would allow him to use his abilities in the service of others. He began to see clear and consistent patterns as he reviewed his vocational development. Verbal-persuasive activities, verbal reasoning and leadership skills, and achievement and altruistic values were woven through his work history and were reflected in his assessment data.

The mid-career alternatives that were identified for Charles' further exploration included fund raising, public relations, institutional development, political campaign management, and community organizing. Together, he and his counselor considered steps that he could take to work his way gradually into paid employment in these areas.

SUMMARY AND EVALUATION

The trait-and-factor approach to counseling is basically atheoretical. This form of counseling makes no pretense of being a comprehensive theory of personality or of counseling. Trait-and-factor theory is best when it is used for describing behavior, and poorest when it is used as a causal attribution theory. Trait theorists are still grappling with some puzzling issues concerning the origin of traits, trait independence, and trait distributions.

The early history of trait-and-factor counseling is an interesting mixture of American social idealism, as shown in the philosophy and works of Frank Parsons, and the empirical approach of differential psychology, as evidenced in the works of E. L. Thorndike and L. M. Terman. These two streams of thinking are interwoven in contemporary trait-and-factor counseling.

This approach includes a variety of counselors within its ranks. A pure trait-and-factor counselor is difficult to envisage. Almost all counselors who use tests in working with clients are to some degree making trait-and-factor assumptions about their clients. Contemporary trait-and-factor counselors cannot be defined by their adherence to particular techniques. For us, the trait-and-factor approach is an abstract model that counseling activities will approximate to some degree.

Still, within the history of counseling psychology there have been identifiable groups of counselors who have focused their efforts on applying concepts and research from differential psychology to the solution of human problems. One of the pioneering experiments was done by a band of psychologists during World War I, a group whose efforts in human measurement provided tools for early trait-and-factor counselors.

A review of the history of the trait-and-factor approach shows threads of philosophical thinking that have their basis in logical positivism and empiricism. The scientific method, systematic observations, and measurement have been held as values to be emulated. Throughout this history, a high value has also been placed upon rationality. In the early models of trait-and-factor counseling, the client's affective concerns, as well as the affective side of counseling, were hardly mentioned. Over the years, trait-and-factor counselors have had relatively little to say about feelings. However, they have referred consistently to the need for viewing clients in a holistic and integrated way.

The philosophical basis for trait-and-factor counseling has been described by Allport (1966) as heuristic realism:

Heuristic realism, as applied to our problem, holds that the person who confronts us possesses inside his skin generalized action tendencies (or traits) and that it is our job scientifically to discover what they are. Any form of realism assumes the existence of an external structure ('out there') regardless of our shortcomings in comprehending it. Since traits, like all intervening variables, are never directly observed but only inferred, we must expect difficulties and errors in the process of discovering their nature (p. 3).

Allport also talks about the counseling process in these words:

As a safeguard I propose the restraints of heuristic realism which accepts the common sense assumption that persons are real beings, that each has a real neuropsychic organization, and that our job is to comprehend this organization as well as we can. At the same time, our profession uniquely demands that we go beyond common-sense data and either establish their validity or else—more frequently—correct their errors. To do so requires that we are guided by theory in selecting our trait slices for study, that we employ rationally relevant methods, and be strictly bound by empirical verification. In the end we return to fit our findings to an improved view of the person (pp. 8–9).

These eloquent statements about science and rationality assume that science and objective knowledge can play a major role in improved human understanding. However, a problem for trait-and-factor counselors has been to develop a model for communicating such objective information. For the most part, trait-and-factor counselors have sorely neglected making theoretical and empirical investigations of the counseling process. In far too many instances, trait-and-factor counselors seem to assume that the counseling process is information-centered rather than meaning-centered. The importance of the client in the interpretation and acceptance of counseling information has not been emphasized fully enough. To be sure, trait-and-factor counselors still need to pay more attention to the processes by which clients attribute meanings to counseling information.

One would be remiss in discussing the trait-and-factor approach to counseling if no mention were made of the social philosophy that is very much a part of this history. We should not forget that Frank Parsons, who was so critical a figure in the early history, was more a restless social reformer than a scientist. Over the years, trait-and-factor counselors have consistently placed considerable emphasis upon social improvement. Examples are numerous. Donald Paterson pioneered the development of the student personnel program at the University of Minnesota, which brought about far-reaching changes in the education of students at that university. During the Depression, he went on to work with vocational counseling problems for out-of-work youth. Then he worked on the problem of improving industrial relations between management and labor. After World War II, the Veterans Administration counseling programs were established as a means of helping returning veterans to find satisfying and worthwhile careers. In the strife-ridden sixties, counselors were cautioned not to turn their backs on the social conflicts over race and war. Williamson and Biggs (1975) urged counselors to give thought to innovating methods for aiding each succeeding generation to understand and to seek to alleviate the many injustices and inequities that are yet to be corrected. Surely people are capable of learning the mode of rational dialogue in facing social problems!

One naturally thinks of counseling in terms of the future of all education—fiscal crises and the conflicts over policy decisions that seem to increase with every edition of the news media. How in the world can the counselor and client converse about purely personal problems, when overriding crises demand attention? Surely the deliberations of counselor and client will be overwhelmed by the cosmic crises that demand attention!

Yet now more than ever, there is a need for sober, thoughtful dialogue about individuals' problems. Perhaps education needs to be retooled to help students prepare themselves for personal crises that arise in the midst of international, ethnic, racial, and fiscal demands. Perhaps this preparation for modern adulthood—learning to think rationally about oneself and about the human situation—is more important than some of the current content of learning. Maybe we can hope to aid students to learn to deal rationally with controversy and conflict. This kind of idealism has been a consistent feature in the history of the trait-and-factor approach to counseling.

BIBLIOGRAPHY

Allport, G. W. Traits revisited. *American Psychologist*, 1966, *21*, 1–10.

Allport, G. W., Vernon, P. E., & Lindzey, G. *Manual: Study of values* (3rd ed.). New York: Houghton Mifflin, 1960.

Baumgardner, S. Vocational planning: The great swindle. *Personnel and Guidance Journal*, 1977, *56*, 17–22.

Berdie, R. F. The uses of evaluation in guidance. In R. Tyler (Ed.), *Sixty-Eighth Yearbook of the National Society for the Study of Education, Part II.* Chicago: University of Chicago Press, 1969.

Berdie, R. F. Differential psychology as a basis of counseling. *The Counseling Psychologist*, 1972, *3*, 76–81.

Berger, E. M. Willingness to accept limitations and college achievement. *Journal of Counseling Psychology*, 1961, *8*, 140–144.

Berger, E. M. Irrational self-censure: The problem and its correction. *Personnel and Guidance Journal*, 1974, *53*, 193–199.

Betz, N. E., & Weiss, D. J. Validity. In B. Bolton (Ed.), *Measurement and evaluation in rehabilitation.* Springfield, Ill.: Charles C Thomas, 1975.

Biggs, D. A. Counseling interviews or counseling letters. *Journal of Counseling Psychology*, 1970, *17*, 224–227.

Bordin, E. S. Diagnosis in counseling and psychotherapy. *Educational and Psychological Measurement*, 1946, *6*, 169–184.

Brown, W. F. Effectiveness of paraprofessionals: The evidence. *Personnel and Guidance Journal*, 1974, *53*, 257–263.

Campbell, D. P. *A study of college freshmen twenty-five years later.* Cooperative Research Project No. 2160, University of Minnesota. Washington, D.C.: Office of Education, U.S. Department of Health, Education, and Welfare, 1963–1965.

Campbell, D. P. *Handbook for the Strong Vocational Interest Blank.* Stanford, Calif.: Stanford University Press, 1971.

Campbell, D. P. *Manual for the Strong-Campbell Interest Inventory.* Stanford, Calif.: Stanford University Press, 1974.

Cartwright, P. A., & Taylor, R. G. *We try harder—recruitment and retention programs of the Institute of Technology* (Paper No. 71CP671PWR, mimeographed. Presented at 1971 IEEE Summer Power Meeting, Portland, Oregon). Minneapolis: University of Minnesota, July 1971.

Castle, E. B. *Ancient education and today.* Baltimore: Penguin Books, 1961.

Cattell, J. M. Mental tests and measurements. *Mind,* 1890, *15,* 373–381.

Cattell, J. M., & Farrand, L. Physical and mental measurement of the students of Columbia University. *Psychological Review,* 1896, *3,* 618–638.

Courtis, S. A. The Courtis tests in arithmetic. In S. A. Courtis (Ed.), Final report, Educational Investigation, Committee on School Inquiry (Vol. I). New York: City of New York, 1911.

Crites, J. O. An interpersonal scale for occupational groups. *Journal of Applied Psychology,* 1962, *46,* 87–90.

Cronbach, L. J. Five decades of public controversy over mental testing. *American Psychologist,* 1975, *30,* 1–94.

Dahlstrom, W. G., & Welsh, G. S. *An MMPI handbook: A guide to use in clinical practice and research.* Minneapolis: University of Minnesota Press, 1960.

Dawis, R., & Lofquist, L. H. Toward a psychological taxonomy of work. *Journal of Vocational Behavior,* 1975, *7,* 165–171.

Dawis, R., & Lofquist, L. H. Personality style and the process of work adjustment. *Journal of Counseling Psychology,* 1976, *23,* 55–59.

Dawis, R., Lofquist, L. H., & Weiss, D. J. A theory of work adjustment (a revision). *Minnesota Studies in Vocational Rehabilitation,* (XXIII). Minneapolis: Work Adjustment Project, Industrial Relations Center, University of Minnesota, 1968.

Dolliver, R. H. Strong Vocational Interest Blank versus expressed vocational interests: A review. *Psychological Bulletin,* 1969, *72,* 95–107.

Erickson, V. L. Deliberate psychological education for women from Iphigenia to Antigone. *Counselor Education and Supervision,* 1975, *14,* 297–309.

Erikson, E. H. *Identity: Youth and crisis.* New York: W. W. Norton, 1968.

Festinger, L. A theory of social comparison processes. *Human Relations,* 1954, *7,* 117–140.

Goldman, L. *Using tests in counseling* (2nd ed.). New York: Appleton-Century-Crofts, 1971.

Goldman, L. Tests and counseling: The marriage that failed. *Measurement and Evaluation in Guidance,* 1972, *4,* 213–220.

Hahn, M. E., & MacLean, M. S. *Counseling psychology.* New York: McGraw-Hill, 1955.

Hall, C. S., & Lindzey, G. *Theories of personality.* New York: Wiley, 1957.

Hathaway, S. R., & McKinley, J. C. *Minnesota Multiphasic Personality Inventory* (Rev. ed.). New York: Psychological Corp., 1951.

Hodgson, M. L., & Cramer, S. H. The relationship between selected self-estimated and measured behavior in adolescents. *Measurement and Evaluation in Guidance,* 1977, *10,* 98–105.

Holland, J. L. *Professional manual for the self-directed search.* Palo Alto, Calif.: Consulting Psychologists Press, 1973.

Holland, J. L. Some practical remedies for providing vocational guidance for everyone. *Student Counseling Bureau Review*, 1974, *25*(2), 1–21.

Holland, J. L., & Nichols, R. C. The development and validation of an indecision scale. *Journal of Counseling Psychology*, 1964, *11*, 27–34.

Hollingworth, H. S. *Judging human character*. New York: D. Appleton, 1922.

Hood, A. B. *What type of college for what type of student?* Minnesota studies in student personnel work, no. 14. Minneapolis: University of Minnesota Press, 1968.

Jones, J. D., & Osborne, T. An educational support program: The results of merging academics and student personnel services. *Journal of College Student Personnel*, 1977, *18*, 251–254.

Kitson, H. D. Analyzing yourself. *I find my vocation*. New York: McGraw-Hill, 1931.

Krumboltz, J. D. Behavioral goals for counseling. *Journal of Counseling Psychology*, 1966, *13*, 153–159.

Levine, M. The academic achievement test: The historical context and social functions. *American Psychologist*, 1976, *31*, 228–238.

Linden, K. W., & Linden, J. D. *Modern mental measurement: A historical perspective*. Boston: Houghton Mifflin, 1968.

Lofquist, L. H., & Dawis, R. V. Vocational needs, work reinforcers, and job satisfaction. *Vocational Guidance Quarterly*, 1975, *24*, 132–139.

McClelland, D. Toward a theory of motive acquisition. *American Psychologist*, 1965, *20*, 321–333.

Meehl, P. E. When shall we use our heads instead of the formula? *Journal of Counseling Psychology*, 1957, *4*, 268–273.

Minnesota Scholastic Aptitude Test. Minneapolis: Student Counseling Bureau, University of Minnesota, 1964.

Mosher, R. L., & Sprinthall, N. A. Deliberate psychological education. *The Counseling Psychologist*, 1971, *2*, 3–82.

Munsterberg, H. *Psychology and industrial efficiency*. Boston: Houghton Mifflin, 1913.

Norris, L., & Cochran, D. J. The SIGI prediction system: Predicting college grades with and without tests. *Measurement and Evaluation in Guidance*, 1977, *10*, 134–140.

Parsons, F. *Choosing a vocation*. Boston: Houghton Mifflin, 1909.

Paterson, D. G. Developments in vocational counseling technique. In E. G. Williamson (Ed.), *Trends in student personnel work*. Minnespolis: University of Minnesota Press, 1949.

Paterson, D. G., Schneidler, G. G., & Williamson, E. G. *Student guidance techniques*. New York: McGraw-Hill, 1938.

Pepinsky, H. B. The selection and use of diagnostic categories. *Applied Psychology Monographs*, 1948, *15*.

Pepinsky, H. B., & Pepinsky, P. N. *Counseling theory and practice*. New York: Ronald Press, 1954.

Reed, R. *Peer-tutoring programs for the academically deficient student in higher education*. Berkeley, Calif.: Center for Research and Development in Higher Education, University of California, Berkeley, 1974.

Rice, J. M. Educational research: The results of a test in language. *Forum*, 1903, *35*, 269–293.

Sheehy, G. *Passages*, New York: Dutton, 1974.

Sorenson, G. *Toward an instructional model for counseling*. (CSEIP Occasional Report No. 6). Los Angeles: University of California, April 1967 (mimeographed).

Sprinthall, N. A., & Ojemann, R. H. Psychological education: Guidance counselors as teachers and curriculum advisors. *Texas Tech Journal of Education*, in press.

Standards for educational and psychological tests and manuals. Washington, D.C.: American Psychological Association, 1966.

Strong, S. R. Counseling: An interpersonal influence process. *Journal of Counseling Psychology*, 1968, *15*, 215–224.

Strong, S. R., & Gray, B. L. Social comparison, self-evaluation and influence in counseling. *Journal of Counseling Psychology*, 1972, *19*, 178–183.

Super, D. E. Transition from vocational guidance to counseling psychology. *Journal of Counseling Psychology*, 1955, *2*, 3–9.

Super, D. E. Multifactor tests: Summing up. *Personnel and Guidance Journal*, 1957, *36*, 17–20.

Super, D. E. Vocational maturity in mid-career. *Vocational Guidance Quarterly*, 1977, *25*, 294–302.

Taylor, R. G. Personality traits and discrepant achievement: A review. *Journal of Counseling Psychology*, 1964, *11*, 76–82.

Taylor, R. G. Tutorial services and academic success. *Journal of Educational Research*, 1969, *62*, 195–197.

Taylor, R. G., Cartwright, P., & Hanson, G. R. Tutorial programs for freshman engineering students: Effect on grades and attrition. *Journal of Engineering Education*, 1970, *38*, 87–92.

Taylor, R. G., & Hanson, G. R. Pre-college math workshops and freshman achievement. *Journal of Educational Research*, 1969, *63*, 157–160.

Taylor, R. G., & Hanson, G. R. Interest and persistence. *Journal of Counseling Psychology*, 1970, *17*, 506–509.

Thomas, L. E. Mid-career change: Self-selected or externally mandated. *Vocational Guidance Quarterly*, 1977, *25*, 320–328.

Thorndike, E. L. *Introduction to the theory of mental and social measurements.* New York: Teachers College, Columbia University, 1904.

Tichenor, J. M. Life work planning: A group career program evaluated. *Vocational Guidance Quarterly*, 1977, *26*, 54–59.

Tollefson, N. *Counseling case management.* Boston: Houghton Mifflin, 1968.

Vandergoot, D., & Engelkes, J. R. The application of the theory of work adjustment to vocational counseling. *Vocational Guidance Quarterly*, 1977, *26*, 45–53.

Varenhorst, B. B. Training adolescents as peer counselors. *Personnel and Guidance Journal*, 1974, *53*, 271–275.

Watley, D. J. Counselor variability in making accurate predictions. *Journal of Counseling Psychology*, 1966, *13*, 52–61.

Widich, C., Knefelkamp, L. L., & Parker, C. A. The counselor as a developmental instructor. *Counselor Education and Supervision*, 1975, *14*, 286–296.

Williamson, E. G. *How to counsel students: A manual of techniques for clinical counselors.* New York: McGraw-Hill, 1939.

Williamson, E. G. *Counseling adolescents.* New York: McGraw-Hill, 1950.

Williamson, E. G. Value orientation in counseling. *Personnel and Guidance Journal*, 1958, *37*, 521–528.

Williamson, E. G. Value commitments and counseling. *Teachers College Record*, 1961, *62*, 602–608.

Williamson, E. G. Value options and the counseling relationship. *Personnel and Guidance Journal*, 1966, *45*, 617–623.

Williamson, E. G., & Biggs, D. A. *Student development through education.* New York: Wiley, 1975.

Williamson, E. G., & Bordin, E. S. A statistical evaluation of clinical counseling. *Educational and Psychological Measurement*, 1941, *1*, 117–132.

Williamson, E. G., & Darley, J. S. *Student personnel work*. New York: McGraw-Hill, 1937.

Wissler, C. The correlation of mental and physical traits. *Psychological Monographs*, 1901, *3*, 1–62.

Woodworth, R. S. In C. Murchison (Ed.), *History of psychology in autobiography* (Vol. 2). New York: Russell & Russell, 1951.

Chapter 4

Psychodynamic Theory

Norman Abeles

INTRODUCTION

A few introductory words about the aim of this chapter seem to be in order. My attempt is to present a reasonably complete and comprehensive discussion of Freud's theory of psychoanalysis as the prototype of psychodynamic theory. I am well aware that Freudian theory is often made more "palatable" to students by the inclusion of materials that add various perspectives to psychoanalytic thinking. The work done by neo-Freudians falls into this category. The neo-Freudians attempted to place Freudian psychoanalysis within a cultural and social perspective, and made major modifications in the psychoanalysis theory. Another group of theorists pursued the area of ego psychology and has made valuable contributions in that sphere. It would not be impossible, then, to present a "here and now" version of psychoanalytic theory that would select from all these morsels a tasty dish indeed. Since it has been my experience that relatively few students read any of Freud's works in their original translated versions, my intent in this chapter is to provide a reasonably complete "there and then" version of Freud's psychoanalytic theory and practice. The reader who is interested in modifications of Freudian theory will have no difficulties in gaining access to writings that cover that material. Finally, it should be recognized that Freud himself was never totally consistent in his theorizing, and made numerous modifications. Sometimes the modifications stood alongside the older version of the theory. By and large, this chapter will emphasize the final synthesis of psychoanalytic theory, and will point out previous versions when this appears to be helpful. My hope is not to gain converts for Freudian theory, but to encourage understanding.

The editorial assistance of Richard Levine is gratefully acknowledged.

History and Biographical Data

Sigmund Freud, the founding father of psychoanalysis, was born on May 6, 1856 in Freiberg, Moravia (located in Czechoslovakia). According to Jones (1953–1957) the citizens of Freiberg discovered in 1931 that the local birth register indicated mistakenly that Freud had been born on March 6. It seems uncannily fitting that the recordkeeping pertaining to Freud's birth should be marked by one of those *parapraxes* (mental slips) of everyday life that Freud was to investigate systematically some 40 years later.

Another portent of Freud's future career may be discerned in an incident that took place when he was about three years old. Freud's family had decided to move to the larger town of Leipzig. While traveling by train to what was to be his new home, Freud glimpsed some gas jets that were illuminating the night. In the crucible of his vivid imagination, the 3-year-old Freud "saw" these gas jets as souls burning in hell. This disturbing fantasy triggered a "phobia"—of traveling by train, which persisted for several years. The origin and the final resolution of this phobia were ultimately revealed to Freud through analysis. Only one year after the move to Leipzig, Freud's family relocated again and settled in Vienna, where Freud remained until the Nazi invasion of 1938. Freud spent the last months of his life in London, where he died on September 23, 1939.

Because he was of Jewish ancestry, Freud was always sensitive to the presence of anti-Semitism. While the evidence is not definitive, Freud believed that his forebears had settled near Cologne during the fourteenth and fifteenth centuries and had moved east subsequently, to escape anti-Semitic persecution. Freud discovered that it was during the nineteenth century that his ancestors retraced their steps westward to Austria. Even in cosmopolitan Vienna, Freud was made inescapably aware that he was a member of an unpopular religious minority. As someone who grew up in Vienna during the 1930s, I can attest to the fact that anti-Semitism was a pervasive current in my environment.

In the fall of 1873, Freud entered the University of Vienna as a student of medicine. Freud did not feel he had a calling to become a physician. Rather, as Jones (1953–1957) recounts, Freud had a keen interest in studying humanity's cultural and historical development. Galvanized primarily by philosophical and intellectual inquisitiveness, Freud did not view himself as a social activist who aspired to reform or to destroy the sources of social injustice. Notwithstanding his natural proclivity to pursue theoretical issues, Freud eventually concluded that enrollment in the medical faculty was most compatible with his aspirations. Even then, Freud meandered through his medical studies, and took three years longer than necessary to complete his work. He tried out a veritable smorgasboard of courses prior to settling finally on physiology as his area of specialization. The requirements of making a living seemed to preclude a career as a theorist.[1]

The antecedents of Freud's later psychological theories can be traced to the

---

[1]Thus he began to turn toward the practice of medicine.

period when he studied physiology under the aegis of Professor Ernst Brücke (1819–1892). Specifically, Freud was influenced by Brücke's conception of physiology as a dynamic interplay of forces combined with an emphasis on evolution of the organism. After he finally was awarded his M.D. degree in 1881, Freud maintained his affiliation with Brücke's institute for over a year. Handicapped by his Jewish background and the tortuously slow pace of advancement in the university system, Freud was compelled by economic necessity to enter the practice of medicine.

In the course of working toward his M.D. degree, Freud had obtained considerable clinical experience by working with diverse patient groups in hospitals. This clinical experience included a five-month stint with psychiatric patients. In 1884, Freud began serving as a physician in the department of nervous disease at Vienna's general hospital. Interestingly enough, according to Jones (1953–1957), there often were no patients with nervous disorders admitted to this institution, because the superintendent was disinterested in such cases and was committed to reducing costs. Despite the superintendent's efforts, the doctors in charge of admissions "conspired" to admit patients with nervous diseases, thus affording Freud the opportunity to study and work with such cases during his 14-month stint in this department.

In 1885, Freud received a travel grant to visit the great French neurologist, Charcot, at the Salpetriere Hospital in Paris. Charcot's views concerning hysteria made a profound impression on Freud. It was Charcot who demonstrated that hysterical symptoms often eluded explanation when approached from an anatomical point of view. Thus, the phenomenon of "glove anaesthsia," that is, a lack of sensation in an area covered by a glove, cannot be accounted for physiologically because no known nerve injury can produce it. Charcot concluded from this and from other medical case studies that psychological processes may play a causative role in symptom production. Charcot was a pioneer in legitimizing the study of hysteria, a malady that virtually all his colleagues accorded indifference or neglect. Captivated by Charcot's work, Freud offered to translate into German the French physician's *New Lectures on the Diseases of the Nervous System*. The offer was accepted.

It is an ironic footnote in the history of psychoanalysis that Freud attempted unsuccessfully to interest Charcot in the now famous case of Anna O. Freud learned of this case in 1882 from the treating physician, Dr. Joseph Breuer, who was a friend of Freud and of Freud's family. Breuer, a man of considerable scientific standing in Vienna, was 14 years Freud's senior. The two men had met while Freud was at the Institute of Psychology.

Breuer saw Anna O. for about 19 months. She had a plethora of symptoms, including paralysis of both legs and of the right arm, anaesthesias, loss of appetite and nausea, disturbances of sight and speech, and a nervous cough. She had periods when she was completely normal, which alternated with episodes when she appeared to be in a childlike, dreamy state. Breuer referred to this latter state of consciousness as an "absence." Anna O. exhibited many of the features of a double personality. During her interludes of lucidity, she would recount to Breuer the events of the day, including many of the disagreeable and terrifying hallucinations that had beset her. Following these recitals the patient felt much better. In fact, Breuer observed that once, while she was telling him of the initial appearance of a particular symptom, that symptom disappeared completely.

After a time, Breuer sought to deal with the massive amount of material produced by his patient with an approach built upon hypnosis. Specifically, Breuer hypnotized Anna and then recalled to her some of the thoughts and mumblings that coursed through her dreamlike "absences." Breuer reasoned that if Anna could be helped to remember the inciting situation in which her symptoms first occurred, and if this memory were accompanied by a full expression of emotion, then her symptoms would disappear. Breuer's willingness to see one patient regularly for over a year was in itself unusual. Patients who were diagnosed as hysterics almost never received such intensive and prolonged care. Anna O. herself described the treatment she received as "the talking cure." Breuer labeled the process as "catharsis," a term still in vogue today.

While some accounts suggest that Anna O. was cured completely, the actual evidence is more equivocal (Jones, 1953–1957, p. 225). Anna O. did suffer some transient relapses, from which she subsequently recovered. She went on to lead a productive life. She became the first social worker in Germany, and she campaigned in behalf of child welfare and the emancipation of women.

It remains moot whether psychoanalysis began with the discovery of the cathartic method or with Freud's modifications of this therapeutic modality. Between 1892 and 1895, Freud continued to revise and refine his implementation of the cathartic method. Initially, patients were asked to lie down (with their eyes closed) and concentrate on a particular symptom, while trying to recall the events surrounding that symptom. If no associations were forthcoming, Freud would place his hand on the patient's forehead and suggest that some recollection would occur. Occasionally, Freud would resort to hypnosis in dealing with intransigent cases. Ultimately, Freud discarded both suggestion and hypnosis in favor of letting his patients say whatever came to mind without giving conscious direction to their thoughts. At this juncture, the cathartic method had become transformed into what was to be the lynch pin of psychoanalytic technique—free association. Jones (1953–1957) assesses the advent of free association as marking the beginning of the psychoanalytic method, even though the term "psychoanalysis" was not used until one year later, in 1896.

In July 1897, while he was afflicted with sharp mood swings, fear of dying, and inability to engage in productive writing, Freud began his self-analysis. Freud described his neurotic symptoms in a voluminous correspondence that he maintained with his friend, Wilhelm Fliess. As part of his self-analysis, Freud used his dreams as a means of exploring his unconscious. In a very tangible manner, Freud's self-analysis helped to illuminate and deepen his burgeoning understanding of the psychodynamic process. For example, Freud's masterpiece, *The Interpretation of Dreams*, was written coincident with his self-analysis. Additionally, by October 1897, Freud had begun grappling with the implications of resistance and repression, and wrote to Fliess "Resistance has . . . become objectively tangible . . . and I only wish I had also grasped what lies behind repression" (Freud, 1887–1902; Bonaparte, Freud, & Kris, 1954, p. 227).

By 1902, Freud had attracted a small coterie of followers who wished to learn more about psychoanalysis. Eventually, what began as an informal study group on Wednesday evenings became the Vienna Psycho-Analytic Society. Among its most renowned early members were Wilhelm Stekel and Alfred Adler. Between 1904 and 1906 Freud published several important works, including *The Psychopathology of Everyday Life* and *Three Essays on the Theory of Sexuality*. This last volume, in particular, shocked many Viennese, who were scandalized by Freud's contention that children have sexual urges that undergo changes as they develop into adults. Singularly reprehensible in the eyes of Victorian society was the view that children's first sexual objects are their parents.

Meanwhile, Freud's reputation was beginning to extend beyond the borders of Austria. In Switzerland, Carl Gustav Jung, the Chief Assistant of Eugen Bleuler, Professor of Psychiatry, began working with word association tests in an attempt to demonstrate experimentally certain of Freud's findings regarding repression. Jung also attempted to apply Freud's discoveries to the study of psychosis in his book *The Psychology of Dementia Praecox*.

In 1908, on the occasion of Clark University's 20th anniversary, its president, Stanley Hall, invited both Freud and Jung to be guest lecturers. Arrangements were made for the two men to travel together. Thus, in September 1909, Freud delivered a series of five extemporaneous lectures, which were later published, delineating the central tenets of psychoanalysis. Stanley Hall, William James, and J. J. Putnam, who was Professor of Neurology at Harvard, all were receptive to the ideas presented by Freud and Jung (Jones, 1953–1957, Vol. II, p. 52). In general, however, Freud's teachings were greeted with considerable skepticism and suspicion. Many Americans viewed psychoanalytic doctrine as a license for eliminating all sexual restraint.

In Europe, opposition to psychoanalysis was even more vehement. Intellectual debate degenerated, at times, into a personal assault on Freud's character. Some adherents of psychoanalysis were denied promotions or were even dismissed from their scientific posts. A witch hunt of sorts was underway.

External opposition did not create internal unity within psychoanalytic circles. With the passage of time, some of Freud's most prominent followers became dissenters. For example, both Carl Jung and Alfred Adler broke with Freud and articulated their own theories. For Adler, who went on to develop his own ego psychology, the rupture with orthodox psychoanalysis took place in 1911. Jung, whom Freud regarded as a close friend, began to question Freud's emphasis on the sexual life of patients. Concomitantly, Jung became immersed increasingly in studying mythology and the occult. As the theoretical gap between Freud and Jung widened, their friendship cooled. By 1914, the estrangement was complete.

Freud's writings and contributions are too prolific to permit a detailed accounting of them in this format, but mention can be made of some of his best-known works. In addition to those cited previously, among the most popular of Freud's books is his *Introductory Lectures on Psychoanalysis*, which appeared in 1917. Freud also published a number of fascinating essays in the form of case histories, including "The Case of Dora" (a partial analysis of hysterical symptoms), "The Case of Little Hans" (an analysis of a 5-year-old phobic boy), and "The Case of the Rat Man" (a lengthy discussion of the analysis of an obsessional neurosis).

Later in life, Freud explored from many perspectives the origins and nature of mental processes (instincts and the vicissitudes, regression, sociological and anthropological contributions). These concerns are central in such works as *Totem and Taboo* and *Civilization and Its Discontents*. In addition, Freud wrote about religion (*Group Psychology, The Future of an Illusion*), about art and the creative process (note his writings on Leonardo da Vinci), and about literature (*Creative Writers and Daydreaming*). It is no exaggeration to term the range of his intellect as encyclopedic.

Freud continued to reside in Vienna until shortly after the Nazi invasion, and died in London after a courageous battle against cancer in 1939.

PHILOSOPHY AND MAJOR CONCEPTS

After being influenced by his early associations at Brücke's institute, Freud made the principle of *psychic determinism*, or causality if you will, one of the cardinal precepts of psychoanalysis. More precisely, Freud incorporated the principle of psychic determinism into a more general historicism that permeates his vision of how human beings navigate and evolve in the course of their lives. In *The Psychopathology of Everyday Life* (1901), Freud made explicit his view that apparently unintentional aspects of actions can be revealed as well motivated, when these behaviors are studied psychoanalytically. Freud thus rejected outright the possibility that one's thoughts and musings are random, accidental, or meaningless. He insisted that there must be some guiding force that determines the direction of these thoughts and musings. This insistence is at the core of Freud's metapsychological genetic point of view.

His commitment to determinism notwithstanding, Freud acknowledged that he could not predict what form of specific behavior a given conflict might produce. To elucidate, while Freud was confident that he could trace a given behavior back to its causative beginnings, he deemed it impossible to predict the strength of one's drives. In the absence of this piece of data, that is, the strength of one's drives, it remains beyond our grasp to make specific predictions regarding the manifestations of conflict. In analyzing a particular aspect of manifest behavior, it becomes possible to suggest that one element of the conflict was stronger than another, but the specific quantitative strength of mental "forces" eludes direct measurement.

As an individual who had been trained in the biological sciences, Freud embraced the viewpoint that psychic phenomena were expressions of biological phenomena. Freud conceded that he had been influenced by Darwin's theory of evolution, and suggested that many of humanity's higher attributes had passed through various evolutionary stages. It is noteworthy that such mental mechanisms as regression and displacement are discernible in the behavior of animals.

Surprisingly, Freud subscribed to the Lamarckian theory of the inheritance of acquired characteristics—the notion that modification in an animal as a result of some unusual experience or effort on its part would be transmitted genetically to future generations. In the Lamarckian framework, these future generations would make further efforts, and then the modification would become cumulative. Despite the discrediting of Lamarck's theory, Freud insisted that some characteristics of mental behavior are inherited from generation to generation. This implies that the id consists of archetypal experiences that can be traced back to primitive progenitors.

Freud's early training at Brücke's institute clearly predisposed him to accept the interrelatedness of mind and body. His teachers, colleagues, and close friend, Breuer all were strongly inclined to describe human behavior in physical terms. Furthermore, in his lengthy correspondence with Fliess, Freud was admonished repeatedly not to forget the necessity of seeking the organic basis of neurotic disorders.

In a draft of a letter to Fliess that was written in 1895, Freud stated that he was certain that such physical phenomena as migraine headaches and sexual stimulation had a chemical basis (Freud, 1887–1902, p. 116). Freud's point of view was consonant with the widespread belief in the late nineteenth and early twentieth centuries that the solution to human psychological problems could be found in physiology, and brain physiology in particular. In fact, in 1895 Freud embarked on an extensive paper that was aimed at providing an overall physical explanation for normal and psychopathological processes. This "Project," as it was called, was Freud's last attempt to link the anatomy of the brain to psychological processes. Shortly after completing this ambitious essay and sending it to Fliess, Freud abandoned the theoretical premises upon which it had been based. Freud continued, however, to believe that heredity played some role in the etiology of mental disorders. Specifically, he hypothesized that heredity could predispose one toward development of certain symptoms, but he discounted the notion of direct genetic transmission of mental illnesses.

In summary, then, Freud was much more concerned with determining the antecedents of human behavior than with unveiling the anatomical structure of mental activities. While he held that heredity was a factor in shaping mental processes, he was cautious in his assessment of its relative importance. Finally, though Freud was a determinist in his belief that psychological symptoms and conflicts could be traced back to their origins, he also deemed it impossible to predict specific symptoms and conflicts solely from detailed knowledge of one's early experiences.

Free Association

As indicated previously, Freud's modifications of the cathartic method led directly to development of the method of free association. Two important changes marked the introduction of free association as the centerpiece of psychoanalytic technique. First, Freud eliminated the use of hypnosis, because he had concluded that it provides incomplete information about psychological processes and fosters resistance to therapeutic intervention. Secondly, Freud insisted that his patients keep their eyes open, in order to maintain greater contact with the therapist. Freud instructed his patients to lie down on a couch and say whatever came to them, without involving conscious direction or self-censorship. The therapist was directed to sit outside of the patient's field of view and to maintain an "evenly hovering," attentive attitude. These conditions were designed to stimulate retrieval of fantasies and unconscious wishes and to minimize the influence of social and physical factors.

Freud's theoretical and technical contributions underwent continued revisions. For example, early in his practice of psychoanalysis Freud invited his patients to dine with him and his family. He also presented detailed explanations of his methods to his patients, in the belief that this would facilitate further production of materials. Later, Freud modified both these practices. Freud did not alter his view that it was more facilitative therapeutically to have patients lie down in a place where their analysts were out of view than to have analyst and patient sit across from each other face-to-face.

Quite evidently, there are presently many therapists the world over who subscribe to Freud's basic method, with various modifications. Many practitioners prefer to have their patients face them in a seated position. In addition, the instructions for free association have been altered in a variety of ways. Paul, in his eloquent book *Letters to Simon*, suggests the following "Basic Instruction": "You can tell me the things you want to tell me, it's up to you. I will listen and try to understand. When I have something useful to say, I will say it" (1973, p. 13). Clearly both the orthodox Freudian approach and Paul's revision of it are predicated on open verbal expression, honesty, and trust. Paul's variation may convey to patients the feeling that they possess more opportunity for interpretation and choice.

As White points out, the key elements in free association are, first, that the patient's recollections, fantasies, and internal wishes have to be communicated to a listener; and, secondly, that the patient comes to the therapist because he or she is suffering and seeks help. Thus, within the context of the therapy situation, the associations that are produced serve a "therapeutic purpose" (1964, p. 30).

Transference and Resistance

Writing in *On The History of the Psychoanalytic Movement* (1914), Freud asserted that psychoanalysis is defined to a significant degree by the conclusion that transference and resistance are manifest starting points of therapeutic work. Other essential tenets of psychoanalysis include acknowledgment of the importance of unconscious determinants and recognition of the role of early history in the personality development of individuals.

In describing the relationship between Anna O. and her physician, Dr. Breuer, Freud (1914, p. 293) talks of a "very intense suggestive rapport on the part of the patient." Freud labels this as a "prototype" of what we describe as transference today. Freud was convinced that the analytic situation itself catalyzed powerful transference feelings in the patient. Specifically, in the course of psychoanalysis the patient engages in a highly intense and intimate endeavor with a relatively unresponsive, nonintrusive authority figure. Freud theorized that the strong feelings generated toward the therapist by the patient in the analytic setting originate in childhood experiences with one's parents and with other important persons. These intense emotions, which are rooted in the past, are carried forward; that is, they are transferred to the analyst and constitute a powerful vehicle for change in the analytic process.

As Freud (1915a) observed, patients commonly fantasize at the outset of treatment that good behavior on their part will elicit their analyst's love. This fantasy is undoubtedly present in many modalities of psychotherapy other than psychoanalysis. The patient typically wishes to cooperate, wants to please the therapist and hopes to receive approval and liking in return. The analytic situation is unique in that it intensifies these feelings on the patient's part. Unlike most other treatment approaches, psychoanalysis provides the patient with only minimal cues regarding the personality and character of the analyst. Additionally, despite strong expectations and often pervasive feelings of dependency, the patient is given relatively little feedback by the analyst. The emotional and ideational reactions that are engendered by these conditions replicate similar responses experienced earlier in life.

Freud soon discovered that the patient's love and affection for the therapist eventually give way to feelings of anger and hostility. In the psychoanalytic vernacular, the patient invariably experiences both positive and negative transference in the course of psychoanalysis. As a rule, positive transference facilitates progress in therapy, while negative transference frequently contributes to a state of impasse. A central objective of psychoanalysis is to reveal to the patient the origins of transferred emotions, so that new ways of dealing with these feelings can be found. In order to help the patient accomplish this task, Freud admonishes the therapist not to respond in an emotional or personal manner to the powerful transference-love and transference-hate that the patient expresses.

Behavior that is based upon transference is termed acting out, since the patient acts out (verbally at least) feelings that originated in childhood. Without the assistance of psychoanalysis, the patient rarely recognizes instances when he or she is being driven by sentiments that are rooted in the long-forgotten (or repressed) past. Since the analytic situation maximizes transference and encourages its exploration, there is, of course, the danger that the patient will continue to "act out" toward relatives, friends and acquaintances outside the therapy hour. "Acting out" behavior is usually inappropriate and detrimental to the patient's self-interest. Because they know this, analysts will routinely caution individuals who are contemplating or undergoing analysis to refrain from making important life decisions (such as marriage) until therapy is completed.

While Freud contended that transference is present from the inception of the analytic relationship, he recognized that the process is often not very apparent when the analysis is progressing smoothly. Moreover, the analyst does not need to focus upon transference feelings as long as the therapy advances. When transference becomes *resistance*, however, then it must be confronted. Freud characterized the kind of transference that interferes with analysis as a special form of resistance. This transference is actually a compulsive repetition of earlier childhood experiences. The task of analysis is to convert this repetition into a recollection (Freud, 1924).

Freud initially discussed resistance in relation to free association. He found that despite his patients' best efforts, they encountered considerable difficulty in telling everything that came to their minds. Resistance takes many forms, ranging from simple expressions of embarrassment to elaborate intellectual arguments purporting to demonstrate the irrelevance of analysis. As suggested earlier, resistance may be expressed in transference. To illustrate, a male patient may, in the course of therapy, reenact past struggles he had with his father in order to gain his independence. This hypothetical patient might well resist cooperating with his therapist (father) as part of his effort to break ties of dependency (Freud, 1924).

Now it may be asked, what is it that elicits transference in any of its variants? Wolstein replies succinctly: "Therapeutic probings of intolerable feelings or thoughts which the patient never felt free to divulge to another person calls forth a distorted reaction" (1954, p. 127). He adds that Freud dealt only inferentially with the relationship between anxiety and transference. Wolstein (1954) tackles this issue by stating that when the therapeutic work between therapist and patient is impeded by the patient's anxiety, the concomitant changes in the verbal or other behaviors of the patient are an indication of transference distortion (p. 137). Obviously, this operational definition encompasses the operation of resistance.

Repression and the Unconscious Process

Freud considered the concept of repression to be one of the cornerstones of psychoanalytic theory, particularly as the concept relates to his ideas about unconscious processes. Freud had observed that his patients could not raise certain memories into awareness without the expenditure of considerable energy and effort. Other recollections seemed to be wholly irretrievable. At first, Freud defined repression as "the function of rejecting and keeping something out of consciousness" (1915c). In a subsequent paper concerning the unconscious, Freud (1915d) emphasized the role of repression in inhibiting the development and expression of affect of any kind. It is noteworthy that Freud recognized that there were flaws inherent in the concept of unconscious feelings. Strictly speaking, feelings have to be tied to thoughts or ideas. In a technical sense, however, it is common to refer to unconscious anger or unconscious love, for example, without always specifying ideational content.

Freud defined the unconscious in more than one way, but he was clear about its relationship to repression. The core of the unconscious consists of wishes that are stimulated by impulses (sexual and aggressive). These wishes continually strive for expression. They are modified as they push toward consciousness, since they must traverse a barrier (or censor) that stands between the unconscious and consciousness. There is also an intermediate agency, the preconscious, which contains material that is capable of being raised to consciousness, although with some effort. In contrast, repressed contents in the unconscious are effectively barred (*censored*) from reaching even the preconscious. This division of the psyche into the unconscious, the preconscious, and the conscious is known as the topographical point of view, since metaphorically it represents configurations of the mind in the same way that a topographical map depicts the natural features of a given area.

Some people mistakenly view the unconscious as a kind of "garbage pail" that contains ideas blocked from reaching consciousness by repression. While Freud did initially regard the unconscious as a repository of sorts, he subsequently broadened this conception by stating that all mental processes originate in the unconscious. This revised view underscores the dynamic character of the unconscious. Unconscious impulses, as well as their ideational and emotional correlates, strive ceaselessly to rise through the barrier into the preconscious and eventually to consciousness. Conversely, *drives*, with their accompanying ideas and affects, are pushed back (repressed) continually from the conscious to the unconscious. Repressed contents, Freud noted, are usually connected with unpleasant, painful affect. Much later in his career (1925), Freud reformulated his theory and concluded that anxiety was the cause of repression. It is widely accepted that painful ideas are repressed into the unconscious ("repression proper" in Freud's idiom). Generally less familiar is Freud's contention that the first phase of repression ("primal repression") consists of the denial of ideas to consciousness. This precludes changes of these ideas, or produces a "fixation" as Freud termed it. Freud was careful to explain that repression is not a "one-shot" process that prevents material permanently from reaching consciousness or causes material to revert to the unconscious. Rather, repression is a continual process that consumes psychic energy. To reiterate, repression takes a variety of forms. While repression is a necessary precondition for the development of symptoms, it also finds expression through dreams, a phenomenon that will be discussed later.

Finally, it is pertinent to outline how repression works—that is, the mechanics of the process. In his approach to this question, Freud looked first at the final outcome of repression and then tried to deduce the nature of its operations. Although Freud suggested that a number of mechanisms may be at work in the process of repression, he pointed to a withdrawal of energy as being an element common to all of them. In a simplified presentation of a case study involving an animal phobia, Freud (1915c) identified as subject to repression a sexual (libidinal) impulse toward a feared parent. Operationally, the sexual impulse toward the parent was repressed, and a fear of an animal was substituted in its place. The end result was withdrawal or diverting of the sexual impulse, which had been directed toward a forbidden object. While the impulse had been withdrawn, its strength remained undiminished. In this particular case, it had simply been converted into anxiety, that is, fear of animals.

Sexual Strivings and Libido

Whenever words are used in unaccustomed ways, there is almost always objection to the new usage. Even today, the word "sexual" has a fairly specific connotation. It is not surprising, therefore, that Freud's usage of the term "sexuality" was criticized severely as being "over-inclusive." The fact that Freud was far from crystal clear or settled concerning the definitions of his terminology only added fuel to his critics' fires.

Initially, Freud (1915b) distinguished between two primal instincts, the self-preservative (ego) instincts and the sexual instincts. A decade later, Freud (1925) reworked his conceptualization to combine the self-preservative and sexual instincts into one category, which he termed Eros. At the same time, Thanatos (the death instinct), which was comprised of aggressive instincts, made its appearance in Freudian theory.

Libido, in the Freudian lexicon, refers to the mental aspects of sexual instincts, or the way in which sexual longing is represented in the mind. It is analogous to hunger, in that both are forces. To the extent that hunger is representative of self-preservation, libido is representative of sexual instincts. Freud first referred to libido theory within the context of the role that sexuality plays in anxiety neuroses and neurasthenia. Later, he utilized libido theory to trace and develop the entire theme of sexuality. Sexuality, in Freud's rubric, referred not only to sexual relations between the sexes, but also to a broad array of behaviors that are common in infancy and childhood. Freud thus viewed the sexual instinct in developmental terms, and contended that its initial aims are not directed toward genital union. Concomitantly, Freud included some adult behaviors (perversions) that are also not directed toward coitus as being expressive of the sexual instinct.

In his *Three Essays on the Theory of Sexuality* (1905), Freud articulated his concept of sexual energy more fully. After discussing deviations in the sexual instincts and focusing on sexuality in the neuroses, Freud introduced the concept of "erotogenic zones." In the broadest sense, any part of the body that yields pleasurable sensations when stimulated is defined as "erotogenic" (erogenous). Freud regarded as highly erogenous not only the genitals, but also the mouth and the anus. The indicators of sexual energy consist of the fairly differentiated and discrete pleasurable sensations that have already been described. Significantly, childhood sexuality is not exclusively autoerotic. Even very young children (ages 2 to 5) are erotically attracted to others.

In addition to the sexual energy that is triggered by direct stimulation of the erogenous zones, sexual arousal can also be catalyzed by inner "processes," once they have attained certain levels of intensity. These direct and indirect sources of sexuality contribute to the evolution of a unified sexual instinct (at about the time of puberty), unless there has been impairment of the individual's normal development.

Finally, Freud (1905) specified that libido is a force that varies quantitatively. This force "has the capacity of measuring processes and transformations in the spheres of sexual excitement" (p. 74). To recapitulate briefly, libido is a special kind of energy that is representative of sexual instincts. It is present in all people, though the amount varies from one individual to another.

Dynamic Emphasis: The Ego and the Id, Primary and Secondary Process

The topographical point of view was discussed previously within the context of relating repression and the unconscious. It provides a partial description of activity within the mind, based upon the perspective of depth. The topographical model is centered around accessibility or inaccessibility to consciousness (Arlow

& Brenner, 1964). A contrasting approach to differentiating the mind focuses on the activity of one's drives (inner world) in juxtaposition to the external environment. This alternate view is often referred to as the "structural theory," even though Freud himself did not use this term.

With the publication of *The Ego and the Id* in 1923, Freud added a new metapsychological point of view to supplement the topographical model. In endeavoring to explain more comprehensively the various aspects of intrapsychic conflict, Freud divided the mind into the ego and the id, while retaining his earlier schema that was based upon the unconscious, the preconscious, and the conscious. The id is situated totally within the unconscious. It is illogical, amoral, and inconsistent. Since the id inhabits the unconscious, it is impervious to the factor of time. The id may harbor conflicting impulses toward the same person at the same time, because it is immune to the constraints of logic or morality. The id is a wholly unorganized, chaotic reservoir of undifferentiated energy.

Although this energy is undifferentiated, Freud (1920) did delineate two components in the course of revising his instinct theory. These components (aggressive and sexual) are present in varying proportions. From this perspective, even the most tender, erotic, and loving impulses contain some aggressive constituents. Freud was unequivocal in stating that the id is present from birth, and that it is influential in an evolutionary sense in the development of later structures.

By adding the concept of the id to the topographical point of view, Freud encompassed more fully the dynamic nature of mental processes. This dynamic emphasis is evident in the view that there is a constant striving for discharge of energy from the id, in accord with the dictates of the pleasure principle.

Primary Process and Secondary Process

In the early stages of developing his theoretical matrix, Freud drew a distinction between what he termed "primary process" and what he termed "secondary process." Primary process, the more primitive of the two modes of functioning, is unorganized and illogical and not subject to the constraints of reality or of time. Although it can be verbal, primary process material most often consists of a flow of images. Dreams are common vehicles for expression of the primary process mode of functioning. Dream images typically meld into one another through the process known as "condensation." *Displacement* is another mechanism that is common to primary process material. Through displacement, one element may be replaced by another that is more remote, or a change in accentuation from an important to an unimportant element may transpire.

In any event, the major aim of primary process is speedy discharge of mental energy. In young children, where the effects of primary process are readily observable, basic drives (aggressive and libidinal) strive for immediate discharge and are unbridled by the mediation of thought processes. Freud attributed the impetus for immediate discharge of energy to an uncomfortable increase in tension in the absence of such discharge. The habitat of primary process, the unconscious, is governed by the objective of avoiding tension (unpleasure). The infant, for example, employs imagery in fantasies, dreams, and "hallucinations" to alleviate its tensions and to satisfy its desires without confronting the impediments that are inherent in external reality. The "pleasure principle" (which was originally called the pleasure-unpleasure principle) is the term used to describe the undifferentiated tension-avoidance effort that is intrinsic to primary process.

Secondary process, on the other hand, is notably more organized and restrained. In sharp contrast to primary process, secondary process is marked by reflection and submission to the exigencies of reality, of time, and of logic. In this more mature mode of functioning, Freud takes into account the panoply of learned responses that are acquired as the individual develops into an adult. Secondary process betokens maturation of the preconscious, which begins to develop in childhood. Secondary process and the workings of the ego comply with the demands of external reality. Freud (1911) formulated the reality principle as a regulatory mechanism for the preconscious and for the conscious. The reality principle is based upon the capacity to delay immediate gratification in exchange for future satisfaction (which assures more predictable consequences). It stands in stark contrast to the pleasure principle that governs primary process.

The Ego

The ego evolves gradually out of the basic id structure. Its development is predicated on awareness of the external environment's potential for reducing or eliminating tensions. The ego, which begins to form in early infancy, is thus highly responsive to the outside world. The ego embodies reason and "common sense." It strives to tame the demands of the chaotic id. The ego, in a sense, performs a balancing act between the pleasure principle on the one hand and the reality principle on the other. More precisely, the ego opposes impulsive discharge of the instinctual drives, while seeking compromise outlets of expression. The ego's array of activities develops over a considerable period of time. In the beginning, the ego simply acts as the executor for the id. The ego will be considered more fully later, in the course of tracing the normal development of the individual.

The Superego

The superego will be mentioned briefly at this juncture, although it too will be accorded more comprehensive attention in the forthcoming treatment of the normal development of the individual. At first, Freud used the term *ego ideal* to describe that inner voice that helps us to choose values and to set moral standards. Later, he referred to the ego ideal as the *superego*. It remains questionable whether Freud meant to supplant the term ego ideal with that of superego. One interpretation is that ego ideal refers primarily to the conglomeration of positive values and aspirations that are held consciously by an individual. According to this view, the superego contains both a conscious and an unconscious component. The unconscious part of the superego resembles what is known in common parlance as a "bad conscience." It consists of harsh, unremitting moral judgments that are experienced phenomenologically as severe guilt. To simplify somewhat, both the ego ideal and the superego can be defined as an internalization of normative social values and ideals that are transmitted to the child by parents and by significant others.

Both the superego and the ego are derived from the id. Both structures are partially conscious and partially unconscious. The superego is a specialized portion of the ego. Since the superego is formed in the crucible of struggles and conflicts that are inherent in the Oedipal stages of development, it is formed comparatively late in life. Identification with parental figures constitutes an essential ingredient in the formation of the superego.

NORMAL DEVELOPMENT OF THE INDIVIDUAL

Toward the latter part of his life, Freud (1925) asserted that the birth process is the prototype of later anxiety. From this vantage point, while the separation from the mother at birth is strictly a biological phenomenon, it is also true that later separations from the mother take on psychological meanings. When Freud described the birth process as a model for later anxiety, he meant that the fetus experiences many unpleasurable sensations during the birth, although its capacity for awareness is strictly limited. Otto Rank, one of Freud's early followers, took a much stronger position. He contended that all neuroses are a product of severe anxiety that is produced by the trauma of birth, and that the infant has visual impressions of the birth process. These visual images remind the individual forever of the birth experience, particularly the jarring separation from the mother and from the comfortable prenatal environment.

Freud raised two major objections to Rank's theory. First, he argued that there was no convincing evidence to support the notion that later neurosis originates in the trauma of birth. Secondly, he insisted that the newborn infant has only limited awareness and is therefore incapable of having visual impressions of its birth.

Psychoanalytic theory does allow, however, that the newborn infant possesses certain basic equipment that influences and shapes personality development. The id is present at birth, as is the unconscious, which soon begins to differentiate into the preconscious and the unconscious. In addition, there are instincts (self-preservative, aggressive, and sexual), the unstructured beginnings of absorption with oneself (primary narcissism), and the prototype of anxiety (initial reactions to unpleasant stimuli).

Energy and Instincts

Although he acknowledged its essentially speculative nature, Freud assessed his concept of instinct as being indispensable to the process of describing and explaining human behavior. It is embodied in the German word *trieb*, which has been translated to mean "instinct." Some theorists argue that the term "drive" would be a more accurate rendering, because it does not carry with it the implication of being an inherited attribute.

Freud (1915c) defined an instinct as the psychological representation of a stimulus from within the body. Thus the *source* of the instinct is biological. Energy is stored in the body. This energy is released because of a physiological excitation within some organ or tissue of the body. This excitatory process is called a "need," while its psychological manifestation is termed a "wish." If we take hunger as an example, the contraction of the stomach's walls produces hunger pangs. The energy catalyzed by this physiological process sets a direction for thoughts, memories, and similar psychological phenomena.

Instincts possess other important qualities as well. First, even in the absence of satisfaction the instinct functions constantly, though its intensity may vary. Thus, in contrast to external stimuli, it cannot be avoided. Secondly, the *aim* of an instinct is to remove its source, that is, the bodily need. Thirdly, the instinct seeks an object or event so as to achieve a state of reduced tension or quiescence. The intake of food, for example, results in a reduction of physiological tension, and thereby vitiates the psychological correlate (that is, the wish for food).

To reaffirm what has been said earlier, Freud posited the existence of self-preservative instincts, sexual instincts, and aggressive or destructive instincts. The self-preservative instincts are those that are required for the maintenance of life. The sexual instincts include all pleasurable sensation, as well as the more specific genital sexuality. The energy of the sexual instincts is called "the libido." Finally, although Freud held that the aggressive or destructive instincts are in opposition to the self-preservative and sexual instincts, he did not propose an antilibido equivalent of libido.

In summary, psychoanalytic theory presumes the existence of psychic energy, as exemplified by the functioning of the instincts. It is this energy that performs the psychological work involved in dreaming, imagining, and thinking. The theory clearly holds that somatic energy and psychic energy are mutually convertible. Thus, we experience hunger pangs and think about food. Conversely, we dream about solar energy and then work purposively to transform the imaginal production into a physical reality.

Phases of Development

The Oral Psychosexual Phase   As the infant develops and matures, differentiation commences. Initially, it is the outside world that facilitates this process. The early stages of awareness are capable of little more than distinguishing between the presence and absence of tension. It follows that when Freud talks about the infant's functioning in terms of the pleasure principle, his reference is to the process of tension reduction. In the first year of life, the mouth is a zone of primary importance. While the act of imbibing nurturance is certainly tension reducing, the act of sucking is in itself a source of pleasure. The ability to discriminate between self and the rest of the environment occurs during this phase of development. More specifically, the infant moves from experiencing a global "oceanic" feeling that is characterized by a sense of omnipotence and absorption with self (*primary narcissism*) to a more refined stage of development.

Freud ascribed symbolic psychological meanings to early physical processes. Within this context, the physical process of eating represents a taking in, or incorporation of, something from the outside. Freud links this ontogenetically to our primitive past, so that by analogy the infant's incorporation of milk from the breast or from the bottle depicts the uncivilized savage devouring a captive. Just as the process of birth is the prototype for later anxiety, so incorporation is the prototype for *identification*. The early identification with important others (usually parents), which is marked by assimilation of their psychological characteristics, is part of the child's narcissism. Substantively, this process is a futile attempt to maintain infantile feelings of omnipotence by modeling oneself after one's parents. The process of identification that is designed to satisfy elemental instincts begins to operate as a modeling mechanism later.

Just how the infant begins to differentiate between self and the outside world remains to be explained. Psychoanalytic theory suggests that this differentiation is a function of the degree to which nurturance is supplied to the helpless infant by the parenting individual. From a strictly theoretical standpoint, unlimited nurturance—that is, complete anticipation and gratification of all the infant's needs— would inhibit development of a sense of reality and would perpetuate primary narcissism. Reality dictates that some deprivation must befall every infant. It is the alternation of nurturance and deprivation that confers upon the infant a sense of differentiation between self and the rest of the environment. Considerable empirical evidence suggests that a preponderance of nurturance, coupled with small doses of deprivation, encourages optimal development in infancy (Ribble, 1943; Spitz, 1945, 1946).

The later part of the oral phase is marked physiologically by the eruption of teeth. The infant derives pleasurable sensations from biting, in addition to sucking and swallowing. This developmental period, which is commonly referred to as the oral-sadistic phase, is highlighted by other maturational advances. The infant becomes much more able to relate to the environment. Objects are grasped more determinedly and successfully. Visual perception is more acute and reliable. In the psychoanalytic idiom, this incorporation of the environment into the self is termed *introjection*.

Galvanized by deprivation, as well as by the wish to maintain narcissistic absorption with the self, the infant's aggressive impulses become more manifest. During the oral-sadistic phase, both pleasurable and aggressive impulses may be directed toward others, even simultaneously at times. Freud (1915b) regarded the infant's ability to recognize another person's separate existence, combined with the wish to "devour" or incorporate, as constituting *ambivalence*. To illustrate, the infant wishes for fusion with the parenting figure (a loving, pleasurable situation), yet at the same time it may desire to bite and hurt that nurturant individual (an aggressive, pleasurable sensation). The antecedents of love and hate are discernible in the ambivalence that is expressed in the oral-sadistic phase. Freud believed that hate originates in the narcissistic ego's rejection of stimuli that impinge upon it from the outside world. Clearly, this model emphasizes the *auto-erotic* nature of infantile sexuality.

Freud laid out a general timetable for the onset and termination of the developmental phases he demarcated. It is important to realize, however, that these phases tend to overlap, and that each individual evolves at a unique pace. Finally, the phases presently under discussion refer to pregenital development because sexuality is manifested, but the ability to reproduce does not yet exist.

The Anal-Sadistic Psychosexual Phase Sometime near the beginning of the second year of life, the sensations surrounding the process of elimination become an important source of pleasure. This heralds a new developmental phase, in which the anal zone supersedes the mouth as the focal point for erotogenic pleasure. By this time, the infant's physical maturation has proceeded to the point that purposeful control of the sphincter muscles that are involved in urination and defecation becomes possible. The infant is now more able to tolerate tensions. Parents encourage the infant to adhere to the *reality principle*, that is, to postpone immediate gratification for later satisfaction.

During the anal-sadistic phase, increasing pressures are placed upon the ego. These pressures—frustrations, really—are created by parental demands that the infant behave differently. For example, constraints are placed upon the process of elimination and upon the pleasurable discharge associated with it. The infant is, of course, highly sensitive to parental reactions and expectations. Although still helpless and massively dependent upon parental care, the infant begins to resist toilet training and other strictures that are designed to accelerate the socialization process. These strictures create a sense of deprivation (Freud referred to this as "privation"). While all this makes early infancy sound very bleak, there is another side to the picture. Compliance with parental wishes is rewarding in that additional attention is lavished on the responsive infant and enhanced self-esteem results from the feelings of being loved.

The anal phase, like its oral counterpart, is divided into two parts. The early phase, which is sometimes called the expulsive period, centers around the active, assertive, somewhat aggressive awareness that the infant develops toward the process of elimination. Naturally, given our society's rather intense preoccupation with toilet training its children, the infant also learns about relations to objects as part of this socialization process. Thus, feces become a symbol of some importance. Anything of so much interest to adults must be valuable!

The later or "retentive" anal phase focuses on the pleasure derived directly and indirectly from withholding feces. The physiological stimulation of the mucous membranes that is created by the retention of bowel movements is in itself pleasurable. In addition, the withholding of feces is likely to elicit a good deal of attention from parents. Of course, although the retention of feces may be pleasurable, it also can be interpreted as a holistic gesture (a punishment of the parent). This is the derivation of the sadistic component of the anal phase.

There is still another facet of this developmental stage that requires elaboration. It concerns the bisexual nature of human sexuality, which Freud linked to physiological function. The rectum is a hollow, tubular organ that performs the function of expelling excretory matter. This organ can also be stimulated by an external source, such as an enema tube or other foreign object. Freud viewed the more active, expelling aspects of stimulation as being related predominantly to masculine traits. Conversely, more passive, receptive modalities of stimulation are tied more to feminine attributes. Toilet training is a crucible in which physiological concerns intertwine with psychological relationships with parents and with significant others. Through the expulsion or withholding of feces, the infant can experience sexual sensations and aggressive feelings. This dualism establishes the pattern of future relationships with people. Concurrent feelings of love and hate are fueled in the child by conflicting parental attitudes toward the process of elimination. These feelings of ambivalence extend back to the oral phase, but now they are etched more sharply in awareness.

Psychoanalytic theory suggests that the ease or difficulty with which the anal phase is negotiated is predictive of future development. If, for example, this phase is suffused with anxiety, a pattern of "anxious compliance" may be established. In contrast, an unremarkable transiting of this phase presages relatively easy mastery of future tasks. Freud believed that an intense clash of wills between parent and child over toilet training was a portent of later conflict, but Blum (1953) tends to discount this hypothesis. Freud (1908) also contended that those individuals who negotiate the anal phase with marked difficulty and tension will subsequently develop the character traits of extreme stinginess, obstinacy, and orderliness.

Freud referred to yet another erotogenic zone, the focal point of which is the urethra. The developmental importance and timing of this zone remain controversial (Fenichel, 1945). Suffice it to say that the canal that carries urine is important in psychosexual development. The act of urination becomes a focal point of pleasurable libidinal sensation during about the third year of life. In a manner that is analogous to the anal phase, the release or retention of urine involves relationships to significant others.

The Phallic Psychosexual Phase. Between the ages of 3 and 5 years, differences in psychosexual development between males and females are accentuated. Freud (1905) called this period of development the genital phase. Actually, this may be something of a misnomer, in that Freud placed much greater emphasis upon the male sexual organ than upon more global genital organization. Thus, in this psychosexual stage, boys and girls become differentiated from each other on the basis of whether or not they have a phallus. This approach is often referred to as phallic primacy. Later, Freud did draw parallels between the functioning of the clitoris and that of the penis, but he continued to emphasize the value that both sexes attach to the penis during this phase of psychosexual development.

During this stage, the boy identifies with his penis, and manifests intense interest in the genitals. Sexual fantasies and curiosity about sex increase, accompanied by more frequent masturbation. The threat of castration becomes frighteningly credible when the boy discovers that girls do not possess penises. Castration anxiety may be expressed in the form of excessive concern about injuries to other parts of the body, fears about minor operations, and alarm about injurious effects of masturbation. The girl, in Freud's schema, feels deprived and envious when she becomes aware that she does not possess a penis. She fantasizes that she once may have had a penis, and that she is now denied the pleasure that a larger phallus might provide (from the point of view of masturbation as well as of urination). Freud is unequivocal in his conviction that both boys and girls value the phallus highly, and have fears about castration.

The Oedipus Complex in the Male   In letters written to his friend, Fliess, in 1897, Freud made one of his most important early contributions—the discovery of the Oedipus complex (Freud, 1887–1902). The name *Oedipus* is extracted from Sophocles' play *Oedipus Rex*, which relates the story of King Oedipus, who unwittingly kills his father and marries his mother. Once he becomes aware of what he has done, Oedipus blinds himself as a self-punishment.

The Oedipus complex presupposes that the child is drawn erotically to the parent of the opposite sex. At the same time, there are angry (even murderous) impulses and wishes directed toward the same-sex parent. Orthodox psychoanalytic theory takes for granted that a strong attachment develops between the male child and his mother. With the onset of the phallic phase of psychosexual development, previous ties, which are based primarily upon dependency needs, assume a decidedly erotic tinge. There is once again a bisexual dimension to the Oedipus complex. The boy can either fantasize about taking the place of his father (that is, becoming his mother's lover), or he can imagine himself supplanting his mother (that is, becoming his father's lover). The former resolution is referred to as the *positive Oedipus complex*, while the latter resolution, which is relatively infrequent, is termed the *negative Oedipus complex*. In between these two theoretical extremes, there are many variations and many degrees to which the Oedipus complex is resolved. Freud also emphasized that biological determinants play a crucial role in shaping the ultimate outcome of the identifications that are made with both parents. The intensity of feminine or masculine predispositions heavily influences the direction in which Oedipal resolution occurs. The Oedipus complex and its resolution are preeminently important in psychoanalytic theory, for it is the ability to master the intricacies of this elemental conflict that distinguishes the normal individual from the neurotic.

The Oedipus Complex in the Female   Freud's ideas concerning the psychosexual development of girls illustrate vividly how his theoretical positions evolved and changed. Early in his career, Freud (1900) minimized the differences that exist between boys and girls with respect to their psychosexual development. Many years later, Freud (1924, 1931) acknowledged that the process of identification is particularly complex for girls. Perhaps Freud was aware of the secondary status that traditional society conferred upon women. In any event, Freud jettisoned his earlier contention that the Oedipus complex was similar for both boys and girls by emphasizing that the intense relationship between the female child and her mother has to be redirected to the father. Girls, like their male counterparts, may relate to the father as a rival for the mother's affections. As a rule, however, girls do not feel so intensely about this rivalry as boys do. In response to the frustrations imposed on her by toilet training and by weaning, the little girl begins to draw away from the mother. The sexual longings (at first unconscious) that begin to be directed toward the father at this time are accompanied by feelings of anger and jealousy toward the mother. This resentment is deepened by the daughter's propensity toward blaming her mother for not having provided her with a penis. As feelings toward the father intensify, the little girl fantasizes both about having her father's penis and about removing her mother as a rival. Ordinarily, the desire to have a penis gives way to the wish to have a child by the father. Needless to say, it is often difficult and confusing for a 5-year-old child to distinguish between fantasy and action.

Freud recognized the fact that boys and girls respond differently with respect to their feelings and anxieties about castration (that is, to the "castration complex"). Usually, the girl's discovery that she lacks a penis enhances and encourages the development of femininity. Orthodox psychoanalytic theory also posits that it is possible to observe the changing identifications from one parent to the other more readily in the case of girls than it is in the case of boys.

The Universal Nature of the Oedipus Complex   Freud regarded the Oedipus complex as a universal phenomenon, though he was far from categorical in delineating its origins. Furthermore, in his commentary on the beginnings of civilization, Freud embraced enthusiastically the notion that the individual's course of development recapitulates the history of all humankind. Put concisely, ontogeny recapitulates phylogeny. This derives from the Darwinian view of evolution, in which the process of human development from a one-celled organism to a complex functioning individual replicates the evolving complexity of animal species. Indeed, as the human fetus is studied, striking similarities between it and other animals emerge.

Freud contended that there was concomitant psychological correspondence between human beings and animals as well. Psychoanalytic theory incorporates Darwin's notion of the *primal horde*. According to this theory, the primitive human social unit was comprised of a strong, fatherlike male and a number of females living in a small group. Using the enormous power that his role conferred, the powerful father acted to banish young males from the group in order to prevent them from having sexual relations with the females. As advancing age began to divest the father of his powers, some of the young males would return to challenge his authority. In the end, this primal horde would murder the father and, in true cannibalistic fashion, devour his remains.

Freud invoked this legend as a possible explanation for the universality of the Oedipus complex. Fenichel (1945), one of Freud's foremost interpreters, is much more guarded concerning the purported universality of the Oedipus complex. He suggests that family structure may be the primary determinant in shaping the specific form that Oedipal conflicts assume.

The Latency Psychosexual Phase   The storminess of the Oedipal phase soon abates, and memories of its strife are repressed at about age 5 or 6. A new period of sexual development commences. Overtly sexualized feelings are supplanted by sentiments of affection. The vigor of hostile impulses wanes. While Freud concluded that the child's sexual energies were diminished during this phase, which he called the "latency period," he was careful to allow for individual differences. Some children, for example, maintain considerable sexual activity and seem to bypass the latency period altogether. Although Freud believed that physiological factors were central in the etiology of the latency period, he attached great importance to societal values and pressures in his explanation of the suppression of infantile sexuality.

During the latency period, the ego is fortified. Sexual energies that only recently have been directed toward parents become "aim inhibited." Substantively, the child begins to engage in increased cognitive activities, spends more time with members of the same sex, and generally adheres more to the exigencies of the reality principle. All these changes are deemed to be indicative of so-called secondary process functioning. The latency period is also characterized by a much clearer separation between ego and superego than has been the case heretofore. Parental values have been introjected, thereby constituting the nucleus of the superego (Freud, 1924).

The strengthened ego and reduced sexual energy make possible a much greater balance between ego and id. In this context, the ego continues to grow and consolidate. The latency period lasts until the onset of puberty, which typically occurs at about the age of 11 but can vary between the ages of 9 and 14.

Preadolescence and Adolescence   Freud viewed sexual development as a two-stage process that is bifurcated by the latency period. Physiological changes that trigger an increase in sexual energy signal the end of latency and the advent of puberty. Old Oedipal conflicts, which are stilled temporarily during the latency period, reawaken. Usually, the more mature ego is able to defend against this renewed Oedipal strife. Puberty is marked by an increase in the energy level of nonsexual impulses as well.

As preadolescence shades into adolescence, there are redoubled efforts to inhibit or to eliminate unbidden impulses that are directed toward parents. Behaviorally, the adolescent frequently engages in self-isolation and other forms of distancing from the family. Crushes on older people (teachers, movie stars, rock singers) and peers alike are common. Often, "causes" are embraced with passionate fervor. These manifestations of adolescence are typically as brief as they are intense. Well into adolescence, the individual begins to search for love objects, as evidenced by dating and other heterosexual activities.

The Genital Phase and Adulthood   This phase witnesses the definitive organization of sexuality, which occurs after puberty. Optimally, the capacity to achieve total genital satisfaction, including the potential to reproduce, is achieved. Freud (1938) asserted cogently that mature genital development entails more than the ability to carry out a sexual relationship with a partner. What Freud had in mind was the capacity to delay gratification and to engage more fully in aim-inhibited behaviors. Thus, feelings of affection ideally accompany more aim-directed sexual impulses. Some sexual impulses are expressed in activities, such as foreplay, that are preparatory to unalloyed sexual intercourse. Still other sexual impulses are modified to form character types (such as the anal character that was discussed previously), or they are wholly suppressed or repressed. The normal adult finds socially sanctioned outlets for utilizing his or her energies and manages to cope effectively with people and with other dimensions of the environment. The ability to love and to work, and to enjoy both these experiences, is a hallmark of effective self-mastery. The ego must be able to mediate between the exigencies imposed by the outside world on the one hand and the demands of the id and the superego on the other. These often conflicting forces help to mold character. The degree of adjustment that the individual has achieved can be assessed by the quality of object relations and the capacity to achieve satisfaction from such life activities as work. Freud's historical determinism assumes, of course, that the content of adulthood is dictated by the conflicts and resolutions laid down in the first year of life.

DEVELOPMENT OF MALADAPTIVE BEHAVIOR

Anxiety and the Neurotic Process

As White (1964) observes, it is not possible to develop a unitary theory to cover all types of maladaptive behavior. Maladjustment can and does assume a plethora of forms. At best, one can look at standards of normal development and note the numerous possibilities for deviant behavior. It may be feasible, however, to promulgate a theory concerning the neurotic process. This is what Freud attempted to do. In the present format, his final formulation will be discussed first. Subsequently, aspects of his earlier theorizing will be reviewed.

Freud (1925) tackled the question of the origin of neurosis. Anxiety is portrayed as a reaction to danger, which calls forth defensive measures. There is no inherent limit to the kinds of situations that can call forth anxiety. The ego is the mental structure that experiences anxiety. Freud differentiated between "real anxiety," whose source is identifiable, and "morbid anxiety," whose origins remain unknown. Most American psychologists tend to label real anxiety as fear, and to reserve the term *anxiety* for the feelings that are generated by obscure or unknown sources.

The ego, which was identified previously as the mental structure that experiences and produces anxiety, is called upon to mediate the often conflicting demands from the outside world, the id, and the superego. At first glance, it may seem baffling that the ego would want to produce anxiety, given the fact that the organism's aim is to avoid this feeling. The apparent riddle is solved through understanding that the ego functions like a safety valve, by permitting itself to experience relatively small amounts of anxiety in order to avoid a more massive onslaught. The ego's safety valve capacity constitutes a partial defense that provides a more manageable substitute for threatening impulses.

The ego, of course, is not totally helpless. It has at its disposal an array of defensive processes that can be mobilized when needed. By means of repression, for example, the ego can and does exclude from consciousness many perceptions and ideas that are associated with impulses it finds unacceptable. Freud interpreted a number of hysterical symptoms as representing a compromise between the realization of a forbidden wish and the need to be punished. Consider the irate son whose arm tightens and refuses to move just as he is about to strike his aged and enfeebled father. This represents conflict between the wish to express strong anger and the fear of unacceptable impulses, a conflict that is compounded by superego anticipation of parental retribution.

Anxiety itself is both a physical and a psychological phenomenon. Physically, it is experienced as unpleasurable tension, coupled with the sensation of being flooded and overwhelmed by powerful stimuli. Psychologically, it is experienced as an amalgam of helplessness, vacillation, and dread of the unknown.

Traumatic Neuroses and the Concept of Repetition Compulsion

It is now opportune to examine the role that anxiety plays in the formation of neurotic disorders that are characterized by a very sudden onset. In times of war and natural disaster, many individuals become overwhelmed by fear, anxiety, and panic. A familiar example is the traumatized soldier who returns from the front and remains trembling with fear, even though he is secure physically in the relative safety of a hospital. His sleep is fitful and is interrupted by persistent nightmares that cause him to reexperience the traumatic battlefield conditions. Freud speculated that this "compulsion to repeat" the traumatic events that led to the neurotic breakdown was a kind of advance warning (after the actual event) of the overwhelming shock about to follow. He further theorized that perhaps the warning or advance preparation had been absent prior to the actual trauma, thereby leaving the individual totally unprepared for what was about to follow. This reenactment was called "repetition compulsion."

While repetition compulsions are most readily apparent in neuroses of sudden onset, the general syndrome of preservative symptoms is found in other circumstances as well. In fact, Freud first developed this concept after observing the tendency of children to seek repetitive activities and to pursue repetitive games, a tendency that often engendered frustration and dismay in onlooking adults. Similarly, Freud found that patients in therapy often repeat over and over again childhood experiences that involve pain and tension.

Primary Defense Mechanisms: Denial and Repression

Neuroses of traumatic onset provide a compressed view of neurotic processes and mechanisms of defense. Although their presence is particularly clear-cut in neurotic disorders, defense mechanisms are employed by normal individuals as well. The neurotic's defenses are more rigid, more intense and indiscriminate, and function in an inhibitory manner (White, 1964). The most primitive of the panoply of defense mechanisms are denial and repression. *Denial*, as its name implies, is simply a way of avoiding painful, unpleasant, anxiety-producing thoughts and feelings by acting as if they did not exist. Expressions such as "Nothing really happened; at worst, it was a bad dream," signal denial. Whereas for the infant, denial is an integral part of the developmental process, its extensive use by the adult is a clear indicator of severe maladjustment.

Repression has been alluded to earlier in this chapter. As a defense mechanism, it is a specific form of denial that effectively blocks anxiety-provoking impulses (usually sexual or aggressive) from reaching consciousness. Both repression and denial represent the operation of defensive processes.

Secondary Defense Mechanisms

Reaction Formation This defense involves the development of conscious attitudes that are the opposite of repressed wishes. Consider the situation of a younger sister who bridles at the attention lavished upon her successful older sister by parents and friends. With the passage of time, resentment may deepen into hate, or even into murderous impulses. Given the ego-threatening and anxiety-provoking nature of these hostile impulses, the impulses may well be repressed. Instead of expressing her unacceptable feelings, the younger sister undergoes a change of personality. She becomes kind and loving toward her older sister. Typically, this kindness is expressed as excessive concern for the older sister's welfare. Coupled with this preoccupation with her erstwhile rival's well-being is continual vigilance to guard against a breakthrough to consciousness of the repressed hostile impulses. In this regard, it is clear that the individual pays a price for containing unacceptable feelings successfully. Specifically, the energy required to prevent the original impulses from gaining control depletes the ego's strength and impairs its functioning to some degree.

Projection This defense involves attributing one's unacceptable impulses, feelings, and thoughts to other people or to objects. At the level of consciousness, projection may be conceptualized as a special form of denial. Returning to the example of sibling rivalry cited above, if projection were at work, the resentful and envious younger sister would attribute her own angry sentiments to her older sister. Thus, the younger sister might wonder why her older sibling was acting in a hostile manner toward her. More behaviorally oriented theorists would call this reversal a type of response substitution.

Displacement Along somewhat similar lines, the defense mechanism of displacement accomplishes the discharge of anxiety-producing impulses and thoughts onto an object or person other than the one toward whom the unacceptable feelings are directed. In this instance, the younger sister might take out her hostile feelings on her best friend or on her dog instead of on the older sister, who is the "real" object of her fury. Through the action of this defense mechanism, strong emotions that are directed at the older sister are transferred effectively. In a more general sense, displacement refers simply to the transferring of energy from one object to another. An example of this is the shifting of accent within a dream, which permits the removal, alteration, or transferral of feelings from one dream fragment to another. This broader definition of displacement needs to be differentiated from those instances in which the term is employed to designate a mechanism of defense.

Sublimation Sublimation consists of a channeling of impulses toward socially approved activities. To pick up our example of the resentful younger sister once again, she might sublimate her hostility toward her older sibling by working in a summer camp for delinquent girls—a situation requiring the frequent and judicious use of disciplinary measures. Within this context, hostile impulses are changed with regard to both aim and object, though only one need be transformed for sublimation to operate. This process in effect neutralizes the original impulse and causes it to disappear.

In his discussion of sublimation, Freud (1932) emphasized the transformation of sexual impulses. He asserted that feelings of tenderness originate in sexual needs whose aims have been modified. Freud also delineated some similarities that exist between the process of sublimation and the process of identification. Both these mechanisms involve neutralization of impulses, both entail some changes in aim and/or object, and both depend upon relationships with significant others who serve as models. In summary, then, Freud stressed the role of sublimation in transforming basic instincts (sexual and aggressive) into socially valued activities. Sublimation is therefore a normative-adaptive mechanism of defense.

Intellectualization *Intellectualization* involves the promulgation of rational and abstract explanations for behaviors that are rooted in irrationality and emotionality. The term "rationalization" has also been used to describe this mechanism of defense. Intellectualization is yet another means for preventing anxiety-provoking impulses from reaching awareness. If this defense mechanism were to operate in the younger sister of our example, she might say to herself: "I have many more important things to do than to be preoccupied with my sister. I ought to concentrate on fundamental issues, such as the nature of truth, the distinction between good and evil, and the question of God's existence. I simply don't have the time to think about my sister." While intellectualization is a very common means of defending against one's impulses, it is particularly prevalent in adolescence.

Undoing The defense mechanism of *undoing* occurs most often in obsessive-compulsive neuroses. It is a form of magical thinking that is built around certain ideas or actions that are designed to circumvent the consequences of unbearable anxiety. The compulsion to repeat activities (repetition compulsion) is in itself an attempt to "undo" or do away with the anxiety attached to a painful experience that has been repressed into the unconscious. Suppose the prototypical younger sister's hostile, even murderous, impulses became so intense as to make her feel dirty and contaminated for harboring such feelings. Without really knowing why, she might find herself going to the front door periodically, opening it, and drawing a deep breath of fresh air. Let us assume further that this activity is engaged in regularly and repeatedly. This compulsive ritual represents a symbolic effort on the younger sister's part to cleanse herself of her corrosively hateful sentiments. The ritual endeavors to "blow away" the painful repressed contents (Freud, 1925).

Another variant of undoing involves the completion of a positive act that nullifies an earlier negative one. Take for example the individual who returns home thinking erroneously that the door has been left unlocked. Most people would discover that they were mistaken and then proceed on their way, satisfied that their concerns were unjustified. This compulsive individual, however, who uses undoing as a defense, would first unlock the locked door and then relock it in a ritualistic manner. This individual would thus feel compelled to undo what had been done previously.

Isolation Another defense mechanism frequently encountered in obsessive-compulsive neuroses, as well as in other forms of maladjustment, is the propensity to separate ideas from feelings. To illustrate, let us suppose that our hypothetical younger sister had a dream in which her older sister was maimed in an automobile accident and was taken to a hospital writhing in pain. Let us assume that the memory of this vivid dream persisted into the waking state. If the mechanism of isolation were at work, the younger sister would be able to recall the dreadful dream scenes, but would experience no emotions whatsoever. Clearly, the withdrawal of emotional meaning from the visualized experience is a form of protection against severe anxiety. Isolation may operate in well-adjusted individuals, given the proper set of circumstances. Individuals who have been subjected to the horrors of war or of natural disaster may be able to revisualize disconcerting events readily without being able to retrieve the emotions that accompanied them.

GOALS OF COUNSELING

The primary objective of psychoanalysis is to alleviate symptoms of psychopathology by raising repressed thoughts and feelings to consciousness. In order for analysis to proceed, the formidable obstacle of resistance must be surmounted. This is a long, arduous, and painful process. In order to be successful, it is essential to engage the emotions as part of this process. The intermingling of cognitive insight and emotional responsiveness in psychoanalysis enhances self-awareness and eventuates in what Alexander (1961) terms a "corrective emotional experience."

The patient who undergoes psychoanalysis is helped to express repressed psychological contents, thereby facilitating recognition of underlying motivations. Optimally, timely and pointed interpretations by the analyst aid in lifting repression and in encouraging verbal expression by the patient. Once conflictual feelings and thoughts are brought into the open, the patient becomes more capable of making conscious choices instead of being a pawn that is pushed by unconscious forces. The patient gains greater freedom in the spheres of feeling and of action. Freud defined the well-adjusted individual as one who is able to love and to work.

Although they are ambitious, the aims of analysis are not all-encompassing. Individuals can never be wholly free of intrapsychic conflict. Moreover, societal constraints and expectations inevitably clash to some extent with unfettered pursuit of individual desires. Nonetheless, a successful analysis would confer upon the individual more effective coping abilities that are derived from expanded self-awareness.

Very early in his career, Freud abandoned the approach of attacking symptoms with direct suggestion. Direct suggestion (as in hypnosis) often is an ineffective and unreliable treatment modality. Cures resulting from the utilization of direct suggestion seem to be transient. Even when it is successful, direct suggestion seems to cover up psychological difficulties instead of dealing with underlying causes.

Analysis, on the other hand, penetrates resistances and reveals unconscious motives. This treatment method contains the promise of more permanent changes. Analysis makes major demands both on the patient and on the analyst. The transference relationship that develops as analysis unfolds is, in microcosm, a reflection of the patient's relationships to people whom he or she encounters outside therapy. As Strupp (1963) suggests, the crucial focus in psychoanalysis is the alignment of psychic forces, as opposed to scrutiny of particular behaviors. Strupp (1963) adds that gains that are achieved within the therapeutic relationship should be matched by similar advances outside the analytic situation. In the long run, of course, psychoanalysis strives to create those conditions that will engender optimal, psychologically mature ego functioning. By bringing about enhanced ego strength, analysis permits the individual to master impulses and to harmonize them with environmental demands. The successfully analyzed patient is then freer to choose and to engage in those behaviors that he or she deems to be essential for achieving a richer and more differentiated pattern of living.

PROCESS AND TECHNIQUES OF COUNSELING

In reviewing the many talks I have had with graduate students who are beginning to learn about different approaches to psychotherapy, I realize that discussions of process and technique usually follow a predictable course. Some students aspire to understand every last detail, so that they can be certain of making no mistakes. Others, who are more skeptical, believe that preoccupation with process and technique bespeaks rigidity and impersonality on the part of the therapist. These questioning students argue further that devotion to a particular technical approach depersonalizes the therapeutic endeavors and precludes spontaneity in the relationship between therapist and client. In their view, the best way to conduct therapy is to follow their instincts and to simply be themselves.

My answer to all this is that, almost invariably, doing what one thinks is best *is* based on theoretical premises, although these premises are implicit rather than explicit. It is in the course of practicing psychotherapy that knowledge of therapeutic process and technique proves to be valuable. I also point out that adherence to a theoretical point of view does not necessarily extinguish the manifestation of humanness between therapist and client. Just as more cognitive understanding of a musical score may deepen one's appreciation and enjoyment of a concert performance, so too a theoretical comprehension of the process of psychotherapy adds to the therapist's self-assurance and effectiveness.

Freud regarded psychoanalysis both as a means of helping individuals in distress and as a vehicle for gaining new insights into the nature of personality. Within this context, he represented a scientist-professional model at its best. To be sure, there are many practicing analysts who place most or all of their efforts on the professional (helping) side, but psychoanalysis continues to inspire research and theory as well.

Population for Whom Analysis Is Suitable

Freud was quite specific in delineating patient characteristics and types of disorders for which analysis was indicated. In an early paper on this subject, Freud (1904) listed the following requirements. Patients should be less than 50 years old, should be endowed with reasonable intelligence, and should be capable of periods of normal functioning. They should not have deep-seated character defects or severe organic disabilities. In addition, Freud (1904) advised against beginning psychoanalysis with patients who are beset by symptoms requiring immediate removal (as in anorexia nervosa, for example). Based upon his extensive experience, Freud concluded that patients who are in the throes of massive confusion, depression, and psychosis are not propitious candidates for psychoanalytic treatment. Finally, a reasonable amount of education was specified as a prerequisite for obtaining benefit from psychoanalysis.

The method itself is demanding and time-consuming for both patient and therapist. Freud willingly acknowledged that patients might wish to avail themselves of simpler, shorter, and less costly therapy modalities, if these modalities held out the promise of effectiveness. He reported that many of his patients came to him only after they had tried many other means of finding help.

Critics have asserted that Freud's criteria for invoking psychoanalysis as a treatment approach seem to favor middle-class, better educated, relatively intact, younger patients; meanwhile, their less prosperous, less educated, more severely impaired counterparts were neglected. In his defense, it should be said that Freud never proclaimed psychoanalysis as a panacea for all psychological difficulties, notwithstanding those people who would have wished him to do so. Obviously there are many problems inherent in the human condition that do not admit of a psychological solution. Despite its limitations, psychoanalysis holds out the promise of a fuller life to larger numbers of individuals.

Contractual and Technical Arrangements

With regard to the technical arrangements for analysis, Freud insisted that his patients commit themselves to hour-long sessions, usually for six days each week. For patients who were well into therapy or were suffering from relatively minor problems, Freud allowed that three times a week might be sufficient. In any event, the hour belonged to the patient, and payment was expected whether or not it was used. Freud contended that leniency regarding "missed" appointments tended to increase the number of such absences, while strict enforcement of his rules minimized "unavoidable" skipping of sessions. Freud estimated the length of psychoanalysis as involving a minimum of six months, and often as extending well beyond a year. Curiously enough, this is much briefer than most present day analyses. Freud refrained from telling patients in advance how long their analyses might last. Likewise, he did not insist on a minimum length of therapy. Rather, he left it to his patients to terminate therapy whenever they wished, although he did not hesitate to let them know when he deemed their decision to be premature. In an interesting aside, Freud observed that in his later years of practice, he encountered difficulties in getting patients to terminate. As part of the technical arrangements, Freud stipulated that the analyst sit behind the patient, who was directed to recline on a couch. While Freud had some personal motives for this practice (he did not care to be looked at for eight hours a day), he also contended that not facing the patient facilitated regression and the development of the transference relationship. In the absence of external cues about the analyst's feelings and demeanor, the patient readily fills that vacuum and in so doing reveals much about his intrapsychic conflicts.

The Opening Phase of Analysis

Freud (1913) recommended that the first few weeks of treatment be regarded as a kind of experimental or trial analysis. The analyst uses these initial sessions to determine diagnostically whether the patient is suitable for analytic treatment. For example, the analyst must differentiate neurotic patients who present obsessive or hysterical symptoms from patients whose manifestations of mental disorders mask a schizophrenic ("paraphrenic" in Freud's terminology) illness. The latter type of ailment does not lend itself readily to psychoanalytic treatment.

At the very beginning of analysis, the patient is told the fundamental rule of free association. This entails expressing everything that comes to mind, without censure and with total honesty. The analyst is keenly attuned to those instances when the patient deviates from the fundamental rule. These moments of resistance are explored through free association. The analyst steadfastly refuses to comply with the patient's request that the analyst supply a topic for discussion. If the patient is unable to think of anything to say, the analyst labels this as resistance to the treatment process and suggests that the patient may be trying to avoid certain thoughts. After all, the patient is participating willingly in analysis and must free-associate verbally in order to help the analyst grasp the dynamics of the case.

Resistance may take many forms. For example, the patient may prepare in advance a presentation of his or her life history, in order to take full advantage of the precious and expensive treatment hour. Alternatively, the patient may try to engage the analyst in conversation. Or, after a period of free association, the patient may begin to describe in minute detail the furnishings in the analyst's office. Whenever resistance occurs, the analyst's task is to encourage the patient to return to the fundamental rule of free association. Free association is much more than an intellectual exercise. It facilitates the experiencing of powerful emotions and helps to lift the curtain of repression that conceals unconscious conflicts. Whenever the analyst suggests that the patient adhere to the rule of free association, there is an implicit message that something is being avoided. This is one kind of interpretation. As rapport between patient and therapist builds, the patient's readiness to accept interpretations about the content of free association, as well as of resistance, increases. The effectiveness of interpretations is contingent upon two important prerequisites. First, the material interpreted should be reasonably accessible to the patient's consciousness. Premature interpretations of deeply repressed thoughts and feelings will almost invariably be rejected by the patient, regardless of how accurate they may be. Secondly, the existence of a trusting relationship (a therapeutic alliance) between analyst and patient is essential for interpretations to have the desired therapeutic impact. Freud (1913) cautioned that as long as the patient was conforming to the fundamental rule of free association, no interpretations should be offered concerning the transference relationship between analyst and patient.

The analytic situation fosters transference. Every one of us learns characteristic ways of relating to significant others at a very early age. The relative anonymity of the analyst, the admonition to free-associate, and other elements in the analytic process all encourage patients to regress and to replay their idiosyncratic patterns of relating, which date back to early childhood. What distinguishes the transference that develops toward the analyst from manifestations of transference toward others outside therapy is its burning intensity (Freud, 1912a). With the vitiation of resistances and the concomitant relinquishing of conscious control, unconscious feelings and ideas that have been repressed for years surface and are expressed in the transference relationship. The intensity, to which allusion has already been made, is a testimonial to the timelessness of material harbored in the unconscious.

Paradoxically, the transference both facilitates and impedes the therapeutic process. *Conscious* positive feelings toward the analyst on the part of the patient assist in moving therapy forward. By way of contrast, unconscious positive feelings that are tinged pronouncedly with erotic overtones, if directed by the patient toward the analyst, constitute resistance. Likewise, negative or hostile feelings about the analyst represent resistance, which must be interpreted and worked through if progress in therapy is to regain its momentum. It is often asked how the analyst reaches a decision concerning which elements of the vast amount of material produced by the patient require interpretation. Freud (1912b) suggested that the analyst adopt an attitude of "evenly hovering attention," while avoiding preconceived expectations as to what material is important. Above all, Freud urged that a therapeutic atmosphere be established and inveighed against imposing interpretations on the patient. Critics of psychoanalysis typically overlook these admonitions.

Dream Interpretation

Psychoanalysis attaches enormous importance to the interpretation of dream material. Freud advised analysts to listen passively to the patient's description of a dream, and then request the dreamer to free-associate to the various parts of the dream. There are several ways in which this associative process can be carried out. The patient may be asked to free-associate to the dream sequences as they unfolded originally. Alternatively, the most vivid elements in the dream may be designated as focal points for free association. Yet another approach involves having the patient free-associate about the dream's connection to waking events.

Freud (1923) proposed that patients who are familiar with dream analysis should themselves choose which path of free association to follow.

Freud made a clear distinction between manifest dream content and latent dream thoughts. *Manifest dream content* is the descriptive representation of the dream, and Freud deemed it to be of little significance in itself. *Latent dream thoughts* depict the dream's meaning as revealed by the dreamer's associations and the analyst's interpretations. The associations themselves often hint at the dream's latent meaning, but a more complete unveiling of the dream's hidden significance requires interpretations by the analyst. Even in the absence of associations, certain dream elements may be interpreted consistently as having a particular meaning. These universal elements are termed "symbols." Thus, birth is usually represented by water, while the human form assumes the form of a house in dreams. Freud concluded that there is a panoply of dream symbols to represent various dimensions of human sexuality. Specifically, the male sexual organ is symbolized by sharp, elongated figures (knives, pencils, rockets), while the female sexual organ is represented by receptaclelike enclosures (boxes, rooms, vessels). While the meaning of some dream material is rendered inaccessible by powerful resistances, Freud believed there are many instances in which his interpretative methods can yield valuable results.

Dream Theory

Dream interpretation consists of moving from manifest content to latent meaning. The process by which latent material is transformed into manifest content is called the dream work. In Freud's view, all dreams blossom from the striving to fulfill a wish. Freud did not insist that all dreams have a sexual component, nor did he assert that wish fulfillment need be pleasurable. For example, the wish fulfillment in dreams that are dominated by the superego is pervaded by the theme of self-punishment. It was only after difficult deliberation that Freud concluded all dreams are rooted in wish fulfillment. Freud acknowledged that with regard to anxiety dreams, and particularly with regard to those that recall traumatic wartime incidents, it is difficult to perceive what wish they may be satisfying. In the end, though, he concluded that even these anxiety dreams represent a partial, if somewhat obscure, attempt at wish fulfillment.

Since dreams function in illogical, nonrational ways (primary process), dream elements can undergo displacement and condensation. *Displacement* causes dream distortions by shifting thoughts toward seemingly unrelated activities. *Condensation* refers to the combining of several dream elements into one thought or image. Since repression lifts markedly during sleep, repressed impulses are able to use dreams as vehicles for expression. However, the presence of condensation and displacement in dreams confirms the fact that censorship still operates, even during sleep.

Finally, Freud emphasized that dreams are psychological (psychic), not organic (somatic), phenomena. The process of dream interpretation reveals much about the dreamer's unconscious dynamics. Dream symbols conform to the strictures of censorship and are also indicative of "archaic repression" (Freud, 1932). Here Freud is alluding to the presence of symbols throughout human history.

ILLUSTRATIVE CASE MATERIAL

It is, of course, impossible to capture all the richness of Freudian theory in any one excerpt of patient-therapist dialogue. Nor would a series of excerpts be much better. I am fully aware that the current mode of presenting case material is to give verbatim accounts of what transpires in therapy, since it is in this way that the techniques can be conveyed directly. Even more desirable are videotapes that can record the verbal and nonverbal interactions between therapist and patient. Nevertheless, I have always encouraged students to read Freud in the original, in order to grasp fully the scope and integration of his theory and praxis. For illustrative purposes, I will present an abbreviated account of one of Freud's case studies, entitled *From the History of an Infantile Neurosis* (1918). This case history is also known as the case of the "wolfman" because the patient suffered from wolf phobias as a child.

The Case of the "Wolfman"

The patient was an 18-year-old man, the son of a Russian landowner who had died three years prior to the beginning of the analysis. At the time he came to see Freud, he was severely incapacitated and was not even able to dress himself. Jones (1953–1957) recounts that the patient had consulted with various psychiatrists, including Kraepelin, and had spent time in a number of sanitoria prior to contacting Freud.

As a child of about 4 years of age, the patient recalled, he had been morbidly afraid of wolves. This "anxiety-hysteria," as Freud termed it, then developed into an obsessional neurosis that lasted until the age of 10. During this time, the patient was very religious and spent many hours in prayer. At times, he would climb on a chair and kiss the numerous holy paintings that hung in his room. In addition, he engaged in other ritualistic behaviors. For example, he remembered that once while traveling to a resort his attention was riveted on individuals who were poor, handicapped, or aged. In order to avoid becoming like them, he forced himself to breathe either in or out forcefully. The patient also recalled having had disturbing associations. Whenever he thought of God, words like "excrement" or "swine" popped into his mind. In a similar vein, when he had seen three mounds of horse dung on the road, he could not help but think of the Holy Trinity.

At about the age of 10, these painful and disturbing neurotic symptoms seemed to disappear spontaneously, though the patient still felt himself to be shy and somewhat odd. Nevertheless, he managed to complete secondary school without undue problems. About a year before he came to see Freud, the patient contracted gonorrhea. Psychological incapacitation followed soon thereafter. Freud contended that remnants of the infantile neurosis were still extant in the patient and that they were affecting his current behavior. Freud, however, chose not to demonstrate directly his view of how the past was shaping the present, even though the patient was willing for him to do so. Freud (1918) stated flatly that it was "technically impractical and socially impermissible" to describe the full history and nature of the adult neurosis. Instead, he focused on the contours and content of the infantile neurosis. Consequently, relatively little is known about the wolfman's adult neurosis, although Jones (1953–1957) reports that during the first analytic session the patient offered to have anal intercourse with Freud and wished to defecate on his head.

Family Background and Interpretations The patient claimed that his parents had been happily married, but they had suffered from poor health. The patient apparently did not have much access to his parents. The mother was not readily available because she was frequently afflicted with abdominal pain. The father suffered from depression and spent much of his time away from home. The patient had an older sister, two years his senior, who was considered to be rather precocious. From the time of his birth, the patient was cared for by an elderly woman who was devoted to him. The parents usually vacationed for part of the summer, and left their children at home. When the patient was about $3\frac{1}{2}$ years old, his parents hired an English governess to look after him and his sister, in addition to the elderly woman who was still in their employ. The patient's grandmother also lived with the children that summer, and he became aware of friction between the governess and the elderly woman.

In face of this contentiousness, the patient sided with "Nanya," his name for the elderly woman. When his parents returned from their trip, they observed a striking change in their son's behavior. He now was irritable, loud, and easily upset. This comportment continued even after the governess was dismissed. It was sometime during this period in the patient's life that the "wolf" phobia first took hold. While looking at a wolf pictured in a book, the patient became frightened that the animal might devour him. His 6-year-old sister, taking pleasure at his discomfiture, made certain he was exposed often to the picture of the wolf. The patient's excessive fear extended to other animals as well, yet paradoxically he obtained pleasure from hurting insects and cutting them into pieces.

Regarding the boy's relationship with his parents, it will be recalled that he was not particularly close to his mother. His relationship with his father, on the other hand, seems to have been close and warm during the very early years of his life. Subsequently, the two grew apart and the father evidenced preference for his daughter. The patient eventually began to fear his father. This then is a partial recapitulation of the background material in this case. The central task of analysis, in this instance, was to uncover the origins of the changes in the patient's behavior when he was a child. His development of phobic and obsessive symptoms was an area of special interest. Hopefully, our brief account of the discoveries that took place during analysis will tempt the reader to read Freud's full description of this case.

The patient had some initial associations concerning the English governess, followed by a series of dreams in which he tried to undress his sister forcibly when both were small children. As this material was worked over and over in analysis, it emerged that the patient's aggressive actions were fantasies that served a protective purpose. Later in the analysis, the patient recalled that his sister had fondled his penis on one occasion, while at the same time telling him stories that insinuated that his beloved Nanya was engaged in various sexual exploits. The aggressive fantasies, Freud points out, now become more comprehensible. Because of his need to maintain an assertive masculine self-image, the patient could not admit to himself that he had been a passive participant in sexual activities with his own sister. Now the loud and abusive behavior manifested by the patient after his parents' return from their summer holiday begins to "make sense." It appears to have been a rage reaction partly attributable to his sister's seductiveness toward him. But this is far from the end of the story.

As noted earlier, the patient and his sister were competitors for their parents' love. Given the sister's favored position, it was unlikely that she would be an appropriate sexual object. Indeed, analysis disclosed that the patient had masturbated openly, as young children sometimes will, in front of his beloved Nanya. Freud interpreted this behavior as an attempt at seduction. Nanya, however, rejected the patient's advances and intimated that continuation of this kind of behavior might produce an injury (a "wound") to his penis. Soon after this threat, he gave up masturbation. In Freud's view, the experience of Nanya's threat, which was coincident with the boy's entrance into the genital phase of psychosexual development, resulted in a regression to the anal-sadistic stage. This regression explains his irritability, and in particular, his propensity to hurt animals, as well as the people he loved. Parenthetically, this development was the harbinger of later problems.

As this material was being retrieved in the analytic process, other fantasies came to the forefront. These dealt with punishment and assaults, including fantasies of being beaten on the penis. Freud regarded the presence of both active and passive fantasies at the same time as being indicative of ambivalence. In effect, *the patient was unable to move smoothly from one psychosexual phase to the next without leaving remnants of earlier developmental periods behind.* Overall, Freud contended, the abrupt shift from a pleasant, docile demeanor to one of aggressiveness, irritability, and general disruptiveness bespoke conflict. Specifically, the child was groping for resolution by letting his parents know that something was wrong, as well as by searching for attention and expiation through punishment.

The analysis was able to determine with reasonable certainty that the seduction had taken place when the patient was about $3\frac{1}{2}$ years old. The ensuing outbursts of intemperate behavior persisted for six months or so after this incident. Interestingly enough, the patient recollected that he began experiencing intense anxiety only after his misbehavior had ceased, at about the age of 4. A vivid, disturbing dream apparently precipitated that anxiety.

The patient dreamt that his window opened suddenly, whereupon he saw six or seven white wolves sitting on a tree. The wolves had big tails, and their ears were cocked attentively. The patient remembered that he awoke screaming in fear, thinking the wolves were going to eat him. Initially, the patient associated this dream with the picture of the wolf that was mentioned earlier. Subsequent associations uncovered a link between the dream and certain fairy tales with which the patient was familiar. In one of these fairy tales, a wolf devours six or seven little goats, though the remaining one escapes by hiding. Additional associations led Freud to conclude that these fairy tales had contributed to the patient's animal phobia. This phobia, Freud later explained, reflected the patient's ambivalent feelings toward authority figures, as well as his fear of his father.

This portentous dream was produced quite early in the analysis, yet it remained the subject of continuing attention. Toward the end of treatment, a further discovery was made. The patient, Freud noted, had always stressed the vividness of the dream, and that the wolves had remained perfectly still while scrutinizing him closely and intensely. In his case history, Freud (1918) summarizes the various elements discussed to this point: "A real occurrence—dating from an early period—looking—immobility—sexual problems—his father—something terrible" (p. 504).

Through yet another series of associations, Freud and the patient concurred that the dream of wolves at the age of 4 represented an earlier waking incident wherein the patient had witnessed his parents' having sexual intercourse. The particular position of coitus afforded the patient a view of both male and female genitalia. It was this primal scene, which was repressed in the child's unconscious, that resurfaced in distorted form via the dream of the wolves. The patient desired closer relations with his father, but the primal scene conveyed the impression that only someone without a penis could be intimate with his father. This reinforced his fear of castration, which had been mobilized earlier in Nanya's warning. According to Freud, the patient's anxiety about being eaten by the wolves in his dream disguised a passive wish to be taken care of by the father and to be a submissive sexual object. This wish was later repressed, and the patient's fear of wolves came to symbolize his feelings toward his father.

Some Concluding Remarks   Freud's case history also includes discussion of many broader therapeutic issues. For example, he asks whether witnessing of the primal scene by a young child necessarily has a profound impact upon future psychological development. He evaluates whether it is really possible for early experiences to be preserved in the unconscious, only to reemerge later in dreams. He also responds to the suggestion of some that interpretations are imposed on the patient by the analyst, and fit preconceived ideas contained in psychoanalytic theory. Finally, Freud presents an intriguing line of speculation concerning the primal scene. He suggests that through displacement, the child may transform actual observations of animals engaged in coitus into fantasized experiences of having seen parents having sexual relations. The effect, however, is the same. That is, the fantasy of having witnessed the primal scene is just as impactful as the reality of having done so.

A few concluding remarks about the overall course of the analysis seem pertinent here. The original psychoanalytic treatment lasted for over four years, though it was only after Freud set a time limit that major progress was made. The patient then returned home and functioned very well. After the Russian Revolution, the patient was left destitute and barely escaped with his life. He was seen again in analysis for about four months by Freud. Jones (1953–1957) reports that during this time Freud saw the patient without charge and, in fact, helped to raise money to assist him and his wife for the next several years. The patient remained in good health for another twelve years, after which he received additional brief periods of treatment from Ruth Brunswick, a female analyst. She reported him to be functioning very well a number of years later.

SUMMARY AND EVALUATION

Freud was the originator of a rich theory of personality, which included a comprehensive approach to psychotherapeutic treatment. Always sustaining a dialectic between conceptualization and experience, Freud developed and refined his theory of personality from contacts with patients in the consulting room. Freud's flexibility and growth are illustrated by his willingness to discard hypnosis as a treatment modality when it proved to be ineffectual or transient in its impact. The method of free association, which was described previously, supplanted hypnosis and revealed to Freud the basic content of mental processes. Within the therapeutic relationship, transference and resistance are the focal points of the therapeutic work. Transference is reflected in the powerful feelings that are generated toward the therapist, which have their origins in the patient's childhood experiences with parents and significant others. Resistance, which can assume a plethora of forms, is in its broadest sense interference with the analytic process.

In working with patients, Freud observed that some memories were recalled only with great difficulty, while others remained inaccessible for long periods of time. He developed the concept of repression to explain the process that keeps certain thoughts, feelings, and images outside the realm of consciousness. Repressed contents may demonstrate their presence indirectly, through blockages, or in disguised form—via dreams, for example.

Freud initially hypothesized that human beings were driven by self-preservative and sexual instincts. Later, he added aggressive instincts and combined self-preservative and sexual drives into a unified concept. Libido, a distinctive source of energy that is present in all of us in varying amounts, also refers to the mental representation of sexual instincts in the broadest sense of the word. For Freud, sexuality encompassed many dimensions, including the multiplicity of developmental aspects of infancy and childhood. Freud also promulgated the concept of "erotogenic" zones to delineate bodily areas that produce pleasurable sensations. He described phases of psychosexual development that focus around these zones.

Freud used at least two different conceptual frameworks to encapsulate the nature of mental processes. The first, which is commonly termed the topographical theory, differentiated between conscious and unconscious mental processes. The second, which is referred to as the structural theory, defined the mental structures known as the id, the ego, and the superego. The id represents the basic instinctual drives (aggressive and sexual), and is situated in the unconscious. The ego develops gradually out of the id, and is partly conscious and partly unconscious. Its function is to mediate between impulsive discharges of the id and the demands of reality—a task worked out through compromises. The superego is a specialized portion of the ego, and it also inhabits both the conscious and unconscious. Essentially, it is an internalized representation of parental prohibitions and societal values to which the individual is exposed in early childhood.

Normal psychological evolution is characterized by broad phases of development that often overlap with one another. During the first year of life, the mouth is the most important physiological zone, and the stage of development centered around it is termed the oral phase. During this period, differentiation of self from others commences largely as a result of gratifications and frustrations that the infant receives from those who care for him or her. By the second year of life, the focus shifts to sensations that are associated with the process of elimination. During this anal phase, the infant begins to delay immediate gratification in return for later satisfactions. In other words, the pleasure principle begins to yield to the reality principle, a development which is essential for future socialization and survival of the individual. The relative difficulty or ease with which this phase is negotiated is one indicator of future ability to master other tasks. From the third to the fifth year of life, the phallic phase of development, there is emphasis on differences in development between males and females.

Both sexes must experience the process of resolving the Oedipus complex. Briefly, the Oedipus complex is comprised of strong sexual feelings toward the opposite-sex parent on the part of the child, feelings that are accompanied by hostile, even murderous impulses toward the same-sex parent. Successful resolution of this complex, a complex that Freud deemed to be universal, implies the transfer of sexual feelings to other objects and closer identification with the same-sex parent who was formerly a hated adversary.

Following this active, conflict-ridden phase, the latency period commences and sexual stirrings typically lapse into relative quiescence. Freud recognized that there were exceptions, however. At the beginning of puberty, there is a renewed upsurge in sexual activity and the impulse life of the individual. Finally, the definitive organization of sexuality, including genital satisfaction, crystallizes after puberty. The well-adjusted, normal adult ought to have command over his or her energies, and ought to be able to cope successfully in relationships with other people. Beyond that, the individual ought to be able to extract pleasure from the potentiality to love and to work, while adapting realistically to life's demands.

Maladjusted or neurotic behavior, in contrast, represents an effort to avoid experiencing the intensity of repressed impulses. In the case of maladjusted individuals, a sudden lifting of repression would unleash overwhelming anxiety. The attempts to ward off unbearable anxiety are aided by an array of defense mechanisms that includes repression and denial.

With respect to the treatment of psychological disorders, psychoanalysis has at its technical core the fundamental rule of free association. Under the aegis of this rule, the patient is encouraged to say whatever comes to mind without censorship. Much of the analytic process involves exploring the resistances to these instructions, as well as the transference relationship that the patient develops toward the analyst.

Another fundamental aspect of psychoanalysis is dream interpretation. Analysis of latent meanings contained in dreams is one of the most effective means of understanding unconscious processes. This endeavor is made difficult by the fact that the recollection of dream material includes much that is distorted and seemingly devoid of meaning. The structure and content of dreams are inherently irrational, illogical, and fragmented—governed, in other words, by primary process. While insight and understanding are highly valued in psychoanalysis, the key elements that result in change have to do largely with emotions. In the final analysis, this modality of therapeutic treatment is, in large measure, a reeducative emotional experience. Much of the emotional power of psychoanalysis derives from the intensity and immediacy of the transference experience.

Finally, we turn to evaluation. If the value of a theory is to be measured by the number of critics and the volume of criticism lodged against it, then psychoanalysis surely occupies a preeminent position. Two major criticisms are perhaps most prominent. The first contends that psychoanalysis, in its obsession with intrapsychic factors, overlooks the importance of social, cultural, and economic circumstances in shaping the individual. A number of Freud's early followers broke with him over this issue. The second major criticism maintains that most of psychoanalytic theory is not subject to experimental verification. Psychoanalysis as a method is charged with being a closed system that is intrinsically unobservable and unquantifiable. In the eyes of theorists who advance such criticisms, the observations obtained as part and parcel of the psychoanalytic process are wholly unreliable. In response to these charges, Rapaport (1959), a brilliant theorist within psychoanalytic circles, has acknowledged that psychoanalytic theory requires "methods to obtain data which can lead beyond the clinical relationships to theoretical relationships" (p. 159).

To balance the ledger, psychoanalysis has proved to be an unusually comprehensive theory that has exercised enormous influence not only on psychology and on psychiatry but also on literature, art, music, anthropology, and sociology. But even more importantly, both for the dedicated student and for the person on the street, psychoanalytic theory is a compelling call to think about human behavior and the process of change. That, I submit, is in itself an historic achievement.

BIBLIOGRAPHY

Alexander, F. *The scope of psychoanalysis*. New York: Basic Books, 1961.
Arlow, J. A., & Brenner, C. *Psychoanalytic concepts and the structural theory*. New York: International Universities Press, 1964.
Blum, G. S. *Psychoanalytic theories of personality*. New York: McGraw-Hill, 1953.
Fenichel, O. *The psychoanalytic theory of neurosis*. New York: W. W. Norton, 1945.
Freud, S. *The origins of psychoanalysis: The letters to Wilhelm Fliess, drafts and notes: 1887–1902*. New York: Basic Books, 1954.
Freud, S. The interpretation of dreams, 1900. *Standard Edition* (Vols. 4–5). London: Hogarth Press, 1953.
Freud, S. The psychopathology of every day life, 1901. *Standard Edition* (Vol. 6). London: Hogarth Press, 1960.
Freud, S. Freud's psychoanalytic procedure, 1904. *Standard Edition* (Vol. 7). London: Hogarth Press, 1953.
Freud, S. On psychotherapy, 1905. *Standard Edition* (Vol. 7). London: Hogarth Press, (1953). (a)
Freud, S. Three essays on the theory of sexuality, 1905. *Standard Edition* (Vol. 7). London: Hogarth Press, 1953. (b)
Freud, S. Character and anal erotism, 1908. *Standard Edition* (Vol. 9). London: Hogarth Press, 1959.

Freud, S. Formulations of the two principles of mental functioning, 1911. *Standard Edition* (Vol. 12). London: Hogarth Press, 1958.

Freud, S. The dynamics of the transference, 1912. *Standard Edition* (Vol. 12). London: Hogarth Press, 1958. (a)

Freud, S. Recommendations to physicians practicing psychoanalysis, 1912. *Standard Edition* (Vol. 12). London: Hogarth Press, 1958. (b)

Freud, S. Further recommendations on the technique of psychoanalysis, I: On beginning the treatment, 1913. *Standard Edition* (Vol. 12). London: Hogarth Press, 1958.

Freud, S. On the history of the psychoanalytic movement, 1914. *Standard Edition* (Vol. 3). London: Hogarth Press, 1962.

Freud, S. Further recommendations in the technique of psychoanalysis, III: Observations on transference love, 1915. *Standard Edition* (Vol. 12). London: Hogarth Press, 1958. (a)

Freud, S. Instincts and their vicissitudes, 1915. *Standard Edition* (Vol. 14). London: Hogarth Press, 1957. (b)

Freud, S. Repression, 1915. *Standard Edition* (Vol. 14). London: Hogarth Press, 1957. (c)

Freud, S. The Unconscious, 1915. *Standard Edition* (Vol. 14). London: Hogarth Press, 1957. (d)

Freud, S. Introductory lectures on psychoanalysis, 1917. *Standard Edition* (Vols. 15–16). London: Hogarth Press, 1963.

Freud, S. From the history of an infantile neurosis, 1918. *Standard Edition* (Vol. 17). London: Hogarth Press, 1955.

Freud, S. Beyond the pleasure principle, 1920. *Standard Edition* (Vol. 18). London: Hogarth Press, 1955.

Freud, S. The ego and the id, 1923. *Standard Edition* (Vol. 23). London: Hogarth Press, 1964.

Freud, S. Remarks on the theory and practice of dream interpretation, 1923. *Standard Edition* (Vol. 19). London: Hogarth Press, 1961.

Freud, S. The dissolution of the Oedipus complex, 1924. *Standard Edition* (Vol. 19). London: Hogarth Press, 1961.

Freud, S. Inhibitions, symptoms and anxiety, 1925. *Standard Edition* (Vol. 20). London: Hogarth Press, 1959.

Freud, S. Female sexuality, 1931. *Standard Edition* (Vol. 21). London: Hogarth Press, 1961.

Freud, S. New introductory lectures on psychoanalysis, 1932. *Standard Edition* (Vol. 3). London: Hogarth Press, 1962.

Freud, S. An outline of psychoanalysis, 1938. *Standard Edition* (Vol. 23). London: Hogarth Press, 1964.

Jones, E. *The life and work of Sigmund Freud* (3 Vols.). New York: Basic Books, 1953–1957.

Paul, I. H. *Letters to Simon*. New York: International Universities Press, 1973.

Rapaport, D. *The structure of psychoanalytic theory*. In S. Koch (Ed.), *Psychology: A study of a science* (Vol. 3). New York: McGraw-Hill, 1959.

Ribble, M. A. *The rights of infants*. New York: Columbia University Press, 1943.

Spitz, R. A. Hospitalism: An inquiry into the genesis of psychiatric conditions in early childhood. *Psychoanalytic Study of the Child*, 1945, *1*, 53–74.

Spitz, R. A. Anaclitic depression. *Psychoanalytic Study of the Child*, 1946, *2*, 313–342.

Strupp, H. H. The outcome problem in psychotherapy revisited, *Psychotherapy: Theory, Research and Practice*, 1963, *1*, 1–13.

White, R. W. *The abnormal personality* (3rd ed.). New York: Ronald Press, 1964.

Wolstein, B. *Transference*. New York: Grune & Stratton, 1954.

Chapter 5

The Rational-Emotive Approach to Counseling

Albert Ellis

INTRODUCTION

I developed rational-emotive counseling, which is better known as rational-emotive therapy (RET), at about the beginning of 1955 (Ellis, 1957a, 1957b, 1962). As a clinical psychologist, I first did marriage and family counseling and sex therapy, but then felt that psychoanalysis was a deeper and more intensive method of helping people to solve their emotional problems. So in the late 1940s I was trained as a psychoanalyst, and practiced classical analysis and psychoanalytically oriented psychotherapy for several years. However, I became quite disillusioned with this type of treatment, largely because of its inefficiency and its unscientific attitude toward theory and practice, and therefore abandoned it in the early 1950s. Gradually I developed, largely at first on pragmatic grounds, rational-emotive counseling. Later, I developed an integrated theory of psychotherapy and of personality on the basis of clinical and experimental findings with RET and with related forms of cognitive-behavior therapy (Ellis, 1957b, 1962, 1971, 1973a, 1974a, 1977a, 1977b, 1977c, 1978a, 1978b).

At first, RET was almost alone as an active-directive form of therapy that consciously and comprehensively employed cognitive, emotive, and behavioral methods; it was opposed violently by most other schools of psychotherapy. Psychoanalysts, Rogerians, and existentialist therapists opposed it because of its highly active, didactic, confrontational approach. Experiential and feeling-oriented therapists fought it because they found it much too philosophic and cognitive. Although Eysenck (1964) endorsed it in one of his early books on behavior therapy, most classical behavior therapists shied away from it, because it dealt extensively and intensively with cognitive mediating processes rather than merely with overt behaviors. Almost all other systems of psychotherapy inveighed against it for one reason or another and tended to label it as simplistic, overintellectual, and too directive.

Following one of the basic principles of RET, that humans enjoy and greatly desire the approval of others but that they do not need this approval absolutistically, I persisted in practicing and teaching RET to thousands of members of the public and to hundreds of mental health professionals. I lectured, demonstrated, wrote, and recorded RET presentations at the Institute for Rational Living and the Institute for Rational-Emotive Therapy in New York City, and in many other parts of the United States, Latin America, Canada, and Europe. In the face of almost overwhelming opposition, I stubbornly refused to make myself feel depressed, guilty, ashamed, or self-downing.

A notable change in the psychotherapeutic climate and in the consequent acceptance of rational-emotive counseling occurred during the late 1960s. The encounter movement, which oddly enough had originated in the highly passive methods of sensitivity training, became very popular. It thoroughly endorsed the active-directive procedure of a group leader's putting people through distinctly organized and straightforwardly taught exercises (Schutz, 1967). Gestalt therapists also began to gain a large following and rigorously emphasized, as did RET practitioners, keeping the client in the present rather than in the past, as well as very direct confrontational methods (Perls, 1969). Transactional analysis gained an immense popularity among readers and therapy participants. It strongly stressed cognitive techniques and a great deal of teaching (Berne, 1964). Existential and humanistic therapists came to the fore with procedures that were largely based upon philosophic analysis and direct dialogue between the therapist and the client (Frankl, 1968; May, 1969). An influential group of therapists began to emphasize an unusually directive problem-solving approach to therapy (Haley, 1963; Watzlawick, Beaven, & Jackson, 1967).

Perhaps even more importantly, classical behavior therapy began to go cognitive in the 1960s. Such outstanding authorities as Bandura (1969) endorsed cognitive restructuring as a major form of behavioral treatment after they had found, by their own practice and research, that simple stimulus-response (S-R) approaches to personality and personality change did not work very well. Notably, too, a host of young and vigorous psychologists and counselors who were working in the field of behavior modification began to do many controlled experiments that clearly demonstrated, as RET holds, that people affect their emotions and behaviors significantly by the kind of things they tell themselves, and that if they are induced to tell themselves one set of statements rather than another, they change their feelings and their actions importantly. Many of these experimenters were clearly influenced by my work, including Davison and Neale (1974), Goldfried and Davison (1976), Goldfried and Merbaum (1973), Lazarus (1971, 1976), Mahoney (1974, 1977), Meichenbaum (1977), and Rimm and Masters (1974). Independently of my work, another psychoanalytically trained therapist, Aaron T. Beck of Philadelphia, also began to discard analytic techniques and to construct a highly cognitive form of therapy; his writings have also influenced many experimenters to verify some of the basic clinical and personality hypotheses of RET or of cognitive-behavior modification (Beck, 1967, 1976).

As a result of this recent experimental work, RET has undoubtedly become one of the most popular brands of psychotherapy and is an essential part, and virtually the cognitive core, of the cognitive-behavior therapy movement. Almost all the recent texts on behavior therapy, as well as the self-help books that tell readers how to apply behavior modification principles to their own lives, include a section on RET or RET-oriented cognitive restructuring. In addition, following my lead, a good many authors have written popular clinical texts applying RET to various kinds of clients. These authors include Wolfe and Brand (1977), Church (1975), Diekstra and Dassen (1976), Hauck (1972), Lange and Jakubowski (1976), Lembo (1976), Morris and Kanitz (1975), and Tosi (1974).

Because the main points of RET theory and practice can be stated in clear and simple form and made available to the average reader, rational-emotive counseling has led to the publication of almost innumerable self-help books that enjoy a wide popularity. Some of the best known of these publications have been by Blazier (1974), Dyer (1976), Ellis (1957a, 1969a, 1973a, 1976a, 1977a), Ellis and Harper (1961, 1975), Ellis, Wolfe, and Moseley (1972), Goodman and Maultsby (1974), Grossack (1978), Hauck (1973, 1974, 1975), Kranzler (1974), Lembo (1974), Little (1977), Maultsby (1975), Maultsby and Hendricks (1974), McMullen and Casey (1975), Powell (1976), Thoresen (1976), and Young (1974).

Somewhat like Freudian psychology, RET has also become enormously influential because many of its basic tenets, and sometimes its entire philosophy and practice, have been incorporated into the writings of many authors and lecturers who fail to give it any public credit and also fail to mention the contributions of its main philosophic ancestors, such as Epictetus and Marcus Aurelius. Thus, unacknowledged RET principles seem to have been included importantly in the popular works of such individuals as L. S. Barksdale, Wayne Dyer, Werner Erhard, William Glasser, Haim Ginott, Ken Keyes, Roy Masters, and Manuel Smith. In view of the profound influence that both acknowledged and unacknowledged RET writings have had on the public, rational-emotive counseling seems to be unquestionably one of the most influential therapies of the twentieth century.

PHILOSOPHY AND MAJOR CONCEPTS

Philosophical Principles

The philosophy of RET has several important aspects or principles, including the following:

1   Humans are human, and are neither superhuman nor subhuman. They have distinct fallibilities and limitations that they can conquer or transcend somewhat. But it is doubtful that they will ever overcome their human and mortal boundaries completely and achieve "higher" states of consciousness or of being that are truly transcendental or omniscient. They may transcend or rise above their

present physical and psychological restrictions, but it is most unlikely that they can become transcendental—that is, can go beyond the material universe into the realm of pure spirit or godhood.

2   At present, all humans die, and there is no evidence that they have any kind of meaningful life after death, or immortality. Therefore, they had better assume that this is their life and make the most of it while it lasts.

3   The main purpose or goal of living, for practically all people, consists of surviving and of surviving in a reasonably happy state—or in a state that is relatively free from needless pain and discomfort. One can choose other goals than this—such as death or a continued miserable existence. But humans are biologically predisposed toward survival and happiness, and it seems wise or suitable for them to go along with their interest in these goals.

4   Happiness or hedonism is a valid choice to make; but since most people live for 75 years or so these days, the goal of long-range rather than short-range hedonism seems wise or rational for them to embrace. "Eat, drink, and be merry for tomorrow we die" seems a self-defeating philosophy, since you probably won't die tomorrow—but will awake with a hangover!

5   Human values are not absolutistic or completely given; they are partially chosen. To some extent our behavior is determined, since there are profound biological and social influences that strongly encourage us to behave in certain ways, and it seems almost impossible to rise above them fully. RET calls for a soft rather than a rigid determinism: the acceptance of the fact that we have strong pressures on us that we cannot very well avoid and control, and that we *also* have some strong element of choice or free will that we can control partially (Ellis, 1962; Kurtz, 1977). As May has noted, "By refusing to accept either determinism or freedom, we diminish ourselves. Without determinism, and the predictability that goes with it, we have *anarchy*. Without freedom, and the exuberance that goes with it, we have *apathy*" (1977, p. 10).

6   The term "rational" is not defined, in RET, in any absolutistic or dogmatic way. Nor can it probably be derived completely from empirical observation. Humans choose to live by values, purposes, or goals, and Alfred Adler (1931, 1964) was one of the first psychotherapists to point out incisively, as noted above, that humans usually choose survival and happiness as their main values. As subvalues, they also choose to be happy (a) by and with themselves, (b) as members of a social group, (c) relating intimately to a few others, (d) vocationally and economically, and (e) recreationally and esthetically. Once they choose such values, it is *then* rational or *efficient* for them to think, emote, and act in such ways as to abet their achieving these values; and it is *then* irrational or inefficient for them to behave in such ways as to interfere with that achievement. Rationality per se does not exist in its own right, but as a method of achieving certain selected goals. RET therapists are often accused wrongly of knowing what rational behavior is and of persuading clients to adopt this kind of behavior. Not so! They start with clients' own values, goals, and purposes, and try to show them how they are pursuing such values ineffectually or irrationally, and how they could pursue them more rationally. But RET therapists do not *give* clients their basic values or goals.

Concepts of Human Personality

RET has a good many major concepts of human personality and personality change, some of the most important of which follow:

Biological Predispositions   Humans are born with a strong predisposition to be rational, self-preservative, and self-actualizing, as has been shown by Ellis (1962, 1971, 1973a), Maslow (1962), and Rogers (1961, 1977). But they also have powerful predispositions to behave irrationally and self-defeatingly (Ellis, 1962, 1976b, 1977a). They think easily and "naturally," they think about their thinking, they are creative, they love, they learn by their mistakes, and they change themselves enormously. But they also tend to be short-range hedonists, to avoid thinking things through, to procrastinate, to be suggestible and superstitious, and to be perfectionistic and grandiose.

Cultural Influenceability   In accordance with one of their strongest innate tendencies, humans tend to be influenceable, particularly during their childhood, by their family members and by other immediate associates, as well as by their culture in general. In spite of their wide individual differences in this respect, virtually all of them add to their emotional disturbability and irrationality by going along with familial and societal teachings and conventions.

Interaction of Thoughts, Feelings, and Actions   All normal humans think, feel, and act, and do so interactionally and transactionally. Their thoughts significantly affect (and often create) their feelings and behaviors; their emotions affect their thoughts and actions importantly; and their acts distinctly affect their thoughts and feelings. To change any one of the modalities, modification of either of the other modalities, or both other modalities, will bring results. Therefore a comprehensive form of psychotherapy, such as RET, consciously and strongly uses all three cognitive, emotive, and behavioral methods of personality change (Ellis, 1971, 1973a, 1976a, 1977a; Ellis & Grieger, 1977; Ellis & Knaus, 1977).

Power of Cognitive Therapy   A significant change in one major cognition can help to bring about important changes in several emotions or many behaviors, while a significant change in a feeling or in an action may bring about only limited cognitive change. Humans are unusually thinking or symbolizing creatures; consequently, virtually all therapeutic procedures include highly cognitive elements, and the most effective forms of treatment tend to be exceptionally cognitive, as well as emotive and behavioral (Ellis, 1968a, 1970, 1974a, 1977a; Ellis & Harper, 1975; Raimy, 1975). RET employs a wide number of cognitive methods but particularly emphasizes the Disputing of irrational Beliefs, and thereby attempts to be a highly depth-centered system of personality change that helps clients to modify profoundly their basic philosophies of life.

Irrational Thinking and Disturbance   RET holds that almost all serious emotional disturbances do not stem from point A (the Activating Experiences or Activating Events) that afflict people; rather, they arise directly from, or are "caused" by, B (the Beliefs that people hold about these events). B consists both of rational Beliefs (rB's), which generally take the form of wishes, wants, and preferences, and of irrational Beliefs (iB's), which almost always take the form of absolutistic demands, commands, and musts.

I originally stated 10 or 12 basic irrational Beliefs (iB's) that are widespread among humans, and these have been quoted and studied by hundreds of clinicians and experimenters. Many irrationality tests based on these beliefs have been devised, standardized, and validated (Bessai, 1975; DiGiuseppe, Miller, & Trexler, 1977; Jones, 1968; Murphy & Ellis, 1979; Zingle, 1965; Zingle & Mallett, 1976). After giving this matter further thought, I reduced my original number of basic irrational Beliefs to three major musts, each of which has several important subheadings (Ellis, 1977a; Ellis & Grieger, 1977). These musts are: (1) I must (or should or ought to) do well and/or be loved by significant others; it is awful if I do not; I can't stand it; and I am therefore a rotten person (RP)! (2) You must treat me kindly and fairly; it is horrible if you do not; I can't stand you and your behavior; and you are therefore a bad individual! and (3) The world must deal with me nicely and fortunately and give me virtually everything I want immediately; and it is terrible if it doesn't! I can't stand living in such an awful world; and it is an utterly abominable place!

Importance of Insight   Although RET is a highly cognitive form of therapy, it does not place any great emphasis upon the value of the usual kind of therapeutic insight—or upon the client's understanding the whys of the individual disturbance or exactly how he or she became disturbed. Unlike psychoanalysis and various kinds of awareness therapy (for example, gestalt therapy), it does not assume that insight of this nature will lead to spontaneous change. Instead, it calls for three different kinds of insight on the part of clients: (1) People's self-defeating behavior has clear-cut antecedent causes, not in terms of past or present Activating Experiences (A) but in terms of their present Belief system (B) and especially their irrational Beliefs (iB's); (2) No matter how people originally become—or, rather, make themselves—disturbed, they feel upset today because they are still reindoctrinating themselves with some irrational Beliefs (iB's) they originated in the past. They keep conditioning themselves rather than getting conditioned by other people or events; and (3) Insights 1 and 2, in themselves, will not help to change people's irrational Beliefs. Only constant hard work and practice on the part of disturbed individuals, in the present and in the future, is likely to make and keep them less disturbed.

Existentialist and Humanist Leanings   RET takes the existentialist and humanist positions that people largely create their own world; that they invariably tend to view things somewhat phenomenologically and subjectively; and that they had better define their own freedom, cultivate individuality, live in dialogue with others, accept their experiencing as highly important, be fully present in the immediacy of the moment, and learn to accept limits in life and the fact that they will eventually die (Braaten, 1961; May 1961; Hartman, 1967; Combs & Snygg, 1961). More than virtually any other form of therapy, it particularly emphasizes unconditional positive regard or full acceptance (Ellis, 1962, 1972); and it takes the highly unusual philosophic stand that humans had better not rate themselves, their essences, or their being at all, but rate only their deeds, acts, and performances— not in order to prove themselves, or to have ego strength, but in order to be themselves or to enjoy themselves (Ellis, 1957a, 1972, 1973a, 1974a, 1976a, 1977c, 1978a). Because of its active-directive outlook, however, RET endorses the active methods employed by existentialists like Viktor Frankl (1968), rather than the more passive methods used by existentialists like Rollo May (1969).

Behavioral Outlook Rational-emotive counseling or therapy does not take the classical behaviorist position that people learn to be or are conditioned to be disturbed, and that therefore they have to learn to feel or be conditioned to feel less disturbed. It takes, instead, the stand that they largely disturb or condition themselves to feel and act dysfunctionally, and that it is their essential nature to do so. However, just because it believes that people are easily disturbable and that they also fall back into disordered pathways easily once they have gotten themselves to change temporarily, RET takes an approach that relies heavily upon behavior modification procedures, and in fact, uses more operant conditioning and in vivo desensitization procedures than many classical behavior therapists employ. Along with the usual behavioral methods, however, it always employs strong cognitive and emotive approaches to therapy, and hence is a form of what Lazarus (1971, 1976) calls "broad spectrum" or "multimodal" behavior therapy.

In its most elegant form, as will be shown below, RET employs a good deal of cognitive reconstructuring or philosophic Disputing (at point D), after clients have been shown their irrational Beliefs (at point B). But some behavior therapists wrongly believe that RET is synonymous with disputing or arguing clients out of their irrationalities. Not so. It uses perhaps 50 different kinds of cognitive re-structuring, including—among others—giving clients new self-statements, reat-tribution training, empirical disconfirmation, positive thinking, thought stopping, hypnotic and nonhypnotic suggestion, and rational emotive imagery (REI) (Maultsby & Ellis, 1974). In its general or inelegant form, RET is synonymous with cognitive-behavior therapy; and in its more elegant form, it specializes in disputing, debating, and discriminating methods of cognitive restructuring (Ellis, 1973a, 1974b, 1977a, 1977d, 1978a; Ellis & Abrahms, 1978; Ellis & Grieger, 1977).

NORMAL DEVELOPMENT OF THE INDIVIDUAL

RET sees the normal individual as developing in terms of personal desires, wishes, and preferences. In this respect, every person is distinctly different from all other individuals; for each of us has almost innumerable traits and preferences, and they range widely from mild to intense, depending upon our heredity and our social experiences. In some respects, we are amazingly similar; all of us who survive, for example, eat, defecate, breathe, move, and grow older. In many normal tastes, moreover, we are also reasonably similar; virtually all of us prefer sugar to acid, caressing to being bitten, being accepted to being rejected by others. We also tend to have very strong desires, which we wrongly view as "needs" or "necessities." Thus, virtually all humans prefer strongly to be sociable, to love others, to be adventurous at times, to have sexual arousal and orgasm, to be free from overweening authority, and to indulge in various kinds of games or pastimes. We will not die if these desires or "needs" are not fulfilled; but we will tend to be much less happy than we otherwise would be, and will tend to lead "bad" or "undesirable" lives. Some of our desires are so strong that we would prefer not to live without their fulfillment.

In certain respects, normal growth and development occur in somewhat regular stages; but these vary within a wide range, and most personality theorists have, out of their own compulsive tendencies to put everything perfectly in order, either invented or greatly exaggerated these stages. The Freudians (Freud, 1965) have by far been the worst offenders in this respect. Freud believed, for example, that normal children first go through an oral and anal stage, then a masturbatory genital stage, then a latency period, then a homosexual stage, and finally a heterosexual stage of development. His oral and anal "stages" seem largely to be figments of his imagination, although it is true that children have a goodly degree of anal and oral pleasure or sensuality—but not of what we would usually call distinct sexuality. His "latency" period is also mostly an invention, since the majority of children seem to have steady or increased sexuality from their sixth to their twelfth years, and by no means absolutely must go into a latency period. Freud's "homosexual period" certainly occurs in the lives of a good many children, often during their teens; but many skip it entirely or have strong homosexual desires much later in life, long after they have first developed heterosexual urges. Finally, Freud's heterosexual stage of sexual "normality" is common among most individuals in many societies; but a much larger number of people than he ever dreamed of engage in considerable masturbation all their lives, or become primarily homosexual, or engage fairly frequently in bisexual activities. Freud's belief that adult masturbators, homosexuals, bisexuals, or inorgasmic women are "fixated" on an earlier, more childish level of development is another hypothesis for which there is virtually no evidence, while there is considerable evidence to contradict it (Ellis, 1954, 1976a; Kinsey, Pomeroy, & Martin, 1948; Kinsey, Pomeroy, Martin, & Gebhard, 1953; Masters & Johnson, 1966, 1970).

Other theories of "normal" human development, such as those of Erikson (1959) and Sullivan (1947), are usually variations on the Freudian theme, and although they have some element of truth, are largely overgeneralizations. As yet, RET has created no such theories—and if it remains wise, it may never create such theories! More empirically based theories of human development, such as those of Piaget (1952, 1954), would appear to be more realistic and could be endorsed by rational-emotive counseling but are not essential to it. RET largely emphasizes how the individual can *re*develop rather than how the individual develops, and it holds that there may only be a mild or moderate relationship between a theory of personality and an effective theory of personality *change* (Ellis, 1978a).

DEVELOPMENT OF MALADAPTIVE BEHAVIOR

Many schools of psychotherapy, especially those stemming from or allied with the psychoanalytic school, have complicated theories of how maladaptive behavior develops. Frequently, they emphasize methodologies, such as the clients' gaining insight into the origins of their disturbances or their reliving and "working through" the early "traumatic" events of their lives. Sometimes these insight-abreactive methods are made the central core of therapy. RET takes a dim view of this kind of "therapeutic" thinking because RET tends to hold: (1) that we really do not know, as yet, too much about the "real" origins and development of maladaptive behavior; (2) that most of the existing theories in this respect dramatically overemphasize one or two special incidents—such as "birth trauma," "primal pain," or "Oedipus complex"—when there is little evidence that such incidents actually occurred or were as crucial as hypothesized if they did occur; (3) that considerable clinical and experimental data now indicate that insight into and abreaction of childhood "traumatic" experiences do little or no therapeutic good; (4) that when effective personality change does take place as a result of insight-abreactive therapy, it most probably results from clients' cognitions *about* such insights and catharses rather than from these "experiences" themselves; (5) that some of the most effective forms of therapy, such as operant conditioning or self-management procedures, occur when clients seem to have little or no understanding of the origins and development of their symptoms; (6) that a considerable amount of both insight and abreaction seems to take place *after* behavioral forms of therapy are used by clients, rather than symptomatic relief's occurring as a result of understanding and catharsis; and (7) that many forms of treatment seem to work quite independently of the theory of the development of maladaptive behavior that supposedly underlies these treatments. Thus, psychoanalytically oriented, transactional analysis, and rational-emotive therapists may all encourage a 40-year-old man to stop living with his mother, and may thereby help him to achieve emotional independence. But all three of these forms of therapy have different theories of the origin and development of his dependency. Again, almost all classical behavior therapists (and cognitive-behavior therapists as well) may employ imaginal or in vivo desensitization with a phobic woman, and almost all of them may agree that this woman originally "learned" her phobic reactions. But they may subscribe to a dozen different learning theories, none of which has as yet been exposited or verified very well.

Does RET, then, have no theory whatever about the origin and development of maladaptive behavior? No, not exactly. It does not purport to come forth, as yet, with a highly detailed theory, nor to relate this theory of maladaptive behavior concretely to its theory and practice of personality change. But it has some tentative ideas in this connection, including the following.

Innate Disturbability

Virtually all humans seem to be born with a strong predisposition to disturb themselves in various ways, and many of them are much more vulnerable in this respect than others (Garmezy, 1975). This does not mean that a very "normal" or "healthy" child could not be "made" or "conditioned" to be neurotic, and possibly even psychotic; for such a child probably could be. But in the usual course of events, children bring "themselves," their "cognitive styles," or their "disturbabilities" to early and later experiences and teachings; and they largely, though by no means completely, *make themselves* needlessly upset or dysfunctional. Highly vulnerable children seem to do this no matter how they are reared; and less vulnerable children do it to a much lesser degree, in spite of the fact that they frequently are "traumatized" early and later in life.

Repropagandizing Tendencies

In addition to their predispositions to upset themselves about innumerable events or things that are not, in themselves, disturbing, practically all humans have strong innate tendencies to repropagandize themselves with irrational ideas and to continue to behave dysfunctionally when (1) they originally accept these ideas from their parents and other teachers, and/or (2) they invent some of these ideas creatively themselves. Once children believe strongly, for example, that some force in the universe will omnisciently know about their wrongdoings and consequently will punish them, they will tend to repeat and "re-prove" this idea powerfully, in spite of the fact that life offers very potent, consistent, contradictory evidence. Children also tend to forget or disconfirm some of their early acquired ir-rationalities; but the tendency to "confirm" them or to continue to believe them despite disconfirming evidence frequently wins out.

Disturbability about Disturbances

Humans are uniquely self-talking and self-conscious creatures; hence, they usually observe their disturbed feelings and behaviors—for example, their anxieties and their withdrawal from certain anxiety-provoking situations—and disturb them-selves very easily *about* these disturbances. Some other animals may do this, too, but hardly to the extent that humans seem to do it. Consequently, the secondary symptoms of their dysfunctioning (that is, their anxiety about their anxieties and their depression about their depressions) frequently become more important and pervasive than their original dysfunctions; and these secondary disturbances often interfere seriously with their understanding and overcoming of their original dysfunctions (Ellis, 1957a, 1962, 1971, 1973a, 1977a; Ellis & Harper, 1975; Low, 1952; Weekes, 1969, 1972). Where original emotional problems, such as test-taking anxiety, may be rather limited in their pernicious effects on individuals' lives, humans' feelings of inadequacy *about* such problems may become so pervasive and pandemic as to affect and violate almost their entire existences.

Payoffs

People usually have some kind of pleasure or payoff in maintaining their dysfunc-tional symptoms, and this makes it harder than ever for them to change (Berne, 1964; Ellis, 1962, 1977a). Psychodynamic therapists tend to see these payoffs in terms of dramatic gains—to hypothesize, for example, that Mary Smith hates her mother, gets great joy in making her miserable, and therefore leads a self-defeating life of prostitution. This sometimes occurs; but much more often the payoff seems to consist of the highly undramatic ease of habituation or comfort of avoiding change. Thus, Mary Smith, even when she intelligently recognizes how she is defeating herself by leading a life of prostitution, refuses to give it up because (1) she would have to train herself for a new profession; (2) she would make much less money temporarily or permanently; (3) she gets immediate ego satisfaction from the admiration of the men she serves; (4) it is easier for her, at this moment, to continue to think and apply her short-range hedonistic philosophy than to change it to one of long-range hedonism; (5) she would suffer a period of anxiety if she faced what she was doing clearly and did something about changing it, and she has abysmally low frustration tolerance about facing this anxiety and doing something basic to overcome it; and so on. Even if *one* of her motives is the dramatic one of remaining a prostitute and thereby "upsetting" her hated mother, Mary's *main,* and highly undramatic, motives probably consist of various kinds of low frustration tolerance or discomfort anxiety. Her *real* payoff is immediate "ease."

Difficulty of Basic Change

Even when people see clearly how they defeat themselves and what they can do to change, they almost always find it exceptionally hard to modify their behavior and to keep it modified. Why? In all probability, it is mainly because that behavior is their natural tendency. They have to force themselves to change an act (for example, their mode of fingering the piano or of hitting a tennis ball) *many times* before they automatically and easily do it differently. Perhaps just as importantly, many of their neurotic or dysfunctional thoughts, emotions, and feelings are biologically natural or enjoyable, and they have to go through severe and continued discomfort to change them. Thus, they get addicted naturally to too much food, nicotine, caffeine, or alcohol; and they can only overcome such addictions painfully.

Once again, even the best-adjusted men and women, once they have overcome a self-defeating habit, tend to fall back into it easily over a period of time. They undertake a rigorous and effective program of exercise—and then, a year or two later, slowly fall back into seldom or never exercising. They work concertedly, for months or for years, at losing 30 or more surplus pounds—and then they slowly or suddenly gain back all the lost weight, and more. Perhaps, as the psychodynamic therapists keep hypothesizing, there are special reasons for their falling from grace and reinstituting the foolish thoughts and behaviors that they held previously and overcame temporarily. More than likely, however, they do it because they do it— because it is exceptionally easy for most humans to take two steps forward and one backward, as well as one step forward and two steps backward!

Unspecialness of Origin of Maladaptive Behavior

RET is one of the few schools of psychotherapy that stresses the unspecialness of the origins of maladaptive behavior, and does not assume that specific causative factors exist in the form of early events, teachings, or experiences. Such factors may indeed exist, and may exacerbate childhood and adult disturbances significantly. But it is highly doubtful whether they are the main "causes" of such disturbances. Indeed, it may be one of the innate irrational tendencies of humans that they more often than not pick special reasons for having healthy or disturbed personality traits, and speciously convince themselves that such reasons truly exist and are enormously important.

RET, along with behavior therapy, reality therapy, personal construct therapy, and various other kinds of psychological treatment, also holds that it is almost completely a waste of time to try to understand the special reasons why a current symptom exists. Such reasons, as just noted, are largely fictional; they are often not truly ascertainable, even if they do exist; they require much time and effort to dig up; and even if relevant, have little or nothing to do with people's *overcoming* their disturbances. Thus, if you know that you play tennis erratically because your mother kept telling you that you could never play it well, or because your father had a fear of being hit by a tennis ball, this knowledge itself will not help you significantly to give up your irrational beliefs that you *have* to play tennis well or that you *must* have a guarantee that you will never be hit by a tennis ball. Your knowing in detail about the origins of your neurotic attitudes about tennis will probably not aid you in seeing exactly what you are now telling yourself to re-create and maintain these attitudes, and it will not show you how you can give up these irrational Beliefs. In fact, this historical understanding, even if accurate (which it rarely is!) will probably sidetrack you from truly understanding and undoing your *present* symptoms.

In other words, RET tends to hold, though not dogmatically, that the real or basic causes of human disturbance lie, first, in the general propensity of an individual to think crookedly, emote inappropriately, and act dysfunctionally, much of which is innate; and, second, in the individual's specific tendencies to behave self-defeatingly, much of which is also the result of biologically based vulnerability and low frustration tolerance. The origins of disturbance seem to stem from this kind of specialness, rather than from some kind of special history that creates the origins and the development of the neurotic or psychotic symptoms.

GOALS OF COUNSELING

RET is often accused wrongly of trying to help people to become less emotional. Quite false! RET assumes that emotion is basic to human living, and that without strong feelings it is unlikely that people would either survive or live happily. RET clearly divides emotion into two distinct types—appropriate and inappropriate—and it tries to help clients have quite strong and sincere appropriate feelings, but to give up their inappropriate or self-defeating feelings.

Appropriate feelings, in RET, normally consist of various kinds of desiring, wishing, or preferring, and of the feelings that occur when these are blocked or frustrated. Thus, appropriate positive emotions include love, happiness, pleasure, and curiosity; appropriate negative emotions include sorrow, regret, frustration, annoyance, displeasure, and irritability. These negative emotions are deemed "appropriate" because they usually help people to change conditions that they find objectionable—such as being rejected or failing to get a job—and thereby to get more of what they want and less of what they do not want in life. *Inappropriate emotions,* in RET, usually consist of feelings like depression, anxiety, despair, hostility, and feelings of worthlessness; they are called "inappropriate" because they normally do not help people to change obnoxious conditions, but frequently help make them worse. Thus, if you are depressed about being rejected by someone (in addition to feeling sorry or frustrated about this rejection), you will frequently do nothing to get accepted by this person or by equivalent people later; and if you feel angry about failing to get a job, you may well act badly with future job interviews and thereby interfere even more with your chances of getting employment.

In RET, inappropriate emotions seem almost invariably to stem from absolutistic demands and commands—from dogmatic *shoulds* and *musts*—rather than from strong desires, wishes, and preferences. A basic RET assumption is that irrational ideas, inappropriate feelings, and dysfunctional behaviors are very frequently created or caused by absolutistic musts—or by *mus*turbation. Without this kind of overgeneralized thinking, most of what we call emotional disturbance would probably never occur.

Once people choose to stay alive and to try to enjoy themselves, there are several goals that usually seem to help them in these respects, and that therefore they had better seek. RET therapists try to help them achieve these goals, which include the following:

Self-Interest

Emotionally healthy people are primarily interested in and true to themselves, secondarily to others in general, and to a few selected others in particular. Since they inevitably have their being-in-the-world, as the existentialists have shown, they had better not be *completely* self-absorbed or "selfish." But they had better put themselves first usually, and had better act kindly and considerately toward others. This is because they themselves want to enjoy freedom from unnecessary pain and restriction, and they see that they are likely to do so only by helping to create a world in which the rights of others, as well as their own rights, are not curtailed needlessly.

Self-Direction

Healthy individuals assume responsibility for their own lives, are able to work out most of their problems independently, and while at times they want or prefer the cooperation and help of others, they do not *need* or absolutistically *demand* the support of others.

Tolerance

Well-functioning humans give others the *right to be wrong* and, while disliking or abhorring others' behavior, do not condemn or damn *them* as persons for displaying this displeasing behavior.

Acceptance of Uncertainty

Emotionally mature men and women accept the fact that we live in a world of probability and chance, where there are not, and probably never will be, any absolute certainties; and they realize that it is not horrible—indeed, in many ways it is fascinating and exciting—to live in such a probabilistic, uncertain world.

Flexibility

Healthy people remain flexible intellectually, are open to change, and view the infinite variety of people, ideas, and things in the world around them unbigotedly, as permissible and acceptable.

Scientific Thinking

Nondisturbed individuals are sufficiently objective, rational, and scientific, and they are able to apply the laws of logic and of scientific method not only to external people and events, but to themselves and to their own interpersonal and intrapersonal relationships.

Commitment

Healthy people are usually vitally absorbed in something outside themselves, whether it be in people, things, or ideas. Preferably, they have at least one major creative interest, as well as some human involvements, which is highly important to them and around which they structure a good part of their lives.

Risk Taking

Emotionally sound persons are able to take risks, to ask themselves what they would really like to do in life, and then try to do this, even though they may fail. They are adventurous (though not necessarily foolhardy); are willing to try almost anything once, to see how they like it; and look forward to some breaks in their usual life routines.

Self-Acceptance

Healthy people are glad to be alive and to accept themselves just *because* they are alive, *because* they exist, and because, as live individuals, they almost invariably have some capacity to enjoy themselves and to ward off unnecessary pain. They do not equate their worth or value to themselves with their extrinsic achievements or with what others think of them; and they preferably do not rate themselves, their totality, or their being at all, but accept their existences and endeavor to *enjoy* life.

Nonutopianism

No one, in all probability, is likely to get to the point where he or she is never frustrated, and consequently is never sorrowful, regretful, and annoyed by frustration; it would seem unhealthy if anyone ever did. But humans are also not likely to achieve perfect joy or happiness, on the one hand, nor total lack of anxiety, depression, despair, self-downing, and hostility, on the other hand. Even though these negative emotions seem foolish and needlessly self-defeating, the best that we can do probably is to minimize their frequency, intensity, and duration—and not to eliminate them completely. Perfect mental health seems like a chimera, at least for as long as humans remain much the way they are.

Process and Techniques of Counseling

RET counseling is a somewhat complicated process, since it rests upon the assumption that people have a combination of cognitive, emotive, and behavioral disturbances when they come for counseling, and that many different kinds of rational, evocative-confrontational, and activity-oriented techniques have to be employed by the counselor to help them overcome their emotional problems. Consequently, RET has no monolithic, invariant process; and it includes, in a seemingly eclectic manner, a wide variety of therapeutic techniques.

Now that I have said this, I can also go on to say something that may seem almost the opposite: that most of the time, in the course of RET counseling, a certain general or overall technique is employed, and that it has a heavily cognitive orientation. This orientation rests upon several therapeutic assumptions, including the following:

1 Human thinking and emotion overlap significantly, so that we tend to largely "cause" or "create" our emotions by our thinking (as well as "cause" some of our thinking by our emoting), and we can change these emotions importantly, particularly when we deem them disordered, by looking at and thinking about the cognitions that underlie them and by disputing or reconstructing these inappropriate cognitions vigorously and persistently.

2 External stimuli or Activating Events (A) contribute significantly to emotional and behavioral Consequences (such as neurotic symptoms), but people's philosophies or Beliefs (B) about A cause these Consequences (C) more importantly and more directly. Effective and elegant counseling, therefore, deals mainly with B rather than with A and C; and it aims at a clear-headed, detailed understanding of clients' irrational Beliefs (iB's) and a concerted attempt to have clients change or surrender such Beliefs.

3 People largely think about what happens to them at A (Activating Experiences) in words, phrases, and sentences. But they also do so in nonverbal but still highly cognitive ways—including images, fantasies, and dreams. These nonverbal cognitions also contribute significantly to their disordered emotions and behaviors and can be used to change such behaviors.

4 Human disturbances often involve or are created by people's expectations about what is happening and about how others "should" act toward them, and when people change their expectancies they frequently change their disturbed feelings.

5 When people view situations, others' reactions, and their own behavior as being out of their own control and think that they cannot cope properly or adequately, they frequently disturb themselves; they will tend to feel much less upset when they come to view important things as being within their own control and think that they can cope properly.

6 Disturbed individuals attribute highly negative motives, reasons, and causes to others and to outside events; when they change their attributions, they frequently feel and act better in regard to these others and these events.

Manifold empirical data exist in the form of experimental studies that have validated the RET and cognitive-behavior therapy hypotheses that I have just listed (DiGiuseppe, Miller, & Trexler, 1977; Ellis, 1977b; Murphy and Ellis, 1979). Other

RET clinical hypotheses for which there are a great deal of clinical supporting data, but which have not as yet been substantiated sufficiently by controlled experiments, include the following:

1   Clients who unconditionally or fully accept themselves, and do not give any pronouncedly positive or negative rating to their "selves" or "essences" at all, but feel determined to live and to enjoy themselves whether or not they perform well and whether or not significant others accept them, are much less disturbed emotionally than those who rate themselves, and particularly those who do so negatively.

2   Although a counselor's giving clients considerable warmth and approval will often help them to feel better, they will tend to *get better* (that is, feel independent and self-accepting even under poor conditions) much more significantly when counseling helps them to change their attitudes about themselves profoundly.

3   Often clients will be helped importantly if they are not only shown how to overcome their fears of failure and rejection and to surrender their self-damnation but also are helped to increase their frustration tolerance and their discomfort-anxiety about their painful emotional reactions to failure and rejection.

4   Elegant counseling or therapy tends to occur when counselors help clients to understand and surrender their secondary as well as their primary symptoms of disturbance; that is, to dispute and extirpate their anxiety about their anxiety, depression about depression, and guilt about hostility.

5   Clients may be helped significantly with many kinds of cognitive restructuring or disputing of their antiempirical notions and irrational ideas. But the most elegant, profound, and long-lasting changes tend to occur when they give up their major *must*urbational ideas, especially (a) "I *must* perform well and be approved greatly, or else I am pretty worthless!" (b) "You *must* treat me kindly and fairly, or else you are a louse!" and (c) "Life conditions *must* be easy and afford me quick and great satisfaction, or else living in this world is unbearable and awful!" When counselors truly help clients to give up these absolutistic demands, commands, and whinings, and to live mainly with desires, preferences, and wants, they do the most efficient types of counseling.

6   In the case of severely disturbed individuals, self-penalization without self-damnation is often a more effective means of effecting behavior change than is self-reinforcement or reward.

7   Semantic reeducation, employing the principles of RET and general semantics, can be quite effective. Clients can be helped to change "I need love" to "It would be better if I received it," change "I should succeed" to "I preferably should succeed," change "I can't do it" to "I find it hard but not too hard; and I probably can do it" (Ellis, 1957a, 1977a).

8   Teaching clients the logicoempirical method of science in regard to their everyday problems can be an effective form of counseling.

Once these basic propositions are accepted by rational-emotive counselors, they try to apply and implement them directly in the course of the counseling process. To this end, they employ three basic techniques consciously and actively: cognitive, emotive, and behavioral methods of psychotherapy. They may seem to use these methods eclectically, in relation to the basic personality, the kinds of disturbance, and the responsiveness to therapy of each individual client. Actually, however, they use CEB (cognitive-emotive-behavioral) procedures on theoretical grounds—on the assumption that such procedures are grounded in the basic nature of humans and of their disturbability and potentiality for change. The "eclecticism" of RET practitioners occurs within the framework of the above kinds of theories about the origin and the modifiability of "emotional" disturbance.

Cognitive Methods of RET

RET deliberately and consciously employs a large number of cognitive therapeutic methods, including philosophical and logical analysis of irrational ideas, teaching and instruction, questioning of antiempirical conclusions, thought stopping, suggestions, and cognitive diversion or distraction. In its most elegant form, it is famous for showing clients the ABC's of their disturbances and then particularly emphasizing D, the Disputing of their irrational Beliefs (iB's). Typically, a young male may come to therapy because he is exceptionally angry with his parents for "unfairly" criticizing and restricting him while he is living at home and going to a nearby college, and because he is also very guilty about his feelings of hostility toward them.

In a case like this, an RET counselor would probably start with this young man's secondary symptom, his guilt, and show him how it fits into the ABC model of RET. At point A, Activating Experience, he feels angry with his parents; and at point C, emotional Consequence, he feels guilty about this anger. "What are you telling yourself," the therapist would ask the client, "at point B, to create your guilt about your anger at point A?" The client would then bring out, with the therapist's helpful questioning, a set of rational Beliefs (rB's) and irrational Beliefs (iB's) about A.

His rational Beliefs (rB's) would be along these lines: "I don't like feeling angry with my parents, because they also do many nice things for me and because anger is a painful, disruptive feeling. I wish I were much less angry. How annoying to fall into this trap of upsetting myself so much about their behavior!" If he stayed *only* with these rational Beliefs that the therapist would show him, he would in all probability merely feel annoyed and irritated by his parents' actions and would not feel hostile and condemning toward them for acting in a certain way. In this case, his feelings of annoyance and irritation would be quite appropriate—they would help him to cope with their "poor" behavior and perhaps to figure out ways to get them to change it, or else to live with it more satisfactorily himself.

But the RET counselor would also get this young man to see that he also has a pronouncedly irrational set of Beliefs (iB's) about his own anger: "I *must* not be as angry as I am! I *can't stand* my foolish anger! It's *awful* that I am this way! What a *worm* I am for hating my reasonably nice and helpful parents!" It is these absolutistic *demands,* rather than his strong *wishes* about his feelings of anger, that make him feel guilty.

The counselor would then show this client how to Dispute (D) his irrational Beliefs (iB's) about his anger, by asking himself several scientific questions about it, such as: (1) "Where is the evidence that I *must* not be angry as I am?" (2) "Why can't

I *stand* my foolish anger?" (3) "Prove that it's *awful* that I am this way." (4) "How does my self-defeating anger make me a *worm?*"

If the RET counselor persists in getting the client to keep Disputing or Debating his irrational Beliefs (iB's), and helps him with this Disputing, the client will most probably be able to get to cE—a new cognitive Effect or revised Belief System about A. His cE's would include Beliefs like these:

1   "There is *no* evidence that I *must* not be as angry as I am. There is evidence that I get bad results this way, and that I could make myself unangry and get better results. But under the present conditions, with my general philosophy of self-condemnation, I really *will* make myself as angry as I do; and in this sense, I *should* and *must* act the foolish way that I indubitably do act. It would be lovely and sensible if I did not make myself angry; but, alas, I am a fallible human person who still behaves, and who in many respects will continue to behave as long as I live, in this self-destructive manner. Why can't I, therefore, accept myself *with* my fallibility, and simply keep trying to act somewhat better, less angrily?"

2   "I damned well *can* stand my foolish anger, though I'll never *like* it. I can stand virtually anything that happens to me, or that I make happen, so long as I am alive. My anger won't kill me; and it need not even make me totally miserable. I can lead a fairly happy existence, even if it continues—though I would doubtless be happi*er* without it. So I might as well stand it—and many other stupid and obnoxious things I do—gracefully lump what I don't like, and work hard at minimizing or eliminating it in the future.

3   "It's clearly not *awful* (or *horrible* or *terrible*) that I am angry, but only highly uncomfortable and disadvantageous. If it were *awful,* that would mean (a) that my anger is *totally* or *100 percent* bad, which it certainly doesn't seem to be; (b) that it is as bad as it could *possibly* be, when it doubtless isn't; (c) that it is *more than* bad, or at least 101 percent bad—which is impossible; and (d) that it *must not* be as bad as it is—when, of course, it must be, if it is! Nothing is really awful or horrible in the universe; though, of course, many things are highly obnoxious. Now, why can't I look at the obnoxiousness of my anger, and therefore try to eliminate it, rather than *awfulizing* about it, and thereby probably making it worse?"

4   "My self-defeating anger never makes me, as a person, *a worm;* it merely makes some of my behavior some of the time *wormy.* My wormy or foolish behavior cannot ever *be* or *equal* me, my totality, since it is merely an important *part* of me. Moreover, no matter how angry I have been up to now and no matter what bad deeds I have wrought as a result of my anger, I always have a future, and I have the potential of changing in the future and making myself less angry. However, even if I am thoroughly angry with everyone for the rest of my life (which is highly unlikely!) I am not a damnable *person* for acting this deplorable *way.* I am merely a person with rotten behavior, and never a totally rotten person (RP). No human is damnable, even though human acts may be consistently poor and immoral."

By helping this young man to Dispute (at D) his irrational Beliefs (iB's) and to come up with a new philosophy or cognitive Effect at E, the RET counselor helps him to restructure his cognitions profoundly and to face his future behavior, including his future anger, with a distinctly different outlook—a rational and efficient, rather than an irrational and inefficient, basic attitude toward himself and others. The counselor would then go on to discuss and get the client to uproot his primary symptom: his feelings of anger (at point C) after his parents presumably treat him critically and unjustly (at point A). Here again, he would be helped to see that he has a distinct set of irrational Beliefs (iB's), such as: "My parents *must* treat me kindly and fairly! I *can't stand* their criticizing me. It's *terrible* that they act so unfairly to me! What *lousy people* thay are for treating me so abominably!" He would also be helped to Dispute these irrational Beliefs (at point D) and to come up with a new set of cognitive Effects (cE's) at point E, such as: "There is no reason why my parents *have to* treat me kindly and fairly, although it would be lovely if they did. I can definitely *bear* their criticism, though I'll never like it. It's never *terrible* or *horrible* that they treat me the way they do, but only a pain in the neck! They are not *lousy people,* but only people who behave badly to me in this respect and who have the right to be wrong because they are fallible humans."

Once the RET counselor has helped the client to give up his irrational Beliefs (iB's) about his feeling of anger toward his parents, the counselor would then go on to the anger itself and work on that cognitively. The therapist would show the client how to Dispute at point D the iB's listed in the previous paragraph and to come to a new cognitive Effect (cE), or new philosophy, at point E.

At the same time, the RET counselor would also attempt to help this client in various other cognitive ways, including: (1) teaching him logical and semantic precision, so that he stops telling himself that his parents will *always* act badly toward him and that he *cannot* give up his anger toward them; (2) showing him how to use DIB's (Disputing Irrational Beliefs), until he convinces himself that even the worst things that might happen—for example, his parents' continually criticizing and restricting him—would not lead to the dire results that he melodramatically fantasizes that they would (Ellis, 1974b; Ellis & Harper, 1975); (3) getting him to fill out, preferably on a regular basis, the Rational Self Help Form published by the Institute for Rational-Emotive Therapy in New York City and to bring it in to the therapist or the therapy group he attends for correction and discussion (this form is printed on pp. 216–219); (4) instructing him in various kinds of skill training, such as assertion training, that could help him express himself to his parents assertively but not angrily; (5) teaching him rational self-statements that would help him cope with his difficulties with his parents, such as, "My parents have severe problems of their own. Tough!" or "I don't have to express myself angrily in order to cope with my parents' criticism"; (6) showing him cognitive distraction or diversionary techniques, such as thought stopping, when he obsesses himself with his parents' unfair behavior; and (7) teaching him the technique of semantic referenting, so that he can see some of the advantages of his parents' criticism as well as some of the disadvantages of his own whining about their criticism (Danysh, 1974; Ellis, 1975a, 1977a).

Emotive-Evocative Techniques of RET

While trying to help this angry client in the cognitive ways just listed (and several others that might also be employed), the RET counselor would almost always use a number of emotive-evocative methods as well. These would tend to include the following:

1   Accepting the client unconditionally, without qualification, no matter how poor his behavior has been or continues to be. This kind of full acceptance of people *with* their disabilities and errors is one of the main philosophic cores of RET; it is taught not only verbally and philosophically but also through the therapist's *showing* the client that, in the case we are considering, he has every right as a fallible human to make errors for which he is criticizable, and to hate his parents childishly instead of merely deploring their unfair behavior. The therapist's attitude and demeanor, therefore, are just as important as his or her words in establishing this kind of unconditional acceptance of the client (Bone, 1968; Ellis, 1971, 1973a, 1977a).

2   Role playing is often employed in RET to show clients exactly what their false ideas are, and how they affect their relations with others. In the case we are considering, the RET counselor (or a member of an RET therapy group) might well enact with the client his parents' unduly criticizing him; in the course of this role playing, he might be shown (a) how he overreacts to this criticism; (b) what he is telling himself to make himself overreact; and (c) how he could assert himself with his parents in a more appropriate, less overreacting manner.

3   Modeling is employed to help clients think, feel, and act differently about the things they use to disturb themselves. Thus, as an RET counselor I might well act *un*angrily myself when an angry client behaves badly in therapy; and I might show how when I make a mistake as a therapist, that mistake is fully acknowledged without any concomitant feelings of guilt or self-downing.

4   Passionate exhortation may be used to persuade clients to give up some of their crazy thinking and self-defeating behaviors and to replace them with more efficient ideas and performances.

5   Humor may be employed incisively and strongly by an RET counselor to reduce some of the disturbance-creating ideas of the client to absurdity (Ellis, 1977e). Rational-emotive therapists sometimes make use of humorous rational songs that are aimed to keep running through clients' heads, to show them how silly and unproductive some of their angry, guilty, and other behaviors are (Ellis, 1977f).

6   Shame-attacking exercises are employed regularly in RET counseling to show clients that they can do "shameful," "humiliating," or "ridiculous" things with almost complete impunity, and not have to put themselves down or feel ashamed in front of the people who witness these acts (Ellis, 1973b). These exercises were invented some years ago for use in rational marathon encounters, but they are used in individual and regular group treatment by RET therapists (as well as by non-RET therapists who have often adopted them) (Ellis, 1969b). In the case of the angry and guilty young man that we are considering here, he might well be given the shame-attacking exercise of deliberately doing something that he knows his parents would find very shameful, and training himself to feel unashamed and unguilty, as well as unangry, when they criticize him severely for this act.

7   A variety of other encounterlike emotive exercises are used often in RET, to help clients to reveal themselves honestly, to acknowledge their negative feelings, to take emotional risks with others, and to open themselves in various other ways so that they can get in touch with their disturbed feelings and do something cognitively and behaviorally about changing them.

Behavior Therapy Techniques of RET

RET is a form of cognitive-behavior therapy, and almost invariably it uses some of the main behavioral methods with its clients. Virtually all the common behavioral methods, such as those outlined by Dr. Kenneth LaFleur in Chapter 6 about behavioral approaches, are well within the theoretical framework of RET and are used at times by RET counselors. Those that are employed most often include the following:

1 Activity-oriented in vivo homework assignments have been pioneered by RET. Where behavior therapists like Wolpe (1973) would tend to use imaginal desensitization for clients who are, let us say, shy about encountering other people, RET counselors would tend to give them gradual or implosive assignments of actually doing such encountering and taking the risk of real rejection. In cases of anger, such as that of the young man whom we are considering in this section, an RET counselor would tend to encourage him not to get away from his parents, but first to stay with them deliberately and to give them every possible chance to criticize or "insult" him unfairly; the counselor would help this client to work through, in vivo, his feelings of hostility toward his parents and to teach himself how to accept his parents with all their unfairness. After that had been accomplished, the counselor might *then* encourage the client to move out of his parents' home.

2 RET homework assignments include a great deal of cognitive homework—especially in the form of clients' doing their written ABC's and Disputing their irrational Beliefs (iB's) actively at D. These assignments are often done on the special Rational Self Help Form published by the Institute for Rational-Emotive Therapy and printed on pages 216–219 of this chapter (Ellis, 1968b, 1977g; Maultsby, 1971b, 1975). People who use this form regularly tend to internalize its outline, and are usually able to do their cognitive homework in their heads thereafter, without necessarily using the form itself.

3 Operant conditioning, especially in the form of self-management procedures, is used continually in RET to help clients work at changing their cognitions and also at changing their emotions and behaviors (Ellis, 1973c). The angry young man in our illustration, for example, might well be given the assignment of reinforcing or rewarding himself (perhaps with reading, listening to music, or socializing with his friends) whenever he worked on his feelings of anger and guilt and gave them up at least temporarily; and the assignment of penalizing himself (with, for example, burning a twenty dollar bill or cleaning the toilet) whenever he failed to work against these feelings.

4 Relaxation and other kinds of physical distractions are often used in RET, not as curative but as palliative measures that interfere temporarily with anxiety. Thus, when the angry young man became angry with his parents or anxious about this anger, he might be shown how to use Jacobsen's (1942), Schultz and Luthe's (1967), or other relaxation techniques, and thereby to block off some of his disturbed feelings. In RET, however, he would not be given relaxation procedures only or mainly, but would also be shown how to face his disordered feelings, get in full touch with them, and change them by changing the basic irrational Beliefs that he subscribes to devoutly and that he uses to create the disordered feelings (Ellis, 1977a).

5   The RET counselor frequently employs rational emotive imagery (Maultsby, 1971b, 1975; Maultsby & Ellis, 1974), a technique that is simultaneously cognitive, emotive, and behavioral. Thus, the angry young man might be asked to fantasize, as powerfully and intensely as he could, his parents' acting very unfairly toward him and criticizing him in a savage manner. He would then be asked how he feels as he engages in this fantasy—and would probably reply, "Very angry!" He would be instructed to keep this same image, get in touch with his anger, and then change it to a feeling of disappointment only, a feeling merely of regret and not of anger. When he had done this, he would be asked, "How did you change your feeling?" He would probably reply, "By telling myself that it isn't the end of the world when they treat me like that; they have a right to think and act the way they do, even if I don't like it." He would finally be instructed, "Fine! That's one way to change your feelings of anger—and you notice how you did it cognitively, by changing some of your ideas about your parents. Now every day, for the next month or so, do this same kind of rational-emotive imagery; imagine your parents treating you unfairly, let yourself feel angry, change your anger to disappointment (the way you did or some other way), and practice feeling disappointed instead of angry. If you keep practicing this new and appropriate feeling, instead of your inappropriate feeling of rage, you will soon do it 'naturally' and easily, whenever your parents actually do treat you unjustly." Rational-emotive imagery (REI), as can be seen, has some pronounced cognitive, emotive, and behavioral aspects, and it is often given as an RET homework assignment (Ellis, 1977a).

What RET Counselors Avoid Doing

As just noted, RET makes wide use of a great number of cognitive, emotive, and behavioral methods of therapy. But it does not do so merely because these methods work and may be validated pragmatically. It does so largely on theoretical grounds, because the many methods it uses tend to be active and vigorous ways of helping clients to dispute their basic irrational Beliefs (iB's) and to arrive at radically new, much more rational and realistic philosophies of life.

Because it has a theoretical basis and is rooted in a distinct theory of personality and of personality change, RET normally avoids or rarely uses some of the most popular methods of various other schools of counseling, particularly the following:

1   The RET counselor does not spend much time, in most cases, listening to clients' A's—the Activating Experiences they tend to relate ad nauseam. The counselor is not interested in all the gory details of what happened and where and when it happened, and is especially not interested in the historical details of clients' existences. These details are largely sidetracking, often have little or nothing to do with clients' disturbances, and can easily lead both client and therapist down the garden path. The RET counselor therefore encourages clients to narrate their A's with relative brevity, and not to become obsessed about them.

2   RET counseling usually starts with C, clients' emotional Consequences or feelings—such as feelings of anxiety, despair, depression, hostility, and worthlessness. But clients are not encouraged to revel in these feelings—merely to acknowledge that the feelings exist and to describe them succinctly. If such feelings

are denied or played down, various dramatic-evocative techniques may be employed to bring them to the surface and to have them acknowledged. But clients who immensely enjoy reveling in their feelings, their feelings, their feelings, are soon stopped, and are brought back carefully and incisively to B—the Beliefs with which they largely created these feelings and by which they keep maintaining them.

3   Abreaction and catharsis are encouraged only rarely or briefly in RET, because considerable research by Bandura (1977), Berkowitz (1970), Geen, Stonner, and Hope (1975), and others has shown that such forms of "treatment" are more likely to exacerbate than minimize hostility. This has been one of the main RET hypotheses for many years (Ellis, 1962, 1977a, 1977b), since it seems obvious that when people express their anger violently, either verbally or nonverbally, and either directly or indirectly, they tend to reindoctrinate themselves with the irrational ideas that others *must* not act the way they indubitably do, and that the others are utter bastards for acting this way. RET, therefore, concentrates on helping people to understand the philosophic sources of their anger and to eliminate the anger, rather than to express it, suppress it, or repress it.

4   RET avoids most of the popular psychoanalytic or psychodynamic methods of therapy, including free association, dream analysis, establishment of an intense transference relationship, explanation of the client's present symptoms in terms of past experiences, and disclosure and analysis of the so-called Oedipus complex. It considers free association and dream analysis largely as wasteful procedures and replaces them with incisive probing and questioning. It gives clients considerable empathy and understanding, but avoids the kind of warmth that will help make them more dependent than they were when they first came to therapy. It considers most explanations of present symptoms that are made in terms of past "traumatic" events to be quite specious and useless. It sees the so-called Oedipus complex as a minor, and usually rare, subheading under the main heading of the client's dire need for approval—a need that RET brings up continually, analyzes logically, and tries to help the client surrender.

5   As noted above, RET makes use of a great many encounter or opening-up-type exercises, but it places them in a philosophic or problem-solving context, and does not concentrate on them simply because they prove fascinating to the client or to the counselor. Thus, it specializes in shame-attacking and risk-taking procedures, both in the sessions themselves and as homework assignments. But it tries especially to help clients see exactly what they are doing in telling themselves to make such procedures "shameful" and "risky," and how they could think and behave differently to undo their feelings of shame or embarrassment in the course of doing these and similar exercises.

From the above dos and don'ts of RET, it can be seen that rational-emotive counselors employ mainly a fairly rapid-fire, active-directive-persuasive-philosophic method. They challenge clients continually to validate their personal observations and ideas. They analyze some of these ideas logically and show why the ideas do not and cannot work. They firmly bring to clients' attention the practical results of their thoughts and feelings. They reduce some irrational Beliefs to absurdity, sometimes in a highly humorous way. They teach clients how to think scientifically so that they can thereafter observe, parse logically, and annihilate effectively the repeated self-defeating ideas and behaviors that they experience.

The RET theory of counseling states that there are many kinds and techniques of psychological treatment, and that most of them have some effectiveness. But an efficient system, such as RET, tends to save both the therapist and client time and effort; helps clients to zero in fairly quickly on their major problems and to start working toward giving them up; works with a large percentage of different kinds of clients; offers an "elegant" or "deep" solution that deals with basic difficulties and encourages clients to solve these basic difficulties in the future, after therapy has ended; and produces relatively long-lasting results.

On all these counts, some amount of clinical and experimental evidence now exists that RET works as well as or better than other commonly used counseling procedures (DiGiuseppe, Miller & Trexler, 1977; Ellis, 1977a, 1977b; Ellis & Grieger, 1977; Ellis & Harper, 1975; Lembo, 1976; Morris & Kanitz, 1975; Murphy & Ellis, 1979). If RET is an unusually effective means of counseling, it is probably because of the depth and hardheadedness of its philosophic position; that is, it zeroes in more intensively on and combats absolutistic thinking more than do other systems. It is designed to be realistic and unindulgent; it tries incisively and determinedly to get to the core of and to undermine the childish demandingness that seems to be the main element of serious emotional disturbance.

ILLUSTRATIVE CASE

Probably the best way to illustrate the process of RET or of any other therapeutic procedure is to give verbatim excerpts from actual counseling sessions. Such verbatim transcripts appear in several of the main RET presentations (Ellis, 1965, 1971, 1973a, 1973d, 1978b; Ellis & Gullo, 1971; Ellis & Knaus, 1977). Here is another verbatim transcript, which will show how I conduct a typical first session of RET:

Co 1: Did anybody refer you here?

Cl 1: Yes, one of my friends. In fact, one of my gay friends.

Co 2: And how did he come to refer you?

Cl 2: I believe he has been here. And so has his lover. They both seem to have been helped by seeing you.

Co 3: All right. (Reading from the personal data form the client has filled out): "Extremely emotional reaction to problems. Irrational reactions. Tremendous depression. Inability to concentrate on anything except things bothering me. I am a homosexual." All right, now. What's the depression about?

Cl 3: Well, the depression has been over a love affair I've been having.

Co 4: Yeah? And it's going badly?

Cl 4: Very badly. I'm normally depressed to begin with, but this has made it really acute.

Co 5: No, it hasn't. Now why am I correct and you incorrect about this?

Cl 5: Because maybe you have better answers than I do.

Co 6: No. Because nothing in the universe ever has or ever will depress anybody! Now, why is that so?

Cl 6:   Because that is not the root of the problem.

Co 7:   The root is your childish reaction to the depression. No, not to the depression—we'll get to that reaction later—but to your disappointment. He is disappointing you by not caring for you—right?

Cl 7:   Right.

Co 8:   And you're saying, "That's awful!" Right?

Cl 8:   Right.

Co 9:   Now, *why* is it awful?

Cl 9:   Because I love him.

Co 10:   That's why it's disappointing, unpleasant. Now, why is your unpleasantness *awful*?

Cl 10:   I can try to intellectualize it and say it's awful because it reminds me, maybe, of the way it was before.

Co 11:   But why was *that* awful? Why is *anything* ever awful in the universe?

Cl 11:   It's awful because—I'm not sure.

Co 12:   If you answer that question correctly, you will change your entire philosophy—and perhaps your entire existence. If you give the right answer and really *believe* it to this question: Why is anything that's unpleasant *awful*? For there's only one really good answer; and if you give it, you'll give up your depression.

Cl 12:   Because it's affecting my happiness. *That's* why it's awful.

Co 13: That's why it's *unpleasant*. You fail to see that you've got *two* propositions, one sane and one completely magical and insane. The first one is "It's unpleasant. I'm not getting my piece of taffy! I like x and I'm getting x minus 10." Well, obviously that's unpleasant. Now your second proposition is, "*Because* it's unpleasant it's awful!" Now that is never true; it couldn't be true; it's just about 100 percent bullshit—which you and others in this world believe devoutly. Now why is that 100 percent bullshit—your statement that because it's unpleasant, and I'm assuming it is, it's *awful*? Why is that bullshit?

Cl 13:   I'm not sure if I understand.

Co 14:   You have two propositions. The first one is sane. Well, maybe we'd better go back to that for a minute. "I'm not getting what I like, and therefore, that's unpleasant, unfortunate." Right?

Cl 14:   Right.

Co 15:   Well, that's obviously true. Now, *why* is that true?

Cl 15:   Because it's hurting me.

Co 16:   Because "I want x and I'm getting x minus 10. My value is x and I'm not getting what I value. But I'm entitled to want whatever x is—even if it's a million dollars, if it's a guy, or a job. I'm entitled to want it. And since I want it and I don't have it, I find that unpleasant. And either I find it moderately unpleasant if I want it moderately; or I find it very unpleasant if I want it very much." In the case of this guy, I assume that you don't often become attached to a guy seriously, is that right?

Cl 16:   Right.

Co 17:   So, therefore, it's very unpleasant not to have him. On a scale from 0 to 100, we might say that you find it 80 to 90 percent unpleasant. So that's provable—its unpleasantness. Provable because you want it and that's the essence of this kind of proof. If you didn't want him, if you fell out of love with him, then it wouldn't even be unpleasant to lose him. But as long as you want anything and you're not getting it, you find it to some degree unpleasant. Now you don't seem to realize that although the unpleasantness of losing your male friend is a provable proposition, you have a quite unprovable addition to it: "Because it's unpleasant, it's *awful!*" Now, you think that's correct. You think it follows from the first proposition, but it doesn't. Now, why doesn't it follow, that because it's unpleasant (which we're assuming that it is—very unpleasant; we'll say 90 percent unpleasant) it's *awful.* Now, why doesn't that follow?

Cl 17: Why *doesn't* it follow that it's awful? Maybe it shouldn't exceed unpleasant; but *unpleasant* is *awful* for me!

Co 18: Let's go back. Let's suppose you only defined it as unpleasant, not as awful. You merely stuck to, "It's very unpleasant," and you believed that, nothing else, only that. How would you feel with that belief?

Cl 18: Just that it was unpleasant?

Co 19: Very unpleasant—right. "It's very unpleasant; it's very unpleasant."

Cl 19: I'd still believe it was *awful.*

Co 20: No, no. You're insisting on this *other* belief, which helps destroy you. Unless you give it up, your happiness is dead. But let's suppose you *were* saying, which you're not, and you really believed, "It's *only* very unpleasant; that's the way it is." *Then* how would you feel?

Cl 20: Much better.

Co 21: Right. But you'd feel disappointed, sorry, sad. And that would be appropriate, instead of your inappropriate feeling of depression. And your depression comes from your *awfulizing.* If you never said anything was awful, terrible, or horrible, you would probably never be emotionally disturbed. It's your crazy belief—escalation of *unpleasant* or *very unpleasant* into *awful, horrible,* or *terrible*—that upsets you, and that probably has upset you all your life. Now, if we can get you to really *not* believe that, you'll solve your problem of feeling depressed.

(Typically, the therapist jumps right into this first session, when he knows practically nothing about the client other than his presenting symptoms. As soon as he knows A, the Activating Experience—the client's love affair that is "going badly"—and C, the emotional Consequence of depression that the client feels, he hypothesizes, according to RET theory, that the depression is most probably caused by irrational Beliefs (iB's) consisting of the client's awfulizing about his affair. As is common, the client immediately admits his awfulizing; and the therapist therefore tries several quick and startling tactics: (1) He tries to get over the revolutionary and probably shocking point that *nothing* is awful, terrible, or horrible, even though many things are very disappointing. (2) He points out that giving up awfulizing will probably change the client's entire existence, as well as eliminate his depression. (3) He attempts to get the client to think for himself and figure out why many things are *unpleasant* or *unfortunate* but that these same things are not *awful.* (4) When the client shows confusion and does not think his way through to the "right" answers, the therapist does not hesitate to supply them; but he also persists in trying to get the client to think things through for himself. (5)

He tries to clearly show the client the difference between rational Beliefs (rB's) and the appropriate emotions of disappointment and displeasure to which they lead, and irrational Beliefs (iB's) and the inappropriate and destructive emotions of depression and despair to which they lead. The therapist, perhaps unjustifiably, assumes that the client is intelligent enough to understand the differences he is pointing out and to start changing his irrational Beliefs and his inappropriate emotional Consequences fairly quickly. If this does not work, the therapist will retreat and start over again at a slower pace. But he thinks that there is little to lose by trying to make a few solid points that will possibly help the client as quickly as possible.)

Cl 21:   Well, that seems to say, though, that it would make you very blasé about everything.

Co 22:   No, see—. Look how you jump! Is the feeling of disappointment, of sorrow and regret, blasé? Is it?

Cl 22:   No.

Co 23:   Of course not! Suppose somebody you loved—. Suppose you were married and had a child and the child died. You could feel 99 percent sad, couldn't you? Would that feeling be blasé?

Cl 23:   No.

Co 24:   But do you ever have to feel 1 percent depressed?

Cl 24:   Do I have to feel 1 percent depressed?

Co 25:   Yes. Let's suppose that occasionally, a few times in your life, you would feel 99 percent sad. It practically would never be that way, but only 70, 80, or 90 percent instead. But suppose you happened to feel 99 percent sad—would that ever have to jump to 1 percent depression?

Cl 25:   I'm not sure about that.

Co 26:   No, it wouldn't have to. Because the feeling of depression includes awfulizing. "It's *awful* that this sad thing has occurred!" is the thought that leads you to feel depression. Don't you see that you have two different thoughts—and that you put them together and think they're the same? And as long as you put these two thoughts together, you are cooked and will feel depressed.

Cl 26:   So the experiences I'm having are not awful experiences? They're merely unpleasant?

Co 27:   Well, that's right. Almost everyone would find being rejected by a lover unpleasant. And to you it's probably a very unpleasant experience. Suppose, though, that your lover dies. Or suppose he tells you to get lost, he doesn't want to see you again. Now, by your legitimate value, "I care for him, I would like him to care for me," that becomes a very unpleasant experience—especially since we're assuming that you can't easily go and find a replacement for him tomorrow.

Cl 27:   Right.

Co 28:   So that's why the experience is unpleasant. If you could find someone else like him tomorrow, whom you could care for just as much, it would only be moderately unpleasant. But you know it's unlikely you'll replace him tomorrow. All right. So, therefore, you'll find it very unpleasant. Now your problem is that you're defining this *unpleasantness* as *awful;* and there isn't anything *awful* in the universe. If you see what the word really means, you'll see that there isn't. Now, if you could figure out why there isn't anything *awful* and really believe there isn't, you'd give up awfulizing and still feel very unpleasant. And then you'd either live with your loss or manage to win your friend back. But *why* isn't there anything *awful*? No matter how unpleasant it is? Suppose I tortured you to death slowly. Now that's practically 100 percent unpleasant.

Cl 28:   I would say *awful.*

Co 29:   But why *wouldn't* it be *awful?*

Cl 29:   Why would it or wouldn't it?

Co 30:   Would *not* be *awful?*

Cl 30:   Being tortured to death would be the end.

Co 31:   And you'd be in dire pain until the end. Let us say that two hours from now you would die.

Cl 31:   I don't see how it could be just unpleasant. *Awful* to me is more than that.

Co 32:   We're talking about 100 percent unpleasantness now, or close to it. We're not talking about a moderate degree of unpleasantness.

Cl 32:   Yeah. But I don't see it.

Co 33:   Because you're not defining your terms. You're not defining what *awful* means.

Cl 33:   And I guess maybe I should.

Co 34:   Yeah; right. Because *awful* means, first, very unpleasant. You don't say a thing is *awful* if it's just moderately unpleasant. If you wanted an ice cream cone and you didn't get it because none was available, you wouldn't say that was *awful*. Right?

Cl 34:   Right.

Co 35:   So, first, it means very unpleasant. Well, that's provable. Occasionally, people say something is very unpleasant when it really isn't. "I didn't get the ice cream cone I wanted, and that's exceptionally unpleasant!" And they may whine about it. But most people know when something is very unpleasant. So, in your case, losing your friend is very unpleasant. And, second, *awful* means 100 percent unpleasant. Doesn't it really?

Cl 35:   Yeah.

Co 36:   Well, is it *really* 100 percent unpleasant?

Cl 36:   My experience?

Co 37:   Yeah, your experience right now, with him.

Cl 37:   No, because I manage to try to find other things to take my mind off it.

Co 38:   Right! But your being tortured to death might be 100 percent unpleasant. You might think so. But it really wouldn't be. Do you know *why* it wouldn't be?

Cl 38:   It wouldn't be if I didn't die.

Co 39:   Oh, no. Suppose you actually die after two hours of torture?

Cl 39:   Now, why wouldn't that be 100 percent unpleasant?

Co 40:   Because you might get tortured and die after *four* hours of torture. Or you might die after *eight* hours of torture. You see, you never can really get to 100 percent unpleasantness. It could always be *worse* that it is! So nothing is really 100 percent unpleasant. We just foolishly, while we're being tortured and while we're dying, say to ourselves something like, "Oh, this is 100 percent unpleasant." But suppose you were given the choice of being tortured for four hours or two hours, which would you pick?

Cl 40: The two hours.

Co 41: Correct! So you can see that two hours of torture isn't really 100 percent unpleasant. But it's nearly 100 percent!

Cl 41: But again, it's almost 100 percent, because I know the outcome in this case is death. So either way, I'm going to die.

Co 42: But death itself, or the state of actually being dead, isn't even unpleasant!

Cl 42: Well, I'll never begin to believe that.

Co 43: Well, because you're building up myths. Do you know what the state of death really is?

Cl 43: There's no more.

Co 44: As far as we can tell, it's exactly like the state you were in before you were born. Now, is that an unpleasant state?

Cl 44: We don't know that either.

Co 45: No, not for certain. But we can pretty well guess! The probability seems to be about 99 out of 100, at least for anybody who faces reality and thinks about it, that when you're dead you're exactly in the same position as you were before you were born. And that was hardly unpleasant. Does anybody feel terribly bad or have very unpleasant experiences before he or she was born?

Cl 45: No.

Co 46: No! So many people just won't face the reality that death is nothingness, utterly insensate nothingness; and most of the beliefs about it seem to be sheer horseshit, crap of the worst sort! Not that life before or after death couldn't exist. But the probability of there being any hereafter, and any hell, is virtually zero. But many people imagine self-defeatingly that something's going to happen to them after death. Did you ever see the play or film *Our Town*?

Cl 46: Yeah.

Co 47: And do you remember that in this Thornton Wilder play the main characters are dead, buried; and they're worrying all the time about what's happening to those they knew who are still living in Our Town? Now, a Martian, if such a person existed, would probably die laughing about that. Do you realize why a Martian would die laughing?

Cl 47: No.

Co 48: Because they're *dead*. You think of zero when you're dead. You certainly wouldn't worry, "Oh, look what I did or didn't do when I was alive!" or "I didn't win So-and-so when I lived, and now someone else is winning him. Isn't that awful!"

Cl 48: You notice that I said, in the form you gave me to fill out, that my religious beliefs were just average.

Co 49: Yes, I see that on the form.

Cl 49:   I think that I have to admit to myself that I happened to have been born and raised Catholic, and that's the only reason why I am a Catholic. I happen to believe though, if I'm honest, that my beliefs in religion are only as strong as they are because it's a crutch to me. I don't see any purpose in life as it stands, when I keep having these experiences that I call *awful.*

Co 50:   I know. And you also seem to be saying, "There *must* be a purpose in life." But why must there be? As far as we know, there's no real cosmic purpose. Nobody up there hates you or likes you. The universe doesn't give a damn about you, a single damn. And if you're wise, you'll make your own purpose, and mainly enjoy yourself as much as you can while you're still living. And if there is anything up there, it's pure gravy. But that's implausible, and you'd better not count on it. You'll be awfully disappointed when St. Peter isn't there! But we can get back to that later. If I can get you to believe one thing, you will stop feeling depressed and rarely feel depressed again for the rest of your life.

Cl 50:   That nothing is *awful?*

Co 51:   Yes, that nothing in the universe is awful! Because *awful* first means very unpleasant—and unpleasant things really exist. Or, at least, things we don't want and that we legitimately view as unpleasant exist. But it also means 100 percent unpleasant—and that practically never exists. The only thing close to it would be something like being tortured to death slowly. That would really be almost 100 percent unpleasant, and it's implausible that that will happen. And your losing your friend's love is not nearly that unpleasant. Maybe 70, 80, or 90 percent unpleasant—which is not *awful,* just damned unpleasant! Thirdly, *awful* means a magical thing, which really never exists. It means something that is *more than* unpleasant, that is at least 101 percent unpleasant. Don't you agree that when you say, "But that's awful!" you don't really mean it's 100 percent bad, but you actually mean that it's at least 101 percent?

Cl 51:   Yeah.

Co 52:   Well, can *anything* be 101 percent unpleasant?

Cl 52:   Not in reality.

Co 53:   Right. You can think something is more than unpleasant; but that's horseshit. Just like thinking that something can be 101 percent pleasant. It can only be exceptionally pleasant—but not more than pleasant!

Cl 53:   Why can't it be?

Co 54:   Well, because there isn't anything more than 100 percent. Logically— if you believe in the rules of logic. When I say "can't," incidentally, I mean almost impossible; for I have no way of proving any absolute "can'ts." There seems to be no absolute certainty. But according to all the normal rules of logic, how can pleasantness or unpleasantness amount to 101 percent?

Cl 54:   I guess if I knew logic I could appreciate it.

Co 55:   You may not know the formal rules of logic; but logic merely means things that normally follow each other. And if we rate pleasantness from 0 to 100— which seems to be the sane way to rate it—we obviously had better not go off the scale to 101 percent unpleasantness. That does not follow, and is therefore illogical. And *awful,* the way you use it, really means 101 percent unpleasant. And if you give up this concept that anything can be *that* bad, you'll probably change your entire outlook. *Awful,* again, means that something is so unpleasant—that it's so unpleasant for you to lose your friend's love—that it *shouldn't* be that way, *shouldn't* exist.

Cl 55:   Would you just repeat that again?

Co 56:   When you say that something like dying of torture or losing your friend's love, which is highly unpleasant, is *awful,* you really seem to mean that it *shouldn't* exist—*shouldn't* be the way it indubitably is. Every time you believe in awfulness, you invent this kind of *should.* Awful means that something *must* not exist because it's so unpleasant, and because it does exist as it *must* not, it's awful. Doesn't it really mean that? Well, is there anything that *should not* or *must not* exist in the universe?

Cl 56:   No.

Co 57:   Even if I tied you up now and began torturing you to death slowly, is there any reason why I *should not* do this?

Cl 57:   Because we're intelligent people.

Co 58:   No, that's why it's wrong for me to torture you. You see, you are again confusing two things. It's wrong for me to do a thing like that; but why *shouldn't* I, why *must* I not, act wrongly? Is the universe going to prevent me from acting wrongly?

Cl 58:   No.

Co 59:   You see, there are no absolutistic *shoulds* or *musts* in the world. We only invent them foolishly!

Cl 59:   But what kind of existence would we have if we did not try to distinguish between right and wrong?

Co 60:   No. I'm not saying we'd better not distinguish between right and wrong. You jumped, you see! It's wrong of me to torture you, and it would be better if I didn't. The reason it would be better is that you would suffer needlessly; and also you or others might be encouraged to torture me, and I don't want to live in a world where people torture each other easily. So as long as I agree to live in society, I agree that it's better for you and me if I don't torture you. Right?

Cl 60:   Yeah.

Co 61:   So we still have right and wrong without the *should.* The *should* says that what is better *must* exist. Now, *must* it?

Cl 61:   No.

Co 62:   Yes, that is horseshit! The Ten Commandments, which include some real nonsense along with sense, say, "Thou shalt not steal." Now the first part of this means that it would be preferable if you didn't steal—because you live in a social group, and if you steal and other people steal, too, chaos might result. This makes sense. But the second part says, "Because it would be better that you not steal, a law of the universe exists that says you *should* not, *must* not under any conditions whatever steal, and that you are utterly damnable if you do what you must not." Now is it likely that such a universal law truly exists?

Cl 62:   Well, it's a typical human law.

Co 63:   Well, think about it. The law is typical, all right; but it typically includes pernicious drivel. It doesn't merely say that it would be better not to steal.

It also says, "Jehovah said you absolutely must not steal," or "The universe commands that thou shalt not steal." Well, if Jehovah really said, "You absolutely must not steal" or the universe commanded this, you obviously *couldn't* steal; it would be impossible for you to do so.

Cl 63: I see what you mean.

Co 64: So we'd better change this commandment to "It would be better not to steal; for if you do, you and your social group get into needless trouble." Then we have morality. But morality doesn't need a *should* or a *must*. Those kinds of commands of the universe just do not exist; we invent them foolishly! And once we invent them, we tend to make ourselves anxious and depressed. Can you see that?

Cl 64: Yes, I think I'm beginning to see that.

(The therapist, seeing that the client has difficulty in distinguishing certain rational from irrational ideas, patiently and persistently tries to teach him how to do so. He especially tries to show him how, if he stays with such rational Beliefs (rB's) as "It would be very sad to be unloved by a lover, but it wouldn't be awful and I wouldn't be an utter failure," he would not only stop feeling depressed and anxious, but he would not lose motivation and become blasé, and would not give up moral thinking and acting. Typically, the client believes wrongly that if he thinks straight, he will become blasé and immoral—as a great many people believe wrongly. But the therapist takes some pains to show him why this is not true, and how he can be rational and still be highly emotional, motivated, and moral. The therapist also continues, quite strongly, to teach the client how to antiawfulize and how to accept the worst things that might happen to him, even death, without defining these things as terrible and unbearable. RET theory says that if the therapist succeeds in helping the client to accept himself and his life when the worst things occur, he will be able to live fairly happily with less obnoxious occurrences and will truly get himself to surrender most of his anxiety creation. Even though the client seems highly unsophisticated at times—does not seem to know any rules of logic, for example, and shies away from applying them to his life—the therapist persists in teaching him to become more sophisticated and to think things through for himself instead of giving up and accepting conventional self-defeating views of himself and of the world. The therapist often uses highly vigorous, strong language to emphasize his points and to get them across to a somewhat reluctant and difficult client.)

Co 65: Now just let me give you a simple little illustration to show you what feelings you're creating when things happen to you. Let us suppose that you leave this office a little while from now, and that you don't know how much money you have in your pocket. It could be a dollar or a hundred dollars; you just don't know. So you say to yourself, "I'd like, I'd prefer to have at least five dollars—because I might take a cab, go to the movies, eat, or buy something. I wish, I'd prefer to have at least five dollars. Not ten, not a hundred, not two hundred; but a minimum of five." That's all you're saying to yourself: "I wish I had at least five dollars in my pocket." Then you look in your pocket and you find only four. How would you feel?

Cl 65: Rotten, disappointed.

Co 66: Disappointed. Exactly. You wouldn't kill yourself? You wouldn't feel depressed?

Cl 66:   No.

Co 67:   O.K. Now forget about this first time and suppose you're going out again. But this time, still not knowing how much money you have in your pocket, you say to yourself, "I *must,* I absolutely *must* have at least five dollars—a guarantee of five dollars at all times." That's what you're telling yourself; that's your devout belief, "I must," and not "I'd like to." Then you look in your pocket and again find four. Now, how would you feel.

Cl 67:   Pretty bad.

Co 68:   Meaning, what?

Cl 68:   Meaning depressed, destroyed, anxious.

Co 69:   Because?

Cl 69:   Because I've convinced myself that I must have it.

Co 70:   Right! But, mind you, you would have, in each case, the same four dollars. The only thing that has changed is that you have made "I would like to" into "I must." So it wasn't the lack of a dollar that made you anxious, depressed, and destroyed in the second illustration. It was the *must*urbational demand, "I *have to* have at least five dollars." See?

Cl 70:   Yes, that seems quite clear. I do see.

Co 71:   Now let's go one step further, to the final part of our model. And this model, as far as I can see, shows what virtually all human disturbance is, and what really causes it directly. The third time you're about to go out into the street, and still don't know how much money you have in your pocket, you say to yourself exactly the same thing as the second time: "I *must,* I absolutely *must* have at least five dollars—a guarantee of five dollars at all times." Not a hundred dollars; not even ten; but a minimum of five. And you look in your pocket, and this time you find six. Now, how would you feel?

Cl 71:   I must have at least five at all times, and I find that I have six?

Co 72:   Right.

Cl 72:   I would feel better. In fact, elated.

Co 73:   Yes, you might well feel elated. But then, about five minutes later, you'd probably feel panicked. Do you know why you would probably feel panicked?

Cl 73:   Because it's still not what I said I must have.

Co 74:   Yes—*at all times.* You have six right now, and feel elated about that. But you could hardly stop wondering, within five minutes or so, "Suppose I spend two; suppose I lose two; or suppose I get robbed?" Wouldn't you?

Cl 74:   Yes, I definitely would.

Co 75:   Now you see what happens to you—or anyone else in the world— when you change a desire, a preference, into a must or a necessity? First, you're destroyed when you don't have what you think you must; and secondly, you're destroyed when you do. Because you're asking for a guarantee of having it at all times. And there seem to be no guarantees!

Cl 75:   Yes, I guess there aren't any.

Co 76:   Now do you see what you are doing with this fellow you have the relationship with? You're saying, first, that "You *must* love me right now, the way I want you to!" And when he doesn't seem to love you that way, you're telling yourself, secondly, "Isn't that awful! I can't stand it!" and you thereby become depressed. Moreover, even if he told you tomorrow—

Cl 76: That he loves me, right?

Co 77: Right. Even then you'd be anxious, wouldn't you?

Cl 77: I sure would. About his possibly not loving me the next day!

Co 78: That's exactly right.

Cl 78: It's sick!

Co 79: Yes, but what you call your sickness is simple, at least to explain: it's your *must.*

(As the therapist persists, seemingly against the odds of the client's crooked thinking and of his undeveloped ability to change such thinking, the therapis·˙ teaching and logic start paying off; the client begins to see not only that he has *musts* about his lover's not caring for him enough, and that they make him "sick," but also that no guarantees exist in the world, so that even if he regains the love he wants, he still will be anxious about retaining it. This is exactly what the therapist is trying to get him to see: that *musts* make people anxious under practically all conditions, and that therefore such musts had better be surrendered. This antimusturbational or antiawfulizing technique constitutes one of the main cores of RET; usually, only after the client starts understanding it and using it are the other main emotive and behavioral methods also employed. In fact, so far as behavioral modes of therapy are concerned, showing clients their *musts* and getting them to work against such notions is facilitated greatly by their seeing the *musts* and starting to give them up.)

Cl 79: My friend who referred me here told me that you do not go into the past at all. But isn't it important to know how this kind of thinking came about?

Co 80: No, because it is highly doubtful that the events of the past caused it. Humans seem to be born with strong tendencies to invent *shoulds, oughts,* and *musts* about what happens to them, including what happens early in their childhood. They *bring* their *musts* to their relationship with their parents. Hence, they disturb themselves as children; and, refusing to give up these *musts* later, they disturb themselves all their lives. Their parents and other early influences may of course help them exacerbate or exaggerate their *shoulds* and *musts;* but they by no means force them to adopt this kind of crooked thinking.

Cl 80: But how do you undo that kind of thinking?

Co 81: By realizing that you have it and then fighting it very strongly and persistently—questioning it, disputing it, challenging it. I used to be a psycho-analyst, and I saw that *mus*turbation starts in childhood, but is not really caused by childhood events. Virtually all humans are sorely afflicted with it. If they don't have it about needing the love of a guy, they have it about needing a woman, about money, or about something else. But they all seem to have it.

Cl 81: Is that *must* part of a value system that I have?

Co 82: Yes, a value system that you created largely because you're human. You don't need special things happening to you to create it about.

Cl 82: So how do I rearrange that system and make it sensible, rational?

Co 83: By giving up your most important *musts* a thousand times, until you no longer believe them.

Cl 83: So that I never feel anything is a *must*? Is that right?

Co 84:   Yes, but don't give up feeling that certain things are important. You can value some things, including the love of your lover, very much; but you try not to absolutely require, demand, need them. I think you are beginning to see this now!

Cl 84:   But what about love?

Co 85:   The same thing as anything else you value highly. Love is not a necessity; it's just a strong desire. You could love your friend or several other people. And you can sanely say to yourself, "Because I love him, I am determined to try to get him to love me, to be with me." So? That seems to be a good value; so you work hard to get it.

Cl 85:   As much as I know what you are saying, and as much as I'm depressed about not having him, I must be very honest with myself and say that many times when we are together my depression can be just as great.

Co 86:   Because when you are with him, what do you then tell yourself *must* be? Are you still asking for a guarantee?

Cl 86:   Yeah!

Co 87:   For what? How can you get a guarantee of love? Now, if you can get yourself to change your *musts* into *it would be better, but it doesn't have to be,*" then you will help yourself get what would be better, or you will see that you don't get it. And if you don't, that's tough shit! So you don't. There's no law that says you have to get what would be better, is there?

Cl 87:   No.

Co 88:   But there really is—in your nutty head! You're making up that law, that lie. You see? And that's where your anxiety and your depression come from. And that nutty law—"Whatever I really want, or at least anything very important I really want, I *must* have!"—will do you in. Right?

Cl 88:   Yeah.

Co 89:   Why *must* you?

Cl 89:   Well, I could say because those are my needs.

Co 90:   No, those are your *wants!* Humans don't have necessities—they just foolishly think they do! Because let's suppose that your lover drops dead. Must you be miserable for the rest of your life?

Cl 90:   No.

Co 91:   But if you really had a *need* for him, you'd have to be totally miserable forever without him.

Cl 91:   It would be a different kind of depression then. One is rejection and the other is—.

Co 92:   That's right. You would depress yourself if he drops dead, because then you could never have him, and you might view that as *awful.* But you would depress yourself more if he doesn't drop dead, and just leaves you. That's the funny part. If he rejects you but still loves you somewhat and is still alive, you'll depress yourself worse! That just shows how nutty humans behave! Because you're saying, "If he rejects me and is still alive, that makes me a shit; while if he's dead and I can't see him any more, I'm not a shit!" Aren't you?

Cl 92:   Yes, I can see that I am.

Co 93:   Well, how does it make you a shit if he rejects you?

Cl 93:   Because someone I feel right now I *must* have so badly tells me to go screw myself.

Co 94:   Right. But if you said to yourself, "This person I want badly doesn't like me enough; isn't it too bad. I have one set of traits and he likes another set more. Tough!" would you then put yourself down?

Cl 94:   No, I can see that I wouldn't. If I could say that.

Co 95:   But of course you can! You have that choice; you're just not making it.

Cl 95:   I think I have too many emotional feelings. But the way you propose seems to be too free of emotion.

Co 96:   No. You're ignoring the distinction I made before. Your emotional feelings are good, but you have two kinds of emotions: appropriate and inappropriate. Your appropriate emotions stem from "I want a relationship with my lover very much, and it's very regrettable and sad when I don't have it." That's one set of emotions. But you unfortunately have a second, inappropriate set: "I absolutely need a good relationship with him, and I'm dead, I'm destroyed without it!" Now you'd better work at giving up the second set but keep the first set of emotions, and you'll still be quite emotional. In fact, you'll probably then love more and love better—because you won't be afraid to love. This way, if you lose him, you're going to scare yourself shitless about getting involved again.

Cl 96:   Yeah, I know.

Co 97:   Yeah, you see? So how does that help you love, if you say, "I need So-and-so?" But if you tell yourself, "I want So-and-so, because I'll have a better life with him? But if I don't have So-and-so, I'll find someone else to love. Even if I were on a desert island, without anybody to love, I still could be a happy person." Then you'll love more. But if you foolishly tell yourself, "If I give up my depression, I wouldn't feel anything; and if I gave up my need for him, I couldn't love," that's nonsense. It's just the opposite!—if you give up your depression and your dire need to have him love you, you can love even more.

Cl 97:   But you said, "a happy person." Has anyone ever defined what a "happy person" is?

Co 98:   I would say that a happy person generally is a nonneedy person. That's what it really means. Actually, a "happy person" may be a bad term. It would probably be better if we used the term, a "nondepressed person" or a "nonanxious person." For a nondepressed person means one who does not need but actively wants very much. If you're nonanxious and nondepressed, you want things very much and try to get them; but you never really get all the things you want—and you definitely don't need what you don't get.

Cl 98:   It's interesting, because I did say on the form I filled out for your Institute that if I were not depressed, I probably would feel pretty good. It's just my depression that makes me feel so bad. And yet I know that I won't have utopia if I'm not depressed. I'll still miss some things.

Co 99:   Yes, you will. But if you were not depressed, you'd still have desires; and then you could spend the rest of your life trying to fulfill them. You wouldn't, of course, get them all fulfilled.

Cl 99:   Of course not.

Co 100:   But you'd get a lot of them fulfilled. You certainly seem to be bright and attractive enough. So if you stopped depressing yourself, you'd get many of your desires, because you'd keep working at getting them fulfilled. But those you don't get, you don't! You might want to be a millionaire, and make only a half-million. Too bad! But not *awful*. Just a pain in the ass. You are now defining the loss of your lover as a horror, a terror; and if we can get you to give up that definition, you'll be fine. Or, at least, you'll feel only sorry and disappointed if you lose his love. And if you feel that way, you won't get everything you want; but you'll probably get a lot more of what you want—and maybe even win him later. See?

Cl 100:   Yes. I'm really beginning to see. I want him but I don't need him. I really don't!

(The client begins to see some of the main points the therapist keeps making during the first session of therapy; but he keeps feeling afraid that he has to understand his past, that he has to feel depressed rather than just sorry if he never wins his lover again, that he will lose all feelings if he only wants and does not need, and that he may not be a "happy person" if he acts as rationally as the therapist is trying to help him act. The therapist persists in disputing his irrational Beliefs, and in showing him the difference between appropriate and inappropriate feelings of Consequences of these iB's. The therapist is hardly convinced, at the end of the session, that the client really has changed any of his basic ideas. But to his surprise, the client opens the second session as follows:)

Cl 101:   I saw what you were saying to me last time, but I must admit that I didn't believe much of it. I could see the advantages of thinking the way you were pointing out, but I really couldn't think, uh, feel that way. But I got the *New Guide to Rational Living,* as you told me to do at the end of the session, and I read nearly all of it. I also read the pamphlets you told the office to give me. They helped me see even more clearly the same things we went over during the session.

Co 101:   What things, exactly?

Cl 102:   Well, well, mainly that I do not need what I want and that it isn't the end of the world, or certainly the end of me as a person, if my lover doesn't want me. I went over those ideas in my head many times during the week, whenever I felt upset about him. At first, it only worked moderately well. But then I really began to believe it, that I don't need him, more and more, and then it really began to work. I learned during the week that I now have practically no chance with him, since he's quite hung up on this other guy. And I can't say I feel good about it. I feel really rotten at times. But it's what you call sorrow or sadness, not depression. I'm not putting myself down. I know I'll live a less happy life, at least right now, without him to care for me. But I'll still live! And I know, certainly after awhile, I'll be happy again. I know I will!

Co 102:   Fine! That really sounds good. Did you in any way act upon this set of rational beliefs this week?

Cl 103:   Well, well, I guess I did. Something. I learned that I have practically no chance with Jim because I decided to confront him about this. And I did. I was terribly afraid to know, really, how he felt. But I decided, especially after reading something in one of your pamphlets, that it would be much better if I took the pain of his refusing immediately instead of prolonging my agony by trying to avoid it. So I invited him to dinner, asked him exactly about his feelings and about his intentions with the other guy, the one he now goes with, and found out that he was really serious about him. I suspected this, but didn't really know. So I took the chance of actually finding out. I did. It was very painful at first, but not as bad as I would have suspected. Maybe because I had prepared myself so much in my head beforehand, by our session and by the reading. But I was very glad that I had forced the issue, taken the chance, and not prolonged the agony. Now I know I have virtually no chance of getting back with him. Not right now. And that's all right. Well, really not all right—you know what I mean. But I can take it. I'm determined to take it and not, as you saw, awfulize about it and put myself down. So I'm doing real good on that.

The client continued to do "real good," with some slipping back from time to time, in the course of the next few months that I saw him. I used various other RET methods with him during this period. Cognitively, I had him fill out a Rational Self Help Form (the one printed on p. 216 of this chapter) several times a week, especially when he felt the slightest depression about the breakup of his affair. He also did DIBS (Disputing Irrational Beliefs) at lease once a week (Ellis, 1974b). And he regularly did Referenting (Ellis, 1957a, 1977a), to bring to his attention the advantages and the disadvantages of the affair's ending, as well as the dis-advantages of continuing the relationship (in case it had gone on) and the advantages of forming new relationships.

Emotively, I fully accepted the client with his problems, including his fixed homosexuality. He knew that I was quite heterosexual, but he also came to feel strongly that I had no prejudice against him because of his homosexuality, and that I was not pushing him in a heterosexual direction. Once in awhile we discussed the possibility of his trying sex with a woman, and he almost did so on one occasion; but even though he felt that being gay was a distinct disadvantage in the social and business circles in which he traveled, he was helped to stop putting himself down, as he did somewhat at the beginning of therapy, for choosing that kind of life. He also was encouraged regularly to practice rational-emotive imagery (REI) (Maultsby, 1975; Maultsby & Ellis, 1974), to imagine himself not getting a suitable lover in the near future, to let himself feel acutely depressed about this, and to change his feel-ings of depression into mere feelings of disappointment and concern. This tech-nique he found particularly helpful in coming gradually to acceptance of the defeats that he met in trying to find a new relationship. Although my relationship with the client was never very strong, he did seem to feel that I was quite encouraging, and he tended to take on some of my optimism about his eventually building a good steady relationship with a homosexual partner.

Behaviorally, the client and I agreed on homework assignments right from the start, including reading assignments and filling out the Rational Self Help Form. More actively, he increased his social activity and made a determined effort, with my encouragement and checking, to look for other suitable partners. He at first tended to cop out in this respect and to withdraw into increased business activity and into sports. But he agreed to make an attempt to have at least one date with a potential partner every week, and to penalize himself by visiting one of his obnoxious relatives if he did not. With the help of this penalty, he usually carried out this assignment. He started with a few purely sexual encounters, but within a few weeks after therapy began he got into a minor affair. Just before therapy ended, he began what seemed to be a major affair with someone he had known for a long time previously, but with whom he had always avoided getting too close for fear of becoming too involved and hurt. He worked through some of his original fear in this respect, and persisted in the affair. When I spoke to him 15 months after therapy had ended, in the course of one of my regular Friday night public workshops at the Institute for Rational Living in New York City, he indicated that the affair was still going on, and that he and his lover were then living together and continuing to work out a better, though still somewhat difficult relationship.

All told, RET seemed to help this client get over his depression about the end of an affair, stop downing himself for being rejected, take the risks of becoming involved again, accept himself with his homosexuality more than he had ever done before, and keep working at maintaining another relationship. Although we spoke rarely about his business ventures during therapy (he ran his own interior design firm), he also reported that he began to feel much less hostility toward his fellow workers and toward his clients than he had felt previously, and that, even when business was not particularly good, he experienced considerably less anxiety about the present and future.

SUMMARY AND EVALUATION

I created rational-emotive therapy in the mid-1950s against great opposition from almost all the other popular schools of counseling at that time. However, it soon became an important part of a revolutionary movement in psychotherapy, one that increasingly stressed active-directive counseling, encounter-type confrontation, and cognitive-behavior therapy. Today it is one of the more popular forms of psychological treatment, as well as one of the main cores of the emotional self-help movement. It overlaps significantly with, and in some ways is practically synonymous with, cognitive restructuring, cognitive-behavior therapy, multimodal therapy, semantic therapy, philosophical therapy, and cognitive-humanistic counseling. In its less elegant or more general form, it has a distinct theoretical framework that is cognitive-behavioral; but it is quite eclectic in its treatment techniques and employs a large number of thinking, affective, and behavioristic methods. In its more elegant form, it emphasizes a clear-cut understanding, on the part of clients, of their basic irrational beliefs (particularly their absolutistic *shoulds* and *musts*), and in addition to using a wide range of cognitive, emotive, and behavioral techniques of counseling, it especially employs logical disputing, philosophic restructuring, semantic analysis, and teaching clients to use the scientific method to uproot their irrational beliefs and dysfunctional behaviors.

Because its hypotheses are stated in distinctly operational and testable ways, RET has already inspired a large number of outcome studies that use control groups to validate its efficacy; and almost all these studies have shown that groups of individuals who are treated with RET make significantly greater changes in personality adjustment and symptom removal than do control groups who are treated with no therapy or with other forms of counseling (DiGiuseppe, Miller, & Trexler, 1977; Smith & Glass, 1977; Murphy & Ellis, 1979). Literally hundreds of controlled experiments have also tested some of the main clinical and personality hypotheses of RET, and over 90 percent of these experiments substantiate these hypotheses (Ellis, 1977b). At the present time, therefore, impressive evidence exists to support both the clinical validity of RET and allied cognitive-behavior therapies and their popularity with the professional and general public.

Research in this area, however, is in most respects still in its formative stages. Many RET hypotheses, such as the advocacy of philosophic disputation in counseling and the view that people act in an emotionally disturbed fashion when they do not rate their "selves" or "personhood," but merely rate their traits, deeds, and performances in terms of how effective these are for joyous living, are yet to be tested substantially; a great deal more investigation in this connection seems called for. One of the basic tenets of RET is that whatever is most useful in counseling and psychotherapy had better be validated by scientific experimentation, and not merely subscribed to devoutly on the basis of brilliant clinical intuition or popular practice. For all its efficacy so far, RET had therefore better not rest on its laurels— instead, it had better encourage continual evaluation of its own and other counseling theories by the most rigorous scientific procedures available.

BIBLIOGRAPHY

In the following list of references, items preceded by an asterisk are particularly relevant to the theory and practice of rational-emotive therapy (RET). Most of these items are published or distributed by the Institute for Rational Living, Inc., 45 East 65th Street, New York, N.Y. 10021, Telephone (212) 535-0822. Anyone interested in such publications may obtain a price list of these and other relevant pamphlets, books, recordings, films, and other materials about RET from the Institute, and may also obtain a current brochure listing the talks, seminars, workshops, and other presentations in the area of human growth, rational living, and rational-emotive therapy that the Institute continues to sponsor.

Adler, A. *What life should mean to you.* New York: Blue Ribbon Books, 1931.

Adler, A. *Superiority and social interest.* (Ed. by H. L. Ansbacher & R. R. Ansbacher). Evanston, Ill.: Northwestern University Press, 1964.

Bandura, A. *Principles of behavior modification.* New York: Holt, Rinehart & Winston, 1969.

Bandura, A. *Social learning theory.* Palo Alto: Stanford University Press, 1977.

Beck, A. T. *Depression.* New York: Hoeber-Harper, 1967.

*Beck, A. T. *Cognitive therapy and the emotional disorders.* New York: International Universities Press, 1976.

Berkowitz, L. Experimental investigations of hostility catharsis. *Journal of Consulting and Clinical Psychology,* 1970, *35,* 2–7.

Berne, E. *Transactional analysis in psychotherapy.* New York: Grove Press, 1961.

Berne, E. *Games people play.* New York: Grove Press, 1964.

Bessai, J. *A factorial assessment of irrational beliefs.* Master's thesis, Cleveland State University, 1975.

*Blazier, D. C. *Poor me, poor marriage.* New York: Vantage Press, 1974.

Bone, H. Two proposed alternatives to psychoanalytic interpreting. In E. Hammer (Ed.), *Use of interpretation in treatment.* New York: Grune & Stratton, 1968.

Braaten, L. J. The main theories of "existentialism" from the viewpoint of a psychotherapist. *Mental Hygiene,* 1961, *45,* 10–17.

*Church, V. A. *Behavior, law and remedies.* Dubuque, Iowa: Kendall/Hunt, 1975.

Combs, A. W., & Snygg, D. *Individual behavior.* New York: Harper, 1961.

*Danysh, J. *Stop without quitting.* San Francisco: International Society for General Semantics, 1974.

Davison, G. C., & Neale, J. M. *Abnormal psychology: An experimental-clinical approach.* New York: Wiley, 1974.

*Diekstra, R. F. W., & Dassen, W. F. M. *Rationele therapie.* Amsterdam: Swets & Zietlinger, B. V., 1976.

*DiGiuseppe, R., Miller, N., & Trexler, L. Outcome studies of rational-emotive therapy. *Counseling Psychologist,* 1977, *7*(1), 64–72.

Dyer, W. Your erroneous zones. New York: Funk & Wagnall, and Avon, 1976.

Ellis, A. *The American sexual tragedy.* New York: Twayne Publishers, 1954 (Rev. ed., New York: Lyle Stuart and Grove Press, 1962).

*Ellis, A. *How to live with a "neurotic."* New York: Crown Publishers, 1957 (Rev. ed., New York: Crown Publishers, 1975). (a)

Ellis, A. Outcome of employing three techniques of psychotherapy. *Journal of Clinical Psychology.* 1957, *13,* 344–350. (b)

*Ellis, A. *Reason and emotion in psychotherapy.* New York: Lyle Stuart, 1962 (paperback edition, New York: Citadel, 1977).

Ellis, A. *Homosexuality.* New York: Lyle Stuart, 1965.

*Ellis, A. What really causes psychotherapeutic change? *Voices: The Art and Science of Psychotherapy.* 1968, *4,* 90–97 (reprinted, New York: Institute for Rational Living, 1968). (a)

*Ellis, A. *Homework report.* New York: Institute for Advanced Study in Rational Psychotherapy, 1968 (Rev. ed., *Rational self help form,* New York: Instidude for Advanced Study in Rational Psychotherapy, 1977). (b)

*Ellis, A. *The art and science of love.* New York: Lyle Stuart and Bantam Books, 1969. (a)

*Ellis, A. A weekend of rational encounter. In A. Burton (Ed.), *Encounter.* San Francisco: Jossey-Bass, 1969 (reprinted, *Rational Living,* 1970, *4*(2), 1–8). (b)

Ellis, A. A cognitive element in experiential and relationship psychotherapy. *Existential Psychiatry.* 1970, *7*(28), 35–52.

*Ellis, A. *Growth through reason.* Palo Alto: Science & Behavior Books and Hollywood Wilshire Books, 1971.

*Ellis, A. Psychotherapy and the value of a human being. In J. W. Davis (Ed.), *Value and valuation: Axiological studies in honor of Robert S. Hartman.* Knoxville: University of Tennessee Press, 1972 (reprinted, New York: Institute for Rational Living, 1972).

*Ellis, A. *Humanistic psychotherapy: The rational-emotive approach.* New York: Julian Press and McGraw Hill Paperbacks, 1973. (a)

*Ellis, A. *How to stubbornly refuse to be ashamed of anything* (cassette recording). New York: Institute for Rational Living, 1973. (b)

*Ellis, A. Are cognitive-behavior therapy and rational therapy synonymous? *Rational Living,* 1973, *8*(2), 8–11. (c)

*Ellis, A. Emotional education at the living school. In M. M. Ohlsen (Ed.), *Counseling children in groups.* New York: Holt, Rinehart & Winston, 1973 (reprinted, New York: Institute for Rational Living, 1973). (d)

*Ellis, A. Rational-emotive theory. In A. Burton (Ed.), *Operational theories of personality.* New York: Brunner/Mazel, 1974. (a)

*Ellis, A. *Disputing irrational beliefs (DIBS).* New York: Institute for Rational Living, 1974. (b)

*Ellis, A. *Sex and the liberated man.* New York: Lyle Stuart, 1976. (a)

*Ellis, A. The biological basis of human irrationality. *Journal of Individual Psychology,* 1976, *32,* 145–168 (reprinted, New York: Institute for Rational Living, 1976). (b)

*Ellis, A. *How to live with—and without—anger.* New York: Reader's Digest Press, 1977. (a)

*Ellis, A. Rational-emotive therapy: Research data that supports the clinical and personality hypotheses of RET and other modes of cognitive-behavior therapy. *Counseling Psychologist,* 1977, *7*(1), 5–42. (b)

*Ellis, A. RET as a personality theory, therapy approach, and philosophy of life. In E. Brand & J. L. Wolfe (Eds.), *Twenty years of rational therapy.* New York: Institute for Rational Living, 1977. (c)

 Ellis, A. Rejoinder: Elegant and inelegant RET. *Counseling Psychologist,* 1977, *7*(1), 73–82. (d)

*Ellis, A. *Fun as psychotherapy.* Paper read at American Psychological Association Convention, Washington, D.C.; September 3, 1976 (published in cassette form, New York: Institute for Rational Living, 1977). (e)

*Ellis, A. *A garland of rational songs.* New York: Institute for Rational Living, 1977 (also published in cassette form, New York: Institute for Rational Living, 1977). (f)

*Ellis, A. *Rational self help form.* New York: Institute for Rational Living, 1977. (g)

*Ellis, A. Toward a theory of personality. In R. Corsini (Ed.), *A sourcebook of personality theories.* Itasca, Ill.: Peacock, 1978. (a)

 Ellis, A. Rational-emotive therapy. In R. Corsini (Ed.), *Current psychotherapies* (2nd ed.). Itasca, Ill.: Peacock, 1978. (b)

 Ellis, A., & Abrahms, E. *Brief psychotherapy in medical and health practice.* New York: Springer, 1978.

*Ellis, A., & Grieger, R. *Handbook of rational-emotive therapy.* New York: Springer, 1977.

*Ellis, A., & Gullo, J. *Murder and assassination.* New York: Lyle Stuart, 1971.

*Ellis, A., & Harper, R. A. *A guide to successful marriage* (original title: *Creative marriage*). Hollywood: Wilshire Books, 1961.

*Ellis, A., & Harper, R. A. *A new guide to rational living* (original title: *A guide to rational living*). Englewood Cliffs, N.J.: Prentice-Hall, and Hollywood: Wilshire Books, 1975.

*Ellis, A., & Knaus, W. *Overcoming procrastination.* New York: Institute for Rational Living, 1977.

*Ellis, A., Wolfe, J. L., & Moseley, S. *How to raise an emotionally healthy, happy child* (original title: *How to prevent your child from becoming a neurotic adult*). Hollywood: Wilshire Books, 1972.

 Erikson, E. H. *Identity and the life cycle.* New York: International Universities Press, 1959.

 Eysenck, H. J. (Ed.). *Experiments in behavior therapy.* New York: Macmillan, 1964.

 Frankl, V. E. *Psychotherapy and existentialism.* New York: Simon & Schuster, 1968.

Freud, S. *Standard edition of the complete psychological works of Sigmund Freud.* London: Hogarth Press, 1965.

Garmezy, N. *Vulnerable and invulnerable children: Theory, research and intervention.* Washington, D.C.: American Psychological Association, 1975.

Geen, R. G., Stonner, D., & Hope, G. L. The facilitation of aggression: Evidence against the catharsis hypotheses. *Journal of Personality and Social Psychology,* 1975, *31,* 721–726.

*Goldfried, M., & Davison, G. *Clinical behavior therapy.* New York: Holt, Rinehart & Winston, 1976.

*Goldfried, M., & Merbaum, M. (Eds.). *Behavior change through self-control.* New York: Holt, Rinehart & Winston, 1973.

*Goodman, D., & Maultsby, M. C., Jr. *Emotional well-being through rational behavior training.* Springfield, Ill.: Charles C Thomas, 1974.

*Grossack, M. *You are not alone.* New York: New American Library, 1978.

Haley, J. *Strategies in psychotherapy.* New York: Grune & Stratton, 1963.

Hartman, R. S. *The measurement of value.* Carbondale, Ill: Southern Illinois University Press, 1967.

*Hauck, P. A. *Reason in pastoral counseling.* Philadelphia: Westminster Press, 1972.

*Hauck, P. A. *Overcoming depression.* Philadelphia: Westminster Press, 1973.

*Hauck, P. A. *Overcoming frustration and anger.* Philadelphia: Westminster Press, 1974.

*Hauck, P. A. *The rational management of children.* New York: Libra, 1967 (Rev. ed., New York: Libra, 1975).

Jacobsen, E. *You must relax.* New York: McGraw-Hill, 1942.

Jones, R. *A factored measure of Ellis' irrational belief system, with personality and maladjustment correlates.* Doctoral dissertation, Texas Technological University, 1968.

Kinsey, A. C., Pomeroy, W. B., & Martin, C. E. *Sexual behavior in the human male.* Philadelphia: Saunders, 1948.

*Kranzler, G. *You can change how you feel.* Eugene, Oregon: G. Kranzler, 1974.

Kurtz, P. *Exuberance.* New York and Buffalo: Prometheus Books, 1977.

*Lange, A., & Jakubowski, P. *Responsible assertive behavior.* Champaign, Ill.: Research Press, 1976.

*Lazarus, A. A. *Behavior therapy and beyond.* New York: McGraw-Hill, 1971.

*Lazarus, A. A. *Multimodal therapy.* New York: Springer, 1976.

*Lembo, J. *Help yourself.* Niles, Ill.: Argus, 1974.

*Lembo, J. *The counseling process: A rational behavioral approach.* New York: Libra, 1976.

Little, B. *So you want a problem!* Chicago: Compco, 1977.

*Low, A. A. *Mental health through will-training.* Boston: Christopher, 1952.

*Mahoney, M. J. *Cognition and behavior modification.* Cambridge, Mass.: Ballinger, 1974.

*Mahoney, M. J. Reflections on the cognitive learning trend in psychotherapy. *American Psychologist,* 1977, *32,* 5–14.

Maslow, A. *Toward a psychology of being.* Princeton: Van Nostrand, 1962.

Masters, W. H., & Johnson, V. E. *Human sexual response.* Boston: Little, Brown, 1966.

Masters, W. H., & Johnson, V. E. *Human sexual inadequacy.* Boston: Little, Brown, 1970.

*Maultsby, M. C., Jr. Systematic written homework in psychotherapy. *Psychotherapy: Theory, Research and Practice,* 1971, 8(3), 195–198. (a)

*Maultsby, M. C., Jr. Rational emotive imagery. *Rational Living,* 1971, *6*(1), 24–26. (b)

*Maultsby, M. C., Jr. *Help yourself to happiness.* New York: Institute for Rational Living, 1975.

*Maultsby, M. C., Jr., & Ellis, A. *Technique for using rational-emotive imagery.* New York: Institute for Rational Living, 1974.

*Maultsby, M. C., Jr., & Hendricks, A. *You and your emotions.* Lexington, Ky.: Rational Self-Help Aids, 1974.

May, R. *Existential psychology.* New York: Random House, 1961.

May, R. *Love and will.* New York: Norton, 1969.

May, R. The paradoxes of freedom. *Dawnpoint,* 1977, *1*(1), 26–35.

*McMullen, R., & Casey, B. *Talk sense to yourself!* Lakewood, Colo.: Jefferson County Mental Health Center, 1975.

*Meichenbaum, D. H. *Cognitive behavior modification.* New York: Plenum, 1977.

*Morris, K. T., & Kanitz, J. M. *Rational-emotive therapy.* Boston: Houghton Mifflin, 1975.

*Murphy, R., & Ellis, A. *A comprehensive bibliography of materials on rational-emotive therapy and cognitive-behavior therapy.* New York: Institute for Rational Living, 1979.

Perls, F. S. *Gestalt therapy verbatim.* Lafayette, Calif.: Real People Press, 1969.

Piaget, J. *The language and thought of the child.* New York: Humanities Press, 1952.

Piaget, J. *The moral judgment of the child.* Glencoe, Ill.: Free Press, 1954.

*Powell, J. *Fully human, fully alive.* Niles, Ill.: Argus, 1976.

*Raimy, V. *Misunderstandings of the self.* San Francisco: Jossey-Bass, 1975.

Rimm, D. C., & Masters, J. C. *Behavior therapy.* New York: Academic Press, 1974.

Rogers, C. R. *On becoming a person.* Boston: Houghton Mifflin, 1961.

Rogers, C. R. *Person centered psychology.* New York: Harper & Row, 1977.

Schultz, J. H., & Luthe, W. *Autogenic training.* New York: Grune & Stratton, 1967.

Schutz, W. *Joy.* New York: Grove Press, 1967.

Smith, M. L., & Glass, G. V. Meta-analysis of psychotherapy outcome studies. *American Psychologist,* 1977, *32,* 752–870.

Sullivan, H. S. *Conceptions of modern psychiatry.* Washington, D.C.: William Alanson White Foundation, 1947.

*Thoresen, E. *Learning to think: A rational approach.* Clearwater: Institute for Rational Living, Florida Branch, 1976.

*Tosi, D. J. *Youth: Toward personal growth.* Columbus, Ohio: Merrill, 1974.

Watzlawick, P., Beaven, J. H., & Jackson D. D. *Pragmatics of human communication.* New York: Norton, 1967.

Weekes, C. *Hope and help for your nerves.* New York: Hawthorn Books, 1969.

Weekes, C. *Peace from nervous suffering.* New York: Hawthorn Books, 1972.

Wolfe, J. L. *Short term effects of modeling/behavior rehearsal, modeling/behavior rehearsal plus rational therapy, and placebo.* Doctoral dissertation, New York University, 1975.

*Wolfe, J. L., & Brand, E. *Twenty years of rational therapy.* New York: Institute for Rational Living, 1977.

Wolfe, J. L. & Fodor, I. G. A cognitive-behavior approach to modifying assertive behavior in women. *Counseling Psychologist,* 1975, *5*(4), 45–52.

Wolpe, J. *The practice of behavior therapy.* New York: Pergamon, 1973.

*Young, H. Rational counseling primer. New York: Institute for Rational Living, 1974.

Zingle, H. W. *Therapy approach to counseling underachievers.* Doctoral dissertation, University of Alberta, 1965.

*Zingle, H. W., & Mallett, M. *A bibliography of RET materials, articles and theses.* Edmonton, Canada: University of Alberta, 1976.

Zubin, J., & Spring, B. Vulnerability—a new view of schizophrenia. *Journal of Abnormal Psychology,* 1977, *86,* 103–126.

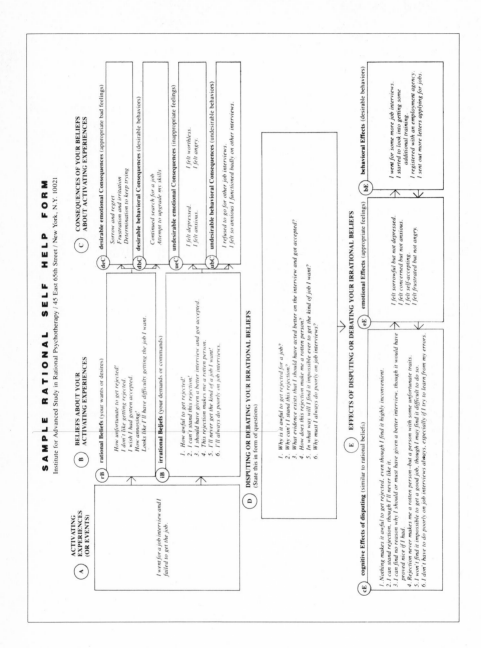

SAMPLE RATIONAL SELF HELP FORM

Institute for Advanced Study in Rational Psychotherapy / 45 East 65th Street / New York, N.Y. 10021

(A) ACTIVATING EXPERIENCES (OR EVENTS)

I went for a job interview and I failed to get the job.

(B) BELIEFS ABOUT YOUR ACTIVATING EXPERIENCES

(rB) rational Beliefs (your wants or desires)

How unfortunate to get rejected!
I don't like getting rejected.
I wish I had gotten accepted.
How annoying!
Looks like I'll have difficulty getting the job I want.

(iB) irrational Beliefs (your demands or commands)

1. *How awful to get rejected!*
2. *I can't stand this rejection!*
3. *I should have given a better interview and got accepted.*
4. *This rejection makes me a rotten person.*
5. *I'll never get the kind of a job I want!*
6. *I'll always do poorly on job interviews.*

(C) CONSEQUENCES OF YOUR BELIEFS ABOUT ACTIVATING EXPERIENCES

(deC) desirable emotional Consequences (appropriate bad feelings)

Sorrow and regret
Frustration and irritation
Determination to keep trying

(dbC) desirable behavioral Consequences (desirable behaviors)

Continued search for a job
Attempt to upgrade my skills

(ueC) undesirable emotional Consequences (inappropriate feelings)

I felt depressed.   *I felt worthless.*
I felt anxious.   *I felt angry.*

(ubC) undesirable behavioral Consequences (undesirable behaviors)

I refused to go for other job interviews.
I felt so anxious I functioned badly on other interviews.

(D) DISPUTING OR DEBATING YOUR IRRATIONAL BELIEFS
(State this in form of questions)

1. *Why is it awful to get rejected for a job?*
2. *Why can't I stand this rejection?*
3. *What evidence exists that I should have acted better on the interview and got accepted?*
4. *How does this rejection make me a rotten person?*
5. *In what way will I find it impossible ever to get the kind of job I want?*
6. *Why must I always do poorly on job interviews?*

(E) EFFECTS OF DISPUTING OR DEBATING YOUR IRRATIONAL BELIEFS

(cE) cognitive Effects of disputing (similar to rational beliefs)

1. *Nothing makes it awful to get rejected, even though I find it highly inconvenient.*
2. *I can stand rejection, though I'll never like it.*
3. *I can find no reason why I should or must have given a better interview, though it would have proved nice if I had.*
4. *Rejection never makes me a rotten person—but a person with some unfortunate traits.*
5. *I won't find it impossible to get a good job, though I may find it difficult to do so.*
6. *I don't have to do poorly on job interviews always, especially if I try to learn from my errors.*

(eE) emotional Effects (appropriate feelings)

I felt sorrowful but not depressed.
I felt concerned but not anxious.
I felt self-accepting.
I felt frustrated but not angry.

(bE) behavioral Effects (desirable behaviors)

I went for some more job interviews.
I started to look into getting some additional training.
I registered with an employment agency.
I sent out more letters applying for jobs.

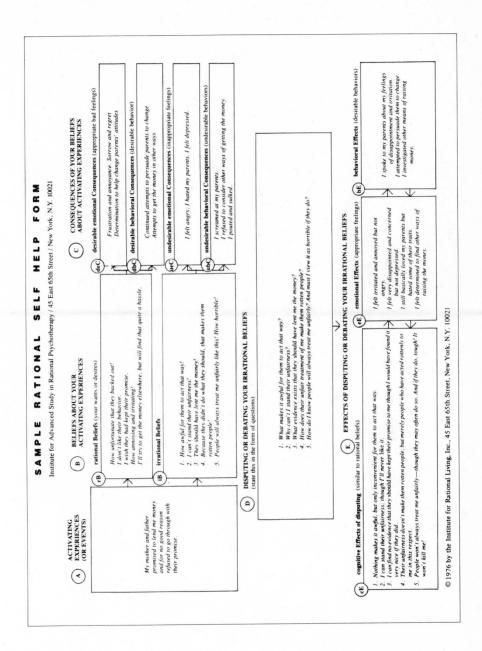

SAMPLE RATIONAL SELF HELP FORM

Institute for Advanced Study in Rational Psychotherapy / 45 East 65th Street / New York, N.Y. 10021

(A) ACTIVATING EXPERIENCES (OR EVENTS)

My mother and father promised to lend me money and for no good reason refused to go through with their promise.

(B) BELIEFS ABOUT YOUR ACTIVATING EXPERIENCES

(rB) **rational Beliefs** (your wants or desires)

How unfortunate that they backed out!
I don't like their behavior.
I wish they had kept their promise.
How annoying and irritating!
I'll try to get the money elsewhere, but will find that quite a hassle.

(iB) **irrational Beliefs**

1. How awful for them to act that way!
2. I can't stand their unfairness!
3. They should have lent me the money!
4. Because they didn't do what they should, that makes them rotten people!
5. People will always treat me unfairly like this! How horrible!

(C) CONSEQUENCES OF YOUR BELIEFS ABOUT ACTIVATING EXPERIENCES

(deC) **desirable emotional Consequences** (appropriate bad feelings)

Frustration and annoyance. Sorrow and regret
Determination to help change parents' attitudes

(dbC) **desirable behavioral Consequences** (desirable behavior)

Continued attempts to persuade parents to change
Attempts to get the money in other ways

(ueC) **undesirable emotional Consequences** (inappropriate feelings)

I felt angry: I hated my parents. I felt depressed.

(ubC) **undesirable behavioral Consequences** (undesirable behaviors)

I screamed at my parents.
I refused to consider other ways of getting the money.
I pouted and sulked.

(D) DISPUTING OR DEBATING YOUR IRRATIONAL BELIEFS

(state this in the form of questions)

1. What makes it awful for them to act that way?
2. Why can't I stand their unfairness?
3. What evidence exists that they should have lent me the money?
4. How does their unfair treatment of me make them rotten people?
5. How do I know people will always treat me unfairly? And must I view it as horrible if they do?

(E) EFFECTS OF DISPUTING OR DEBATING YOUR IRRATIONAL BELIEFS

(cE) **cognitive Effects of disputing** (similar to rational beliefs)

1. Nothing makes it awful, but only inconvenient for them to act that way.
2. I can stand their unfairness; though I'll never like it.
3. I can find no evidence that they should have kept their promise to me though I would have found it very nice if they did.
4. Their unfairness doesn't make them rotten people, but merely people who have acted rottenly to me in this respect.
5. People won't always treat me unfairly—though they may often do so. And if they do, tough! It won't kill me!

(eE) **emotional Effects** (appropriate feelings)

I felt irritated and annoyed but not angry.
I felt very disappointed and concerned but not depressed.
I still basically loved my parents but hated some of their traits.
I felt determined to find other ways of raising the money.

(bE) **behavioral Effects** (desirable behaviors)

I spoke to my parents about my feelings of disappointment and irritation.
I attempted to persuade them to change.
I investigated other means of raising money.

© 1976 by the Institute for Rational Living, Inc., 45 East 65th Street, New York, N.Y. 10021

RATIONAL SELF HELP FORM

Institute for Advanced Study in Rational Psychotherapy / 45 East 65th Street / New York, N.Y. 10021

INSTRUCTIONS. Please fill out the **ueC** section (undesirable emotional Consequences) and the **ubC** section (undesirable behavioral Consequences) **first.** Then fill out all the A-B-C-D-E's. PLEASE PRINT LEGIBLY. BE BRIEF!

(A) ACTIVATING EXPERIENCES (OR EVENTS)

(B) BELIEFS ABOUT YOUR ACTIVATING EXPERIENCES

(rB) rational Beliefs (your wants or desires)

(iB) irrational Beliefs (your demands or commands)

(C) CONSEQUENCES OF YOUR BELIEFS ABOUT ACTIVATING EXPERIENCES

(deC) desirable emotional Consequences (appropriate bad feelings)

(dbC) desirable behavioral Consequences (desirable behaviors)

(ueC) undesirable emotional Consequences (inappropriate feelings)

(ubC) undesirable behavioral Consequences (undesirable behaviors)

(D) DISPUTING OR DEBATING YOUR IRRATIONAL BELIEFS
(State this in the form of questions)

(E) EFFECTS OF DISPUTING OR DEBATING YOUR IRRATIONAL BELIEFS

(cE) cognitive Effects of disputing (similar to rational beliefs)

(eE) emotional Effects (appropriate feelings)

(bE) behavioral Effects (desirable behaviors)

1. FOLLOW-UP. What new GOALS would I now like to work on? ....

....

....

....

What specific ACTIONS would I now like to take? ....

....

....

2. How soon after feeling or noting your undesirable emotional CONSEQUENCES (ueC's) or your undesirable behavorial CONSEQUENCES (ubC's) of your irrational BELIEFS (iB's) did you look for these iB's and DISPUTE them? ....

....

....

How vigorously did you dispute them? ....

....

If you didn't dispute them, why did you not do so? ....

....

3. Specific HOMEWORK ASSIGNMENT(S) given you by your therapist, your group or yourself: ....

....

....

4. What did you actually do to carry out the assignment(s)? ....

....

5. How many times have you actually worked at your homework assignments during the past week? ....

....

6. How many times have you actually worked at DISPUTING your irrational BELIEFS during the past week? ....

....

7. Things you would now like to discuss with your therapist or group ....

....

....

Behavioral Views
of Counseling

N. Kenneth LaFleur

INTRODUCTION

Behavioral counseling is one approach to counseling.[1] It does not purport to have the qualities of theory as described in Chapter 1. The approach provides broad guidelines that demand specificity but that do not provide a "standard way or cookbook" for the practice of counseling. Within the behavioral approach, *counseling* is viewed as the systematic use of a variety of procedures by a counselor and client to effect changes that are relevant to mutually established goals that are based on achieving a resolution of the client's concerns (Thoresen, 1969a). "Behavioral counseling is a process of helping people to learn how to solve certain interpersonal, emotional, and decision problems" (Krumboltz & Thoresen, 1976, p. 2).

The use of the term *behavioral counseling* was first promoted publicly by John Krumboltz of Stanford University, during a presentation at the 1964 American Psychological Association Annual Convention in Los Angeles, California. In a later article that was based upon the APA paper, Krumboltz explained that the adjective *behavioral* was used to provide a constant reminder that a counselor's activity is focused upon changes in client behaviors (Krumboltz, 1965). What was termed by some as a "revolution" and by others as an "evolution" in counseling now had a public national forum through the activities of Krumboltz. The activities did not begin in 1964, but had begun to emerge in the 1950s.

The decade of the 1950s experienced counseling as a philosophy of life that was carried out through a relationship with a client in an interview setting. Counselors were adamant in their objections that, as a philosophy of life, counseling should not be examined with scientific rigor. The scientific methodology of observation and experimentation was considered inappropriate for the investigation

[1]In this chapter the term *counseling* is used as a synonym for *therapy*.

of counseling. A counselor-client relationship was the method of counseling and was the necessary and sufficient ingredient for providing help to clients. For practical and philosophic reasons, the relationship process components, which were conceptualized to be the heart of counseling, were not amenable to investigation. The counseling relationship was not considered to be scientific subject matter.

Psychodynamic and psychiatric approaches to client assessment and treatment techniques dominated the field of counseling in the 1940s and 1950s. Yates (1970) cites the growing dissatisfaction with these traditional approaches as emerging with force in the years immediately following World War II.

Differences between the traditional and emerging behavioral approaches were highlighted during a symposium with Carl Rogers and B. F. Skinner at the 1955 American Psychological Association Convention in Chicago, Illinois. The topic of the symposium was the control of human behavior. The essential concepts addressed were the use of scientific methodology, the role of the subjective self in human change, and the view of a philosophy of life. While not directed to the work of counselors, the 1955 debate of Rogers and Skinner served notice that several clear lines were being drawn between the existing traditional approaches of counseling and the developing behavioral approach.

Several other instances of a break from traditional approaches occurred during the 1950s. Dollard and Miller (1950) challenged psychodynamic views by using concepts of Hullian learning theory to describe psychodynamic therapy. Skinner (1953) criticized psychoanalytic procedures by using operant learning terminology to detail psychotherapeutic methods. Wolpe (1958) provided a bridge between the laboratory learning studies and clinical intervention in his publication, *Psychotherapy by Reciprocal Inhibition*. In his book, Wolpe described the acquisition and change processes for human behaviors in terms of learned responses. Wolpe posited an intervention strategy that was based upon expansions of Hullian learning theory to help clients inhibit, eliminate, or weaken debilitating responses. The works of Lazarus (1958) and Eysenck (1952) helped to close the gap between basic experimental learning laboratory research and theory and the application of the results of the learning studies to the conceptualization and treatment of human concerns. The 1950s provided the environment for a clash between two forces—the traditional psychiatric and psychodynamic approach and the emerging behavioral approach. O'Leary and Wilson (1975) suggest that this environment included a failure of existing procedures, and the availability of an alternate paradigm for conceptualizing the development and alleviation of human concerns.

The field of counseling experienced the effects of the debate during the 1960s. Michael and Meyerson (1962) called for the use of learning principles in an approach to counseling and guidance. It was the work of Krumboltz and his students at Stanford University that led the move away from the existing presuppositions and the intervention and research practices of counseling during the decade of the 1960s. In the field of counseling, Krumboltz must stand as the pioneer and prime motivator of the behavioral approach to counseling.

Articles written by Krumboltz (1964, 1965, 1966a) outlined the major features of a behavioral view of counseling as distinguished from the traditional approaches. Under the direction of Krumboltz, the 1965 Cubberley Conference at Stanford focused on the innovative experimental procedures that had been developed and used by counselors during the early 1960s. The conference provided four major addresses, informal sessions, and learning-based technique demonstrations by counselors. The major addresses by S. W. Bijou, J. D. Krumboltz, H. B. McDaniel, and E. J. Shoben, Jr. with a summary paper by C. G. Wrenn were published under the apt title *Revolution in Counseling: Implications of Behavioral Science* (Krumboltz, 1966b).

Thoresen (1966) provided impetus for the direct application of behavioral counseling to school counseling work by outlining the basic propositions of behavioral counseling and the application of these features with a high school student. Through this publication, two later publications by Thoresen (1969a, 1969b), a major review of behavioral counseling by Hosford (1969), and a text called *Behavioral Counseling: Cases and Techniques* (Krumboltz & Thoresen, 1969), Krumboltz and his students effectively defined the meaning and features of behavioral counseling. Repeatedly throughout these writings there is the proposition that the term "behavioral" is used as an adjective to promote a constant reminder that counselor activity should be focused on what clients are doing. In that sense, all counseling is behavioral.

Krumboltz and his associates were aided by corresponding developments in fields other than counseling during the decade of the 1960s. The expanding role of behavioral approaches in the clinical setting gave rise to, and prospered by, the increased publication of behaviorally oriented clinical research in the professional journals. The emergence of four major behavioral journals between 1963 and 1970 helped to establish the behavioral approach as a dominant force in the helping professions: *Behavior Research and Therapy*, *Journal of Applied Behavior Analysis*, *Behavior Therapy*, and *Journal of Behavior Therapy and Experimental Psychiatry*.

Several books also aided the foundation of the approach to helping others that was based upon the findings and concepts of the behavioral sciences. Bandura (1969), Eysenck (1960, 1964, 1966), Franks (1969), Goldstein, Heller, and Sechrist (1966), Kanfer and Phillips (1970), Ullman and Krasner (1965, 1969), Wolpe (1969), Wolpe and Lazarus (1966), and Yates (1970) were some of the writers who, through their books, provided evidence for a growing compilation of experimentally validated helping techniques. From small steps in the 1950s to large leaps in the 1960s, the behavioral approach became a force in the helping professions.

In the preface of their 1969 *Behavioral Counseling* book, Krumboltz and Thoresen stated their hope that in the future the adjective "behavioral" could be dropped. Largely because of their efforts and the corresponding work of allied professionals, the desire they expressed in 1969 had met with some degree of fulfillment by 1976. The recent publication of *Counseling Methods* (Krumboltz & Thoresen, 1976) did not require the use of the adjective. The revolution had come, and counseling had experienced an evolutionary stage that provided for continued growth based upon the principles of "behavioral" counseling. The main features of this behavioral approach are detailed in the next section.

MAJOR FEATURES

The behavioral view of counseling began with several major features that were outlined by Krumboltz (1965). Because the growth of behavioral counseling was fostered by a dissatisfaction with the predominant views of counseling in the 1950s, the main features are distinguishing factors—guidelines that make behavioral counseling distinct from the psychodynamic and psychiatric approaches. It should be noted that the same distinct features of behavioral counseling that were proposed by Krumboltz in the mid-1960s continue to be both the hallmarks and distinguishing features of the contemporary behavioral approach.

Educational Process

Counseling is an educational process. The focus in counseling is on helping the client to learn new actions in order to resolve concerns. As such, principles of learning, research reports examining the application of learning principles, and learning procedures that have been found effective in the behavioral sciences are used to form the basis for providing aid to clients. The activities of clients are the issues for counselor-client attention and are viewed initially by the counselor as being neutral. Client behaviors are judged not to be good or bad, well or sick, adaptive or maladaptive in and of themselves. The behaviors are viewed as behaviors that have been learned or as the absence of behaviors that either have not been learned or are not being performed by the client. Value judgments about behavior are made through societal forces and are dependent upon the context in which they occur. Clients are not seen as *basically* lazy, nonassertive, undecided, neurotic, nonactualized, or sick; rather, a client's actions are viewed as the central issue for counseling and as individually learned actions that the client uses in specified settings. Counselors help clients learn new ways to act. Counseling is an environment that is essentially educational, and the counseling process is an educational process.

Individually Tailored Techniques

Techniques in counseling are tailored to individual clients and to specific client concerns. The individuality of clients is a hallmark in the behavioral approach. Not all clients should experience the same technique. The same counseling technique should not be necessarily be employed in helping each individual client to resolve a variety of concerns. There is no standard counseling technique for all clients. Different clients and different concerns require the use of different helping strategies by different counselors. The methods of assessment, counseling goals, and techniques are tailored on an individual client basis. Client problems are the guide to the use of a specific technique, rather than the technique itself. Counseling is not locked into a counselor's office but often takes place in the environment where the client experiences the concern. Often the environment may *be* the client, and thus may be the focus of a counselor's change strategies (Thoresen & Hosford, 1973). If a client's actions are a result of a person-situation interaction, then attention to the client's environment and the use of techniques outside the counselor's office are imperative.

Experimental Methodology

Behavioral counseling employs an experimental methodology for the development of helping techniques. There is no encyclopedia of approved techniques for
counselors. The profession is a constantly changing one, and its health depends
upon the continual evaluation, development, refinement, and birth of "new" and
"old" helping activities. The counselor employs the experimental method in all
counseling activities. Thoresen (1969) has called for counselors to approach their
work as "applied behavioral scientists." Counseling is a complex activity, and
counselors should be questioning and examining their activities at all times. The
core of the behavioral approach is the experimental methodology with which each
helping activity for each client is examined (Yates, 1970). The experimental nature
of a helping agent's work is the cornerstone of the behavioral approach (Craighead, Kazdin, & Mahoney, 1976).

Scientific Methodology

The final distinguishing feature of behavioral counseling is the adoption of scientific methodology to guide the course of its activities. Counseling is a process
that is amenable to rigorous investigation. Counseling is scientific subject matter,
and testable statements can be made about the activity of counseling. Use of
systematic observation, quantification of data, and careful control and analysis
procedures are the methods for improving counseling. Replication, review, and
revision that are based upon relevant evidence are major features of scientific
methodology, and stand as a distinguishing feature of behavioral counseling.
Counseling effectiveness is determined by the application of scientific methodology to individual counseling activities.

Summary

There are several distinct features of behavioral counseling. Counseling is viewed
as an educational process in which effectiveness is judged in terms of how differently clients act as a result of counseling. The focus is on the client and on the
client's environment. Techniques are formulated to help individual clients act
differently. Guided by the counselor's creativity, by learning principles, and by the
client's learning history, techniques are tailored to fit an individual client. Working as applied behavioral scientists, counselors use experimental methodology
and treat counseling as scientific subject matter in order to develop their counseling skills.

DEVELOPMENT OF BEHAVIOR

Normality

Behavioral counseling does not distinguish client actions on an abnormal-normal
continuum. All client actions, whether labeled as abnormal or normal by some
judging agent, are learned behaviors, and the principles by which they are learned
are the same. Counselors help clients to achieve specific changes in their behaviors.

Hypothetical constructs of personality are not useful to counselors because they do not provide any aids in the development of techniques. Indeed, hypothetical constructs are often a deterrent to counseling when the counselor's job is to fit the client's concern into predetermined assessment and helping techniques. Traditional views of personality serve to provide counselors with a professional rhetoric that attracts attention away from the client's specific actions, which are the focal point of counseling.

Clients, their actions, and their environment comprise the life blood of counseling. Whether clients are labeled "abnormal" or "normal" is not crucial to what happens in counseling. Given the structure of personality development as a learning process, counselors must look to the learning literature both to understand and to help clients. Just as there is no standard counseling technique, there is no one learning theory that is applicable to describe clients and to provide the basis for technique development. Several theories of learning exist, and behavioral counselors use the constructs, principles, and research evidence of all learning models in their work with clients.

Conceptual Models

Mahoney and Thoresen (1974) have conceptualized client behaviors as occurring between two major events: antecedents and consequences. Antecedents precede the behavior, and consequences follow the behavior. There are functional relationships among all three of the events in the antecedent-behavior-consequence chain, antecedents that affect each event. Antecedent and consequence events influence what clients do, and control over either or both of these events will help clients to resolve their concerns. The role of antecedents and consequences and the domain of these events have been used to categorize various learning theories. Frequently used categories include classical conditioning, operant conditioning, and observational learning.

Classical Conditioning   Classical conditioning focuses upon the antecedents of behavior. It is also referred to as "respondent conditioning" because the antecedent event is a stimulus that, following the conditioning process, produces a response. The focus of classical conditioning is upon the stimuli or antecedents that elicit reflexive responses. The theory posits that, following the pairing of an unconditioned stimulus and a neutral stimulus, the presentation of the neutral stimulus will elicit the reflex response that occurred previously only when the unconditioned stimulus was present. The theory states that the process (see Figure 6-1) for new stimuli to gain the ability to elicit reflexive responses is classical conditioning. Classical (respondent) conditioning conceptualizes client behaviors as conditioned links between stimuli and responses. Once the link has been established through a pairing and conditioning process, the response is a conditioned reflexive action elicited by the presence of the conditioned stimulus. In classical conditioning, behavioral control is held by events that precede the behavior and have the power to elicit the behavior.

The classical conditioning theory of learning was fostered through the pio-

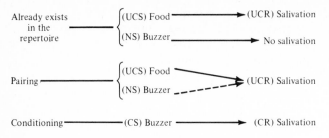

Figure 6-1   Illustration of classical conditioning principles.

neering work of a Russian scientist, I. P. Pavlov (1848–1936). Pavlov and his colleagues applied the experimental animal-laboratory classical conditioning research to the realm of psychiatric disorders. Through the work of Pavlov, the principles of classical conditioning as a learning paradigm were used to describe the development of client concerns. In a series of studies, Pavlov and his coworkers were able to demonstrate classical conditioning principles by teaching dogs to salivate when a bell or a light was presented in the absence of food aroma. The classical conditioning process for these studies is graphically displayed in Figure 6-1.

In the United States, J. B. Watson was influenced greatly by the work of Pavlov and accepted the classical conditioning theory as the sole explanation for all learning. In a classic report by Watson and Rayner (1920), the fright of a young boy in the presence of a loud noise and a white mouse was established as a fear of mice. The boy's fear of mice later generalized to other furry, shaggy items, such as a bearded mask, other animals, and several articles of clothing. Watson's work is noted for his extension of the classical conditioning theory of learning to all human behavior. While Pavlov used the theory to explain the development of psychiatric disorders, Watson expanded the explanation to include the broader spectrum of all human behavior.

Two other contributions of Watson are important in the development of classical conditioning theory and of the behavioral approach to counseling. First, the role of the environment in classical conditioning was stressed by Watson. Providing increased attention to the environmental variables enabled a greater application of the classical conditioning paradigm to behavior change. Secondly, it was Watson who held for the demands of the experimental nature of the behavioral approach and insisted on an adherence to scientific methodology. It is this latter contribution that causes many to identify Watson as the father of methodological behaviorism.

Variations of the classical conditioning theory of learning and its application to human behavior were proposed by Guthrie, Hull, and Dollard and Miller. All variations had as the learning basis the fact that client behaviors are the result of the presence of a conditioned stimulus that has preceded the behavior.

Operant Conditioning   Operant conditioning focuses upon the consequences of behavior. It is also referred to as "instrumental conditioning." The operant theory of learning states that the consequences of a response are the controlling factor that determines the frequency, rate, and intensity of the exhibited response in the future. Antecedent events are viewed as cues to provide information about the coming of consequences. In this sense, antecedents do not control the response, but rather set the stage for the response by providing predictive information about the consequences. Behaviors that influence the environment by generating consequences are termed *"operants."* Client behavior (operant) changes are the result of the alterations of consequences in the antecedent-response-consequence chain. A consequence gains control over the operant when presentation of the consequence is contingent upon the performance of the response. Systematic client behavior usually is not possible without the development of the response-consequence contingency relationship.

The architect of the operant or instrumental conditioning theory of learning is B. F. Skinner. It was Skinner (1938, 1953) who proposed the operant view as providing the basis for explaining how behavior is learned and the procedures for changing behavior. While not denying the influence of antecedents or stimuli in learning, Skinner believed that the most significant behaviors of people are operants, and that these behaviors are controlled by their consequences. Behavior consequences are termed either "reinforcers" or "punishers." In a series of controlled animal and human laboratory studies, Skinner developed his theory of learning in terms of operant conditioning. What started as a scheme by which Skinner organized his behavioral observations has evolved to Skinner's use of operant learning theory to explain individual and societal behaviors.

Social Learning   Social learning has also been referred to as imitative learning, observational learning, and modeling. Aided by the work of the classical and operant conditioning theorists who emphasize external controlling events, and by the efforts of the cognitive theorists who focus upon the role of internal events, integrated views of learning were formulated (Bandura, 1969; Kanfer & Phillips, 1970). Social learning theory is an integrated view, and it provides evidence that the internal and external environments of clients act in an interdependent fashion. Learning occurs as a result of the interdependent interactions of both environments.

Mischel (1977) has highlighted the effects of these interacting internal and external events upon human behavior. A social-cognitive conceptualization of personal learning is the result. Mischel (1973) has proposed examining behavior as it is affected by five interacting person variables: construction competencies (client knowledge and skills), encoding strategies and personal constructs (client classification schemes for observations), outcome expectancies, stimulus values, and self-regulatory systems and plans.

Bandura (1977) has placed emphasis upon internal events and upon the ways in which they affect an individual's interpretation of antecedent and consequence events. Values of the cues and consequences are determined by each individual in conjunction with external standards and feedback. Once clients receive the cues of the environment, they interpret these antecedent events in terms of a cognitive self-efficacy process. The four major sources of the self-efficacy process are performance accomplishments, vicarious experiences, verbal persuasion, and emotional arousal. These four sources of self-efficacy, in conjunction with situational characteristics, provide the expectancies that are important determinants of client learning. The expectancies can vary in terms of magnitude, generality, and strength. In a sense, a client's cognitive expectancies can be conceived as thoughts of personal mastery.

Similar to the control that self-efficacy presents for behavior change, the processes of internal consequence events also provide controlling powers. These internal consequence events are the performance, judgment standards, and self-evaluative reactions that clients make of their behaviors. The standards for these reactions are learned, and often have more controlling power over present and future client behavior than do external consequence events.

Largely through the research and writings of Bandura (1969, 1977), social learning theory developed the details of observational learning. Observational learning occurs when the behavior of a model is observed by an individual, without any performance of the modeled actions by the observer and without the provision of consequences for the absence of performance. Behavior is learned by observing the model through an internal coding of the modeled events. Bandura distinguishes between the acquisition and the performance of learned behaviors. While the learning of a behavior can be acquired solely through the observation of a model, performance of the modeled behavior is dependent upon a series of factors, including the response consequences of the model and/or observer, the characteristics of the model, and the number of models observed.

Summary   Behavioral counselors are constantly using experimental methods to devise tailored techniques for their clients. The techniques attend to the client's learning history, the change desired, and the counselor's skills. The basis for techniques is found in the theories and research of learning. The theories of classical or respondent conditioning, operant or instrumental conditioning, and modeling or observational learning provide solely or in consort a strong foundation for technique development. Behavioral counseling is not limited to these three theories, but to date most client change strategies have been based upon concepts from one or from a combination of the theories outlined. These concepts are detailed in the next section.

Learning Concepts

The actual components of the learning processes within the major theoretical models presented are vital to behavioral counselors. The component learning concepts provide a basis for understanding how clients have learned current behavior, and suggest technique strategies to help clients learn new behaviors or perform already-learned behaviors in a different fashion.

Reinforcement   The concept of reinforcement was developed mainly in terms of the operant conditioning theory. "Reinforcement" refers to the learning process where the presentation of a consequence following the performance of a response (behavior) results in an increase in the probability that the response will recur. The consequence events are the reinforcers if their presentation results in the increased probability.

There are two major categories of reinforcers: primary and secondary. *Primary reinforcers* are unconditioned consequence events, in that they have acquired reinforcing value without any special training. Typically, the primary reinforcers are consequences such as water, food, and other items that are vital to the existence of life. They have an automatic reinforcing value, provided that a need for life maintenance exists. If no need exists, they lose their reinforcing value. *Secondary reinforcers* are consequence events that have a reinforcing value as a result of conditioned learning experiences. Items such as praise, money, and attention are consequence events that have a learned reinforcing value, typically as a result of the fact that they have been presented initially in conjunction with a primary reinforcer. The value and classification of a consequence event as a secondary reinforcer are determined individually and depend upon the previous learning experiences of the client. It is also important to note that the reinforcing value of a particular consequence may vary among situations for the same client.

Consequent events that are used to reinforce or to increase the probability of the occurrence of a behavior may be characterized as either pleasurable or aversive items. Whether the reinforcing event is viewed as a pleasurable or aversive experience is also dependent upon the learning history of each individual client and may vary across situations with the same client. Attention may be a pleasurable experience for one client, and it may be aversive for another. The presentation of attention in one situation may be a pleasurable experience, and in another experience it may be aversive. The important concept is that both pleasurable and aversive events can have reinforcing value.

The presentation of a pleasurable event as a consequence is termed "positive reinforcement." The event is desired by the client and leads to increased or continued performance of the behavior by the client. "Negative reinforcement" refers to the removal of an aversive event. If the removal of an aversive consequence following the performance of a behavior leads to increased occurrence probability of the behavior, then the removal activity is called negative reinforcement.

Reinforcement can occur on either a continuous or an intermittent schedule. Generous and constant, continual presentation of reinforcers following the performance of a behavior is classified as a *continuous schedule*. Continuous reinforcement schedules are most helpful in the learning of a new behavior. The learning occurs rapidly, but is relatively weak in that it is easily extinguished when reinforcement ceases. *Intermittent schedules* are presentations of reinforcers that follow only selected performances of the target behavior. The selection may be based upon a *ratio schedule* that is determined by the number of responses performed. It can also be based upon an *interval schedule* when the amount of time between the performance and the presentation of the reinforcer is the determining factor. Learning new behaviors by using an intermittent schedule of reinforcement is a slower process than one employing continuous schedules. However, once the behavior is established, extinguishing the behavior is more difficult than it would be if the behavior had been taught solely through the use of a continuous schedule. To help clients learn quickly behaviors that will be firmly established, a process of first using continuous reinforcement and then transferring to intermittent schedules may be the most effective mode.

Counselors often use attention as a reinforcer in counseling. Providing attention to a client when client self-disclosure occurs, and not when client self-disclosure is absent, often increases the frequency of client self-disclosure. Helping teachers to provide attention to desired student behavior rather than only to undesired behavior will increase the desired actions by students. Reinforcement is used in a multitude of situations in counseling, with a resulting increase in the frequency of those client actions upon which the reinforcement is contingent.

Punishment   The presentation of a consequence that is viewed as aversive or the removal of a consequence event that is viewed as pleasant is the process of punishment. Punishment has taken place if the event decreases the occurrence probability of the behavior with which it is paired and which it follows. Punishment functionally produces the opposite effect of reinforcement. As with the guides for the use of reinforcement, punishment consequences are determined by the individual client's value for the event, and the same punishment event can vary across clients and across situations with the same client. The relationship between reinforcement and punishment, with presentation and removal modes, is displayed in Figure 6-2.

The usefulness of punishment is limited. Its effects are often brief in duration, and the behavior that is stopped temporarily often returns to a level that is higher than the one existing before punishment was used. Punishment also can produce long-term debilitating effects. Clients may continue to perform the target behavior outside the control arena of the punishing agent, which could actually have secondary reinforcing value. In most instances, techniques to help clients reduce or eliminate the performance of a behavior should utilize processes other than punishment.

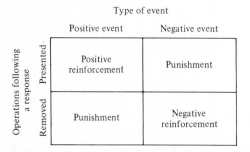

Figure 6-2   Illustration of operant conditioning principles based on event presentation or removal and event value.

Extinction   The termination of reinforcement for the performance of a response is termed *extinction*. It is the procedure in which a previous consequence event is no longer available following a response. The use of extinction assumes that previous reinforcement was available. Ignoring a response that has received attention following its performance is a form of extinction. If the attention was a reinforcing consequence that increased the probability of the occurrence of the response, then stopping the attention and presenting no consequence serves to decrease the performance.

Extinction procedures have been used in a variety of situations. Tantrums, client negative talk, persistent self-depreciating comments, social isolation, and various habitual actions are several of the client actions that have been altered through the use of extinction. Combining reinforcement with extinction is desirable. Such a combination encourages the development of desirable client actions to take the place of the removed behaviors.

Generalization   The effect of reinforcement may spread or generalize to situations or responses that are similar to those in which the learning occurred. Such as effect is termed *stimulus generalization*. The effect can be evidenced when a client performs assertively in one situation with reinforcing consequences, and later performs assertively in a similar situation. *Response generalization* occurs when the reinforcement of one response aids the performance of a similar or related response. Reinforcement for a client's use of a decision-making paradigm to help in postsecondary school selection may result in the client's use of the same paradigm in purchasing an automobile.

Discrimination   Reinforcing a response can have the effect of making the antecedent event a cue that provides information regarding the probability of reinforcement for the performance of the response. Often, responses are reinforced in some situations and not in others. When this occurs, the particular antecedents or situations take on informational or cue meanings for the client. The process is termed "differential reinforcement," and clients learn to discriminate under which antecedent conditions the performance of a behavior is likely to be reinforced. Once discrimination takes place to the point that a behavior is only performed under certain antecedent conditions, the process of *stimulus control* has been established for that behavior. Clients perform differently in similar but subtly different situations, as a result of their ability to discriminate and because of the fact that a stimulus control condition has been established. Often, clients are unable to make necessary situational discriminations, and the counselor's task is to help them learn discrimination skills so that stimulus control can be fostered.

Assertiveness-training counseling procedures often include the use of discrimination skills as part of the intervention process. Clients are aided in learning to identify various cues in different situations, cues that trigger their unassertive actions. An important part of this counseling procedure is for clients to use their acquired discrimination skills to help determine in which situations they will be assertive.

Shaping   The movement from simple to complex related terminal behaviors is the process of *shaping*. A gradual successive approximation procedure is often used to help a client learn a complex behavior. Taken in small steps, the behavior is learned by successive movements toward performing all components of the behavior in the desired environment. The concepts of reinforcement, discrimination, extinction, and generalization, which were discussed earlier, are used individually or in combination to help the shaping process.

Vicarious Processes   The effects of the concepts described as reinforcement, discrimination, extinction, generalization, and shaping can all be provided through observing the responses of others. These modeling effects are the products of vicarious learning processes. The capacity to teach new behaviors and to inhibit existing behaviors via a vicarious process reduces the cost and time constraints that are often imposed on counselors. Vicarious processes permit clients to observe the reinforcing consequences of a model's performance, with a resulting performance by the client. Much of what clients learn initially is through vicarious processes, and the use of modeling components provides for continued learning that is based upon these same procedures.

In one instance, a series of counseling procedures incorporating vicarious reinforcement techniques was used to help clients perform information-seeking actions. Clients listened to audiotaped descriptions of information-seeking actions that were provided by similar individuals. The descriptions included observations by the taped individual of the positive results of the various information-seeking actions. In these instances, the audiotapes provided vicarious reinforcement to the clients.

Summary   Behavioral counseling utilizes all the learning concepts derived from various learning theories, as well as the research examining theories. The effect of employing the learning concepts in counseling is the formulation of a process to understand and help clients. An analysis and understanding of the external *and* internal events that have an effect on the learning and behavior-maintenance actions of the client is critical in behavioral counseling. A knowledge of the effect of the internal and external antecedent and consequence events, in terms of the learning concepts summarized, will aid the counselor and client in developing effective counseling strategies to help the client perform differently.

GOALS OF COUNSELING

The goals of counseling in the behavioral framework are dependent upon the client's concern. As has been suggested in previous sections, behavioral counseling has the individual as its focus. Behavioral counseling goals are individualized for each client—no goals exist that would necessarily be the most appropriate counseling goals for all clients. Unlike other counseling approaches, behavioral counseling does not accept the uniformity concept as related to counseling goals.

The definition of behavioral counseling underscores this individuality of counseling goals. Recall that no "standard way" is provided for counseling, and in the same context there is no "standard goal." What occurs in counseling is determined in part by goals that are mutually established by the counselor and the client. These goals are specified in terms of what the client will do, where the actions will occur, and how well the actions will be performed.

Goals in behavioral counseling serve many functions. As Bandura states:

> Behaviorally defined objectives not only provide guidance in selecting appropriate procedures, but they serve an important evaluative function as well. When desired outcomes are designated in observable and measurable terms, it becomes readily apparent when the methods have succeeded, when they have failed, and when they need further development to increase their potency. This self-corrective feature is a safeguard against perpetuation of ineffective approaches, which are difficult to retire if the changes they are supposed to produce remain ambiguous (1969, p. 74).

The goal criteria that are used in behavioral counseling facilitate the development of appropriate techniques, enable constant evaluation of the efficacy of utilized techniques, and provide the necessary effectiveness data for evaluating the work of the counselor.

The details of goal setting in counseling are provided in the next section. The purpose and goals of counseling as summarized in this portion of the chapter are presented to indicate that the goals are congruent with the basic features of behavioral counseling. Goals of counseling are tailored to individual clients in the same way that counseling techniques are tailored to individuals.

PROCESS OF COUNSELING

Attempts to identify basic stages or steps in the counseling process have resulted in a number of different divisions (Cormier & Cormier, 1975; Gottman & Lieblum, 1974; Hosford & deVisser, 1974; Stewart, Winborn, Johnson, Burks, & Engelkes, 1978; Watson & Tharp, 1977). The rationale for identifying the steps of the process was founded on the need to provide a framework for the teaching of counseling skills. The framework also enabled an examination of the counselor-client process variables at each step and the effects of these variables on client learning during counseling. Behavioral counseling conceptualizes the counselor-client process variables as part of the learning environment and therefore as vital to counseling effectiveness.

While the devised frameworks have a varied number of steps, four basic stages are held in common: assessment, goal setting, technique implementation, and evaluation-termination. Behavioral counseling considers each of the four steps as being necessary and as being related to one another. Each stage is concerned with internal and external factors and with the interdependent reciprocal relationship between these covert and overt events.

Assessment

The purpose of assessment in behavioral counseling is to determine what the client is doing presently. Overt activities, feelings, values, and thoughts of clients at the present time are the items at issue during the assessment phase. Counselors use a wide range of activities to determine and help clients make a current "status report." Assessment focuses upon client strengths as well as upon weaknesses. The specifics of client activities in terms of their response, temporal, and situational properties must be determined. Behavioral counseling requires assessment of what the client is doing presently, how well or poorly the activities are being performed (frequency, duration, intensity), when they are performed, and in which situations the client completes the activities. The assessment phase is necessary to gather information that is required to construct a model of client concerns (Stewart, Winborn, Johnson, Burks, & Engelkes, 1978) and to guide the development of appropriate techniques to resolve the client's concerns. The assessment information centers around the specifics of what clients are doing and the antecedent and consequence factors that control their actions.

Kanfer and Saslow (1969) have suggested seven topical areas for assessment information. In summary form, the seven areas are:

1 Analysis of the problem behaviors presented by the client. The focus of the analysis is on specific behaviors that are described by the client as being excessive or deficient. Behavioral assets of the client are also analyzed, so that those strengths can be used, where possible, to help in the learning of new behaviors.

2 Analysis of the situations in which the problem behaviors occur. The analysis attempts to identify the antecedent and consequence events that are associated with the problem activity. Changes in the situations providing successful counseling (behavior is not problematic) should be explored with the client.

3 Motivational analysis. The reinforcing events in the client's living are identified. Utilization of some of the events to aid new learning is explored, as well as the possibility of a reduction of the present reinforcing events if new learning occurs.

4 Analysis of developmental history. Information is gathered regarding biological, social, and behavioral changes of the client. The client's view of the effects of changes in one area on the other two areas is of interest. Also, clients' perceptions regarding the amount of personal control they have had in such changes should be explored.

5 Analysis of self-control. The degree of client control over the presenting problem behaviors is assessed, both in terms of how the control is exercised and in terms of the events that delimit the success of self-control.

6 Analysis of social relationships. The significant others in the client's life are identified, as well as the relationship of these people with the client. The methods used to maintain these relationships are analyzed.

7 Analysis of the social-cultural-physical environment. This analysis is in terms of the norms and restrictions of the environment.

The information gathered in each of these seven areas is used to provide a better understanding of the client problem and to aid in the formulation of appropriate counseling goals and techniques to resolve the client's concern.

Behavioral counseling is not based upon the notion that the ways in which clients act are the result of some underlying problem. Behaviors are not viewed as symptoms. Psychological diagnostic tests are not primary tools of assessment for behavioral counselors. Information is gathered from data provided by the client and possibly by others. The information is taken from interviews and questionnaires, survey and schedule responses, client records, rating scales, and direct observations of the client when performing the problem behaviors. There is no set handbook of approved information-gathering techniques. Often, counselors and clients become creative and formulate individually tailored techniques to gather assessment information. It is important to remember that the client can be an effective data collector, and that often the act of collecting data can help a client to resolve that concern. Mahoney and Thoresen (1974) and Watson and Tharp (1977) have presented excellent suggestions and examples for client data collection methods. Whatever methods are devised and utilized, the main point to be kept in mind is that descriptions of the problem behavior in terms of its response level and temporal-situational characteristics are the goal of assessment in behavioral counseling.

Goal Setting

Based upon the information collected and analyzed in the assessment phase, the counselor and client set mutually acceptable goals for counseling. Goals are important in behavioral counseling because they direct the learning activity. The goals establish targets for the actions of the counselor and of the client in counseling. Often, goals serve to motivate clients to achieve changes in their behavior, in addition to providing guides for technique choice and/or formulation.

The process of goal setting is helpful because it provides the counselor with evaluative feedback related to the accuracy of the assessment analyses. Stewart, Winborn, Johnson, Burks, and Engelkes (1978) suggest that the goal-setting phase is composed of three steps: (1) helping clients to view concerns in terms of desired and attainable goals; (2) considering a client's goal in terms of possible situational constraints, and in terms of developing an attainable and measurable learning objective; and (3) breaking down the objective into subobjectives and arranging these intermediate objectives into an appropriate sequence.

Krumboltz (1966) has suggested that goals in behavioral counseling must meet three criteria: (1) the goal must be desired by the client, (2) the counselor must be willing to help the client attain the goal, and (3) it must be possible to assess the extent of goal achievement. To meet these criteria, the goals must be stated in terms of specific actions that will be performed by the client, the level of performance desired, and the conditions under which the performance will occur. Goals and objectives are to be in the form of client behaviors. Unless the goal is for the client to make a promise to perform, the goals and objectives must be stated by the client in terms of behavioral performance. The goals must not be in terms of the consequences received for the performance, but in terms of the performance necessary to receive the consequences.

Establishing goals is not an easy task. Behavioral counselors use a variety of skills to aid clients in the goal-setting phase. Several possible goal-setting difficulties and suggested counselor skills to help overcome the difficulties have been proposed by Krumboltz and Thoresen (1976). Their propositions may be summarized as follows:

1 The problem is the behavior of another party. In most instances, the counselor must view the person presenting the problem as being the client. The client then has several choices: to help the other party change, to learn to "live with" the other's behavior, or to withdraw from it.

2 The problem is expressed as a feeling. Counselors can help clients to learn and perform activities that are incompatible with the problem feeling.

3 The problem is the absence of a goal. Clients can explore the goals of others and the ways in which they were established. Identifying alternative goals and beginning initial ownership of one or more of them may lead to complete ownership of that goal or to the development of the client's own goal.

4 The problem is that the desired goal is undesirable. Counselors can help the client to evaluate the possible consequences that would result from achieving the goal and to weigh the opinions of important people concerning the client's choice of a goal. The responsibility for the choice is the client's. The counselor's responsibility is to aid the client in the decision-making process and to make a personal decision whether to help the client achieve the "undesirable" goal.

5 The problem is that the client does not know that the behavior is inappropriate. Clients can learn "investigative" techniques to gather information from the environment.

6 The problem is choice conflict. A "brainstorming" activity can be helpful to uncover hidden alternatives for choice that are not conflictual. Once all alternatives have been discovered, clients can engage in activities that are similar to a feasibility study. The range of decision-making skills must be performed by the client.

7 The problem is a vested interest in not identifying any problem. Clients with such a problem can be listened to, can be aided in making friends who will listen, or can be dismissed. It is the counselor's decision whether the time and interest in listening to the client are available.

The importance of goals in behavioral counseling cannot be denied. Counselors must use all their resource skills to help clients establish goals.

As the process of determining and establishing goals progresses and is concluded, counselors must make decisions that are related to those goals. Counselors must decide whether they will help clients work toward achieving the goals. Krumboltz (1965) has suggested that the three limitations counselors experience are in terms of counselor interest, counselor competency, and ethics. Behavioral counseling goals must be mutually agreed upon by the counselor and the client. Counselors and clients must agree to focus their energies and resources upon achieving the attainment of the established goals. As counseling progresses through the stages that lead to termination, the goals may be altered and new goals established. At each alteration and establishment, the altered goal must receive the mutual acceptance of the counselor and the client.

Technique Implementation

Following the establishment of mutually acceptable counseling goals, the counselor and client must decide what are the best learning strategies or counseling techniques to implement in order to help the client achieve the desired behavior change. Behavioral counselors discuss or "brainstorm" with clients concerning possible alternative techniques to be used. As previously stated, the techniques utilized are tailored to the specific client goal and are based upon the information gathered during the assessment and goal-setting phases. The process of devising counseling techniques is focused upon the current internal and external environmental factors that affect and maintain the client's actions. The intent is to construct and implement counseling techniques that will help the client change behavior within the environments where the behavior is manifested and the change is desired. Thus, counseling techniques are often constructed for implementation outside the counselor's office. Some counselors have argued convincingly that the environment should *be* the counselor's "office."

Multiple methods of learning are utilized in behavioral counseling. The traditional semantic counseling strategies are not the limits for helping clients. People learn via methods other than words. The techniques implemented may be constructed as a "multimedia" event. The media that are chosen to facilitate client learning are based upon the research investigations of media use in learning and upon the most effective learning strategies used by the client in other settings. Counseling may focus upon helping clients to learn more effective learning methods that could be used in a behavior change strategy.

Often, the changes that clients desire involve complex behaviors. This is not to deny the presence of "simple" behavior changes as being appropriate for counseling, but to posit the fact that behavioral counseling deals with complex client behaviors. Behavioral counseling is often more than the reduction of a behavior to a simple goal, and then picking a rudimentary learning technique to help the client attain the goal. An acknowledgment of the complexity of many client behaviors requires the behavioral counselor to be creative in devising the counseling techniques with each client. Most counseling strategies employ several learning concepts in different variations and combinations.

The use of counseling techniques that are based upon multiple learning concepts makes it difficult to categorize the techniques devised to date in terms of the concepts utilized. An emerging categorization system utilizes the client's presenting problem or the counseling goal as the major classification basis. Krumboltz and Thoresen (1976) have categorized techniques according to the following broad counseling goal areas: altering maladaptive behavior (behavioral deficits, behavioral excesses, inappropriate behavior, fears and anxieties, physical problems), decision making, and prevention. Gottman and Lieblum (1974) use the categories of response decrement, response increment, response acquisition, and cognitive restructuring. Stewart, et al. (1978) describe techniques in three broad categories as follows: helping clients learn new responses, motivating clients for behavior change, and helping clients become self-directed. Craighead, Kazdin, and Mahoney (1976), Leitenberg (1976), and O'Leary and Wilson (1975) also utilize client problems as the organizational scheme to present the learning concepts used in a variety of techniques. In each instance, multiple learning concepts are used in a variety of combinations to tailor-make counseling techniques appropriate for diverse counseling goals that fit within each of the broad categories.

Techniques focusing on individualized client learning are the goal of the behavioral counselor. Constructing the best technique aids the counselor's effectiveness in helping the client. Counselor work can also produce decreased effectiveness. Some of the counseling activities which would increase the chances of failure have been suggested by Gottman and Lieblum (1974) and Haley (1969). In summary, these authors warn against:

1 Insisting that the client's presenting problem is only a symptom of a "deeper" problem.
2 Refusing to construct techniques that would be focused upon changing the behaviors thought by the *client* to be the target.
3 Confusing diagnosis and technique implementation.
4 Emphasizing a single "best" method for all problems and all clients, and suggesting that a client who does not change by means of this approach is "unsuitable for counseling" or cannot be changed "by means of counseling."
5 Possessing an untestable theory of behavior change.
6 Insisting that "real" change can occur only after years of therapy.
7 Ignoring the real world in which clients live, and in which their problems exist.
8 Refusing to define counseling goals in specific terms that can be understood by the client and are understandable to others.
9 Avoiding an evaluation of counseling and a follow-up of clients to assess the effectiveness of counseling.

Effectiveness in counseling can be increased when counselors avoid these pitfalls and concentrate on the creative, sensitive activity of developing individualized techniques that are focused upon specific counseling goals.

Evaluation-Termination

Evaluation in behavioral counseling is a constant process, rather than one that occurs only at the end of counseling. The evaluation is made in terms of what the client is doing. The specific client actions that form the basis for evaluation are detailed in the goal statements for each client. These client behaviors are used to evaluate the effectiveness of the counselor and the effectiveness of the particular techniques being utilized. Evaluation must be an ongoing process to enable the monitoring of the technique implementation. Behavioral counselors do not assume that once a technique has been devised and implemented, there will be no "adjustments" or possible abandonment of the technique. The evaluation phase examines whether the technique is *working*, as well as whether it *worked*. Evaluation providing information that the utilization of a technique is not productive in helping a client to change a target behavior is used to change the technique. Behavioral counseling is not tied to any specific techniques or set of techniques, and the experimental characteristic of behavioral counseling includes the counseling process activity with each individual client. The methods of evaluation that facilitate the ongoing examination of counseling activity have been detailed by Gottman and Lieblum (1974), Hersen and Barlow (1976), Kratochwill (1978), and Thoresen (1978). Thoresen and Hosford (1973) have termed this procedure the intensive examination of the individual client.

Termination is more than just a "stopping" of counseling. It is a phase of counseling that includes:

1 Examination of what the client is doing currently, relative to the counseling goal behaviors and stated levels of behavior
2 Exploration of possible additional counseling needs
3 Helping the client to transfer what was learned in counseling to other behaviors
4 Providing an avenue for continued monitoring of client behaviors

Behavioral counseling encourages the view that counseling termination is a phase focused on the transfer of the learning process to other client behaviors, and on the ongoing nature of behavioral change. What happens in counseling is not a series of isolated events. The activities of counseling help clients to learn new methods of living that are applicable to their activities after formal counseling has ceased.

ILLUSTRATIVE TECHNIQUES

Behavioral counseling does not have a set of "approved" techniques. A variety of techniques is used to help clients achieve the desired behavior changes. The techniques are based upon learning concepts and are constantly being used and revised in an experimental method to examine the effectiveness for specific clients and for different goals. Often, the techniques are based upon several or a combination of learning concepts and result in a technique "package." At all times, a technique or "package" is considered tentative and does not become "the way" to help clients. Counselors, clients, and counseling goals differ, and the task for behavioral counselors is to devise the most appropriate "package" for the individual client and to examine its effectiveness.

Four technique "packages" are presented below. They represent general behavioral techniques that have been utilized with effective results. The procedures are not "etched in stone," but continue to be examined and revised by behavioral counselors. All procedures have been used in group situations, as well as during individual counseling.

Systematic Desensitization

Wolpe (1958) was one of the first to use the systematic desensitization procedure in the therapeutic setting. The procedure has been used with a variety of anxiety-related behaviors, fears, and phobic reactions. During its development, systematic desensitization was based upon the theories of classical conditioning. Wolpe considered the client anxiety response to be one that was learned and maintained via the classical model. To help clients eliminate the anxiety response, Wolpe helped them learn new responses to the stimuli that elicited the anxiety. As conceptualized by Wolpe, new responses could be learned through the process of reciprocal inhibition. *Reciprocal inhibition* is a counterconditioning procedure in which an incompatible behavior is paired with the anxiety-producing stimulus. The pairing is systematic and graduated, until the anxiety is no longer elicited by the stimulus, but rather the "antagonistic" or incompatible response is elicited instead. The basis for the procedure is the idea that two competing antagonistic responses cannot occur at the same time. As an incompatible response for anxiety, Wolpe used muscle relaxation.

The systematic desensitization procedure consists of the following three steps:

1 Clients are trained to relax. Relaxation is viewed as a skill, and the training is an educational endeavor. The most widely used approach helps clients to perform deep muscle relaxation. The methods for relaxation can be taught by the counselor or through the use of audiotapes or written materials. Other relaxation methods have been used, some of which permit the client to relax at the same level as deep muscle relaxation but can be learned more efficiently (Benson, 1975). The important point is for clients to be trained to perform, at a high level, a behavior that is incompatible with anxiety.

2 Clients construct a hierarchy of stimulus situations in which they experience the anxiety. The counselor helps the client to identify and arrange the situations in a graduated order from lowest to highest anxiety experienced. Ten to twenty such items should be identified and ordered. The ordering should be accomplished so that the spacing, in terms of anxiety experienced, is equal between the events listed. Marquis, Morgan, and Piaget (1973) have detailed the methods of rank-ordering, subjective units of disturbance scaling, equal-appearing intervals, and just-noticeable differences used in hierarchy construction. The most widely used method is the subjective units of disturbance scaling (suds), in which each item of the hierarchy is placed on a scale from 0 to 100 according to the amount of anxiety experienced (Wolpe & Lazarus, 1966). As originally conceptualized, the hierarchy was constructed to include gradations of the anxiety associated with one situation. The use of a hierarchy to include gradations of anxiety experienced in multiple situations has been proposed by Goldfried (1971). Illustrative examples of both types of hierarchies are presented in Table 6-1. In

Table 6-1   Illustrations of Hierarchies Established in the Initial Stages of Systematic Desensitization (Low to High Values)

Theme-based	Situation-based
Enrolling in a speech class	Conversing with a stranger
Receiving the assignment to present a speech	Asking my supervisor for a "day off" without pay
Completing the research for the speech	Making a large, reasonable purchase
Composing the speech	Expressing a point of view
Practicing the speech	Entering competition
Reviewing the speech on the way to class	Making an overt expression of compliment
Entering the classroom where the speech is to be given	Entering into a conversation at a professional meeting
Walking to the podium to give the speech	Telling a charity that I do not want to donate
Looking at the faces of the audience before beginning the speech	Asking a guest to leave my apartment when it is late and I am tired
Beginning the speech	Questioning the price of an item

both types of hierarchies, the intervals between items should be equal in terms of anxiety experienced. The same methods can be used in determining the appropriate intervals within each type of hierarchy. It is important that the various items on the hierarchy be significant enough so that the client can imagine the event vividly. The events listed must also be sufficiently potent so that the client can identify them as anxiety-producing situations.

   3   A pairing of the hierarchy items with the response that is incompatible with anxiety is completed during the third step. In the case of using relaxation as the incompatible response, the counselor would help the client to move up the hierarchy of events while the client is performing the relaxation skill. The movement on the hierarchy listing is from the event identified as least anxiety-producing to the items listed in succession as being more anxiety-producing. The hierarchy items are experienced one at a time in imagination by the client. The images, which are induced by the counselor, must be vivid. Images should be held for a minimum of 25 seconds. Often the skills of vivid imagery must be learned by the client when systematic desensitization is the "treatment of choice." Clients who are unable to move up the anxiety items on the hierarchy listing without experiencing anxiety are asked to go back to the next lower item and attempt again to achieve vivid imagery of that item while remaining relaxed. If after three attempts an item cannot be imagined while the client remains relaxed, then the hierarchy should be examined for proper spacing, and/or the client should be aided in the performance of the relaxation skills. Hierarchies often must be revised during the third step to permit the pairing of each item listed with the incompatible response.

Many variations of the three steps summarized above have been utilized. The procedure and the individual steps of the procedure have been used with groups of clients as well as with individuals. Methods of training clients in relaxation skills have been varied, and other responses that are incompatible with anxiety, besides relaxation, have been used. Standard hierarchies, rather than individualized hierarchies of the two types mentioned previously, have been used with some success. The pairing of the incompatible response and the hierarchy items has been conducted in vivo rather than through the use of imagery. In each instance, the variations have been made in an attempt to identify the best procedure for the specific client.

Extensive research reviews of systematic desensitization have been completed by Bandura (1969), Davison and Wilson (1973), Kazdin and Wilcoxon (1976), Murray and Jacobson (1971), Paul (1969a, 1969b), Wilkins (1971), and Wilson and Davison (1971). These reviews examined the efficacy of the procedure and provided a component analysis. Current controlled investigations involving the role of client expectancies as an important variable are being conducted. Additional variations of the basic procedure are being attempted and examined. Explanations of the efficacy of systematic desensitization in terms of operant theories (extinction concepts) have been proposed, and will generate additional study of the basic procedure and classical conditioning paradigm. The basic procedure utilizes a variety of steps effectively to help clients eliminate or reduce anxiety. Behavioral counselors continue the creative act of devising new variations based upon the research evidence to date, the specific client learning histories, and the established counseling goals.

Wark (1976) has reported a counseling case study that utilized a theme-based systematic desensitization procedure with a female adult client. The specific goal for counseling was to reduce the client's anxiety about asking questions in an adult course on study methods. The counselor helped the client to understand the purposes of systematic desensitization, to learn relaxation procedures, and to develop a theme-based hierarchy of anxiety-provoking scenes that were associated with asking questions in class.

The client derived the following four hierarchy scenes, presented in increasing anxiety-provoking order:

1   Only the professor is present when you raise a question.
2   Students are present when you raise a question.
3   Only the professor is present when you cannot answer a question.
4   Students are present when you cannot answer a question.

The counselor helped the client to pair relaxation with the visual imagination of the hierarchy scenes. The counseling process of moving from the least to the most anxiety-provoking scene during the pairing component of systematic desensitization was used.

The client's class comments were used as a measure of counseling effectiveness. As the counseling comments progressed during a six-week period, the client moved from answering general questions in class, to asking questions with a known answer, to volunteering comments and asking questions when not sure of or not knowing the answers. Originally a person fearful of asking questions and making comments in class, the client had been helped by counseling to become more like the person she wanted to be.

Modeling

The use of models in counseling is based upon the social learning posited by Bandura (1969, 1977). The use of models to help clients can be employed for three general client goals:

1   Learning of a new or novel behavior. Observing a model perform a behavior can help clients learn the necessary skills to perform the behavior.
2   Weakening (inhibiting) or strengthening (disinhibiting) a behavior already learned. The client may already know how to perform the behavior but may not be performing it at a desired level. The use of modeling in counseling can have the effect of increasing or decreasing the rate of performance of the behavior by the client. Viewing the consequences as experienced by the model alters the self-expectancies of the client. Clients' self-expectancies are the thoughts that they have a probability of experiencing similar consequences if they perform the modeled behavior.
3   Response facilitation. Viewing a model perform a desired behavior affects the client's performance of a previously learned behavior in situations where there are no constraints. Observing the model perform provides the client with cues to enact the learned behavior.

The observation of a model is used typically with a counselor and provides needed attentional cues, feedback, and rehearsal guides.

The act of learning through observation of a model has four major processes. As described by Bandura (1977) these processes involve:

1 Attentional processes—processes dependent upon the modeling stimuli (distinctiveness, complexity, functional value) and the characteristics of the observer (sensory capabilities, perceptual set, learning history) to regulate the sensory registration of the actions modeled.

2 Retention processes—processes that govern how well the modeled actions are converted and stored cognitively by the client for use as future guides for behavior (coding, cognitive organization, symbolic and motor rehearsal).

3 Motor reproduction processes—governing processes for the integration of the components of the modeled behaviors into patterns that are necessary for future performances of the behavior by the client (physical capabilities, skills, feedback accuracy).

4 Motivational processes—the processes of external, vicarious, and self-reinforcement, which serve as motivators for the client to perform the modeled behavior overtly.

Attention to all these processes is required in order to use models in counseling effectively. The processes summarized above provide guides to the counselor for the construction of the modeling aids to be used and for the manner in which they are to be used with clients.

Following the establishment of a counseling goal, modeling can be used to help clients attain their goal. The four major processes of modeling are integrated into the utilization of models in counseling. While the specific choices of the modeling technique components vary for each client, the procedures employed typically include attentional variables and preorganizers, presentation of a model, and guided practice.

Prior to and during the presentation of the model, preorganizers can be provided. These cues set the stage and prepare the client for the presentation. The preorganizers are used to help the client focus attention upon the specific model behaviors, the environmental antecedents that are present prior to the performance of the behavior by the model, and the consequences following the behavior. The cues enable the client to gain an appropriate set by providing instructions to focus upon the enumerated highlights of the model's behavior.

Attention to the modeled behavior can also be enhanced by using a model with characteristics that are evaluated by clients as competent, possessing prestige, and being similar to them. As a general rule, models should be similar to the client and not too superior to the client's own capacity. The situations in which the model performs the behaviors should be similar to the settings in which the client desires to perform. Consequences presented to the model should be similar to those of value to the client. The choice of models and the environmental situations used with the models are important counselor considerations to help facilitate the attentional process.

Models may be presented in a variety of fidelity levels. Live models are at the highest fidelity level. Symbolic models in the form of films, videotapes, audiotapes, and written descriptions are at lower levels of fidelity. Research has indicated that the use of symbolic models is often as effective in producing behavior changes as the use of live models. Different fidelty levels will be effective with different clients and counseling goals. Also, models of various fidelity levels can be used in a graduated procedure with the same client and goal, to aid the learning of increasingly more finite components of the behavior modeled.

An opportunity for the client to practice the observed model behaviors should be provided following the presentation. This opportunity to approximate the modeled behavior will enable the client to receive accurate feedback regarding the rehearsal and will provide an opportunity for the counselor to reinforce the appropriate aspects of the performance. It can serve as a practice session and warm-up exercise in a "safe" environment, prior to the performance in the client's "real" environment.

The probability that the client will perform the modeled behavior is affected by the consequences received by the model. Processes of vicarious learning affect the consequence expectancies regulating the behavior of the client. Vicarious reinforcement and vicarious extinction processes will have an effect on the inhibiting and disinhibiting of client behaviors, as well as on client motivation for performing the modeled tasks.

Much of what clients learn is through observation. The use of models in counseling provides a viable medium to facilitate client learning. Utilization of symbolic models is of particular interest in behavioral counseling because the model can be varied in an efficient manner. Multiple models have been found to be more effective than single models and can be employed easily through symbolic modeling. The ability of the counselor to devise tailor-made model presentations and to have the model presented in controlled settings that are free from distractions enables symbolic modeling to be more efficient and effective than live modeling in most counseling situations.

Research in the arena of using modeling procedures in counseling has established the ability of the procedure to produce behavior change. Continued investigation and experimental use of modeling will focus upon a component analysis of the various steps involved, thus providing the basis for a more exacting use of the procedure.

Komechak (1976) has detailed an innovative modeling technique that utilizes a live model to help a mother increase her use of positive parental behavior with her young daughter. The daughter had been brought to a guidance center by her parents because they were at their wits' end as to how to manage the girl. They had tried a variety of punishment techniques to get the girl to behave at home, but nothing appeared to help.

Initial assessment revealed that the mother did not use positive comments while interacting with the child, and often scolded the child. The mother and social worker observed via one-way glass the interaction between a counselor and the daughter in a play room. As they observed the interaction, the social worker pointed out to the mother the affectionate consistent words and actions of the counselor, and how these words and actions resulted in cooperative behavior on the part of the daughter. A plan was devised in which the mother would monitor the frequency of her praises, her scoldings, and the daughter's misbehaviors. The monitoring helped the mother to see the relationships among these three items. As the relationships became clear, the mother started to use more of the affectionate and consistent comments that she had observed the model perform.

Information collected by the mother and confirmed through spot-checks by the father indicated that within a period of three weeks the child's misbehavior had reduced by 47 percent. The ratio of scoldings to praising comments by the mother reversed and appeared to be related directly to the decrease in the daughter's misbehavior at home. Modeling had helped the mother learn new ways to interact with her daughter, which helped the daughter to act in a cooperative manner.

Self-Management

Based upon the belief that clients can often become their own counselors, many behavioral counselors have focused their attention upon the development of self-management techniques (Thoresen & Mahoney, 1974). A comprehensive description of the necessary skills and of the process stages of self-management has been provided by Mahoney and Thoresen (1974). The techniques of self-management have been based upon a social learning theory model, and include covert and overt processes. The major strategies of self-management are self-observation, environmental planning, and behavioral programming.

Self-observation serves several functions. First, it provides both the counselor and the client with data describing the behavior of concern. Often, the act of making observations will help the client to become more aware of the interacting situational variables associated with the behavior. Second, the process of observing and recording behavioral data can be a reactive agent in that it affects the goal behavior. In this sense, self-observation is in itself a treatment strategy. Third, the data gathered during this phase can be used to assess changes in the behavior during counseling. The data tell the story, and information from the self-observation phase can be compared with information from other phases as counseling progresses.

Often clients must be trained in observation and recording skills. It is important that accurate and objective data be gathered. For this reason, clients should be given positive expectancies regarding the act of self-observation. What to observe and how to record the data must often be practiced prior to beginning actual use of the skills.

Environmental planning procedures involve actions by clients to arrange the antecedent and consequence events of their environment in such a manner as to help achieve the counseling goal. There are two basic types of environmental planning activities that are useful in self-management: stimulus control and consequence prearrangement. Stimulus control, or the prearrangement of cues, involves having the client make breaks and modifications in the stimulus-response chain. Avoiding situations that elicit undesirable behavior is one technique of stimulus control. Modifying the presentation of the stimuli to facilitate desired behavior is another technique. Modification of covert cues provides yet another technique. Research has provided evidence that the modification of external cues (Stuart, 1967) and/or internal cues (Meichenbaum & Cameron, 1974) results in the behavioral changes that clients desire. As such, the prearrangement of the cues serves as an effective self-management strategy.

The prearrangement of response consequences is the second type of environmental programming technique. Contractual agreements with others is one form of response consequence arrangements. Social contacts can agree with clients to provide desired consequences for performance of the desired behavior or to deliver punishments for nonperformance. Such a procedure is a *contingency contract* and includes a specification of the levels and conditions of performance by the client. The posting of a client's data record from self-observations can be another form of response consequence arrangement. Other persons who know the client's goal can monitor the movement toward the goal and provide the appropriate social consequences for progress or the lack of progress.

Behavioral programming is based upon the assumption that what clients say to themselves has a controlling effect on their behavior. There is evidence to suggest that internal (covert) events follow learning concepts that are similar to those of external (overt) events. As a self-management technique, behavioral programming involves the presentation and/or removal of both covert and overt rewards and punishments. Similar to the concepts in operant learning theory, these presentations and removals will affect the occurrence of the behavior in the future. Central to the use of behavioral programming methods is the necessity of a contingency contract. The consequences either can be self-administered or can be under the administrative control of others. An example of covert rewards would be clients' focusing on highly valued characteristics in themselves. Permitting oneself to attend a basketball game is an example of a self-administered overt reward. Similar events of the opposite nature can be used as self-administered consequences to decrease a behavior.

Self-management techniques vary with the client and with the counseling goal. As with all techniques, the procedures must be tailored to the individual client and are limited only by the creativity of the counselor and the client and by the research evidence concerning the potential effectiveness of the devised techniques.

A variety of self-management techniques have been proposed for helping clients who desire weight reduction. Mahoney and Mahoney (1976) report a counseling program utilizing self-management procedures with a middle-aged housewife. The client was aided by the counselor in learning and performing a series of self-management strategies during an initial 10-week counseling contact. Self-observation, environmental planning, and behavioral programming all were used in conjunction with the following components of counseling intervention:

1 Self-monitoring—use of a diary to record food quality, food quantity, and situational eating

2 Nutrition—an education phase to emphasize the importance of a diet that was balanced and adequate in terms of nutritional value

3 Exercise—utilization of moderate exercise to aid initial loss of weight and continued weight control

4 Stimulus control—separating eating from other activities, altering size and appearance of food, and making high-calorie foods unavailable

5 Relaxation training—making available an alternative to food intake as a method of reducing anxiety

6 Family support—engaging family members as reinforcing agents via providing positive comments about weight loss and not offering food between meals

7 Self-reward—use of contrasts that included provisions for rewards for the client at specified times, with intervals dependent upon achieving detailed goals

8 Cognitive ecology—monitoring, evaluating, and altering self-statements that held to perfectionist standards

The client was able to use the above procedures with a resultant weight loss of 18.5 pounds during the initial 10-week counseling contact. During a one-year follow-up contact, the client provided information that she had continued to keep her weight 18.5 pounds below the beginning level. At the time of a 16-month follow-up she was 20.5 pounds less, and at a 20-month follow-up she was 42 pounds less than her initial weight.

The client had not only achieved the desired loss in weight, but had learned techniques that enabled her to make the loss permanent and continual. She had utilized self-management techniques to govern her own life in the realm of physical weight.

Cognitive-Behavioral

Central to the use of cognitive-behavioral techniques is the evidence that internal (covert) events influence the overt behavior of clients (Bandura, 1969, 1977). Mahoney (1974) and Meichenbaum (1977) present a review of the research evidence and behavior change techniques that were developed within the cognitive-behavioral perspective. The role of client perceptions, thoughts, and beliefs on the overt behavior of clients has been emphasized by cognitive psychologists as a mediational role (Bandura, 1977; Ellis, 1977; Kanfer & Phillips, 1970). The extensions of cognitive theory to the development of client behavior change began in earnest during the 1970s, and initial evaluation suggests that these techniques can be used effectively by counselors.

Based upon the use of imagery, Cautela (1972) and Cautela and Baron (1977) have devised a series of techniques in the broad category of covert conditioning. The major characteristic of these techniques is the engagement of the client in two phases of imagery: (1) clients imagine themselves engaging either in the behavior they desire to change or in the behavior they wish to develop, and (2) clients imagine experiencing specified consequences following the imagined performance. The entire sequence is completed in the form of imagery and is guided by the counselor's instructions. The specific imagined behavioral performances and consequence experiences are dependent upon the client and the counseling goal.

Variations of the basic paradigm have been developed under the following categories: *covert reinforcement*—a pairing of pleasant imagery with the word "reinforcement" is followed by imagery of a pleasant event prompted by the counselor's stating the word "reinforcement"; *covert negative reinforcement*—client imagery of an aversive event is removed by imagery of the client performing a desired behavior; and *covert extinction*—imagery of performing the undesired behavior is followed by imagining no consequences. Another covert technique, *covert modeling* (Cautela, 1971; Kazdin, 1974, 1976), employs the same procedures as those used in the overt modeling procedures discussed previously. Clients are instructed in a similar manner, with the exception that the observations are completed in imagery format. Guidelines used in the development and presentation of overt modeling that is directed toward fidelity levels, model characteristics, attentional cues, and consequences are appropriate in the use of covert modeling.

Several counseling strategies based upon the cognitive-behavioral perspective have been developed for use in helping clients change their covert behaviors. *Coverant control* (Homme, 1965) is an example of such a technique. During coverant control strategies, the client is encouraged to focus upon particular cognitive behaviors (coverants). Coverants can be either positive or negative, and can be viewed as a form of self-reward or self-punishment. Ellis (1962, 1977) has conceptualized client problems as being influenced by irrational thoughts that are held by the client. Use of Ellis' *rational-emotive therapy* focuses upon the identification of the irrational beliefs that are held by the client and that cause the undesired behavior. The specific techniques of rational-emotive therapy are detailed by Ellis in Chapter 5. In summary, counselors use confrontation and client training in self-instructions and self-verbalizations to help clients rid themselves of the irrational beliefs.

A self-instructional counseling technique based upon a cognitive-behavioral model has been developed and investigated by Meichenbaum (1974, 1977). Meichenbaum's strategy attempts to focus upon the client's "internal dialogue." Through the use of modeling, instructions, and rehearsal techniques, clients are taught self-instructions that provide guides for the performance of the desired behavior. The guides focus client attention upon the situational events, self-efficacy and expectancy variables, and the component activities necessary for the completion of the performance. The strategy can be used as a prevention as well as an intervention counseling technique. Coping with stress, pain, and problem-solving concerns has been facilitated by using Meichenbaum's strategy.

Mahoney (1977) has summarized the state of cognitive-behavioral theory and techniques as being in a stage of recognition and challenge. To further the growth and refinement of such theory and techniques, Mahoney suggests attention to three major areas:

1 Demonstration of lasting effects in the counseling environment
2 Refining the conceptual and analysis procedure in cognitive-behavioral strategies
3 Clearer specifications of the procedures used

Cognitive-behavioral techniques offer an exciting challenge for behavioral counselors. As with all techniques, continued development, experimentation, analysis, and refinement based upon the effectiveness of the technique to aid client behavior change is the arena for attention.

Many of the illustrative cases presented for the preceding three counseling strategies include the components of cognitive-behavioral techniques. Many of the steps of the counseling program described by Mahoney and Mahoney (1976) and summarized in the previous section were developed to engage the client in the use and alteration of covert actions. Observing the weight loss provided the client with an opportunity to congratulate herself—a form of covert reinforcement. Similar strategies have been used for counseling goals directed toward a decrease in smoking, an increase in the quality of marital interactions, the elimination of homosexuality, and an increase in the frequency of positive thoughts about oneself, among other goals. The influence and interaction between covert and overt actions were central in the development of counseling strategies for each of these goals.

Summary

Behavioral counselors utilize a variety of techniques in their efforts to help their clients. The techniques presented in summary form above are not a complete compilation. The development of the techniques described also is not complete. Behavioral counselors use counseling strategies as sensitive, applied behavioral scientists (Mahoney, 1975; Thoresen, 1969). Techniques are based upon learning concepts from one or a combination of theories. The concepts from all the behavioral sciences are utilized in the development and employment of the techniques. For all technique usage, the individual client and the desired behavioral change direct behavioral counselors in their work.

SUMMARY AND EVALUATION

Behavioral counseling has come a long way since the counseling revolution of the 1960s. The growth has not been easy, but the major features established in its infancy have enabled behavioral counseling to meet the challenges. Use of the adjective *behavioral* has worked and is no longer needed. The features that focus upon the educational nature of counseling, the individuality of clients and techniques, the use of experimental methodology, and an application of the scientific method have provided the necessary self-refining characteristic of behavioral counseling. The same features will continue to guide the future evolution of behavioral counseling.

Formulation of social learning theories has opened new doors for behavioral counseling. During the initial stages, development of techniques was based upon concepts from the classical and operant literature. Techniques were focused upon overt client behaviors as the targets for change. The conceptualization and supporting research in social learning, which attended to the reciprocal interaction of both covert and overt events, enabled behavioral counselors to attend to client feelings, thoughts, and perceptions as behavioral change target goals. Thoresen (1973) and Mahoney (1975) have proposed the methods by which behavioral counseling techniques can be used to meet humanistic aims.

The utilization of self-recording, time series data collection, and single-case designs has been an aid to examine the efforts of behavioral counseling as it progresses (Kazdin, 1975). These procedures enable the intensive study of the individual in terms of performance as the techniques for change are being used, and permit a redesigning of the techniques if the client is not moving toward attainment of the counseling goal.

Behavioral counseling will continue to focus upon intervention, but increased efforts will be given to helping clients cope with (rather than master) difficult situations and to the teaching of prevention strategies (Krumboltz & Thoresen, 1976). Helping clients to learn and to perform general problem-solving and decision-making skills as preventive as well as intervention measures will continue (Krumboltz & Baker, 1973; Horan, 1978). The skills necessary to help clients become their own behavioral counselors or applied behavioral scientists via self-management techniques will be given increased emphasis.

As behavioral counseling ends its age of puberty and enters adolescence, its major features will enable it to meet the challenges of Bandura (1974) and Cronbach (1975) to focus on contemporary problems and to help clients by providing the means to achieve required and requested personal and social change. The future appears bright and exciting—not only for behavioral counselors, but more importantly, for the clients who will receive their aid.

BIBLIOGRAPHY

Bandura, A. *Principles of behavior modification.* New York: Holt, Rinehart & Winston, 1969.

Bandura, A. Behavior theory and the models of man. *American Psychologist,* 1974, *29,* 859–869.

Bandura, A. *Social learning theory.* Englewood Cliffs, N.J.: Prentice-Hall, 1977.

Benson, H. *The relaxation response.* New York: Morrow, 1975.

Cautela, J. R. Covert conditioning. In A. Jacobs & L. Sachs (Eds.), *The psychology of private events.* New York: Academic Press, 1971.

Cautela, J. R., & Baron, M. G. Covert conditioning: A theoretical analysis: *Behavior Modification,* 1977, *1,* 351–368.

Cautela, J. R., Flannery, R. B., & Hanley, S. Covert modeling: An experimental test. *Behavior Therapy,* 1974, *4,* 494–502.

Cormier, W. H., & Cormier, L. S. *Behavioral counseling: Initial procedures, individual and group strategies.* Boston: Houghton Mifflin, 1975.

Craighead, W. E., Kazdin, A. E., & Mahoney, M. J. *Behavior modification: Principles, issues, and applications.* Boston: Houghton Mifflin, 1976.

Cronbach, L. J. Beyond the two disciplines of scientific psychology. *American Psychologist,* 1975, *30,* 116–127.

Davison, G. C., & Wilson, G. T. Processes of fear-reduction in systematic desensitization: Cognitive and social reinforcement factors in humans. *Behavior Therapy*, 1973, 4, 1–21.

Dollard, J., & Miller, N. E. *Personality and psychotherapy*. New York: McGraw-Hill, 1950.

Ellis, A. *Reason and emotion in psychotherapy*. New York: Lyle Stuart, 1962.

Ellis, A. Rational-emotive therapy: Research data that supports the clinical and personality hypotheses of RET and other modes of cognitive-behavior therapy. *Counseling Psychologist*, 1977, 7(1), 2–42.

Eysenck, H. J. *The structure of human personality*. London: Methuen, 1952.

Eysenck, H. J. *Behavior therapy and the neuroses*. London: Pergamon Press, 1960.

Eysenck, H. J. The nature of behavior therapy. In H. J. Eysenck (Ed.), *Experiments in behavior therapy*. London: Pergamon Press, 1964.

Eysenck, H. J. *The effects of psychotherapy*. New York: International Science Press, 1966.

Franks, C. M. (Ed.). *Behavior therapy: Appraisal and status*. New York: McGraw-Hill, 1969.

Goldfried, M. R. Systematic desensitization as training in self-control. *Journal of Consulting and Clinical Psychology*, 1971, 37, 228–234.

Goldstein, A. P., Heller, K., & Sechrist, L. B. *Psychotherapy and the psychology of behavior change*. New York: Wiley, 1966.

Gottman, J. M., & Lieblum, S. R. *How to do psychotherapy and how to evaluate it*. New York: Holt, Rinehart & Winston, 1974.

Haley, J. The art of being a failure as a therapist. *American Journal of Orthropsychiatry*, 1969, 39, 691–695.

Hersen, M. H., & Barlow, D. H. *Single case experimental designs: Strategies for studying behavior change*. New York: Pergamon Press, 1976.

Homme, L. E. Perspectives in psychology, XXIV: Control of coverants, the operants of the mind. *Psychological Record*, 1965, 15, 501–511.

Horan, J. J. *Decision-making counseling: Toward a cognitive-behavioral perspective*. N. Scituate, Mass.: Duxbury Press, 1978.

Hosford, R. E. Behavioral counseling—A contemporary overview. *Counseling Psychologist*, 1969, 1(4), 1–33.

Hosford, R. E., & deVisser, L. A. J. M. *Behavioral approaches to counseling: An introduction*. Washington, D.C.: American Personnel and Guidance Association, 1974.

Kanfer, F. H., & Phillips, J. S. *Learning foundations of behavior therapy*. New York: Wiley, 1970.

Kanfer, F. H., & Saslow, G. Behavioral diagnosis. In C. M. Franks (Ed.), *Behavior therapy: Appraisal and status*. New York: McGraw-Hill, 1969.

Kazdin, A. E. Covert modeling, modeling similarity, and reduction of avoidance behavior. *Behavior Therapy*, 1974, 5, 325–340.

Kazdin, A. E. *Behavior modification in applied settings*. Homewood, Ill.: Dorsey, 1975.

Kazdin, A. E. Effects of covert modeling, multiple models, and model reinforcement on assertive behavior. *Behavior Therapy*, 1976, 7, 211–222.

Kazdin, A. E., & Wilcoxon, L. A. Systematic desensitization and nonspecific treatment effects: A methodological evaluation. *Psychological Bulletin*, 1976, 83, 729–758.

Komechak, M. K. Changing a preschooler's misbehavior by decreasing parental punishment. In J. D. Krumboltz & C. E. Thoresen (Eds.), *Counseling methods*. New York: Holt, Rinehart & Winston, 1976.

Kratochwill, T. R. (Ed.). *Strategies to evaluate change in time-series research*. New York: Academic Press, 1978.

Krumboltz, J. D. Parable of the good counselor. *Personnel and Guidance Journal*, 1964, *43*, 110–126.

Krumboltz, J. D. Behavioral counseling: Rationale and research. *Personnel and Guidance Journal*, 1965, *44*, 383–387.

Krumboltz, J. D. Behavioral goals for counseling. *Journal of Counseling Psychology*, 1966, *13*, 153–159. (a)

Krumboltz, J. D. (Ed.). *Revolution in counseling: Implications of behavioral science.* Boston: Houghton Mifflin, 1966. (b)

Krumboltz, J. D., & Baker, R. D. Behavioral counseling for vocational decisions. In H. Borow (Ed.), *Career guidance for a new age.* Boston: Houghton Mifflin, 1973.

Krumboltz, J. D., & Thoresen, C. E. (Eds.). *Behavioral counseling: Cases and techniques.* New York: Holt, Rinehart & Winston, 1969.

Krumboltz, J. D., & Thoresen, C. E. (Eds.). *Counseling methods.* New York: Holt, Rinehart & Winston, 1976.

Lazarus, A. A. New methods in psychotherapy: A case study. *South African Medical Journal*, 1958, *32*, 660–664.

Leitenberg, H. (Ed.). *Handbook of behavior modification and behavior therapy.* Englewood Cliffs, N.J.: Prentice-Hall, 1976.

Mahoney, M. J. The sensitive scientist in empirical humanism, *American Psychologist*, 1965, *30*, 864–867.

Mahoney, M. J. *Cognition and behavior modification.* Cambridge, Mass.: Ballinger, 1974.

Mahoney, M. J. Cognitive therapy and research: A question of questions. *Cognitive Therapy and Research*, 1977, *1*, 5–16.

Mahoney, K., & Mahoney, M. J. Cognitive factors in weight reduction. In J. D. Krumboltz & C. E. Thoresen (Eds.), *Counseling methods.* New York: Holt, Rinehart & Winston, 1976.

Mahoney, M. J., & Thoresen, C. E. *Self-control: Power to the person.* Monterey, Calif.: Brooks/Cole, 1974.

Marquis, J. N., Morgan, W. G., & Piaget, G. W. *A guidebook for systematic desensitization.* Palo Alto, Calif.: Veterans Workshop, 1973.

Meichenbaum, D. *Cognitive behavior modification.* Morristown, N.J.: General Learning Press, 1974.

Meichenbaum, D. *Cognitive-behavior modification: An integrative approach.* New York: Plenum Press, 1977.

Meichenbaum, D., & Cameron, R. The clinical potential of modifying what clients say to themselves. In M. J. Mahoney & C. E. Thoresen, *Self-control: Power to the person.* Monterey, Calif.: Brooks/Cole, 1974.

Michael, J., & Meyerson, L. A behavioral approach to counseling and guidance. *Harvard Educational Review*, 1962, *32*, 382–402.

Mischel, W. Toward a cognitive social learning reconceptualization of personality. *Psychological Review*, 1973, *80*, 252–283.

Mischel, W. On the future of personality measurement. *American Psychologist*, 1977, *32*, 246–254.

Murray, E. J., & Jacobson, L. I. The nature of learning in traditional and behavioral psychotherapy. In A. E. Bergin & S. L. Garfield (Eds.), *Handbook of psychotherapy and behavior change.* New York: Wiley, 1971.

O'Leary, K. D., & Wilson, G. T. *Behavior therapy: Application and outcome.* Englewood Cliffs, N.J.: Prentice-Hall, 1975.

Paul, G. L. Outcome of systematic desensitization I: Background, procedures and uncontrolled reports of individual treatment. In C. M. Franks (Ed.), *Behavior therapy: Appraisal and status*. New York: McGraw-Hill, 1969. (a)

Paul, G. L. Outcome of systematic desensitization II: Controlled investigations of individual treatment, technique variations, and current status. In C. M. Franks (Ed.), *Behavior therapy: Appraisal and status*. New York: McGraw-Hill, 1969. (b)

Skinner, B. F. *The behavior of organisms: An experimental analysis*. New York: Appleton-Century, 1938.

Skinner, B. F. *Science and human behavior*. New York: Macmillan, 1953.

Stewart, N. R., Winborn, B. B., Johnson, R. G., Burks, H. M., Jr., & Engelkes, J. R. *Systematic counseling*. Englewood Cliffs, N.J.: Prentice-Hall, 1978.

Stuart, R. B. Behavioral control of overeating. *Behaviour Research and Therapy*, 1967, *5*, 357–365.

Thoresen, C. E. Behavioral counseling: An introduction. *The School Counselor*, 1966, *14*, 13–21.

Thoresen, C. E. The counselor as an applied behavioral scientist. *Personnel and Guidance Journal*, 1969, *47*, 841–848. (a)

Thoresen, C. E. Relevance and research in counseling. *Review of Educational Research*, 1969, *39*, 263–281. (b)

Thoresen, C. E. Behavioral humanism. In C. E. Thoresen (Ed.), *Behavior modification in education* (72nd Yearbook of the National Society for the Study of Education). Chicago: University of Chicago Press, 1973.

Thoresen, C. E. Making science better, intensively. *Personnel and Guidance Journal*, 1978, *56*, 279–282.

Thoresen, C. E., & Hosford, R. E. Behavioral approaches to counseling. In C. E. Thoresen (Ed.), *Behavior modification in education* (72nd Yearbook of the National Society for the Study of Education). Chicago: University of Chicago Press, 1973.

Thoresen, C. E., & Mahoney, M. J. *Behavioral self-control*. New York: Holt, Rinehart & Winston, 1974.

Ullman, L. P., & Krasner, L. (Eds.). *Case studies in behavior modification*. New York: Holt, Rinehart & Winston, 1965.

Ullman, L. P., & Krasner, L. *A psychological approach to abnormal behavior*. Englewood Cliffs, N.J.: Prentice-Hall, 1969.

Wark, D. M. Teaching a student to ask questions in class: A case report. In J. D. Krumboltz & C. E. Thoresen (Eds.), *Counseling methods*. New York: Holt, Rinehart & Winston, 1976.

Watson, D. L., & Tharp, R. G. *Self-directed behavior: Self-modification for personal adjustment* (2nd ed.). Monterey, Calif.: Brooks/Cole, 1977.

Watson, J. B., & Rayner, R. Conditioned emotional reactions. *Journal of Experimental Psychology*, 1920, *3*, 1014.

Wilkins, W. Desensitization: Social and cognitive factors underlying the effectiveness of Wolpe's procedure. *Psychological Bulletin*, 1971, *76*, 311–317.

Wilson, G. T., & Davison, G. C. Processes of fear reduction in systematic desensitization: Animal studies. *Psychological Bulletin*, 1971, *76*, 1–14.

Wolpe, J. *Psychotherapy by reciprocal inhibition*. Stanford, Calif.: Stanford University Press, 1958.

Wolpe, J. *The practice of behavior therapy*. New York: Pergamon Press, 1969.

Wolpe, J., & Lazarus, A. A. *Behavior therapy techniques*. New York: Pergamon Press, 1966.

Yates, A. J. *Behavior therapy*. New York: Wiley, 1970.

Chapter 7

Recent Approaches to Counseling: Gestalt Therapy, Transactional Analysis, and Reality Therapy

Steven E. Elson

In some ways, it is a misnomer to refer to the three approaches included in this chapter as "recent." The rudiments of gestalt therapy were introduced by Perls in 1947, Berne published his first article on transactional analysis in 1957, and Glasser first presented reality therapy concepts at a convention in 1962. Yet, in spite of these dates of origin, there are several important respects in which the three approaches are relatively new. It was not until the mid-1960s that they caught the public's eye or were given more than a glance by the professional community. It has been less than a decade since most standard texts on counseling approaches have begun to include them regularly as legitimate counseling theories, and each of the three theorists has published at least one major book in the 1970s. Clearly, all three theories are recent in terms of the attention they have generated.

These three approaches were selected for this chapter not only because they qualify as recent but also because, among their many competitors (for example, see Harper, 1975), they are practiced more widely and have been given more careful consideration by professionals than other new counseling approaches. Each has established itself as an approach to be taken seriously. The differences among them were also a consideration in their selection. Taken together, they can be viewed

The helpful comments, editorial assistance, and emotional support of Bonnie Elson are gratefully acknowledged.

as being representative of most recent counseling theories. Gestalt therapy, with its high view of emotional experience; transactional analysis, which places great emphasis on cognition and insight; and reality therapy, which stresses the importance of overt behavior, cover the gamut of the newer approaches.

In spite of the differences, however, they have many features in common. All three hold, to varying degrees, a positive view of human nature; all have rejected the medical model as a satisfactory model of human behavior; and none employs the standard psychiatric system of classifying "mental illness." All, to a greater or lesser extent, view the goals of counseling as basically the same for each client; counselors using these approaches play a fairly active role in counseling; and for all three, groups are the preferred treatment modality.

There are also striking personal parallels among the founders of the three theories. Perls, Berne, and Glasser were born to Jewish parents. Each graduated from medical school and was trained in the conventional psychiatric tradition of his day. All three were clinicians, and their ideas grew out of their frustration with the inadequacy of traditional psychiatry as applied in their clinical practice. Each published books that became popular with the lay public but were ignored initially by professional colleagues. All three eventually migrated to California and founded institutes in that state.

The most significant similarity, however, is that each approach has established a wide following and has made a major impact upon the helping professions in this country.

GESTALT THERAPY

In 1951, Frederick S. Perls—Fritz to his friends—and two coauthors published a book entitled *Gestalt Therapy: Excitement and Growth in the Human Personality* (Perls, Hefferline, & Goodman, 1951). Although many of the concepts presented in this book had been formulated earlier (Perls, 1947/1969a), its publication marked the first time the term "gestalt therapy" was used in print. In the less than three decades since that time, gestalt therapy has become a well-known treatment approach, and its techniques are widely practiced. As evidence of its growth, Fagan (1974) noted that, up until 1974, more than 25 books about gestalt therapy had been published. More recently, it is becoming common practice for authors of counseling and therapy texts to include a chapter on the gestalt approach (for example, Binder, Binder, & Rimland, 1976; Corey, 1977; Hansen, Stevic, & Warner, 1977). Perls' (1969b) prediction of a gestalt explosion by the early seventies was, if anything, an underestimation of its rapid acceptance and popularity.

Introduction

Fritz Perls, the father of gestalt therapy, was born in Berlin, Germany in 1893. After what has been described as a happy childhood and rebellious adolescence (Shepard, 1975), he matriculated at medical school in response to family pressures to enter a suitable profession. Because he was studying medicine at the time, Perls served as a medical officer in the German army during World War I. He returned to medical school after the war, received the M.D. degree in 1920, and established a practice in neuropsychiatry in Berlin.

During the 1920s, Perls was aware of the controversial new approach to treating psychological problems called psychoanalysis. However, his fascination with this method of treatment did not begin until he entered psychoanalysis himself in 1926. His first analyst was Karen Horney, who encouraged him to pursue formal training. Following her advice, Perls received psychoanalytic training in Berlin, Frankfurt, and Vienna, and during his first years as an analyst he practiced as an orthodox Freudian.

Perls left Germany when efforts to stop Nazism failed. In 1935, he moved his family from Holland to South Africa, where both he and his wife Laura established successful practices as analysts. Perls also founded a psychoanalytic institute in South Africa. During the next few years, however, his discouragement with the rigidity of the psychoanalytic establishment on the continent and his attempts to develop more efficient modes of therapy led him away from orthodox psychoanalysis. The basic concepts of gestalt therapy were formulated while he lived in South Africa and culminated with the publication of *Ego, Hunger, and Aggression* (Perls, 1947/1969a). Perls came to the United States in 1946 and spent the next 25 years—until his death in 1970—developing and practicing gestalt therapy and training gestalt therapists, mostly in New York, Florida, and California.

In addition to his first two books, Perls also published *Gestalt Therapy Verbatim* (1969b) and *In and Out of the Garbage Pail* (1969c). A fifth book, *The Gestalt Approach and Eyewitness to Therapy* (1973), was published posthumously.

In many ways, Perls' concepts of human functioning and growth have been bold and even revolutionary. Yet, Kempler (1973) states that "there is nothing in gestalt therapy that can be considered original" (p. 251). Indeed, Perls himself eschewed the term "founder" of gestalt therapy in favor of the less pretentious "finder" (Perls, 1969b, p. 15). It is apparent as one reads Perls that he borrowed concepts and terms freely from many others. Shepard (1975, Chapter 14) sees this as a testimonial to his openmindedness.

With the exception of Freud, perhaps the most significant influence in the development of gestalt therapy was Wilhelm Reich, with his notions of "body armor" (Polster & Polster, 1973, Appendix A). From Reich, Perls learned an appreciation for bodily attitudes and for the importance of posture, movement, and muscular phenomena. His notions about how body rigidity is used to block awareness and free-functioning were influenced directly by early training with Reich. Also influential in Perls' thinking were the European phenomenologist-existentialists (for example, Martin Buber), to whom he had been exposed as a young man. In fact, Perls (1969b, p. 15) frequently referred to gestalt therapy as "existential therapy" because of its emphasis upon awareness in the "here-and-now."

Obviously, that for which gestalt therapy was a namesake, gestalt psychology, had a profound influence on Perls. He became familiar with gestalt psychology while in psychoanalytic training in Frankfurt during the 1920s (Shepard,

1975), and he used several of its concepts, as well as its name, in developing his own theory of human behavior.

Philosophy and Major Concepts

View of Persons In stark contrast to his Freudian heritage, Perls believed that people are capable of being free of their own "historical baggage" and capable of living fully in the present. He viewed human beings as having the capacity to cope effectively with their environments, to direct their own growth, and to solve their own problems. He felt that each person was potentially free to make choices; thus, the responsibility for one's behavior and experience was placed directly on the individual.

Self-Actualization The reason for Perls' optimistic view of persons was his assumption that all living things strive inherently for self-actualization, that is, for being all that they are capable of being. "Every individual, every plant, every animal has only one inborn goal—to actualize itself as it is" (Perls, 1969b, p. 31). This inborn, self-actualizing tendency is the motivation behind a person's behavior and activity. All other needs are viewed as stemming from and grounded in this basic need to actualize oneself.

Hansen, Stevic, and Warner (1977, pp. 146–150) note that, although this position sounds very similar to that of self-theorists such as Rogers, there is a fundamental difference. For gestaltists, this striving toward self-actualization or "becoming" is present-centered, while for self-theorists it is future-focused. According to Kempler (1973, p. 262), becoming is not striving to become; rather, it is being what one is.

Self-Regulation Closely allied with the concept of self-actualization is a belief in the person's inherent ability for self-regulation. Perls, Hefferline, and Goodman (1951, Chapter 11) maintained that every organism tries to achieve an equilibrium or balance by gratifying or eliminating the needs that emerge and disturb that balance. This homeostatic process, called "organismic self-regulation," functions to reduce tension within the individual.

Perls (1947/1969a) postulated that any disturbance of organismic balance is experienced as pain, while returning to homeostasis is pleasant. Pleasure, pain, and all other emotional experiences have a twofold purpose. First, they alert the organism that something is wrong, and, secondly, they supply the incentive or energy necessary to take care of the need that caused the imbalance. When it experiences some form of pain, the organism can regulate itself either by discharging tension through intense emotional experience or by motivating the individual to take the necessary action to meet the need. In gestalt therapy, then, emotions are central to self-regulation.

An implication here is that persons have the capacity to know their own balance and to attend to needs as they emerge. However, this capacity is realized only insofar as a person remains in the "here-and-now." Individuals cannot utilize self-regulatory functions when they are diverted by ruminations about the past and preoccupations with the future. For Perls (1969b), "The past is no more and the future not yet. Only the *now* exists" (p. 41). The satisfaction of needs—maintaining balance—proceeds most effectively and efficiently when the individual attends to what is happening now.

Awareness   An integral part of organismic self-regulation, then, is awareness. "In order to know their own balance and to find and obtain what they need to meet imbalances, organisms must be aware of themselves" (Latner, 1973, p. 17). Awareness is a key concept in the gestalt approach; it is seen as the process of being in vigilant contact with the most important event or need in the person's life space. As the predominant need arises and is dealt with effectively, awareness shifts to the next "most important" need, and so on. Thus, awareness is always here and now and is always changing.

Suppose, for example, that I am conversing with a colleague. As I am listening carefully to what this colleague says, I notice a "tickle" in the back of my throat. It is somewhat uncomfortable. I swallow to suppress the irritation. Again, I concentrate on my colleague's words and try to ignore the discomfort. Within moments the tickle in my throat increases in intensity. This time it feels scratchy, dry, irritating; I swallow hard, take a deep breath, and cough. Barely abated, the irritation continues, then worsens, and I try to cough it away again. Still trying to pay attention to my colleague, I bend over slightly, take a breath, then sit up straight, and throw my head back to cough. My colleague frowns and suggests that I get a drink of water. I nod, aware now that a drink is exactly what I need. As I walk to the drinking fountain, I continue coughing and swallowing. I am aware of the cool water rushing into my mouth, and I take several gulps. The water soothes my throat. The irritation fades quickly. I walk back to my colleague, take one last swallow, apologize, and we resume our conversation.

In this example, my awareness shifted from event to need and back, as each in turn emerged in prominence. Note that my efforts to divert my awareness from the need only exacerbated the problem. Avoiding awareness inevitably backfires, because energy is spent either in suppressing the need itself or the emotions signaling the need. Only when I let my awareness stay with the need was I able to take care of it.

Gestalt Psychology Principles   Gestalt psychology evolved in Germany during the early twentieth century as a reaction to the rigid and analytical behaviorism in vogue at that time. Behaviorism, with its emphasis upon small units of the environment called "stimuli" and small units of behavior called "responses," was viewed by gestalt psychologists as too restrictive and molecular to account for all psychological experience. The gestalt view was that psychological phenomena are organized into synthesized wholes whose meaning would be lost by separating them into parts. This view stood squarely against the behaviorists' approach of separating out and analyzing individual units of stimulus and response.

The fundamental notion in gestalt psychology is that individuals tend to organize stimuli perceptually into meaningful wholes. Indeed, the German word "gestalt" embodies the concept of a whole that has meaning. A figure that has been organized meaningfully out of a perceptual field is called a "gestalt"—for example, the irritation in my throat in the illustration above.

Several gestalt principles describe the process by which the perceptual field is organized. Most important for Perls was the principle of closure—perceiving separate or unconnected stimuli as being related to one another in meaningful ways. For example, four unconnected lines might be perceived as a square, as a person "closes" the lines and forms the square in his or her mind. Depending upon the arrangement of the four separate lines, the same person might also perceive, in accordance with the principle of closure, a Christmas tree, a cross, or a capital L. The proximity—the relative distance and juxtaposition of the lines to one another— and the similarity of the lines also affects how "closure" is reached with that part of the perceptual field. The important point here is that individuals have a strong need to impose meaning upon, and achieve closure with, relevant portions of their perceptual field. Perls extended this concept to include the phenomenological or psychological field as well; that is, gestalt psychology principles were broadened to include people's perceptions of their own experiences, emotions, and body sensations.

The concept of emerging and receding needs, which has already been discussed relative to awareness, is based upon the gestalt view that individuals organize their phenomenological field into a figure and a ground. A *figure* is what occupies the center of the person's attentive awareness—what the person pays attention to—while the rest of the field serves as the *ground*. Put another way, the figure is the foreground, and the ground is the background. Together they form a gestalt. In the illustration of awareness in the previous section, the figure shifted from my colleague, to the irritation in my throat, to the drinking fountain, and back to the conversation with my colleague. Perls (1947/1969a) calls this continuous flow of figures that are emerging out of and receding back into the background the formation and destruction of gestalts. Gestalts are formed as some portion of the phenomenological field—the predominant need—intensifies and is differentiated from the ground to become the figure. It is destroyed as closure is achieved or a saturation point is reached. This is the way people experience their world.

In the gestaltist view, the phenomenal world is organized by the needs of the individual (Wallen, 1970, p. 3). Individuals attend to aspects of the phenomenal field according to their needs at the time. For example, a hungry traveler is likely to notice the food on the passing billboards; the same traveler, trying to calm his or her active children, may attend to the letters on the billboards, while playing the alphabet game with them. In other words, needs organize an individual's phenomenal world and energize behavior so that they are satisfied.

An important aspect of the figure/ground conceptualization is that figures have meaning only in relation to the ground. The well-known phrase, "The whole is greater than the sum of its parts," epitomizes this idea. Consider for a moment my colleague in the above example. If any of the phrases from the conversation were to be isolated from the rest of the conversation, their meaning would be unclear. Only within the context of the rest of our conversation do the phrases achieve their full meaning. Likewise, only within the context of the ground does the figure become meaningful. Stated another way, the meaning a person gives a figure depends upon the perceived ground in which it exists. For Perls (1969b), "Meaning is the relationship of the foreground figure to its background" (p. 60).

Perls and other gestalt theorists have developed a view of normal growth and functioning, of maladaptive behavior, and of the therapeutic process that is based upon these major concepts. These more practical aspects of gestalt counseling are discussed below.

Normal Development of the Individual

In his writings, Perls does not present a systematized, concrete description of personality development, as such. Unlike some of his contemporaries, he did not view development as a sequence of identifiable, chronological stages in which the developing person attempts to resolve certain stage-specific problems. Nor did he see development as an unfolding of the personality toward an end-product— an ideal, finished person. For Perls, development is growth—a continuous, dynamic, life-long process of "creative adjustments." This ongoing growth process continues throughout life and is terminated ultimately only by death.

In many personality theories, the outcome of development is maturity. Often, adulthood is seen as a necessary, though not a sufficient, condition for maturity. Perls places no such age- or stage-restriction on his concept of maturity. In fact, he feels that most adults are not mature, because they merely play the role of being adults, and Perls sees role playing as a highly immature activity. Gestaltists view maturity in terms of process rather than in terms of product. *Maturing is the transcendence from environmental support to self-support* (Perls, 1969b, p. 28). The emphasis is upon the process of moving toward self-support. From a developmental perspective, it involves the individual's taking on the functions necessary for self-support, or the capacity to mobilize one's own resources in order to deal effectively with the environment (Perls, 1975, p. 76).

The shift from environmental support to self-support is evident in the physical development of the individual. While in utero, the fetus is utterly dependent upon environmental supports; all its needs are provided. After birth, most needs continue to be met by the mother, but the provision of certain needs, such as breathing and extracting nourishment from its environment (its mother), for example, must be supplied by the infant itself. During childhood, individuals assume more and more of their own support: locomotion, speaking, grooming, and so on. Taking over for oneself the physical supports of the environment continues in ongoing fashion into adulthood.

This example of physical development also illuminates the gestalt view of personality development. Immediately following birth, the infant is largely dependent upon its mother to meet its needs. The major reason for this dependency is obvious: the infant simply does not possess the physical and social capabilities necessary to support independent functioning. Additionally, from the gestalt perspective, the infant cannot care for itself because it cannot differentiate between itself and the environment. It has no awareness of "self" as opposed to "not self." This awareness is achieved over time as the infant "bumps into its surroundings again and again and is modified. It learns about separateness, differences, and relatedness" (Kempler, 1973, p. 262). Stated another way, it comes to know what its boundaries are.

Slowly, as awareness increases, children learn to organize their phenomenological fields to meet simple, basic needs. In accordance with the figure-ground principle, emerging needs are organized into gestalts. Successful gestalt formation—a sharp, clear differentiation of figure and ground—leads to the mobilization of the aggressive energy necessary to destroy (destructure) the gestalt, which, in turn, allows the individual to assimilate selectively what is needed and to discard what is unhealthy. This process of *assimilating* (biting off, chewing, and swallowing, in Perls' words) what is vital, and *discarding* (refusing, eliminating, excreting) what is unnecessary is as fundamental in personality development as it is in physical development. In both, old gestalts are destroyed in order to form new ones. This is the process of growth. As material is assimilated from the environment, a person's boundaries (self) are enlarged, and his or her capacities for contacting, organizing, breaking down, and assimilating larger aspects of the environment are expanded. This growth cycle is an ongoing, moment-to-moment process, which Perls calls "creative adjustments" (Perls, Hefferline, & Goodman, 1951, p. 230).

Along with his or her personal development, significant others in the child's life continue to give support in important ways. This is necessary because the child is aware of only a few of the components in the phenomenological field, and the capacity to mobilize energy and deal effectively with the environment is still minimal. In order to facilitate growth, Perls argues that parents must allow their children to experience frustration.

Removing frustration from the child's world is tantamount to preventing growth. Instead of learning to allow self-regulatory processes to function—that is, instead of growing—children learn to use their energies to avoid frustration. They do this by depending upon others, by acting helpless, and by manipulating the environment in many other ways so that they avoid frustration. Perls (1969b) states emphatically that "without frustration there is no need, no reason to mobilize your resources, to discover that you might be able to do something on your own" (p. 32). Learning to overcome frustration, then, although painful, is essential for growth.

If parents make proper use of both frustration and support, children can learn how to use their own resources to overcome difficulties and to function independently. Over time, they will become competent in organizing more and more of their perceptual field into gestalts, in making greater use of their own capabilities, and in relying less upon environmental supports. In other words, as they grow, children become capable of forming and destroying more complex gestalts.

Parents, however, do not always allow adequate frustration nor provide appropriate support. Often, children are spoiled, because parents are too quick to remove frustrating obstacles. In addition, parental support is frequently in the form of approval, when all children really need is simple acknowledgment (Kempler, 1973). Approval for a given activity or behavior is, in essence, a "should";

and the shoulds and should nots of childhood soon become an external standard against which children are encouraged to measure themselves. Thus, children come to invest their energies in attempts to "measure up" to what they think they should be. This now-internalized standard is called "self-image."

Self-image, also called "self-concept," is a part of everyone's personality. It is the part that impedes growth, because it diverts energy toward becoming what one is not. The self (as distinguished from the self-image) and what Kempler (1973) calls "being" are also integral parts of the personality. The self is concerned with the process of adjusting creatively to the environment to meet its own needs. This fundamental characteristic of the self is the formation and destruction of gestalts. Passons (1975) describes the self as "the system of creative adjustments that are present at any given moment" (p. 16). Being, the other entity of personality, is the basic, essential core of the organism.

At any moment, self and self-image have the potential for development. As the individual contacts the environment, either the self-image or the self may emerge to deal with it, each in its own way. When people identify with their self-image, they attempt to exert deliberate control over their natural, self-regulating tendencies. On these occasions, people do not trust their own capacities; they block their awareness and attempt to become what they are not. This interferes with the healthy working of the organism, and growth is stunted.

When individuals identify with self, on the other hand, control is left to the situation, as they adjust creatively to it. Their self-regulating capacities are united in an integrated, holistic, complete way. Although Perls did not use the term "gestalt" to describe personality, it is obvious that, in a sense, the healthy person is a gestalt—a unified, meaningful whole. Becoming whole, however, can only be attained through identification with self, and not with self-image.

Clearly, the process of growth—shifting from dependence to independence—is a hazardous one. People are reorganizing themselves and their relationships to the environment continuously. They are constantly confronted with competing needs and with a variety of possibilities in forming gestalts to meet those needs. Their self-image confronts them with what they "should" do, and their self with what they naturally want to do. In spite of these conflicting demands, healthy individuals identify more with the self than with the self-image. Rather than acquiesce to external standards (albeit *internalized* external standards) to govern their behavior, they establish their own standards, based simply upon who they are. For the most part, they allow the natural, spontaneous, self-regulatory processes to guide their actions. They are aware of themselves. They are present-centered. They come to trust their own capabilities and take responsibility for their own behavior. Functionally, this is self-support. It involves faith in one's inherent ability to deal effectively with the environment, and it involves acceptance of the responsibility for doing so.

Development of Maladaptive Behavior

Gestaltists view personality as a product of individuals' interacting with the environment. If their interactions involve the successful formation and destruction of gestalts, then they are healthy persons. Thus, in the normal course of events, a need emerges out of the background to become figure—to activate awareness—and a gestalt is formed. Energy is mobilized to meet the need, and as the need is satisfied, the gestalt is completed (destroyed), which allows new gestalts to be formed in an ongoing, freely functioning process.

This rather simple definition of healthy functioning yields an equally simple definition of malfunctioning: something is wrong when gestalt formation is blocked or hampered in some way. Blocks arise when people try to be something they are not, when they identify with their self-image. The result is that their energy is expended in trying to block their natural, self-regulating tendencies rather than being directed toward interacting with and assimilating the environment selectively. Much energy is expended in blocking feelings, in particular. These blocks cost individuals their ability to meet their needs and to be aware of and experience the present moment fully.

There are several characteristic ways in which individuals deviate from healthy functioning and growth. All involve identification with the self-image. Gestalt-ists, however, do not use diagnostic categories to classify people. All maladaptive behavior, regardless of the form it takes, is viewed as a growth disorder—a dis-engagement from the self. Three characteristic ways of thwarting growth and the consequences they produce are reviewed below.

Projection   Projection is the act or process of disowning parts of oneself that are inconsistent with the self-image. Unacceptable thoughts, feelings, at-titudes, or actions may all be "projected" onto others. In turn, what has been pro-jected is then viewed as being directed back toward the projector. In other words, via projection, people tend to locate in others their own personal attributes and to deny that these attributes are a part of themselves. Perls (1947/1969a) defined it poetically: "We sit in a house lined with mirrors and think that we are looking out" (p. 158).

As an example: Ms. Potter is awaiting the arrival of a late appointment and views the tardy person as being contemptuous of her. Ms. Potter, who is herself contemptuous, disowns her contempt by attributing it to her appointment. Thus, the mechanism of projection is used as a way of avoiding the disagreeable aspects of one's self-image. In this case, the self-image tells Ms. Potter she should not feel contempt toward others, and so she projects this unwanted aspect of herself.

Though unwanted qualities of oneself are "thrown out" through projection, this manipulation does not eliminate them. Perls offers the solution: "The only way actually to get rid of an 'unwanted feeling' is to accept it, express it, and then discharge it" (Perls, Hefferline, & Goodman, 1951, p. 221).

Introjection   If projection is a way of dealing with the should nots of self-image, then introjection is a method of handling the shoulds. It involves taking into oneself aspects of other people, particularly of parents. The problem is two-fold. First, as a result of their self-image, people adopt patterns of behavior that are foreign to them. They play roles that others have imposed. Secondly, these ways of behaving are adopted wholesale. They have not been broken down successfully and assimilated selectively; rather, they have been swallowed whole.

To illustrate: A man who, after meeting someone who epitomizes his self-image, indiscriminately takes on the other person's mannerisms, ideas, and life-style, has used the mechanism of introjection in an attempt to actualize his self-image. Ironically, the self-image itself has been introjected, swallowed whole. The shoulds and should nots of the self-image have been adopted without being destructured and assimilated appropriately. Perls (1969b) views aggression as being the proper "cure" for introjection. Aggression, as Perls has used the term, does not mean annihilation or assault. Rather, aggression is defined as a positive, healthy, mobilization of energy, which is an essential part of organismic self-regulation. By mobilizing aggressive energies, introjects can be "destroyed." What is needed can then be assimilated, and what is unhealthy can be rejected.

At this point, it is important to note that the self-manipulations used to identify with self-image are closely related to one another. Each is present in all forms of malfunctioning. The interrelationship of projection and introjection illustrates this point. What is projected onto others, that is, thrown out, leaves a hole in one's personality. What people take in indiscriminately, or introject, fills these holes. Thus, in limited and pathetic ways, individuals attempt to make themselves whole.

Retroflection In projection, a part of oneself is directed into the environment; in introjection, a part of the environment is taken in; in retroflection, both directions are operative. Thus, energy directed outward meets resistance and bounces back toward the individual. Consequently, "in retroflection, the environment we act upon is us" (Latner, 1973, p. 126). For example, Mr. Burge loses his job because his employer miscalculated and sustained financial losses in other unrelated business ventures. Now he lays off part of his payroll to reduce his expenses. Although Mr. Burge is laid off as a result of his employer's carelessness, he blames himself for the loss of his job. His pattern is to retroflect blame. That is, blame and reproach that would be directed properly toward his employer is retroflected back toward himself.

Typically, retroflection occurs when behavior directed toward persons in the environment is unsuccessful, and the individual directs it toward him- or herself. Retroflection is also involved when, because people are unsuccessful in obtaining what they want from others, they give it to themselves instead. Thus, "a person who feels a need to be taken care of or nurtured in a particular situation, might wrap his arms around himself, in essence hugging himself instead of being hugged by another person" (Ward & Rouzer, 1974, p. 25).

Developmentally, retroflection occurs when an impulse directed toward a parent is met with harsh, overwhelming hostility. The impulse is held back and eventually turned inward. The child becomes both the instigator and the recipient of the impulse. He or she is split apart into "doer" and "done to," and energy is trapped between the two points. Immobility is often the result.

Retroflections are always manifested physically (Perls, Hefferline, & Goodman, 1951, p. 161). This is obvious in the example of the person who hugs himself when affection from the environment is not forthcoming. It is also the case with the person who avoids crying by clenching her teeth, or the one who pounds his fist into his hand when anger would be expressed more appropriately toward others. Consequently, directing awareness toward how retroflections are being carried out muscularly is a major means of freeing the energy that is bound up in retroflection.

The manipulations of projection, introjection, and retroflection have several common consequences: avoiding responsibility, lack of awareness, and character. These consequences are in themselves significant malfunctions.

Avoiding Responsibility   In all instances of malfunctioning, personal responsibility is avoided. Naranjo (1970) has pointed out that "responsibility is not a *must*, but an unavoidable fact: we are the responsible doers of whatever we do. Our only alternatives are to acknowledge such responsibility or deny it" (p. 50). Each of the maneuvers discussed above involves a denial of responsibility for oneself. In projection, for example, the individual disowns his or her own feelings of contempt, and thus refuses to take responsibility for those feelings by projecting them onto someone else. Perls (1969b) has defined responsibility as "*response-ability:* the ability to respond, to have thoughts, reactions, emotions in a certain situation" (p. 65). This means, for example, that people are willing to "reown" their projections, to become what they project. It means identifying with self rather than with self-image. When responsibility is lacking, attempts are made to maintain one's dependence upon the environment by continuing to manipulate it in order to satisfy needs.

Lack of Awareness   Like avoiding responsibility, lack of awareness is a universal aspect of all maladaptive behavior. Indeed, responsibility and awareness are closely related concepts in gestalt therapy. Yontef (1976) notes that awareness is always accompanied by "the process of knowing one's control over, choice of, responsibility for one's own behavior and feelings" (p. 68). Conversely, a lack of awareness is associated with one's failure to accept responsibility.

As discussed earlier, awareness is an integral aspect of gestalt formation and destruction—the single most important feature of healthy functioning. When awareness is blocked by any of the self-manipulations described above, or by any attempt to override the naturally functioning self, then gestalts cannot be formed clearly, and destruction and assimilation are not accomplished. Closure is not achieved, and incomplete gestalts result. Incomplete gestalts involve unmet needs or unexpressed feelings, and in accordance with the principle of closure these unfinished situations clamor for completion; they clutter one's phenomenal field with emotional material, what Perls, Hefferline, and Goodman (1951) called "unfinished business." Unfinished business, in turn, interferes with successful gestalt formation and destruction because it distracts the person continually. Energy is expended in suppressing the need or feeling. The resulting division of awareness— returning either to the past in thought or to old behaviors in futile efforts to complete situations—prevents creative adjustments in the present.

Fortunately, most people are able to tolerate much unfinished business, since it would be impossible to have closure on every situation with which they are faced—conversations are interrupted, distractions force us to leave tasks undone, events prevent us from resolving minor hassles. However, people are still prone to seek closure on all such incomplete activities or emotions, "and when they get powerful enough, the individual is beset with preoccupation, compulsive behavior, wariness, oppressive energy, and much self-defeating activity" (Polster & Polster, 1973, p. 36).

The cure for lack of awareness is directed awareness. As awareness is focused in the present, the most important unfinished feeling, situation, or experience will come to the fore. Once a disowned characteristic becomes figure and is acknowledged or "owned," closure is achieved and the characteristic can be integrated into the personality. Each incomplete gestalt with which closure is achieved will release additional energy for free functioning.

Character   As with other maladaptive behavior, character develops in childhood. A brief discussion of this development will illustrate the development of all maladaptive functioning. During childhood, individuals are more dependent upon others to provide for them. At some point, however, before self-support has been developed, a child will face a situation in which environmental (parental) support is not forthcoming. The child's reaction is typically one of confusion and helplessness. In order to regain some kind of environmental support, the child will often attempt to manipulate others for support. These maneuvers are employed by the child to maintain control and to avoid coping with the realities of life. When successful, the child acquires manipulative skills and begins to develop rigid and predictable behavior patterns—character. As character is formed, the child can act only with a limited, fixed set of responses and comes to depend upon these responses to garner continuous environmental support. Thus, the pain and process of growth are short-circuited.

The various self-manipulations and their consequences demand considerable energy. As less energy is available to meet the needs of the individual, and as needs are unfulfilled and feelings unexpressed, they continue to clamor for attention; the individual experiences greater anxiety and behaves in unsatisfying and inappropriate ways. Eventually, such an individual may seek help from a counselor.

Goals of Counseling

The major, overall goal in gestalt therapy is to facilitate the client's move from environmental support to self-support, to help the client to grow up, to mature, and to move toward self-actualization. This goal is not achieved easily, for as Perls (1969b) notes, "Very few people go into therapy to be cured, but rather to improve their own neurosis" (p. 39). Typically, clients manipulate the therapist for support in the same way they have learned to manipulate others. These self-defeating manipulations are calculated to enhance the self-image—a product of the demands of others. Thus, "the aim of therapy is to make the patient *not* depend upon others, but to make the patient discover from the very first moment that he can do many things, *much* more than he thinks he can do" (Perls, 1969b, p. 29). Of utmost concern to the gestalt therapist, then, is helping clients to realize their own power and their own self-regulating capacities.

In addition to maturity, a parallel goal of counseling is personality integration. Individuals seeking help come to therapy as fragmented and incomplete persons. In trying to maintain an externally imposed self-image, they have split themselves apart through projections, introjections, and retroflections. Energy directed toward the playing of roles, and limited by character, is not available to the person's self-regulating capabilities. Consequently, a central task of therapy is to reunite, to reintegrate disparate or disowned parts of the person. As these parts are integrated, gestalts are closed, which frees bound-up energy and enables the person to deal with new gestalts. This is a critical goal of therapy, because clients need to achieve enough integration so that they can carry on the process of their own development, without the help of a therapist. It is important to remember that integration, like maturity, is a process; it is ongoing and never completed.

Clearly, the movement from environmental support to self-support and the achievement of integration require awareness. Perls (1969b) has stated that awareness in and of itself is curative. When persons are aware, they function in accordance with "the healthy gestalt principle: that the most important, unfinished situation will always emerge and can be dealt with" (p. 51). Consequently, the restoration of awareness is a significant aim of the therapist.

Responsibility is also an important therapeutic objective. Assisting clients in assuming responsibility for their actions, decisions, and reactions is a major therapeutic task. As clients accept responsibility for disowned and split-off aspects of themselves, they move toward becoming whole persons. Individuals must accept responsibility for themselves if they are to realize any therapeutic gains. Indeed, growth is directly related to the degree of responsibility a person is willing to assume.

The four goals discussed above—maturity, integration, awareness, and responsibility—are interrelated. Making progress toward one goal will effect changes in the others. For example, as people begin to accept responsibility, they also become aware of the behaviors for which they are responsible; split-off parts are integrated as they accept responsibility for and reown them; a gestalt is closed, and, consequently, more energy is available for self-regulation.

Not only are these goals interrelated, they are also global in scope. Regardless of the specific concern a client brings to counseling, the gestalt therapist views the problem as defective self-regulation. Kempler (1973) states that "the identified problem is not the problem. It merely signals the problem" (p. 280). Accordingly, specific changes in behavior, cognitions, or emotions are not direct goals of therapy. Indeed, the client may use presenting problems to manipulate the therapist in order to gain environmental support. If the therapist agrees to help solve the client's immediate concerns, he or she runs the risk of keeping the client dependent and manipulative. When progress is made toward the general goals of maturity, integration, awareness, and responsibility, then clients will discover how they hamper themselves, what their capabilities are, and what they should do to deal with specific concerns.

Process and Techniques of Counseling

One important gestalt technique is to refuse to answer the direct questions of clients, and instead to ask them to frame their questions as statements. This technique is used because not all questions are simple, straightforward requests for information. Often, they are manipulative attempts to obtain support from others or to avoid responsibility. By having to turn questions into statements, clients are forced to see their own manipulations. A question such as, "Don't you think I ought to quit my job?" might be a means of avoiding the responsibility for making a decision. When the questioner is asked to make a statement out of the question, the responsibility can be shifted back to the questioner: "I think I'd be better off if I quit my job."

This technique can be used to help define the process of gestalt counseling. If the question, "What is the process of gestalt therapy?" is turned into a statement, it might read, "Gestalt therapy is process." The technique of changing this question into a statement has helped to answer the question. Gestalt therapy is highly focused on process.

Process is used here in much the same way as in the earlier definition of maturity. In gestalt terms, maturity is not defined by *what* a person does or does not do (content) but by *how* one interacts with the environment (process). Rather than placing importance on exhibiting certain "adult" behaviors, the definition emphasizes the free-functioning gestalt formation process: the how. Similarly, counseling is viewed as a growth process. Gains made in counseling are the result of the process of forming and destroying gestalts in a spontaneous, self-regulating way.

Perls (1969b) states that an understanding of the process of gestalt therapy requires an understanding of the "*now* and *how*" (p. 44). "Now" suggests that only the present exists. People can live neither in the past nor in the future; they limit themselves as they try to do so. Indeed, because all malfunctioning basically involves anachronistic living, any return to the now—to present experiences—is in itself therapeutic. Awareness must always be in the immediate "here and now," although content may involve the past or the future. For example, if a client brings up unfinished business with a deceased mother, the client works in the present by imagining or role playing the mother as if she were present in the counseling session. Rather than just "talk about" mother, the counselor must help the client to experience with vivid immediacy the unexpressed feelings about his or her mother. Closure can be achieved only by working in the present.

"How" becomes important at those points where the client appears to be avoiding particularly painful unfinished business. Here the counselor is extremely sensitive to everything that is going on now: how the client behaves, sits, talks, and moves. This focus on behavioral minutiae provides the counselor with clues about how the client avoids contacting emotional experiences. The counselor can then instruct the client to use awareness techniques to experience the emotion, free the emotional block, and let it recede into the background. Basically, the process of gestalt therapy is a process of focusing on the now and on the how in order to enlarge the awareness of the client.

Role of the Counselor   Unlike other counseling approaches, gestalt counseling sees both the content of counseling and the outcome of counseling as being secondary to the counseling experience or process itself. Therefore, the gestalt counselor does not set goals, demand changes, interpret experiences, solve problems, or even speculate about what might emerge from the client. In fact, by playing the "expert" role, the counselor would actually serve to continue to provide external supports to the client and thus hinder the development of the client's own self-support system. Consequently, the primary function of the counselor is to provide an atmosphere that enables the client to remove growth-preventing obstacles by discovering his or her natural, self-regulating capacities. The counselor acts to facilitate such discoveries by suggesting techniques that expand awareness. This is a major skill of the gestalt counselor.

A related function of the counselor is the use of frustration in counseling. When clients attempt to manipulate counselors into responding the same way that others have responded, counselors must refuse to be manipulated. Clients then are thrown back on their own resources and face the frustrating decision of whether or not to develop their potential. As Perls (1969b) stated, "We apply enough skillful frustration so that the patient is forced to find his own way, discover *that what he expects from the therapist, he can do just as well himself*" (p. 37).

Throughout the counseling process, the responsibility for change is left in the hands of the client. Clients are active, responsible participants; they make their own discoveries and progress at their own rate. Although counselors cannot be responsible for their clients, they are responsible for themselves. To be effective, they should be exciting, alert, and aware individuals who are in tune with themselves and can use themselves as "instruments" for counseling. They should bring their own experiences and humanness to the counseling enterprise. They serve as catalysts for the learning experiences of clients, and they should be skilled at employing a number of techniques designed to help clients discover their self-governing capacities.

Techniques Techniques are limited only by the creativity of the counselor. The following sampling of techniques is not a list of do's and don'ts, but it is suggestive of the ways in which gestalt counselors help clients to expand their awareness and to reintegrate themselves. The techniques listed here, as well as others, can be found in Levitsky and Perls (1970), Harman (1974), and Passons (1975).

1 *Directed awareness.* Virtually all techniques in gestalt therapy are designed to increase awareness in some way. Simple, direct questions to help focus client awareness are often most effective in achieving this objective. Counselors use their own awareness to pick up discrepancies and splits in the verbal and nonverbal communication of clients. By asking "what" and "how" questions, counselors lead clients to face these discrepancies. "What are you now aware of in your body?" "How are you doing your anger?" "What are your hands doing?" "How do you feel right now in your gut?" Directing clients' awareness helps them to stay in the present, to be attuned to themselves, and ultimately to make use of their potential.

2 *Games of dialogue.* Clients are asked to develop a dialogue between two conflicting parts of themselves. First one part talks to the other. For example,

"You should never express your anger." Then roles are reversed, with the other part responding: "But I'm angry." The dialogue is intended to help clients experience both parts of themselves more fully and is used whenever splits or fragments (typically introjects) are observed within persons. Through this dialogue, the conflict can be brought into the open, accepted, and integrated by clients.

3 *Playing the projection.* This technique is used when clients complain and blame and are unaware of how they project their own traits onto others. Clients who accuse another of being selfish and conceited are asked to role-play just such a selfish, conceited person and thus discover that they have those same qualities. Reowning and integrating alienated parts of oneself are the objectives of playing the projection.

4 *Reversal techniques.* With a reversal, clients act out behaviors that are the opposite of what they typically do. This is similar to the projection awareness strategy. A deferential, nonassertive person, for example, might be asked to play a domineering, uncooperative person. Reversals help clients become aware of a part of themselves they did not know existed and thus help to initiate the process of accepting personal attributes that they have tried to deny.

5 *Assuming responsibility.* Clients are asked to use the phrase, "and I take responsibility for it," after each statement they make. This technique is designed to help sensitize clients to the fact that only they are responsible for their own behavior, thoughts, and feelings. Thus, a client might say, "I feel lousy, and I take responsibility for it."

6 *Staying with a feeling.* This technique can be used to help clients experience the unpleasant feelings they strongly wish to avoid. Counselors simply ask clients to continue to feel whatever pain or fear they are experiencing and even to exaggerate the feeling. "Going with" the avoided feeling and making it fully figured will help to saturate the need for the avoidance, and closure can be achieved. Facing, experiencing, and enduring the feeling forces clients to accept their emotional experiences as parts of themselves.

7 *"May I feed you a sentence?"* Here the counselor phrases a statement for the client to say. The statement captures an attitude or feeling that the counselor observes in the client, an attitude or feeling of which the client is not aware. The client "tries out" the sentence by repeating it. In this way, the client can become aware of the previously denied attitude or feeling.

8 *Personalizing pronouns.* Since much everyday conversation is laced with the "it-talk" or "you-talk" that separates people from responsibility for their own judgments and opinions, counselors attempt to help clients talk in a way that acknowledges responsibility. For example, "It sure was a tough meeting" or "You could cut the tension in there with a knife" would be changed to "I was very upset and tense in that meeting." With this technique, clients may become more aware of their experience and may become better integrated as they own and accept responsibility for that experience.

Gestalt counseling is a fluid, ongoing, spontaneous flow of experiences and exercises. Counselors must adapt techniques to the immediate situation and to the unique interactions between their clients and themselves. This requires awareness and skill on the part of counselors and a willingness to participate in the process on the part of clients.

Illustrative Case Material

Jill has been frustrated in her attempts to lose weight. Although the counselor sees that Jill is inordinately concerned about her weight, she does not express this feeling directly to Jill. Rather, she attempts to keep awareness focused in the present, because she believes that Jill's own self-regulating capacities will bring the most important aspect of Jill's imagined weight problem to the fore so that it can be dealt with. Prior to the interchange presented below, the counselor has led Jill through several body awareness exercises. Jill seems agitated.

Cl: Sometimes I feel so fat; I just hate it. You know, I have tried to diet, but I can't seem to stick with it. Mary and I started at the same time, and now she's lost 10 pounds, and I've already gained back what little I lost. It's just no use; dieting is impossible.

Co: Jill, try saying that last sentence again, only this time, use "I" in the sentence.

Cl: What do you mean?

Co: Well, you've stated that Mary lost 10 pounds on her diet, and that dieting is impossible.

Cl: I meant I can't diet.

Co: Tell me that again.

Cl: I can't diet.

Co: Again, but change "can't" to "won't."

Cl: (Hesitantly) I won't diet.

Co: Now, what do you feel as you say that?

Cl: Frustrated . . . I know that's the problem. I simply won't stick to a diet. It seems I sabotage myself somehow every time I begin to see results.

Co: How do you sabotage yourself, Jill?

Cl: Well, I guess that the main way is just to say, "I'm not that fat; I don't really need to lose much weight, and certainly not nearly so fast." And then I break my diet. Then I go back on it, and the same thing happens. It's so frustrating!

Co: Jill, it sounds as if a part of you wants to lose weight but another part really doesn't.

Cl: Yeah . . . that seems to be the case.

Co: Let's try something. Have the part that wants to diet start to talk to the part that doesn't.

Cl: I don't know how to start.

Co: Well, the part that wants to diet believes you're too fat, right?

Cl: Yes.

Co: Start with that part, and have that part talk to the other part.

Cla: You are so fat. Just look at you. No one likes fat girls. And just as bad, you're too lazy to do anything about it. What's wrong with you?

Co: That's it. Now answer with the other part.

Clb: Well, you're partly what's wrong with me. You're always badgering me to diet and lose weight, while sometimes I think I look just fine. If you would just leave me alone, maybe I'd lose a little weight without making such a big production out of it.

Co: OK. Keep the dialogue going. Let's see what happens.

Cla: That's ridiculous. You know you're overweight, and how will you ever lose weight unless you stick with a diet? And how will you ever stick with a diet unless I keep reminding you?

Clb: The only thing you're reminding me of is my mother.

Cla: At least she was interested in how you look and what kind of image you present.

Clb: That's right. How I looked was so important to her. It made me so mad, sometimes I would wear certain clothes just to spite her. You know, that's how I feel about you, too, right now. I'd like to gain 20 pounds just to spite you.

Cla: No, you wouldn't, not really. You care more than that about yourself.

Clb: That sounds like something Mother would say.

Co: Jill, I want you to switch now, and talk to your mother.

Cl: Mom, can't you just leave me alone? No one else comments about my weight except you.

Co: (Playing mother) I just want what's best for you, honey. That's all.

Cl: (Whining) But, Mom, I'm trying, really I am. Just give me time.

Co: Is that what you really want to say to your mother?

Cl: No, no, it's not.

Co: Tell your mother what you want to say.

Cl: Get off my back, Mom. I'm not overweight. I don't want to hear your nagging anymore. I don't care what you think. I refuse to live my life to please you.

Co: Say that last sentence again, louder.

Cl: I refuse to live my life to please you, Mom. From now on, I please myself, and that means no dieting.

Co: Now, who is that part that wants you to diet, Jill?

Cl: It's Mother. I never really thought of it before.

Co: Is there anything more you wish to say to her?

Cl: No.

Co: How do you feel now?

Cl: I feel good . . . free . . . maybe a little guilty.

Co: How does your body feel?

Cl: Light, relaxed. I feel as if I'm not fighting myself. I'm satisfied with who I am. I may want to diet in the future but not right now. And I think I'm through giving myself a hard time about my weight.

In this case transcription, the active role of the gestalt counselor in directing Jill's awareness is obvious. She asked Jill to personalize pronouns, to play the game of dialogue, to focus awareness, and to stay with a feeling. Jill was also an active participant in this process and was willing to cooperate in the endeavor. The result: expanded awareness, finished business, more responsibility, and greater reliance on herself. This example illustrates the classic paradox that gestalt counseling addresses. Attempting to exert deliberate control to conform to one's self-image always fails. Only by accepting one's right not to change is change possible.

Summary and Evaluation

As a theory, the gestalt approach is a complex amalgam of psychoanalytic, existential-experiential, and gestalt psychology concepts. It emphasizes people's inherent capacity to regulate themselves and places a premium on awareness as an essential ingredient in the self-regulation process. As a clinical method, gestalt therapy is experiential and active and stresses awareness in the here-and-now. It encourages full expression of emotion and accentuates immediate experience, thus minimizing the cognitive aspects of human functioning.

Gestaltists see people as developing maladaptive ways of behaving because they have tried to conform to the demands of others rather than relying on their internal, self-regulating mechanisms. This dependence upon others prevents effective functioning in the present. Consequently, the major effort of counseling is to challenge clients to move from environmental support to self-support. Basically, the client makes this move by reexperiencing the unfinished business of the past as though it were occurring in the present. Often this involves verbalizing or acting out repressed feelings.

The process of counseling is an active and confrontive one that is directed at expanding the awareness of the client. The what-and-how of ongoing behavior in the counseling session is emphasized as a major means of expanding awareness in the present. The role of the counselor is to ensure that the client does not continue to avoid responsibility, awareness, and growth. The counselor does this by observing specific behavioral and emotional cues that signal the blocks and avoidances of the client. Focusing the client's awareness on these growth-stunting manipulations is accomplished through the counselor's suggestions for exercises and use of techniques that are designed to enhance awareness. Thus, counselors enable clients to experience the capacities they already possess and help clients to express and "reown" lost parts of themselves.

As the originator of gestalt therapy, Fritz Perls was active in promulgating his concepts and methods. He often demonstrated his approach in gestalt workshops and gained a reputation as a brilliant and gifted clinician. He was an actor at heart and enjoyed working with a client before a large audience. "I feel best when I can be a prima donna and can show off my skill of getting rapidly in touch with the essence of a person and his plight" (Perls, 1969c, no pagination).

Perls' dynamic personality and charisma were at least as instrumental as his books in providing the initial impetus for the growth of gestalt therapy. These personal attributes present a problem, however, because counselors who attempt to imitate his style run the risk of being inauthentic. Kempler (1973) believes that such attempts on the part of counselors pose the greatest danger to the gestalt movement. An overreliance on Perls' personal style and methods is clearly a potential hazard for a therapeutic approach that places a premium on the spontaneity, honesty, and authenticity of the counselor.

Another limitation of the gestalt approach is the narrow client population with which it can be used. The confrontive role of the counselor, and the fact that gestalt exercises are powerful and are capable of creating intense emotional experiences, necessarily restrict its use with fragile, severely disturbed clients and with those who have many social or personal skill deficits. Shepherd (1970) cautions that gestalt counseling should probably be limited to "overly socialized, restrained, constricted individuals . . . whose functioning is limited or inconsistent, primarily due to their internal restrictions" (p. 235).

The applicability of the gestalt approach is also reduced because of its individualistic focus, which fails to reckon with the social systems in which behavior is embedded. In groups, for example, the counselor typically ignores interpersonal dynamics and works with only one client at a time. Moreover, in spite of efforts to employ its concepts and principles in schools and other settings (for example, Brown, 1971), the gestalt approach remains largely confined to the modalities of individual and individual-within-group treatment.

One reason for this limitation may be the fact that the gestalt approach is not grounded in solid theory. Its loosely presented concepts are difficult to follow, particularly as discussed in the Perls, Hefferline, and Goodman (1951) book. Nowhere in the gestalt literature is there a clear, systematic presentation of a theory of human functioning, nor is there an orderly elaboration of therapy. Rather, Perls has combined a number of varied and seemingly unrelated concepts into his own unique system of treatment, which concentrates more on exercises and techniques than on a sequential, progressive therapeutic process.

Another limitation of gestalt counseling is its overemphasis on here-and-now emotions, to the exclusion of both the cognitive activities of individuals and their relevant life circumstances. To ignore cognitive functioning is to ignore one of the major dimensions of human functioning. Furthermore, a failure to address directly the problems experienced in daily life means that clients do not receive training in specific living and coping skills, which they could use to help solve those problems. An exclusive focus on emotion as a means of effecting lasting change is not supported by research evidence. In fact, there is no research support to cite for the effectiveness of gestalt therapy (Smith & Glass, 1977).

The highly egocentric "I do my thing; you do yours" philosophy, as expressed in Perls' (1969b, p. 4) gestalt "prayer," can also be seen as a problem. This philosophy ignores the reciprocal nature of influence among people and their shared social responsibility. Instead, individuals are encouraged to "get in touch with themselves" and "go with their feelings," whatever they are. This kind of thinking leads to hedonistic reductionism, a logical consequence of which is illustrated poignantly by a popular poster. Hitler stands in full military regalia with the gestalt prayer superimposed on his image. In counseling, the "I please myself first" emphasis, coupled with the counselor's power to manipulate the client with techniques, could lead to abuses and game-playing by counselors.

Despite these criticisms, the gestalt approach to counseling has many positives. It avoids abstract intellectualization and encourages people to use the full range of their emotional repertoire. In this way, it is a corrective for strictly verbal approaches. It has been a particularly useful approach in helping to free up individuals who are essentially "normal" but are inhibited and intellectually controlled.

With its emphasis on the present, gestalt counseling is also a corrective for therapeutic approaches that devote inordinate attention to the past. By bringing the past into the present through the client's fantasies and role playing, the gestalt approach makes significant personal history more relevant to the current life of the client. Another strength is the positive view of persons and the stress on the responsibility each person has for his or her own actions, decisions, and feelings.

Finally, Passons (1975) has observed that "it is in the enhancement of awareness that counselors from various points of view can apply gestalt approaches" (p. 29). When used in a prescriptive way, and particularly in combination with other approaches, gestalt techniques have their greatest value as additions to the counselor's repertoire.

TRANSACTIONAL ANALYSIS

From its beginning, transactional analysis (TA) "was to be a therapy for the people." So reports TA chronicler Fanita English (1973, p. 45), and so it has been. With group treatment as its major modality, it is relatively inexpensive and therefore accessible to the general public. With its emphasis upon a simple, colloquial language, it is easily understood by the layperson. With its rational approach, which focuses upon observable behavior and is characterized by a confidence in people, it has been applied in such diverse fields as criminal justice, education, pastoral counseling, management, literature, advertising, and communications.

Few counseling theories have enjoyed the broad appeal and popularity accorded transactional analysis. Three TA books have been best sellers: *Games People Play* (Berne, 1964), *I'm OK—You're OK* (Harris, 1969), and *What Do You Say After You Say Hello?* (Berne, 1972). Several books have been translated into foreign languages, and millions of readers in over 15 countries have been exposed to its concepts (Goldhaber & Goldhaber, 1976). In his recent survey of current psychotherapies, Robert Harper (1975) summarizes the popularity of this approach saying, "Probably more than any other contemporary psychotherapy, TA has reached the masses" (p. 75).

Developed during the late 1950s and 1960s by San Francisco psychiatrist Eric Berne, transactional analysis has also gathered a professional following. From an original group of three therapists meeting informally to discuss Berne's ideas, an international organization had grown to over 7000 professionals by 1976. Training institutes have been established in several states. Many undergraduate colleges offer courses in transactional analysis. Despite criticism from helping professionals concerning its simplicity and colloquial language, TA is clearly expanding its impact upon those who provide human services.

The acceptance of transactional analysis by the general public, and to a lesser extent by the professional community, has prompted English (1973) to describe it aptly as a "populist movement."

Introduction

Eric Berne, the originator and developer of transactional analysis, was born Eric Leonard Bernstein in 1910. The son of a physician, he grew up in a poor Jewish section of Montreal, Canada. Berne was proud of his father and decided at an early age that he would follow in his father's professional footsteps. He received his M.D. in 1935 and moved to the United States to take a psychiatric residency at Yale University. It was at that time, given the prewar antisemitism in this country, that he shortened his name to Eric Berne. He also took American citizenship, and in 1941 he began training at the New York Psychoanalytic Institute.

Two years later, Berne entered the Army as a psychiatrist and started to experiment with group therapy techniques. After his discharge in 1946, he settled in California and established a private practice. He continued to work with groups and to look for effective therapeutic procedures within a psychoanalytic framework. He was committed seriously to "curing" patients and was not content to simply help them improve. During this time, he resumed his psychoanalytic training at the San Francisco Psychoanalytic Institute. All told, Berne spent the first 20 years of his professional life pursuing formal credentialing as a psychoanalyst. However, in 1956, his application for membership in the Psychoanalytic Institute was rejected. Steiner (1974) attributes this rejection to Berne's unorthodox group method of treatment and to his insistence on active involvement with his patients. Consequently, in the middle of his career, Berne turned away from the psychoanalytic establishment and began to develop his ideas about human personality, social interaction, and psychotherapy.

Transactional analysis grew out of Berne's clinical practice, as he listened more to his clients than to his teachers. What he heard was his clients talking from three distinct patterns of feelings and experiences, which he called ego states. He labeled these ego states "Parent," "Adult," and "Child," and observed how they were used in both verbal and nonverbal communication between people. For Berne, the smallest unit of communication—a stimulus and a response—was called a *transaction*, and as he examined transactional exchanges between people, they became the building blocks of his theory.

As Berne developed his approach, he initiated weekly meetings with interested colleagues. At these meetings, which took place in his living room, he began to systematize, present, and discuss his concepts.

His first formal presentation of transactional analysis was at a professional conference in Los Angeles in 1957. Four years later he published *Transactional Analysis in Psychotherapy* (1961), which outlines the basic philosophy and major concepts of his theory. Berne continued to lead the informal weekly meetings until his death in 1970. His colleagues—who earlier had been the impetus for creating the International Transactional Analysis Association—have continued to carry on his work, and in the years since his death, TA's influence has flourished.

In addition to the obvious and acknowledged influence of Freudian theory upon his conceptualizations of human behavior, Berne also was influenced by Alfred Adler's notions of life-styles and his positive view of human nature; by Carl Jung and his concepts of archetypes and wholeness; and by such neo-Freudians as Horney, Fromm, and Sullivan, through their emphasis upon the social and interactional aspects of human behavior. The influence of others upon Berne's thinking, however, does not overshadow the originality, imagination, and creativity of his conceptualizations and descriptions of human behavior and motivation.

Philosophy and Major Concepts

View of Persons The essence of the TA view of human nature is captured in Berne's assertion: "People are born princes and princesses, until their parents turn them into frogs" (Steiner, 1974, p. 2). This aphorism suggests that people are, by nature, capable of living full and autonomous lives. It also implies that past experiences—particularly during early development, when parents are critically important—profoundly affect behavior in the present. In spite of the deterministic thrust of this view, Berne also believed that each individual is ultimately responsible for his or her own basic life decisions.

Steiner (1974) sees the positive, antideterministic aspects of this view of persons as the first and most important assumption of TA. Closely related to this optimistic belief about human beings are two other basic assumptions that have obvious implications for counseling. One of these is Berne's assertion that people who suffer from emotional problems are, nonetheless, intelligent and capable human beings. This point of view significantly influenced his treatment of clients. They became equals in the counseling enterprise, and shared responsibility for the direction and objectives of counseling. As partners, clients had the right to know and understand about themselves whatever the counselor knew and understood (Holland, 1973). Consequently, Berne developed a simple, understandable language of human behavior, so that clients could learn it and use it as readily as counselors did. He was also known to invite clients to any consultations he had with other professionals about them, so that the clients could be informed and could share responsibility for their treatment.

A third important assumption was that all clients, regardless of the extent of their emotional difficulties, could not only be helped in counseling but could be cured completely (Steiner, 1974). This radical notion was based upon Berne's belief that, because people have chosen their psychological positions in life, they can choose to change those positions. Given the proper approach and adequate knowledge of human behavior and motivation, Berne believed that clients could remake the old decisions that led to their emotional problems in the first place.

Motivation In addition to the basic physiological needs for air, water, food, and protection from the elements, Berne postulated several psychological needs. In TA terms, the most important needs are "stimulus hunger," "structure hunger," and "position hunger." Berne believed that the very survival of individuals depends upon their ability to meet these needs. Thus, the way in which individuals have learned to survive affects their transactions with people, the nature and quality of their relationships with others, and their basic outlook on life.

Stimulus hunger Most of us like to be acknowledged by others—to be engaged and stimulated, both physically and emotionally. Berne's view was that, not only is stimulation, or *stroking*, pleasant to people, it is essential for life. Research evidence from both animal laboratories and foundling homes supports his contention (Harlow, 1958; Spitz, 1945). Berne asserts that the need for stroking continues throughout life, although over time, physical strokes are replaced by symbolic ones in the form of words, looks, gestures, and attention.

In TA terms, strokes consist of any kind of recognition from others. They can be positive—hugs, smiles, words of approval—or negative—slaps, frowns, words of disapproval, or rejection. They are the basic units of social interaction and are viewed as being so important to human functioning that persons will seek negative strokes when positive ones are not forthcoming.

Structure Hunger "What do you say after you say hello?" Berne's (1972) classic question underlines the basic human dilemma involving the use of time. As social creatures, much of our time is spent with others. Thus, the question of what to do after the greeting is exchanged becomes highly relevant. Structure hunger refers to people's need to utilize their time in ways that maximize the number of strokes they can receive. Consequently, Berne (1972) views time structuring as an extension of stimulus hunger.

Time can be structured in six different ways. The most limiting and least rewarding way is *withdrawal*. People who structure their time by withdrawing cannot take risks; they avoid communicating with others by escaping into the safety of their own thoughts. They live on "stored" strokes from the past, or they fantasize satisfactory relationships with others in order to procure artificial strokes.

Rituals are the safest form of social interaction. They involve highly stylized and predictable ways of exchanging low-involvement, low-risk strokes, such as greetings. *Pastimes* are less predictable than rituals but are only slightly more emotionally involving. They typically include non-goal-oriented discussions, such as the weather, sports, children, and food. Pastimes are designed to minimize emotional arousal and serve a useful function in stabilizing and confirming one's social position, as well as in providing a means of acquainting oneself with strangers.

Activities include any goal-oriented behavior, such as that related to work or hobbies. The task itself dictates the type of interaction between people, and its accomplishment typically brings strokes from others.

In *games*, the fifth category of time structuring, the safety and low emotional involvement of the preceding categories are exchanged for excitement and drama. Games consist of ongoing transactions that appear to be adventurous and spontaneous. In reality, however, they follow unwritten rules. They are essentially dishonest, because they have covert, though unconscious, motives. The outcome of a game is always a payoff between the people involved. The payoff is typically a sought-for negative feeling, such as anger, jealousy, depression, or guilt. Games are the most common disturbance in interpersonal behavior, and like the first four levels of time structuring, they serve to keep people apart.

Beyond games is *intimacy*, "a candid, game-free relationship, with mutual free giving and receiving without exploitation" (Berne, 1972, p. 25). Intimacy refers to open, honest relationships and affectionate and appreciative feelings between people. Of all the ways to structure time, intimacy carries the greatest interpersonal rewards and the greatest personal risks. By being intimate, a person is vulnerable to the betrayal of trust by others. Hence, experience teaches people to avoid intimacy, and if not constrained by experience, intimacy may be constrained by parental admonitions about how strokes should be exchanged.

Hite (1976) suggests that the notion of time structuring can be used to construct a model of "transactional space" (p. 57). Excluding withdrawal, people can structure their time in the five ways discussed above. These methods of interacting with others can be viewed as five concentric circles surrounding each person. The circles progress (according to the information exchanged, the emotional arousal, and the degree of risk involved) from rituals at the outermost boundary, to intimacy, the inner circle. Acquaintances are typically given access only to the outer circles of a person's transactional space, while close friends are permitted to move freely across boundaries.

Healthy persons will make use of all their transactional space as they interact with others. They use the outer boundaries to assess the risk of allowing someone to enter their intimate space, as well as to deal with routine, short-lived, recreations and relationships. Although games are nearly always destructive, they also may be used adaptively as a defense against unwanted intimacy when others intrude beyond their welcome.

Position Hunger   The third psychological motivator, position hunger, refers to the need to have one's basic decisions about life confirmed constantly. It is related to both stimulus and structure hunger in the following way. At some point early in life, people experience a need to take a position regarding their own intrinsic worth. They have two choices: either "I'm OK" or "I'm not OK." The necessity to commit oneself to one of these two positions comes about as people are bombarded with conflicting and confusing information about themselves during their early years. Incompatible messages such as "You're a good girl" and Can't you ever do anything right?" are unsettling. Once a judgment about oneself is made, it provides a means of processing environmental input in a consistent way, and it furnishes a kind of security and predictability about life.

Evaluating the conflicting information received about others also leads the individual to one of two judgments: "You're OK" or "You're not OK." Taken together, these two decisions—a decision about oneself and a decision about others—constitute the basic life position. Once a life position is chosen (usually very early in life, with limited data and with little evaluative skill), the way in which a person structures time and the kind of strokes he or she seeks are fairly well dictated. In fact, Berne suggests that the life position is a rudimentary blueprint for how people will live their lives. As youngsters grow, they flesh out the blueprint to form a life drama, or "script," which they then attempt to act out in unknowing, yet planful, ways.

The life script helps the individual to structure time in order to ensure that transactions maximize strokes and confirm one's basic life position. This is accomplished each time a payoff is earned by playing a game. To understand how this process works, consider the negative feelings a person experiences after successfully completing the game Berne (1964) identified as "Why don't you—Yes, but" (YDYB). Player X states that she would like to learn to play the guitar but has no time. Player Y offers several time-saving suggestions, each beginning with, "Why don't you . . . ?" Each suggestion is rebuffed by Player X as not being feasible, with a "Yes, but" response. Finally silence ensues, until Player Y says to

Player X, "It sure is tough to make time for yourself when you have such a demanding schedule."

In the game of YDYB, Player X takes a helpless role and seeks confirmation of the role by thwarting all suggested solutions. The outcome is the successful frustration of all solutions offered, and a payoff in the form of an "I'm helpless" feeling. Berne calls this kind of interaction a game, because there is an ulterior or psychological basis to the game, which is disguised by an apparently rational, mature exchange of comments. The initiator of the game collects her favorite feeling—helplessness—and advances her life script of joylessness (Steiner, 1974).

Games such as these are played with utmost seriousness, and with purposeful intent. They are designed to maintain psychological homeostasis. When environmental input throws people off-balance because it does not conform to their basic life script (for example, when the input is inordinately positive), a game can be played to regain a more comfortable, negative feeling.

More specifically, games are designed to net a sought-for payoff, called a "trading stamp." Trading stamps are nongenuine, enduring negative feelings that are collected, or saved to be cashed in, for "free" major actions, such as drinking binges, temper tantrums, suicide attempts, and so on. The justification for a person's collecting stamps is called a "racket." Accordingly, people may be in the guilt racket, jealousy racket, or helplessness racket. A racket is a part of their life script, and it dictates the kinds of games they play.

Berne's creativity, imagination, and humor are evidenced in his analysis of games. This is demonstrated to some extent by the titles he assigns to games: "Now I've got you, you S.O.B.," "If it weren't for you," "See what you made me do," "Buzz off, Buster," "Look how hard I'm trying," and "Why does this always happen to me?" Berne's descriptions of the course and dynamics of games are also clever. His ability to strip away a game's social mask in an incisive, insightful, and humorous way, and so reveal the deadly serious and ulterior motivation inherent in the game, is remarkable. The interested reader is encouraged to peruse Berne's (1964) analyses in *Games People Play*.

Personality Structure According to Berne (1961), personality can be divided into three ego states, called "Child," "Parent," and "Adult." Unlike the Freudian trilogy of personality, ego states are not hypothetical constructs. Each is composed of a coherent, independent set of behaviors, thoughts, and memories that are readily identifiable to the careful observer. Typically, people operate out of only one of these three ego states at a time.

The Child The Child ego state is composed of all the feelings and ways of behaving that were experienced during the early years of childhood. In the mature adult, the Child represents the person through the age of about six. When people act in a childlike manner—for example, jumping up and down gleefully, clapping and yelling "Yippee!"—they are said to be acting out of their Child ego state, or, more precisely, they are "in their Child." This part of the personality contains the person's spontaneous and natural feelings. Berne (1972) states that "it is important for the individual to understand his Child, not only because it is going to be with him the rest of his life, but also because it is the most valuable part of his personality" (p. 12).

TA theorists identify three different forms of Child behavior. The impulsive, carefree, unsocialized, emotionally expressive part of the Child is called the Natural Child. The Adapted Child, on the other hand, is that part that has been socialized by parents and modulates and constrains the behavior of the Natural Child. Finally, the Little Professor is a precursor of adult thinking and reasoning. It is a product of the child's first attempts at figuring things out for him- or herself.

The Parent   The Parent ego state contains behavior, attitudes, and feelings that the person has incorporated from emotionally significant others who served as parent figures during childhood. Copied or recorded uncritically by the developing child, this part of the personality consists mainly of commands, injunctions, and rules that the parent has given. When people act in a critical, authoritarian manner, they are said to be acting from their Parent. The Parent can also be nurturing and helpful. Thus, the Parent is composed of two parts: Critical Parent and Nurturing Parent.

According to Berne (1964), the Parent serves several useful personality functions. First, it is a source for effective child rearing in later life. Secondly, it is a repository for traditions and values passed down from generation to generation, and as such, it has survival value for the culture. Thirdly, the Parent helps to conserve time and energy by responding automatically in many situations—routine actions are performed because "that's how things are done." Because the Parent does not require delay and reflection, the individual is free to invest energy in other more important concerns.

The Adult   Objective information processing, probability estimating, and decision making are functions of the Adult ego state. The Adult receives and evaluates data from the Child, Parent, and environmental sources; discards inappropriate, archaic, and unrealistic messages and feelings; and makes its own decisions. Through one's Adult, a person can "tell the difference between life as it was taught and demonstrated to him (Parent), life as he felt it or wished it or fantasied it (Child), and life as he figures it out for himself (Adult)" (Harris, 1969, p. 30).

The Adult develops gradually over many years, as the person makes validity checks and reality tests upon the environment. This testing process is concerned with facts, not with feelings. Unlike both the Child and the Parent, the Adult is devoid of feelings, although it can evaluate the emotional experiences of the other ego states. The Adult also differs from the Child and Parent in that it continues to gather information and to update what it has stored, while the content of the Child and Parent can remain relatively static after about the age of six. A basic function of the Adult is to keep the ego states updated, appropriate, and useful to the person.

Transactions   Transactions—the basic units of communication—provide the means by which people meet their needs. They consist of an exchange of strokes, or a stimulus and a response. A "hello" exchanged for a smile, for example, is a transaction.

Transactions take place between the ego states of two people and occur between the Parent, Adult, or Child of one person and any one of the ego states of another person. Berne (1964) discusses three types of transactions: complementary, crossed, and ulterior. *Complementary transactions* between Adult and Adult are the simplest kind. For example: Agent or initiator: "Where are the car keys?" (Adult). Respondent: "On the coffee table" (Adult). Such transactions are complementary because both parties are in the same ego state. Another example: Agent: "Kids these days have absolutely no sense" (Parent). Respondent: "Boy, is that the truth!" (Parent). As long as the ego states of both participants are the same, the transaction is complementary, and communication can proceed smoothly.

Another kind of complementary transaction occurs when the ego state of the agent, say the Parent, directs a comment to a different ego state in the respondent, say the Child. If the respondent, in turn, directs a comment from his or her Child back to the agent's Parent, the entire transaction is viewed as complementary. In this case, the agent sends and receives communication with the same ego state (Parent), and the respondent receives and sends from the same ego state (Child). To illustrate: Agent: "Why are you always late?" (Parent). Respondent: "Can't you just leave me alone?" (Child). Theoretically, as long as transactions are complementary, communication can continue indefinitely.

Crossed transactions occur whenever the respondent returns a communication from an ego state that was not addressed originally by the agent. Stated differently, when a message sent by one ego state gets an unexpected response, communication breaks down. To use a previous illustration: Agent: "Where are the car keys?" (Adult). Respondent: "You always blame me for everything that's missing" (Child). This transaction is crossed, because the respondent switched out of the addressed ego state and answered the question from a different ego state. A crossed transaction always terminates the discussion, unless it can be replaced by a complementary one.

A more subtle and complex transaction, which has both a social and a psychological message, is called an "ulterior transaction." Berne (1964) cites salespeople as classical examples of those who engage in ulterior transactions. To illustrate: Salesperson: "This item is a great buy, and we're expecting it to be a very hot seller this year." The salesperson's message on the overt level is an evaluative statement, plus a prediction. However, a covert message is directed at the customer's Child: "You can be the first on your block to have one." The customer thinks, "Wow, I can be first!" (Child) and says, "I'll take it!" (Adult). On the social level, this appears to be an Adult to Adult transaction. On the psychological level, it is Adult to Child. Thus, along with the social message (the spoken words), a hidden, nonverbal message is sent.

Ulterior transactions always involve two or more ego states (one for the overt message and one for the covert) on the part of the agent, the respondent, or both. Such transactions are the basis for the games that people play.

Normal Development of the Individual

For transactional analysts, personality is a product of the child-rearing practices of parents. Healthy parenting behaviors will result in a child's having a positive view of him- or herself and others (the crux of a healthy personality). Unhealthy parenting, on the other hand, will produce a negative self-concept or a negative set toward others, or both. Despite this emphasis on proper parenting, the TA perspective asserts that individuals are responsible for making the major decisions concerning their own lives. However, these decisions are not made in a vacuum, and in order to make decisions that facilitate health and autonomy, people must be given proper nourishment and trust from their parents.

Parents exert enormous influence on their children and consequently on their children's ultimate decisions. Parents can make their children do some things and prevent them from doing other things. They can deliver and withhold strokes. They can teach their children to play games or to be game-free. In Berne's words, they can help their children maintain a "princely" state, or they can turn their children into "frogs." Although such factors as family size, birth order, and even the child's name form an important backdrop, it is primarily the parents who set the stage upon which their children make decisions about basic life positions.

All children begin life with an attitude of basic trust—the "I'm OK–You're OK" position. This original orientation "is rooted in the biological mutuality of mother and child, which provides for the unconditional response of the mother to the child's needs" (Steiner, 1974, p. 71). This is even true of those children who lose their mothers immediately after birth, or who have extremely limited and inadequate mothers. At least in utero they have experienced enough unconditional protection and stroking to start from the "I'm OK" position. A most important task for parents, then, is to help their children decide to maintain the basic trust position, for it is only from this position that development leads to an autonomous, full life.

Steiner (1974) views the most important parental function as that of maintaining a basic faith in human beings and a "firm belief that people, including children, are OK, and, if given a chance, will do OK" (p. 303). Early studies on childhood nutrition lend some evidence to support this assertion. Most children in these studies demonstrated an ability to select nutritionally balanced foods from the wide variety that was presented to them (Holland, 1973). In much the same way, children will do what is right for themselves in all areas of life if they are given the opportunity and support. Based upon this assumption, Steiner (1974, Chapter 26), proposes 10 rules for child rearing, all of which are variations on the theme "Trust human nature, and believe in your children." This guideline translates into allowing youngsters to explore, discover, and express themselves fully.

If parents foster this kind of self-discovery and expression, the messages recorded in the Child ego state during early development will include the full range of emotional experience, the acceptability of spontaneous expression, the joy of intimacy, and the pleasure of creativity. These messages can then be replayed throughout adolescence and adulthood in an adaptive and healthy way and so can contribute to the autonomy and game-free life of the normal adult.

During the first six years of life, the Parent ego state is also developing. It incorporates—wholesale—the parental instructions and examples it experiences. Healthy parents, who operate from their own Nurturing Parent, will allow their youngsters to be themselves, to express themselves and to explore their environments fully, and to be largely free of constraints. These nurturing, protecting, and caring actions of the parents are recorded in the youngster's Parent ego state. They form the basis for the Parent and will eventually guide the individual in exercising caring control over persons for whom he or she becomes responsible.

During the early teenage years, the Adult ego state finally becomes fully operative. As the dispassionate decisionmaker and arbiter of the personality, its function is to make a decision concerning the basic life position that the person will take. If the developing person has been neither constrained nor pressured by his or her own parents, then the Adult is free to maintain the "I'm OK" position. Such a person does not experience the need for a life script to help confirm one of the other life positions. From this basic trust position, the Adult is uncontaminated and can appropriately perform its major function of evaluating circumstances, deciding the ego state from which the person should operate, and keeping the Child and Parent ego states updated and in balance.

In summary, healthy, autonomous individuals make appropriate use of all three ego states, maintain the "I'm OK–You're OK" life position, are relatively script-free, and have no need for game playing. They are aware of and understand themselves and others, are able to express themselves freely, and can give and receive love. Because they have received healthy parenting, they have developed in a normal fashion.

Development of Maladaptive Behavior

Just as parents or parent figures are highly significant in normal personality development, so they are critically important in the development of maladaptive behavior. Steiner (1974) contends that parenting patterns that lead to maladaptive behavior are typical of American culture. He refers to child rearing as "basic training" (p. 125), because, in so many nuclear families, the process of parenting is like the rigorous, rigid, and even oppressive induction process into the military. Parents drill their children in the basics of how to get along in life. This often involves an unintentional, though systematic, attack on the child's potential for intimacy, awareness, and spontaneity—Berne's three ingredients of autonomy. As a result of basic training, children give up their natural status as princesses and princes to become frogs.

The parental arsenal in this basic training process contains conditional and negative strokes, discounts, and injunctions. Strokes—actions or statements that convey recognition of another—have been described as being essential for human survival. They can be conditional or unconditional, positive or negative. *Conditional strokes* are given for what a person does, while *unconditional strokes*—critical for normal personality development—are given for what a person is. When strokes are delivered on an exclusively conditional basis, they reinforce the behavior patterns upon which they are made conditional. As children begin to channel their behavior in the direction of conditional strokes, exploration and free expression are limited. Stated another way, conditional strokes imply a demand, and children soon learn to conform to the demand in order to receive strokes. Being "forced" to conform in this manner eventually takes its toll on children's faith in themselves, and, over time, they give up the basic trust position of "I'm OK–You're OK."

Negative stroking also has an impact upon the child's major decisions. If the developing person receives primarily negative stroking, he or she may conclude that this particular diet of strokes is the only kind available and so may choose a life script that ensures a continuation of the "needed" negative strokes. Although both negative and conditional stroking are harmful, perhaps most devastating to the developing child are parents' discounts—for example, ignoring—of their children's need for strokes. The basic message is "You are insignificant and not worth my time."

Injunctions, another type of negative parenting behavior, are edicts from parents to children that require the children to behave in certain prescribed ways. Typically, injunctions are "don't" messages that inhibit the child's free expression. Although they can be simple, straightforward commands ("Don't touch the hot stove"), injunctions can also be subtle, confusing, double messages. For example, the verbal injunction to "grow up" is canceled out when parents deprive the child of the opportunity to complete tasks because he or she takes too long. Injunctions may also involve harsh, unreasonable orders that are enforced by severe physical punishment and fear.

Conditional and negative strokes, discounts, and injunctions from parents constitute the environmental input that leads children to give up their "I'm OK— You're OK" life position for one of three alternative maladaptive life positions.

Of the three alternatives to the healthy, autonomous basic trust position, the "I'm not OK–You're OK" position is the most frequently adopted (Harris, 1969). Feelings of worthlessness and depression accompany this position. The history of conditional stroking involved in this "depressive" position may lead people to be productive only as a means of gaining strokes from others, rather than for the intrinsic value they might derive from their own competence. Because they are unsure of themselves, people who are stuck in this position may experience severe depression, may withdraw from others, and in extreme cases, may commit suicide.

Persons who adopt the "I'm OK–You're not OK" position typically feel victimized or persecuted, and blame others for their situations. This is the "paranoid" position, and people who take it have difficulty being realistic in their appraisals of self and others. Delinquents and criminals who treat others contemptuously are typical of those who decide on this arrogant orientation. Negative stroking is a key element in its development (Harris, 1969).

The "I'm not OK–You're not OK" position is the consequence of parents' discounting a child's need for strokes. It is the "futility" position and is typically adopted by rejected children, who eventually give up hope and, in extreme cases, must be cared for in state institutions.

The adoption of one of these three positions leads to the time-structuring strategy of game playing. Although the necessity for games is created by taking an unhealthy life position, the specific games a person plays are taught by parents. The child learns that only certain transactions will garner the kinds of strokes and give rise to the types of feelings that are acceptable to parents. Over time, these simple transactions expand into the more complex and subtle manipulations of which games are made. Often, they originate in the classic child-parent struggles, such as feeding and toilet training, in which both participants attempt to gain the upper hand. Depending upon how these transactions are resolved, the child may learn to play games that lead to feelings of helplessness, anger, or mistrust. Eventually these games become a routine part of life and can then be described as a racket. Basically, they are designed to advance the life script and to confirm the life position of both participants in the game. As a result, both child and parent have a stake in continuing to play the game.

In addition to influencing the child's choice of a basic life position and teaching game playing to the youngster, negative parenting behavior also contributes significantly to the development of ego-state boundary problems (James, 1977). *Contamination*, one of two potential boundary difficulties, occurs when the logical, clear thinking of the Adult ego state is interfered with by the prejudiced or irrational ideas and attitudes of the Parent or by the archaic feelings of the Child. In either case, the Adult does not function properly, because information from one of the other ego states is mixed in with it. Consequently, the Adult processes data as though they were accurate, and actions based upon this processing are inappropriate.

Exclusion, the other boundary problem, exists when one or more ego states are effectively prevented from operating. In such cases, the individual uses one or two ego states to the exclusion of the other(s). Ego boundaries are said to be rigid, because the necessary flexibility and permeability between ego states appears to be absent. Hence, the constant Parent is judgmental, demanding of others, and duty-bound. The constant Child is impulsive and conscience-free, and does what it wants without regard for others. The constant Adult is highly rational and objective, and exhibits little feeling and little spontaneity.

As with the life decision about position, personality difficulties that are related to the malfunctioning of the ego states are a product of the quantity and quality of parental stroking and injunctions. Despite the powerful influence of parents on their children, it is the children who make decisions in response to real or imagined parental attitudes, behaviors, and injunctions. The tragedy is that these decisions are made most often by little children, who do not yet have a fully functioning Adult to help sort out the meaning and reality of environmental data. The hope for adaptive, healthy living lies in the fact that since the basic life position is the person's own decision, that decision can be revised. Counseling is a setting in which people can examine such decisions and make new ones.

Goals of Counseling

The goals of transactional analysis have been stated in characteristic TA language: to make losers into winners (James & Jongeward, 1971, p. 6), to turn frogs into princes and princesses (Berne, 1972, p. 37), to obtain a friendly divorce from one's parents (Berne, 1964, p. 183). These colloquialisms express the global goal of TA, which is to help people achieve autonomy (Berne, 1964). *Autonomy* is characterized by (a) awareness (a realistic understanding of one's world), (b) spontaneity (the ability to express emotion in an uninhibited, game-free fashion), and (c) intimacy (the capacity to share love and closeness with others). Although autonomy is the birthright of every person, for most people it is an unrealized potential rather than a fact. It has been stamped out by parents during basic training. Thus, TA is a tool designed to help people reclaim their birthright.

Related to the basic goal of autonomy are four general objectives. First, the counselor is concerned with freeing the client's Adult of the contamination and negative influence of the Child and Parent (James, 1977, p. 96). This is an important first step in counseling, because the counselor must do business with the client's free-functioning Adult to ensure that initial progress is made.

A second, closely related objective is to help the client establish the freedom to make choices apart from parental injunctions. This freedom requires a decontaminated Adult, as well as an understanding of the importance of the Parent and Child ego states in everyday functioning. According to Harris (1969), freedom comes with understanding. "If a patient can put into words why he does what he does and how he has stopped doing it, then he is cured, in that he knows what the cure is and can use it again and again" (p. 206).

A third objective is to assist the client in using all three ego states appropriately. The client should be able to shift ego states readily in order to interact effectively with others. This means eliminating exclusions where ego boundaries are too rigid and establishing boundaries where they are too lax (James, 1977, p. 65). Finally, the counselor seeks to help clients change those decisions that led to a "loser" life position. Individuals become winners when they give up their old life position in exchange for the "I'm OK–You're OK" stance.

In addition to these generic objectives, which are applicable to some degree to all those who seek help, clients are asked to state their own individual goals for counseling. These goals are specified in contracts between client and counselor and typically involve desired changes in behaviors, feelings, or psychosomatic symptoms (James, 1975, Chapter 5).

Process and Techniques of Counseling

One of the most important techniques in transactional analysis is the establishment of a contract between the client and the counselor. The *contract* includes a statement about what the client hopes to achieve in counseling, a statement about what the counselor will do to facilitate the client's progress, and a statement about the conditions that need to be met in order for the contract to be fulfilled. In order for it to have any therapeutic value, transactional analysts insist that the contract must be expressed in specific, observable, behavioral terms, and that it must be realistic. Steiner (1974) stresses the importance of simplicity and clarity in writing contracts and suggests that "words of two or more syllables are largely unusable in contracts because of their vagueness" (p. 244).

James (1975) lists three areas in which contracts are made: (1) Contracts can be made to change behavior, for example to stop drinking or to initiate more social contacts; (2) they can be established to change feelings, for example to feel less angry when frustrated, or to be more accepting of criticism; and (3) they can be implemented to decrease psychosomatic symptoms, such as high blood pressure, ulcers, or lower back pain.

Initial contracts usually involve relatively simple, easily accomplished goals that, when reached, serve to give the client confidence and to reinforce the first efforts at change. When one contract is completed, a new one is established. Thus, each TA client is always working toward a specific, individualized goal. In order to facilitate growth and to capitalize on improving skills and competencies, some clients may work on several contracts at a time.

Contracts serve a number of important therapeutic functions in transactional analysis: They keep the counseling task clearly focused; they give direction both to the counselor and the client; and they provide a means of measuring progress. In addition, because contracts necessarily involve Adult-to-Adult transactions, the process of developing a contract can serve also to help decontaminate the client's Adult, an important general goal of TA. Perhaps most importantly, contracts help to clarify the relationship between the counselor and client. The very process of contract negotiations elevates the client to an equal status with the therapist. Contracting implies trust between partners and conveys a sense of positive expectation from counselor to client.

Although establishing a contract takes place between two people, working on the contract usually occurs within the context of a group. Indeed, because transactional analysis is a learning tool rather than a procedure for exploring the individual psyche, it is ideally suited for use in groups. The group situation expands learning opportunities for members and facilitates "getting well" (Harris, 1969, p. 204). It provides a safe, social forum in which members can interact with one another and can observe and experience their own ego states, their transactions with others, the games they play, the stamps they collect, and so on. The group setting also furnishes models of successful change, as members see one another complete contracts, make new decisions, and alter old, self-defeating patterns of behavior. Moreover, groups serve as "practice fields" for everyday life; members are encouraged to give up games, rackets, and scripts and to "try out" new ways of viewing themselves and of relating to one another.

Individual contracts within the group vary, both in their complexity and in the speed with which they can be completed. These differences notwithstanding, counseling generally progresses through the same series of stages for every client, with each stage building upon the preceding one (Berne, 1966). Depending upon their complexity and difficulty, contracts may be fulfilled during any one of the four stages of counseling.

Structural Analysis In the first stage of counseling, clients are taught to recognize and identify their three ego states. They learn about the content and functioning of each ego state, and they learn how to be careful and accurate self-observers. To help develop familiarity with TA concepts, clients are encouraged to read TA literature and to attend workshops or introductory courses about it.

The counselor plays a particularly active and didactic role during structural analysis. To facilitate learning, questions such as, "Which ego state is talking now?" or "Which part of you made that gesture?" are asked frequently. The counselor makes use of video- and audiotapes, as well as other group members, to provide feedback to clients. In addition, counselors may borrow specific techniques from other counseling approaches to facilitate the awareness of and the differences among the Parent, Adult, and Child ego states. For example, the "empty chair," a gestalt technique, might be used to help people become more aware of their Parent ego state by asking them to imagine their Parent in an empty chair and then to carry out a dialogue with that part of themselves. The counselor expects members of the group to become experts in identifying the ego states of others, as well as to recognize the ego state from which they are operating at any given time. Transactional analysts assume that an "awareness of which particular ego state is functioning in the group at various times, and in response to various stimuli, is a necessary series of steps for the patient to go through in order to fulfill his contract successfully" (Harper, 1975, p. 86).

At times during this first stage of counseling, it may be necessary for the counselor to give clients "permission" to experience all their ego states; this may be done directly or indirectly, verbally or nonverbally. This technique of giving permission is designed to override the injunctions and rules of parents. The simple statement "I give you permission" can have powerfully freeing effects on clients. Permission to experience new ways of behaving or feeling can also render the client vulnerable, however, so the effective counselor always provides "protection" along with the permission. Protection may involve making oneself available to clients between sessions or stopping group transactions at critical times.

In order to help clients toward the fulfillment of their contracts, then, counselors must be skilled at identifying ego states and at teaching clients how to identify them as well. Also, they must be sensitive experts who know when to give permission and protection. For some clients, the knowledge and insight gained in structural analysis, and the support and encouragement given by the counselor, may be all that is necessary to complete their contracts. However, most clients need to progress further.

Transactional Analysis   This second stage of counseling involves helping clients to understand their transactions with others. Counselors teach the concepts of complementary, crossed, and ulterior transactions, and this includes analyzing the ongoing transactions of group members. Knowledge gained through this experience can be helpful in improving communications of group members, both inside and outside the group.

Game Analysis   At some point, it may become obvious that the games people play block the fulfillment of their contracts. Game analysis, the third stage of the counseling process, requires that the counselor have the ability to determine the payoff a client receives by playing a game and the racket that the game supports. Because games may be difficult for a client to give up, the counselor will provide permission and protection regularly during this stage of counseling as well.

Script Analysis   A complete understanding of payoffs and rackets will involve script analysis, the fourth stage of TA counseling. Ultimately, script analysis will explore the decisions that clients have made about their life positions.

These decisions—made in childhood—and the roles, staging, and climax that stem from them, can be discovered by using such techniques as a script checklist (Berne, 1972), analysis of favorite fairy tales (Karpman, 1968), or autobiographical exercises (James & Jongeward, 1971). The purpose of script analysis is to give clients an opportunity to understand their life positions and life dramas, and to make new decisions about themselves. Not only will a redecision free them from the games, self-defeating behavior, and feelings that have prevented the fulfillment of specific contracts, it will also move clients toward having autonomous lives that are characterized by awareness, spontaneity, and intimacy.

The four stages of counseling and the various techniques that transactional analysts use or borrow are designed to help clients gain both emotional and intellectual insight. The concepts and language of TA are structured to give clients a cognitive tool that can be used for self-observation and self-understanding. A major role of the counselor is to teach clients the analytical skills necessary to collect relevant personal and social information and to evaluate it appropriately so that rational, unconstrained decisions can be made. In short, the basic purpose of counseling is to help clients acquire the necessary tools to make their own decisions and to effect their own changes.

Illustrative Case Material

The following transcript is a condensed version of a TA group counseling session. In this particular segment, the focus is upon Bob, a recent group member who has been complaining about problems at work. Bob established a contract, which included as a major goal improving his work situation. He agreed to read Harris' (1969) book before he joined the group.

Cl 1: So, he did it to me again. He got his report to me too late to do anything with it and, of course, I'll get the blame.

Cl 2: Bob, isn't that basically what happened at your job before you were transferred? You told us about that last week.

Cl 1: No . . . No; that was just the opposite. Instead of expecting the impossible from me, my former supervisor used to take all the credit for my work. It was unbelievable! I knocked my brains out for that woman and never heard a word of appreciation from her. Everyone thought she was doing a great job, and she let them believe that it was all her doing. No question that she rode my back to her promotion. If anyone was to get a promotion, it should have been me!

Cl 2: But, isn't the same thing going on now with your present supervisor?

Cl 1: Not at all! My boss now always hands me too much work, too close to the deadline. It's just impossible for anyone to do what he expects. I can't believe how I always seem to wind up with losers for bosses.

Cl 2: Don't you think you might have something to do with how your bosses treat you?

Cl 1: I don't see how . . . I have really tried to do my best. What do you mean, anyway?

Cl 2: Well, it may be that you're not aware of how you sabotage yourself at work, and you're not taking responsibility for yourself. You seem to be blaming your bosses for some of your own hassles.

Cl 1: That's ridiculous. I can't help it if I get stuck with crummy people for bosses. I give my jobs my best shot . . . always have. As a matter of fact, if it weren't for them, I'd be in a much better position at work.

Cl 2: Well, I'm not so sure. . . .

Cl 3: Wait a second, Mollie . . . You're really stretching things, aren't you? Let's go easy on Bob, huh? After all, he's new to the group.

Co: Let me interrupt here. Bob, what ego state were you just coming from?

Cl 1: My Child . . . I think.

Co: Right! How about Mollie and Jim?

Cl 1: Hmmm . . . Well, Jim was definitely coming on Parent. Mollie . . . I'm not so sure.

Co: Was she being objective? Mostly asking for information?

Cl 1: Yeah, I guess so.

Co: And that would be what ego state?

Cl 1: Adult.

Co: Right. Now, I'd like us to take a look at that interchange on the videotape and see if there are any patterns here. (Counselor plays videotape of above transactions).

Co: Anyone pick up anything?

Cl 4: I agree with Mollie; I think Bob is trying to make excuses for the problems he's had at work.

Co: Sara, would you give that feedback directly to Bob?

Cl 4: Bob, it seems to me that you're avoiding your own responsibility in this thing with your supervisors. From what you said last week, and what I heard today, it's almost like you don't want to succeed at work, so you sabotage yourself and blame your bosses.

Co: Good feedback, Sara. Bob, how does that set with you?

Cl 1: I suppose it's possible . . . I must say, I was relieved not to be promoted.

Co: The added responsibility was kind of scary, huh?

Cl 1: Yeah, for sure.

Co: Bob, I want you to consider the possibility that you're playing a variation of the "If it weren't for you" game. In fact, you used that very phrase earlier in referring to your bosses. Basically, it appears that you are blaming your superiors for your own lack of achievement at work. And, from comments you've made about your wife, it looks like this is a favorite game of yours. The stamps you collect in this game are ones of reassurance and resentment. You're saying to yourself, "It's not that I'm undeserving; it's that he's keeping me back." I'd say it's fairly convenient that your supervisors have been so obliging!

Cl 1: Boy, that has a ring of truth to it.

Co: Bob, what do you remember your parents saying to you as a kid?

Cl 1: Well, my father died shortly after I was born, so I never knew him. My mother seemed to feel like I was a big bother. I remember she always had trouble finding a babysitter for me, and she used to complain about that a lot.

Co: How did she complain?

Cl 1:   (Smiling) She would say, "If it weren't for you, I could go out at night."

Co: She was a fairly influential model, wasn't she?

Cl 1:   Yeah, I guess she was . . . But, you know, I never really believed she would go out; she didn't have many friends.

Co: Did she seem afraid of social relationships?

Cl 1:   I think so . . . She wouldn't ever let me bring my friends to the house.

Co: So she used you as an excuse to avoid social contacts?

Cl 1:   It sounds like it, doesn't it?

Co: And you're doing the same thing now at work . . . blaming your boss for holding you back but really glad that you won't have to take the risks of more responsibility.

Cl 1:   Yes . . . I guess that's true.

Co: Bob, I am going to give you permission to take the risk to do your best at work and to quit playing the "If it weren't for him"game.

In the weeks that followed, Bob was able to see the recurring pattern in his transactions with his boss at work. He became skilled at identifying his own and others' ego states, and he was able to interrupt the games he played and to use his Adult more effectively. Not too long after this interchange, Bob negotiated a new contract concerning his feelings about himself and others. He undertook script analysis, and among other things completed a script checklist and wrote and analyzed his autobiography. Eventually, he was able to make a new decision about his basic life position.

Summary and Evaluation

Developed by psychiatrist Eric Berne, transactional analysis is a cognitive and didactic approach to counseling that emphasizes insight and understanding as the basis for change. It employs a clear-cut, simple set of terms within a systematic, carefully elaborated theory. Although deterministic in its basic view of persons, TA also assumes that people are capable of altering the childhood decisions that have determined their life course. In practice, TA proceeds on the premise that once individuals understand how their personality operates, the manner in which they interact with others, and the content and consequences of their basic life decisions, they will be able to effect change in their own lives.

Transactional analysts emphasize the importance of the first five years of life in the development of personality. During this time, the three components of the personality—Adult, Parent, Child—are shaped, and youngsters make a relatively permanent judgment about their own worth and about the worth of other people. After making this critical decision, children unconsciously formulate a plan concerning the course of their life. Once formed, this life script orchestrates the interpersonal transactions through which they meet their needs.

The goals of counseling include helping people to free themselves from the constraints of their early decisions and to make full and effective use of all three ego states. Reaching these major goals will enable them to live game-free, autonomous lives and to enjoy intimate, rewarding relationships with others.

The counselor functions as a teacher, trainer, and consultant as the client acquires the cognitive tools necessary for redecisions and change. Usually, within a group context, counseling progresses through four stages: (1) structural analysis, in which an understanding of the three ego states is emphasized; (2) transactional analysis, which involves a study of interaction patterns between people; (3) game analysis, which is concerned with the transactions that lead to feelings that advance the life script; and (4) script analysis, which provides the format for understanding one's unconscious, basic life decisions and plans.

During each stage of counseling, the emphasis is upon intellectual understanding and insight. The counselor is clearly the expert in this process, although transactional analysts view the relationship as egalitarian. Certainly clients, like counselors, must master a basic understanding of TA concepts if progress is to be made. In addition, clients enter into specific behavioral contracts with the counselor. Both the intellectual insights and the behavioral gains achieved in counseling move clients toward changing their transactions with others and altering the decisions that form the basis for their life scripts.

Although transactional analysis has been called overly simple (for example, by Harper, 1975), it relies on considerable cognitive activity. Because it emphasizes the importance of a basic understanding of its concepts and of the necessity for insights, decisions, and plans, it may not appear simple to some clients. Indeed, because of its cognitive, conceptual focus, its effectiveness is likely to be related to the intellectual skills of the client. Not only will this approach be limited by the conceptual capacities of certain clients, but it will also be of little value to those who require professional help in basic life skills or to those whose problems stem from environmental hardships such as unemployment. Learning to identify ego states and exploring one's early life decisions will do little to help such clients acquire money management skills or to find jobs.

Another limitation resulting from TA's intellectual focus is a neglect of the affective domain of human functioning. Emotionally inhibited, overly cerebral clients do not find TA facilitative in helping them experience and enjoy their feelings.

A related criticism concerns the vocabulary that TA employs. While some view it as a creative and engaging language, others view it as jargonistic and constraining (Corey, 1977). Rather than enhancing self-understanding, the terminology can become a hindrance. This is particularly true when other explanations of human behavior may contribute to a larger understanding but are rejected because the TA vocabulary does not incorporate them. Persons who are that provincial about TA may also make exclusive and aggressive use of its language and concepts. In such cases it may actually become a game in itself, a game designed to obtain feelings of superiority. While this criticism can be directed at any theory, TA seems especially vulnerable to misuse of this type because of its clever conceptualization and interesting language.

Another potential misuse of TA is that counselors may employ it as a means of avoiding genuine contact and involvement with their clients. It does not place much emphasis upon the therapeutic relationship, and some counselors may be attracted to TA because of its cerebral emphasis and because they are reluctant to deal with emotional experiences. Again, this criticism can be leveled at several other cognitive, highly verbal approaches to counseling. But for the reasons noted above, TA may be particularly vulnerable to this problem.

Steiner (1974) has expressed another concern. He sees the easy marketability and popularization of TA as possibly watering down its fundamental distinguishing features and rendering it impotent. Likewise, Goldhaber and Goldhaber (1976) fear that a TA "cult" might develop which could ultimately limit its usefulness by "turning people off." They note that some advocates have become overly zealous and have come to view TA as the answer to all of life's problems. Seeking to temper such expansive enthusiasm, the Goldhabers (1976) respond, "Despite the claims of these many, TA will not cure the common cold" (p. 12).

Enthusiasm for TA should also be tempered by recognizing the lack of empirical data on all aspects of the theory. The theory is both heuristic and testable, and its proponents can be criticized for their failure to study its hypotheses scientifically. Research is necessary to establish the adequacy of its conceptualizations of human behavior and functioning and to verify or discount its effectiveness as a therapeutic strategy.

Criticisms have also been directed at TA because of its apparent lack of counseling techniques. Holland (1973) states that the frequent combination of techniques from other approaches with TA "suggests a dearth of inventiveness at the process level" (p. 378). However, this problem might also be viewed as a strength, in that it gives TA counselors flexibility and encourages innovative combinations with other approaches. Goulding and Goulding (1976), for example, report success when using TA with the techniques of gestalt therapy and behavior modification. Gestalt techniques are used extensively by some transactional analysts (James & Jongeward, 1971). In her recent book about TA techniques, James (1977) also includes a number of contributions from therapists who have combined TA with such diverse therapeutic approaches as psychoanalysis, client-centered therapy, psychodrama, and Adlerian psychology.

Perhaps TA's most important asset is its engaging and simple vocabulary. Despite the hazards already mentioned, the language of TA can be credited with giving the layperson quick and easy access to its principles and concepts and elevating the client to a status of equality with the counselor. By eschewing a mysterious and esoteric vocabulary and by teaching clients their language planfully, transactional analysts demonstrate concretely a basic trust in human nature and convey a sense of confidence in their clients' ability to understand themselves and to make changes in their own lives as a result of their understanding. In the same way, TA's use of contracting gives the client parity with the counselor and helps the client to assume responsibility for the outcome of counseling.

Because of its broad appeal and its applicability as an educational tool, TA is a particularly attractive approach to helping people. By simply reading the literature or by taking introductory courses in TA, individuals can learn its concepts and begin to use them for self-understanding and self-direction, without the necessity of formal counseling. Thus, it can be a self-help psychology that provides people with a "cognitive map" with which to explore, monitor, and change their own behavior and feelings.

REALITY THERAPY

Introduced by William Glasser in 1962 (Glasser, 1976b), reality therapy has attracted increasing attention in the last decade and a half. Elementary and secondary educators have been particularly interested in its concepts, as have workers in the juvenile justice system. In fact, reality therapy has been accepted much more enthusiastically by professionals in these two fields than by persons who are active in the mental health professions. A major reason for this rather anomalous situation has been Glasser's (1965) own emphasis upon the prevention of aberrant behavior, rather than upon its remediation. The school system has been the primary target of his preventive efforts. As a treatment approach, reality therapy has been applied most frequently and most successfully in residential facilities for delinquent youths and "emotionally disturbed" children.

Glasser has been a caustic critic of traditional treatment approaches, which serves to alienate him and his ideas further from the mental health establishment. He has deemphasized the significance of unconscious motivation, the importance of personal history, the preeminence of emotional experience, and the necessity for insight. Instead, he has emphasized personal responsibility, ignored historical events, asserted that cognitive activities and reasoning skills are a person's highest functions, and focused therapeutic attention upon behavior change rather than upon insight. Glasser's simple, straightforward, and common-sense approach makes his ideas an immediately practical tool for educators, probation officers, and other front-line youth workers.

Reality therapy, however, is not exclusively the province of schools and juvenile halls. It is an appealing alternative to those who are interested in an efficient and effective means of helping others help themselves. Glasser's books are very readable and have been widely circulated. The Institute of Reality Therapy and its sister organization, The Educator Training Center, have trained thousands of human service professionals and educators. Glasser is a young and vigorous 54, and it seems a safe prediction that he will continue to be successful in promulgating his ideas to larger and larger audiences.

Introduction

Born in 1925, William Glasser spent all of his childhood and adolescent years in Cleveland, Ohio. Growing up was a relatively painless process for him. He remembers himself as being a "good boy" and, in an interview given several years ago, opinioned, "I don't think I've given my parents a moment's worry in 48 years" (Reilly, 1973, p. 21). Remaining in his hometown, Glasser entered college and obtained a bachelor's degree in chemical engineering, a master's in clinical psychology, and a degree in medicine from Case Western Reserve University. He was married while still in college, and after medical school Glasser moved his young family to the West Coast in order to take a residency in psychiatry at UCLA. The Glassers have made southern California their permanent home, and the impact of reality therapy is particularly pronounced in the Western United States.

Glasser spent his last year of residency at the West Los Angeles Veterans Administration Hospital, an affiliate of UCLA's psychiatry residency program. It was a classic example of conventional psychiatry at work. Assigned to Building 206, which housed the chronic psychotic patients at the hospital, Glasser (1965) characterized the therapeutic program as "the traditional mental hospital approach, in which the patients were accepted as mentally ill and were given good, standard care" (p. 107). A discharge rate of about two patients per year was silent testimony to the ineffectiveness of standard psychiatric treatment. Totally dissatisfied with the status quo, Glasser began to consider alternative treatment possibilities and to try new procedures. He was encouraged by his supervisor at the hospital, but his colleagues at UCLA were not pleased with his maverick ideas, and a potential teaching position at UCLA never materialized.

At about this same time (in 1957), Glasser was offered the position of chief psychiatrist at the new California state facility for female juvenile delinquents in Ventura. He began to implement the concepts he had developed at the Veterans Administration Hospital and worked out a program that placed responsibility for their present situation and future planning upon the girls themselves. Institutional rules were few and fair, and the consequences for violations were spelled out. Punishment was eliminated from the program. When the girls broke the rules, excuses were not accepted; personal responsibility was emphasized, and the girls were questioned about their plans and commitments to change their behavior. Above all, Glasser (1965) expected his staff to demonstrate their care and concern for the girls by becoming involved in their lives and by dishing out liberal helpings of honest praise. The program worked. The staff was enthusiastic; the girls began to live up to the positive expectations of the staff; and, most significantly, the recidivism rate was cut to 20 percent.

Back at the VA Hospital, Glasser was helping his former supervisor to implement a similar program for Building 206. Again the results were dramatic. A discharge rate of 2 patients per year gave way to 25 the second year and 75 the third, and culminated in a complete turnover each year thereafter of nearly all the 200 patients. Just as importantly, returns to the hospital were virtually eliminated. The positive effects of reality therapy were holding over time.

In 1961, Glasser published the rudimentary concepts of reality therapy in his first book, *Mental Health or Mental Illness*. These concepts were expanded, refined, and repackaged in the 1965 publication of *Reality Therapy: A New Approach to Psychiatry*. It is still considered Glasser's main work.

Shortly after the 1965 publication, Glasser founded the Institute of Reality Therapy, which was geared to train human service professionals. As word spread about his success, schools invited his consultation, and Glasser was able to adapt his procedures to fit educational settings. He published these ideas in *Schools without Failure* (1969) and established the Educator Training Center, through which teachers receive instruction in his methods.

In addition to his institutes and consultation activities, Glasser keeps up a hectic speaking schedule. He has written two more books, *The Identity Society* (1972) and *Positive Addiction* (1976a). Probably more than any other contemporary theory of human behavior, reality therapy has been used in the prevention of behavioral and emotional problems.

Although some have viewed Glasser's ideas as radical, Koenig (1974) states that "Glasser's originality is marginal" (p. 66). Clearly, his works are reminiscent of Alfred Adler, O. H. Mowrer, Thomas Szasz, and Norman Vincent Peale. He has been called a behavior therapist (Bratter, 1976), and his ideas are often compared to Ellis' rational-emotive therapy (see Hansen, Stevic & Warner, 1977, Chapter 9). His emphasis upon the counseling relationship is hardly distinguishable from that of Carl Rogers. If Glasser has borrowed heavily from others, however, his hybrid ideas, because they are packaged in a fresh, attractive way, have "force behind them" (Koenig, 1974, p. 66).

Philosophy and Major Concepts

View of Persons Glasser's positive view of persons is evident in his approach to education. Traditionally, education has treated the learner as an empty vessel into which the all-knowing teacher pours facts, figures, and concepts. Glasser (1969) believes that this is the approach taken by educators today. It emphasizes rote memory and factual knowledge and deemphasizes problem solving, critical thinking, and the relevance of the subject matter to the student. The focus is upon the teacher rather than upon the student.

In contrast, Glasser (1969) places great faith in the ability of students to determine the relevance of their educational experience and to help make good decisions concerning both the curriculum and the rules of their school. Problem solving, critical thinking, and social skills are emphasized rather than facts. The teacher is seen as a facilitator or catalyst who draws out the learning potential that the student brings to the classroom. This approach eschews a deterministic view of human behavior and assumes that students are rational beings who have the capacity to discover and make use of their own potential for learning and growth.

For life, as well as for education, Glasser holds the fundamental belief that each person is ultimately self-determining. By depending more upon their decisions than upon their situations, people can live responsible, successful, and satisfying lives. According to Glasser, people are what they do; thus, a change in an unsatisfactory existence can be initiated by deciding to change behavior.

This antideterministic, positive view of persons, which places responsibility for people's behavior and emotions upon themselves, is summarized by Glasser and Zunin (1973): "We believe that each individual has a health or growth force. Basically, people want to be content and enjoy a success identity, to show responsible behavior, and to have meaningful interpersonal relationships" (p. 297).

Motivation From a reality therapy perspective, all people must create a feeling of who they are (Glasser, 1969, p. 15). They must identify or define themselves as individuals—important, separate, and unique. Called "identity" by Glasser, this need is just as basic to each person as the psychological needs for food, water, and air. It is a "single, basic requirement of all mankind" (Glasser & Zunin, 1973, p. 294).

Glasser distinguishes between two kinds of identities. What he calls a "success identity" indicates that an individual defines himself or sees herself as a basically competent, capable, and worthwhile person who has the power to influence his environment and the confidence to govern her own life. The other kind of identity, a "failure identity," is held by people who have not established close personal relationships with others, who do not act responsibly, and who feel helpless, hopeless, and unworthy.

People are intrinsically motivated to attain a success identity. However, a success identity requires that two other basic needs be met: *the need to love and to be loved, and the need to feel worthwhile.* A prerequisite to satisfying these needs is being involved with others. In fact, involvement is the only access to a success identity. "It is an integral part of the organism and is the primary, intrinsic driving force governing all behavior" (Glasser & Zunin, 1973, p. 296).

Interpersonal involvement is clearly essential if people are to fulfill the need to love and to be loved. It is a less obvious requirement, however, in meeting the need to feel worthwhile. It appears to be more important how people evaluate their behavior. Positive self-evaluations lead to feelings of worth, while negative evaluations of oneself result in a sense of failure. However, inasmuch as these two needs are related—people who love and are loved tend to feel worthwhile, and those who feel worthwhile usually love and are loved—involvement is an essential aspect of satisfying both.

The need to love and to be loved is so important in Glasser's view that he sees it as a continuous, lifelong necessity that drives us to seek involvement with others. The minimum requirement for satisfying this need, according to Glasser (1969), is to find at least one person to love who reciprocates that love. "If a person succeeds in giving and receiving love, and can do so with some consistency throughout his life, he is to some degree a success" (p. 12).

Consistent with his emphasis upon behavior, Glasser defines love by what people do, rather than by how they feel. Within the context of school, for example, love is defined as social responsibility—"to care enough to help one another with the many social and educational problems of school" (Glasser, 1969, p. 14). Another definition of love is offered by Dr. G. L. Harrington, Glasser's supervisor at the Veterans Administration Hospital in West Los Angeles. He relates an incident in one of his group therapy sessions. The question, "What is love?" had been posed by a group member. "Everyone was very quiet for awhile, and then someone said, 'Love is someone saying, Get out of bed; it's time for school. Eat your vegetables. Take your vitamins. Wash your hands. Brush your teeth.' That person got it exactly right," said Harrington. "Love is unrelenting concern and involvement" (Reilly, 1973, p. 17).

Although critical, the need for love is no more important than the need for self-worth. "*To be worthwhile,*" Glasser (1965) asserts, "*we must maintain a satisfactory standard of behavior*" (p. 10). Also called self-respect and self-esteem, self-worth requires that individuals evaluate their behavior and work to correct it when it is not up to standard. Feelings of worthwhileness come as a result of solving problems, acquiring knowledge, completing tasks, and doing what one knows is right.

Two points should be made about self-worth. First, it is earned by what a person does. It cannot be given to or bestowed upon someone by another person.

Only by behaving in ways that meet their own internal standards and by coping successfully with the problems they face can people credit themselves and thereby attain a sense of accomplishment, satisfaction, and worthwhileness. Secondly, self-worth requires that individuals judge their behavior positively. This includes moral judgments, and Glasser views morality and values as highly relevant aspects of good mental health. In fact, for Glasser (1965) morality is part and parcel of meeting one's needs: *"When a man acts in such a way that he gives and receives love and feels worthwhile to himself and others, his behavior is right or moral"* (p. 57).

Identity has been discussed as a person's highest psychological need, which is built into the biological system from birth (Glasser, 1969, p. 15). If people are unable to establish an identity through the two pathways of love and self-worth, they will resort to other avenues such as delinquency and withdrawal. Whatever alternative routes a person may use to attain an identity, however, the end result is always the same: a failure identity.

Fortunately, the identity a person has established is not necessarily a permanent fixture. Identities can be changed, but only by changing behavior in such a way that the needs for love and self-worth are met. The process of meeting one's needs by changing behavior will be accomplished by doing what is responsible, realistic, and right—the three R's of reality therapy.

Responsibility   A fundamental tenet of reality therapy is personal responsibility. Defined by Glasser (1965) as *"the ability to fulfill one's needs and to do so in a way that does not deprive others of the ability to fulfill their needs"* (p. 13), responsibility also implies accountability. People are viewed as being accountable for their own behavior and responsible for fulfilling their own needs, regardless of mitigating circumstances. Neither the conditions of the past, factors in the present, nor the behavior of others can be used as excuses for one's actions. Glasser (1969) insists that until an individual accepts responsibility for his or her life and begins to act on that responsibility, change is impossible. He stresses the importance of this concept in discussing schoolchildren: "We must work to make them understand that *they are responsible* for fulfilling their needs, for behaving so that they can gain a successful identity. No one can do it for them" (p. 16).

Reality therapists equate responsibility with mental health—the more responsible people are, the healthier they are; the less responsible, the less healthy. Glasser has even suggested that the term "mental illness" and the whole psychiatric classification system, which are based upon the illness model, be discarded in favor of an accurate description of each individual's responsibility or lack of it. As long as people perceive themselves as sick, they have a ready-made reason for their irresponsibility. Removing the label will help to remove the excuse, and responsibility can be taught to clients more easily.

It is important to note the direction of causality in Glasser's suggestion to abandon the labels and concepts of mental illness. Unlike the proponents of the term, Glasser does not believe that mental health causes responsible behavior; rather, he asserts that behaving responsibly results in mental health. Likewise, unhappiness and personal suffering are the result of irresponsibility, not its cause.

Reality   Accepting responsibility requires that individuals face reality.

This means that they must perceive the real world accurately and understand that their needs must be met within the constraints that that world may impose. Current behavior is emphasized as a part of reality because it is one of the observable, hard facts of the real world. Feelings are less tangible, and Glasser argues that reality dictates that behavior, rather than feelings, be emphasized in counseling. Indeed, in the longstanding psychological "chicken and egg" debate, Glasser takes the position that behavior must change before feelings can change.

In addition to behavior, the present is also viewed as an integral part of the definition of reality. The fact is that we cannot alter the past, and attempts to understand it only divert us from the reality of the present. Moreover, when people are taught that to change themselves they must understand the past, historical events become an excuse for what they are doing now. Consequently, the reality therapist insists that clients face reality, that is, face their present behavior.

If irresponsibility can be equated with mental illness, then the kind of mental illness people suffer is defined by the manner in which they choose to deny reality. Some people, for example, claim to be certain historical figures, thus denying the reality of their own existence; others harbor debilitating phobias, thus denying the improbability or irrationality of the feared mishaps. Such denials of reality always carry with them a failure to assume responsibility for one's life. Reality therapy, then, is designed to help people "face the reality that they can solve their problems by more responsible behavior" (Glasser, 1965, p. 6).

Right   Value judgments are an essential feature of a responsible person's cognitive repertoire. Without evaluating their behavior as being either right or wrong, good or bad, people's actions and activities would be capricious and arbitrary. Not only do moral judgments guide people's behavior, they are also a necessary part of meeting the need for self-worth. "Morals, standards, values, or right and wrong behavior are all intimately related to the fulfillment of our need for self-worth" (Glasser, 1965, p. 11). In addition, the value judgments individuals make about certain behaviors may provide them with the impetus to change those behaviors.

Although Glasser does not offer a specific moral code by which people should live, he does believe that certain generally accepted moral principles—for example, that cheating is wrong and honesty is right—should be affirmed by the reality therapist. His own therapeutic approach is imbued with the particular values that he cherishes—for example, care and concern for others, honesty, and commitment. His definition of responsibility itself sounds suspiciously like the golden rule.

Glasser is careful to urge caution in imposing one's values upon others, but he is equally careful to emphasize that the reality therapist has the responsibility to confront the client with value choices and to point to the possible consequences of those choices.

Development of the Normal Individual

Reality therapists see personality as developing out of the individual's attempt to meet his or her basic needs of love and self-worth. Those who learn to fulfill these needs develop normally, are responsible and reality-oriented, and identify themselves as successes. Those who fall short of meeting their needs are irresponsible, deny reality, and have developed failure identities.

From a reality therapy perspective, development does not occur in stages, although Glasser (1969) does stress the importance of the years between two and five and between five and ten. These two time periods correspond to the child's initial exposure to the social structures that have the most significant impact upon personality formation: the family and the school.

Because the ability to meet one's needs must be learned, parents bear the major responsibility for teaching their children the requisite skills. Particularly crucial are the years between two and five, for it is during this time that children most readily learn the social, verbal, and intellectual skills that they must acquire to be able to satisfy their needs. In helping their children to develop these abilities, parents should ensure that they get much exposure to and involvement with other children and adults. Contact with a variety of people will provide opportunities to practice their developing conversational and social skills. Because they must learn to cope with the realities of life, children should not be rescued from the social bumps and bruises they experience in these interactions with others. They will learn best by experiencing the natural consequences of their behavior, not by being shielded from the frustrations of daily living.

A major parenting effort should be expended to teach youngsters how to talk and how to listen. Verbal skills are extremely important assets as children seek the interpersonal contact necessary for satisfying their basic need to love and be loved. Also important are the child's reasoning and problem-solving abilities. These skills can be sharpened when parents ask their children interesting and thought-provoking questions. Feelings of self-worth are enhanced as children discover that they can think clearly, make value judgments, and cope with problems.

It is essential that parents hold their children to a responsible course of action throughout childhood. This may mean that parents bear the brunt of their child's anger on occasion, but it is of vital importance that parents show their concern by firmly setting limits and refusing to condone irresponsible behavior. Enforcing rules in a planful, consistent, and fair way is discipline, not punishment, and Glasser (1972) encourages its use. Punishment, on the other hand, should be abandoned completely as a parenting technique because it is typically reactive, capricious, and arbitrary.

Most important in the child-rearing endeavor is the involvement of parents with their children. It is the basic ingredient of all successful parenting. Without parental involvement, children will not learn to give and receive love, they will have no foundation upon which to build self-worth, and they will not accept discipline and guidance. Although Glasser does not offer a precise definition, it is accurate to say that parental involvement begins with eyeball-to-eyeball, skin-to-skin contact. It means that parents spend time with their children; show an interest in their activities, thoughts, and concerns; share emotional experiences with them; and treat them respectfully. It also implies that children come to know their parents as persons. Basically, involvement is establishing and maintaining a warm, emotional relationship in which the child feels loved for what he or she is.

Within the context of a loving relationship, responsible parents who teach their children actively, who discipline them when it is needed and refuse to accept excuses, who set an example by modeling responsible behavior, and who allow their children the freedom to learn by doing, create a growth environment in which their children will gain the necessary skills to satisfy their needs. Such children will develop normally and will identify themselves as successes.

Because a school-age child spends almost as many waking hours in the classroom as at home, Glasser (1969) believes that school can be instrumental in helping a child to develop and maintain a success identity. From age five to age ten, school is particularly important if students are to continue the process of learning to meet their needs satisfactorily. Glasser emphasizes that teachers must get involved with their students, make education relevant, and provide many success experiences. He asserts that teachers have influence enough so that if a child's parents have provided poor learning opportunities at home, a positive school experience can help the child salvage a success identity. Unfortunately, most teachers in most school systems hinder, rather than facilitate, the child's normal development.

Given the proper home and school environments, a person will develop normally. Normal development leads to maturity—the ability to stand on one's own two feet psychologically (Glasser & Zunin, 1973, p. 296). Mature individuals identify themselves as successes and take responsibility for who they are, what they do, and what they want. They are also able to develop responsible plans to achieve their goals and to meet their needs.

In summary, personality is formed as an individual attempts to meet his or her needs to love and be loved and to achieve self-worth. Learning to meet these needs requires involvement from parents and from significant others. By example, direct instruction, and discipline, parents teach their children to accept responsibility for their lives, face reality squarely, and make proper value judgments. Children also learn and develop as they try out new behaviors and experience the consequences of their actions. This process of normal development leads youngsters to become personally responsible and to identify themselves as healthy, successful persons.

Development of Maladaptive Behavior

When people are unable to satisfy one or both of their needs for love and worth, they experience psychological pain (Glasser, 1965, p. 11). Pain signals a problem and motivates people to try to alleviate it. Instinctively, people attempt to reduce the pain through involvement with others. If they become involved successfully with another person, the discomfort diminishes and they are well on their way to learning how to meet their needs effectively. If their attempts at involvement are unsuccessful, however, they will be unable to meet their needs and will experience even greater pain.

The failure to become involved with others—a biological prerequisite for satisfying basic needs—initiates a vicious failure cycle. Lack of involvement with another person leads to an inability to fulfill one's needs, which leads to a denial of those needs, which leads to a denial of responsibility, which removes the person even further from successful involvement with others, and the cycle begins again. For example, because Jane is not involved with others, she is unable to love; she chooses to deny her need for love in order to avoid further rejection; in her loneliness she creates a fear of going out of the house and then blames her situation on the phobia. The phobia prevents even the opportunity for involvement with others, and so the cycle perpetuates itself. Much as success breeds success, failure breeds failure. Depending upon where one breaks into this cycle, maladaptive behavior could be viewed as a function of irresponsibility, a lack of involvement with others, an inability to fulfill one's needs, or a denial of reality.

The example above illustrates what Glasser (1972) refers to as self-involvement—looking to oneself to ease the pain that results from failure. Becoming involved with oneself always takes the form of a psychological, social, or physical symptom. Glasser believes that these "symptoms" are selected to fit the person's situation best. Because people treat them as living things, Glasser calls these symptoms "companions." Lonely people, who see them as faithful friends, substitute these companions for involvement with others. Companion symptoms include, among others, depression, phobias, psychoses, antisocial behavior, alcoholism, and many physical ailments. Virtually all social and emotional difficulties, and many physical problems, have self-involvement at their core. "I believe *every* psychologically diagnosable condition is an example of involvement with one's own idea, behavior, symptom, or emotion, or some combination of them" (Glasser, 1972, p. 47).

Self-involvement includes a failure to operate on the principles of responsibility, reality, and right. Self-involved persons identify themselves as failures. They have not learned to act responsibly; that is, they have not learned to meet their needs in a realistic way.

Parents who have not involved themselves adequately must share much responsibilty for their children's failure. Schools also contribute to the development of failure identities. Indeed, Glasser and Zunin (1973) note that the "*formation of a failure identity* seems to occur most often at age four or five, coincidental with the age at which the child enters school" (p. 294). Before that time, most children view themselves as successes, but as school forces them to memorize rather than to think, fails them and then labels them as failures, and foists an apparently irrelevant curriculum upon them, they begin to see themselves as failures. A failure identity is virtually assured when overworked teachers cannot become involved with their students.

Although others may share responsibility for an individual's failure to learn how to meet his or her needs, they do not share in that person's present failure to learn. Regardless of etiology, Glasser (1972) insists that "*we have the symptom now, because we are lonely and failing now*" (p. 56). Looking to the origins of a particular symptom will only serve the same purpose as employing a diagnostic label for that symptom—namely, as an excuse for maladaptive, irresponsible behavior. But whether the maladaptive behavior begins in childhood or last week, it exists now in the present, and all persons must take the responsibility for their present behavior, look at it honestly, and determine whether it contributes to fulfilling their needs.

Glasser (1969) points out that even persons whose need to love and be loved

is not being fulfilled can nonetheless behave responsibly by adjusting their behavior to adhere to a satisfactory standard. By so doing, they "may gain enough
self-confidence to learn to give and receive love" (p. 13).

Reality therapists believe that, regardless of its history, maladaptive behavior can be changed, and that people can become involved with others and take
responsibility for their lives at any point in time. People come to counseling seeking change. Their denial of reality, their self-involvement, and their irresponsibility have not succeeded in reducing their pain more than temporarily, and
therefore they seek professional help.

Goals of Counseling

While involvement is a prominent concept, it is not the goal of reality therapy.
Rather, it is the process by which goals are attained. It is a means and not an end.
The major goal of reality therapy is to help clients to assume personal responsibility (Glasser & Zunin, 1973, p. 292). By definition, responsibility is the ability
to act in ways that fulfill one's needs, which in turn leads to a success identity.
Consequently, in a roundabout way the goal of reality therapy is to assist clients
in achieving a success identity.

However, Glasser deliberately does not discuss success identity as a specific
counseling goal. His reason for not doing so can be illustrated by referring to a
paper he deliverd at a Canadian convention of correctional officers in the early
1960s. In that paper, Glasser (1976b) is highly critical of the traditional view that
unhappiness is the cause of delinquency. This fallacious notion, he asserts, has
spurred all too many well-intentioned but misguided professionals into attempting to bring happiness to youthful offenders. These people have falsely assumed
that if delinquents feel happy, they will not commiit unlawful acts. Glasser points
out that unhappiness does not cause youngsters to engage in delinquent activity;
rather, it is a feeling they experience when they act irresponsibly. His contention
is that feelings and attitudes grow out of a person's behavior and not the reverse.
Likewise, identity—an attitude a person holds about him- or herself—is a by-
product of that person's behavior and cannot be dealt with independently. To
change their identity, people must first change their behavior. Consequently,
responsible behavior is the goal of counseling.

In addition to the global goal of personal responsibility, clients establish
their own particular life goals, to include both immediate and long-term aims. An
immediate objective, for example, might be to stop smoking, while securing a
good engineering job after finishing a college degree could be a long-range goal.
The counselor, then, helps clients to evaluate their present behavior and to determine whether it will help them to achieve these objectives and assists clients in
developing plans to reach their goals.

In the broadest sense, the reality therapist attempts to teach the client an
approach to life. This involves helping the client learn general, cognitive, coping
skills, rather than simply altering specific maladaptive behaviors. The counselor
encourages each client to live by the three R's of reality therapy: responsibility,
reality, and right. Thus, a broad goal of reality therapy is to assist the client in

developing "a system or a way of life which helps a person to become successful in almost all of his endeavors" (Glasser & Zunin, 1973, p. 292).

Process and Techniques of Counseling

From a reality therapy perspective, counseling is a learning process that emphasizes rational dialogue between the client and the counselor. Counselors are active verbally and ask many questions about the client's current life situation. They use questions throughout the counseling process to help the client become aware of his or her behavior, make value judgments, and construct plans for change.

Besides asking questions, reality counselors are active verbally in several other ways. They engage the client in interesting and enjoyable conversations, which at times are unrelated to the presenting problem; they make use of humor; and an occasional heated discussion may be an important part of counseling. Verbal confrontations are also used frequently, particularly because the counselor does not accept excuses. Prolonged silence between counselor and client, on the other hand, is a rare occurrence in reality counseling. Glasser & Zunin (1973, p. 311) view it as a useless therapeutic technique and encourage counselors to be as active verbally as is necessary to stay involved with their clients.

The characteristics of a reality therapist have been detailed by Glasser (1965, Chapter 1). Briefly, they include a high degree of personal responsibility; a sincere interest in and concern for others; a willingness to be open, to share personal struggles, and to allow personal values to be challenged; the strength never to condone irresponsible behavior; and the ability to establish a warm, personal relationship with the client. These qualities are necessary to help the counselor become involved with the client.

Reality counselors do not have a bag of therapeutic tricks from which they can draw during the process of counseling. Rather, Glasser's (1969; 1972; Glasser & Zunin, 1973) eight general principles serve as a guide to the counselor. These principles can be used flexibly, depending upon the needs of the client. The order in which Glasser has presented them, however, illustrates the typical course that counseling takes.

1 *Involvement.* Involvement with at least one successful person is a prerequisite for any client change. People come to counseling because they have failed to become involved with others. Therefore, counselors must communicate quite early that they are concerned about and care for the client. They must be personable, warm, and friendly, and they must develop intimate, emotional relationships with their clients. Glasser (1965) stresses the importance of involvement: "The ability of the therapist to get involved is the major skill of doing reality therapy" (p. 22).

Glasser and Zunin (1973) offer a number of specific suggestions that, if implemented, can help counselors to establish involvement. They suggest that counselors use personal pronouns and never refer either to themselves or to the client in impersonal third-person terms. Self-disclosure is encouraged, since relationships are solidified when counselors reveal themselves as genuine persons.

A friendly, optimistic demeanor on the part of counselors is also important. Clients should sense that their counselor believes in them and is confident that they can effect positive changes in their lives.

Most important is talking with the client about a wide range of subjects. Particular attention should be given to what the clients' interests and successes are— what they are doing right in their lives. Exclusive focus on problems actually retards progress, because it maintains the client's self-involvement, while discussions about other aspects of the client's life not only keep the focus off the problem but also enhance the client's conversational skills. "Talking enjoyably about worthwhile subjects is the best way to help oneself get involved" (Glasser, 1972, p. 83).

Another important aspect of therapeutic involvement is to set the limits of the involvement and to define the relationship as clearly as possible. Rather than being detrimental to the relationship, definition keeps the involvement realistic and guides the expectations of the client.

2 *Focus on behavior.* Many approaches to counseling focus on feelings as the most important part of human experience. Ventilating and understanding feelings are viewed as the best means of therapeutic change. Glasser, as noted earlier, maintains just the opposite. Because he believes that a change in how a person feels follows a change in behavior, the reality therapist is interested in what the client is doing. In dealing with clients who say, "I'm very unhappy," the reality counselor does not ask them to elaborate on their emotional state or on how long they have felt this way. Rather, the counselor focuses attention on behavior: "What are you doing to make yourself unhappy?"

The major purpose of stressing the client's behavior is to help the client become aware of what he or she is doing. "Unless we become aware of our behavior, we cannot learn to behave more competently" (Glasser, 1972, p. 85).

3 *Focus on present.* Another way of getting the problem behavior out on the table is to keep focusing attention upon what is happening now in the life of the client. This emphasis is different from that of some other approaches to counseling, for example gestalt, in which the present is defined as the immediate moment. By present, Glasser means the current events and activities of the client's life. This means finding out about the client's strengths as well as the weaknesses, because as changes begin to take place it will be important to build upon them.

Focusing upon the present also means ignoring the past. Reality therapy rejects the archeological expeditions of many counseling approaches, which assume that in order to make progress, clients must uncover the original trauma that caused their present condition. Indeed, these historical searches often serve the counterproductive purpose of giving clients an excuse to persist in their present maladaptive behavior. If past problems are discussed at all, the reality counselor attempts to relate them to current functioning by asking clients what they did to prevent even further dysfunction (emphasizing assets), or what other alternatives they might have chosen in that situation (practicing problem solving).

4 *Value judgment.* Once counselors have become involved successfully with their clients, and clients are aware of their current behavior, the issue of right and wrong must be raised. Clients must be forced to examine the quality of what they are doing and determine whether it is in their best interests and in the best interests of those around them. That is, does their present behavior help them to meet their needs? This is a value question that clients must answer. Unless clients see that their present behavior is debilitating, and judge it to be wrong, they will not work to change it.

If a client answers "I don't know" or "It made me feel better," the reality counselor presses the question, "Did this behavior do you any good?" Once the client evaluates the behavior as wrong, the counselor must not condone it (Glasser & Zunin, 1973, p. 301). On the other hand, if the client states that he or she did the right thing under the circumstances, the counselor should not argue or debate the point. Only the client can make value judgments about his or her own behavior. Hopefully, time and the natural consequences of the behavior will eventually change the client's perspective.

5 *Planning responsible behavior.* This stage is often the most time-consuming. It begins as soon as clients have made reasonable judgments about their irresponsible behavior. Plans can then be made to change that behavior. The counselor might begin the process by asking, "What is your plan? Do you have any ideas? Shall we put our heads together and figure something out?" A brainstorming session could be suggested in which as many solutions as possible are generated. The counselor must ensure that the agreed-upon plan is neither too ambitious nor too limited. Failure could result, on the one hand, or minimal progress on the other. In either case, the client might lose the motivation to change. The plan should also be realistic and should help the client to move toward his or her goal in logical step-by-step increments. Changing one's social life, for example, should not begin by throwing a party for 50 people. A reasonable plan might include engaging in selected social contacts that are brief and superficial at first and, as the client's confidence builds, allowing them to become longer and more personal.

When plans don't work, they should be discarded. In that event, the counselor should remain encouraging and convey confidence that an option that will work can be found. On occasion, the counselor may need to refer clients temporarily to someone who is more knowledgeable and who can help them make detailed plans. However, more important than expertise is good common sense, and to be effective, counselors must continuously sharpen their common-sense "savvy."

6 *Commitment.* Having a good plan does not ensure that the client will implement it. Therefore, the reality counselor asks the client to make a commitment to carry out the plan. Often, commitments take the form of written contracts, which clients are asked to sign. When plans for change are actually written down in contract form, the contract can serve both as evidence of the agreement to change behavior and as a reminder of the specifics of the plan.

A commitment may initially be made to the counselor in the form of an "I'll do it for you" statement. To expect a client with little self-respect to keep a commitment made for him- or herself is often unrealistic; therefore, Glasser (1972) does not object to a promise to another person. In fact, it may be an important first step toward eventually making and keeping an "I'll do it for myself" promise. Over time, as the client gains a sense of self-worth, the focus should move to commitments made for self.

7 *No excuses.* A fact of therapeutic life is that clients fail in their commitments. It is a temptation to attempt to discover why a plan was not successful, but the reality counselor must resist that temptation. The past is over; the failure is a fact that cannot be altered, and to search for its cause will do little more than provide clients with excuses for their irresponsibility. Thus, "Why?" is an irrelevant question, which is avoided altogether by reality counselors.

When clients return to counseling without having carried out their plans, the value judgment upon which the plan was based should be reviewed. If it still holds, then the counselor will want to know only one thing: "When do you intend to fulfill your commitment?" There is no effort made to fix blame; there are no accusations, no sarcasm, no excuses. The counselor simply insists that commitments that are worth making are worth keeping, and assumes "that a commitment according to a reasonable plan is always possible" (Glasser & Zunin, 1973, p. 303).

8 *Eliminate punishment.* As important as not accepting a client's excuses for irresponsibility is not punishing a client's failure. Critical statements, sarcasm, and even a strategic silence only serve as punishment, even though the intention of the counselor may be to motivate the client. Most often, punitive comments simply reconfirm the client's failure identity. Furthermore, punishment harms the therapeutic relationship.

Glasser and Zunin (1973, p. 303) note that allowing a client to experience the agreed-upon consequences of failing to keep a commitment is quite different from punishment. For example, a plan might include a clause stating that if the client fails to complete the plan, then a postdated $50 check is to be mailed to the campaign fund of the client's least-favored political figure. The counselor is obliged to mail the check, even though the client may wish to renegotiate. Follow-through activities of this kind are not punishment, but emphasize to clients that only they are responsible for their behavior, and only they bear the consequences.

Glasser's eight principles of reality therapy are applicable in both formal treatment settings, such as the counseling office, and preventive settings, such as the school classroom. With minor modifications and the addition of the principles of relevance and no-failure, school personnel have been able to assume the role of therapists.

Class meetings in school and group counseling meetings in treatment settings are the ideal modality for implementing reality therapy principles. The potential for involvement with a number of significant people is inherent in groups. In addition, plans and commitments may be enhanced within the context of a group of involved people. Regardless of modality, however, Glasser believes that these eight principles will help clients become more responsible, realistic persons who are better able to judge their behavior properly and meet their own needs.

Illustrative Case Material

Norman is a 14-year-old first-year high school student whose grades have plummeted. To help him improve his academic performance, Norman's parents have tried to implement several homework and study plans with his junior high school counselor. So far, none has worked. Because they are frustrated and feeling helpless, his parents have referred Norman to a reality therapist in private practice. At the initial interview with Norman's parents, the counselor learns that Norman is doing poorly at home as well as at school. He often refuses to do his chores, speaks disrespectfully to his parents, fights with both his older and younger sisters, and has twice stayed out all night without permission. Subsequently, the counselor has met once with Norman and his parents and twice with Norman alone. In this third session, most of the conversation has revolved around Norman's growing interest in cooking.

Co: So, because you've enjoyed the home ec class so much the last couple of weeks, you think you might like to be a chef someday?

Cl: Yeah! I think it would be interesting . . . I hear chefs get paid pretty good too, don't they?

Co: I don't know, but we could sure find out. What do you have to do to become a chef, do you know?

Cl: Naw . . . I'm not sure . . . I guess go to cook's school or something like that.

Co: Hmmm, I think you're right. How do you get into cook's school, anyway?

Cl: I don't know.

Co: Do you have to finish high school?

Cl: I don't know . . . I think so.

Co: What do you think about that part of it? Finishing high school, I mean . . .

Cl: I don't know . . . probably impossible for me.

Co: But, if you did graduate from high school, you would want to go to cook's school, huh?

Cl: Yeah, I think I would. How come you have to finish high school to go? . . . that's ridiculous.

Co: I'm not sure. I suppose they want to make sure their students can read and follow directions . . . and add and subtract and things like that.

Cl: Well, I can do all that. How come I have to graduate?

Co: I don't know, Norman . . . but it sounds like that's how it is.

Cl: Boy, I might as well throw in the towel then . . . I just got my grades for the quarter.

Co: You did? How did you do?

Cl: Not so hot.

Co: What exactly did you get, Norman? I'd like to know.

Cl: I got a B in home ec, D's in art and music, and an F in English, an F in math, and an F in social studies.

Co: So, home ec is definitely your best subject. How about gym?

Cl: Well, I was working out with the swim team instead of going to gym. I made the team last month.

Co: Great . . . I had forgotten that. You like swimming too, huh?

Cl: Yeah . . . yeah.

Cl: What did you mean, *was* working out with the swim team?

Cl: Coach told me last Friday that I'm off the team until I pull up my grades. I guess I can't have three F's and be on a school team.

Co: Boy, that's rough.

Cl: I'll say.

Co: Norman, let me see if I understand this. You want to be a chef, and that means graduating from high school; and you want to be on the swim team, and that means you've got to do better in school . . . yet, you don't like school.

Cl: That's about it.

Co: What are you doing that makes you not like school?

Cl: Nothing . . . it's those lousy teachers.

Co: Tell me what you're doing anyway. What's your toughest class?

Cl: English . . . I hate it.

Co: So, what happens in English class? What did you do today?

Cl: Huh? I just went, that's all.

Co: Did you get there on time?

Cl: Yeah . . . I don't know . . . I guess I was a little late.

Co: After the bell rang?

Cl: Yeah, I guess so.

Co: Then what?

Cl: Well, I sat down and . . .

Co: Where . . . what part of the room?

Cl: In the back, I think.

Co: Who did you sit next to?

Cl: Huh? George was on one side and Mary . . . I think it was . . . was on the other side.

Co: What kind of work do they do in English? George and Mary, I mean.

Cl: Not very good . . . like me, I guess.

Co: Then what?

Cl: Well, nothing . . . just sat there and fooled around.

Co: Did you ask any questions? Did you do your work?

Cl: Naw . . . I hate that class.

Co: Norman, let me ask you something. You want to swim on the team; you want to go to cook's school. Both require that you do better in school. Would you be doing better if you thought it was possible for you to do better?

Cl: Yeah, but it's hopeless . . . the teachers will never give me better grades.

Co: Well, you're right about that. They won't give them to you. Do you think you could somehow do better work and change the teacher's minds?

Cl: I doubt it.

Co: Let's think about that for a minute. Let's see . . . you arrived at class late . . . does that help you do better work or hurt your work?

Cl: Probably hurt.

Co: I think so, too. How about sitting in the back of the room with George and Mary?

Cl: Probably hurt.

Co: How about never raising your hand . . . never acting interested?

Cl: Probably hurt.

Co: Yep. I'll ask you again, Norman. Do you want to change and to do better work?

Cl: Yes, I do.

Co: So . . . what's the plan? How can we help you?

Cl: Well, I guess I could change what you were talking about.

Co: You mean come to class on time? What else?

Cl: I could change my seat and act more interested.

Co: Great! We've got a three-point plan. What say we write it down?

After writing down the plan, the counselor asked Norman to agree to carry it out in the coming week. Although Norman fulfilled his commitment in the first week, he failed when the plan was expanded to include his math class. The counselor refused to accept his excuses for failure, but the plan was modified, and as Norman kept his commitment, it was slowly expanded to include all his classes. Success led to success. Norman was reinstated to the swim team, and his behavior at home began to improve. Before they terminated, Norman and his counselor explored several chef training programs.

In this example, the counselor began by taking a genuine interest in Norman's strengths. Problems were discussed only briefly until the third session. Once involvement was established, the counselor probed more carefully. She questioned Norman about his current circumstances, while his past was left untouched. She recognized that Norman's school performance was the major stumbling block in keeping him from his goals and did not attempt to tackle home problems simultaneously. The counselor did not ask why, nor did she accept excuses. She simply asked Norman to take stock of what he was doing and to evaluate it in the light of both his immediate and his long-range goals. Finally, she asked him to formulate a plan and asked him to commit himself to it.

Although the transcript cannot reveal the nonverbal cues and verbal inflections, the counselor was warm and accepting and able to make emotional contact with Norman. Her involvement and skillful use of questions to confront Norman with his behavior and its consequences gave him the motivation to begin to take control of his life, and to accept responsibility for his present and his future situation.

Summary and Evaluation

Reality therapy, as developed by California psychiatrist William Glasser, is a verbally active, largely rational approach that is directed at behavior change. In terms of clients served, reality therapy is more a preventive strategy than a therapeutic strategy. Its principles are applied increasingly in the public schools—the social institution in Western culture that is perhaps best suited to preventive mental health efforts. With a fundamentally positive view of persons, an emphasis upon individual responsibility, and a relatively simplistic theoretical structure, reality therapy provides a humane, common-sense approach to the development and management of human behavior.

At the core of the theory are Glasser's concepts of responsibility, reality, and right. Responsible behavior—acting to satisfy one's needs in a way that does not deprive others of doing the same—is viewed as the cause and not as the consequence of happiness. Thus, it is the major goal of counseling. Reality, a related concept, requires that people understand the world—imperfections included—

and recognize that their needs must be fulfilled responsibly within the limits it imposes. Right refers to the objective standard by which people judge their behavior as either right or wrong. Thus, the morality of one's behavior is an essential consideration during counseling.

Reality counselors help their clients learn how to meet their needs—to love and to be loved and to be worthwhile—by using as a guide the three R's: responsibility, reality, and right. Adequately meeting one's needs results in a success identity; inability to do so yields a failure identity. The behavioral changes necessary to satisfy one's needs and to be responsible are achieved as the counselor assists the client to become aware of his or her present behavior, evaluate it, and make and implement a plan for change. During the course of counseling, reality counselors never ask "why"; they ignore personal history; they refuse to accept excuses; and they believe that change is always possible if clients will commit themselves to reasonable plans for change. Most importantly, the counselor establishes a warm, open, emotional relationship with the client. This counselor-client involvement is the foundation of the counseling process. Only by involvement with another person can clients learn how to fulfill their needs and to achieve a success identity.

Although Glasser and Zunin (1973) point to the broad applicability of reality therapy, they also note its limitations. Since it is a highly verbal, highly rational approach, they point out that it is not effective with autistic and severely mentally retarded persons (p. 309). Extending their observation, it seems logical that, in general, the success of reality therapy will probably covary with the verbal and cognitive abilities of the client. Persons who are skilled verbally and cognitively will benefit most, while people with poor verbal skills and critical thinking powers will benefit least.

Another limitation that is not mentioned by Glasser and Zunin, but is related to the verbal/rational thrust of reality therapy, is the excessive emphasis upon verbal exchanges and behavior, to the exclusion of feelings. Although Glasser's contention that changes in feelings generally follow changes in behavior is supported by research (for example, Bandura, 1969, Chapter 7), it does not follow logically that feelings should therefore be ignored in counseling. Often, however, opportunities for therapeutic attention to affect are missed. This happens as reality counselors attempt routinely to tie behavior to feelings (Glasser & Zunin, 1973, p. 299) and thereby obviate valuable chances for exploring client feelings. For example, if a client says, "Boy, was I angry with him," the reality counselor asks: "What are you doing to make yourself angry?" rather than the more facilitative, more empathic, "You seem very upset about that incident." Given the extensive literature about the importance of empathy in relationship building, and given Glasser's emphasis upon involvement, it is odd that he would reject the exploration of feelings in counseling as, at the very least, a relationship-enhancing technique.

Glasser might argue the above point by noting that he encourages frequent "anything goes" conversations about mutually interesting subjects as a means of establishing the counseling relationship and solidifying involvement. However, this technique itself can be criticized as potentially perpetuating a kind of paid friendship. Counselors might not use their unique professional skills and training to help the client because it is too easy to engage in pleasant talk. Reality counselors may be particularly vulnerable to using conversation as a way of avoiding needed confrontation with certain clients. Friendship has a place in counseling, but its importance should never serve as a ready-made excuse for evading the hard work of helping people change.

The lack of a specific change technology can also be viewed as a weakness of reality therapy. In lieu of planned-change expertise, reality counselors rely upon the pooled common sense between themselves and their clients to create necessary plans to help clients alter their behavior. This might be an especially glaring weakness for the noncreative counselor. The problem could be eliminated by training reality counselors in the use of specific behavior and cognitive change techniques, which they could then employ during the planning and commitment phases of counseling.

Finally, because Glasser has not been careful in defining some of his terms, reality therapy is occasionally confusing on the conceptual level. For example, he defines responsibility as "the ability to fulfill one's needs" (1965, p. 13); yet the term is most often used to indicate accountability. Using the same word to refer to both these important reality therapy concepts weakens its meaning and clouds understanding.

Another perplexing use of the term responsibility is in relation to the concept of involvement. Glasser (1972) states emphatically that "without warm, emotional involvement, there is no possibility of success" (p. 78). At the same time, he says, "No matter what happened to him in the past, he still has the responsibility for what he does now" (Glasser & Zunin, 1973, p. 314). If by responsibility Glasser means ability to meet one's needs, the two statements appear to be contradictory. On the one hand, involvement is a precondition for progress; on the other hand, the individual has the ability to fulfill his or her needs now—without preconditions.

The limitations and problems discussed above, however, are minor compared to the strengths and contributions of reality therapy. Glasser has put together a simple, short-term treatment package that works. He boasts an 80 percent success rate with delinquent girls (1965, p. 67), and other more recent research corroborates his understandable enthusiasm (Glasser & Zunin, 1973, p. 308).

From Glasser's perspective, several of the limitations cited above are viewed as strengths, not as weaknesses. Clearly, feelings can be and often are overemphasized in counseling, and Glasser's caution in this regard is helpful. Conversation and friendship, also, are important facets of counseling and can help counselors avoid a preoccupation with problems, which in itself is debilitating for clients. Furthermore, Glasser's focus upon commitment and action offers welcome relief to a field that is overburdened with the notion that insight is the necessary and sufficient condition for change. His incorporation of values and morals into the counseling process has also helped to shatter the longstanding myth that such matters must be left outside the counselor's door.

Reality therapy's most significant strength, however, is its applicability to preventive mental health. As an approach that builds upon people's strengths instead of attempting to eliminate their weaknesses, reality therapy's prevention potential is enormous. Its positive philosophical base, which emphasizes personal responsibility and human concern, coupled with large amounts of common sense, is an approach to life that could have incalculable benefits both for individuals and for the society as a whole. Not only could reality therapy principles be taught to parents and teachers, they might also be applied to such social problems as pollution and prejudice. Whether it is employed in such grandiose ways or not, reality therapy will make an increasing impact upon the helping professions.

REFERENCES

Bandura, A. *Principles of behavior modification.* New York: Holt, Rinehart & Winston, 1969.

Berne, E. Ego states in psychotherapy. *American Journal of Psychotherapy*, 1957, *11*, 293–309.

Berne, E. *Transactional analysis in psychotherapy.* New York: Grove Press, 1961.

Berne, E. *Games people play.* New York: Grove Press, 1964.

Berne, E. *Principles of group treatment.* New York: Oxford University Press, 1966.

Berne, E. *What do you say after you say hello?* New York: Grove Press, 1972.

Binder, V., Binder, A., & Rimland, B. *Modern therapies.* Englewood Cliffs, N.J.: Prentice-Hall, 1976.

Bratter, T. E. A group approach with adolescent alcoholics. In A. Bassin, T. E. Bratter, & R. L. Rachin (Eds.), *The reality therapy reader.* New York: Harper & Row, 1976.

Brown, G. *Human teaching for human learning.* New York: Viking Press, 1971.

Corey, G. *Theory and practice of counseling and psychotherapy.* Monterey, Calif.: Brooks/Cole, 1977.

English, F. T.A.'s Disney world. *Psychology Today*, 1973, *6*, 45–50, 98.

Fagan, J. Gestalt therapy introduction. *The Counseling Psychologist*, 1974, *4*(4), 3.

Glasser, W. *Mental health or mental illness?* New York: Harper & Row, 1961.

Glasser, W. *Reality therapy: A new approach to psychiatry.* New York: Harper & Row, 1965.

Glasser, W. *Schools without failure.* New York: Harper & Row, 1969.

Glasser, W. *The identity society.* New York: Harper & Row, 1972.

Glasser, W. *Positive addiction.* New York: Harper & Row, 1976. (a)

Glasser, W. A realistic approach to the young offender. In A. Bassin, T. E. Bratter, & R. L. Rachin (Eds.), *The reality therapy reader.* New York: Harper & Row, 1976. (b)

Glasser, W., & Zunin, L. Reality therapy. In R. Corsini (Ed.), *Current psychotherapies.* Itasca, Ill.: Peacock, 1973.

Goldhaber, G. M., & Goldhaber, M. B. *Transactional analysis: Principles and applications.* Boston: Allyn & Bacon, 1976.

Goulding, R., & Goulding, M. Injunctions, decisions, and redecisions. *Transactional Analysis Journal*, 1976, *6*, 57–62.

Hansen, J. C., Stevic, R. R., & Warner, R. W., Jr. *Counseling: Theory and process* (2nd ed.). Boston: Allyn & Bacon, 1977.

Harlow, H. F. The nature of love. *American Psychologist*, 1958, *13*, 1–9.

Harman, R. L. Techniques of gestalt therapy. *Professional Psychology*, 1974, *5*, 257–261.

Harper, R. A. *The new psychotherapies*. Englewood Cliffs, N.J.: Prentice-Hall, 1975.

Harris, T. A. *I'm OK–You're OK: A practical guide to transactional analysis*. New York: Harper & Row, 1969.

Hite, R. W. Transactional time structuring and interpersonal communications. In G. M. Goldhaber & M. B. Goldhaber (Eds.), *Transactional analysis: Principles and applications*. Boston: Allyn & Bacon, 1976.

Holland, G. A. Transactional analysis. In R. Corsini (Ed.), *Current psychotherapies*. Itasca, Ill.: Peacock, 1973.

James, M. *The ok boss*. Reading, Mass.: Addison-Wesley, 1975.

James, M. *Techniques in transactional analysis for psychotherapists and counselors*. Reading, Mass.: Addison-Wesley, 1977.

James, M., & Jongeward, D. *Born to win: Transactional analysis with gestalt experiments*. Reading, Mass.: Addison-Wesley, 1971.

Karpman, S. B. Fairy tales and script drama analysis. *Transactional Analysis Bulletin*, 1968, *7*, 39–43.

Kempler, W. Gestalt therapy. In R. Corsini (Ed.), *Current psychotherapies*. Itasca, Ill.: Peacock, 1973.

Koenig, P. Glasser the logician. *Psychology Today*, 1974, *7*, 66–67.

Latner, J. *The gestalt therapy book*. New York: Julian Press, 1973.

Levitsky, A., & Perls, F. S. The rules and games of gestalt therapy. In J. Fagan & L. L. Shepherd (Eds.), *Gestalt therapy now*. New York: Harper & Row, 1970.

Naranjo, C. Present-centeredness: Technique, prescription, and ideal. In J. Fagan & L. L. Shepherd (Eds.), *Gestalt therapy now*. New York: Harper & Row, 1970.

Passons, W. R. *Gestalt approaches in counseling*. New York: Holt, Rinehart & Winston, 1975.

Perls, F. S. *Ego, hunger, and aggression*. (Originally published in London: Allen & Unwin, 1947.) New York: Random House, 1969. (a)

Perls, F. S. *Gestalt therapy verbatim*. LaFayette, Calif.: Real People Press, 1969. (b)

Perls, F. S. *In and out of the garbage pail*. LaFayette, Calif.: Real People Press, 1969. (c)

Perls, F. S. *The gestalt approach and eye-witness to therapy*. Palo Alto, Calif.: Science & Behavior Books, 1973.

Perls, F. S. Gestalt therapy and human potentialities. In F. Stephenson (Ed.), *Gestalt therapy primer: Introductory readings in gestalt therapy*. Springfield, Ill.: Charles C Thomas, 1975.

Perls, F. S., Hefferline, R. F., & Goodman, P. *Gestalt therapy: Excitement and growth in the human personality*. New York: Julian Press, 1951.

Polster, E., & Polster, M. *Gestalt therapy integrated*. New York: Brunner/Mazel, 1973.

Reilly, S. Dr. Glasser without failure. *Human Behavior*, 1973, *2*, 16–23.

Shepard, M. *Fritz*. New York: Saturday Review Press, 1975.

Shepherd, I. L. Limitations and cautions in the gestalt approach. In J. Fagan and I. L. Shepherd (Eds.), *Gestalt therapy now*. New York: Harper & Row, 1970.

Smith, M. L., & Glass, G. U. Meta-analysis of psychotherapy outcome studies. *American Psychologist*, 1977, *32*, 752–760.

Spitz, R. Hospitalism, genesis of psychiatric conditions in early childhood. *Psychoanalytic Study of the Child*, 1945, *1*, 53–74.

Steiner, C. M. *Scripts people live: Transactional analysis of life scripts*. New York: Grove Press, 1974.

Wallen, R. Gestalt therapy and gestalt psychology. In J. Fagan & I. L. Shepherd (Eds.), *Gestalt therapy now*. New York: Harper & Row, 1970.

Ward, P., & Rouzer, D. L. The nature of pathological functioning from a gestalt perspective. *The Counseling Psychologist*, 1974, *4*(4), 24–27.

Yontef, G. M. Gestalt therapy: Clinical phenomenology. In V. Binder, A. Binder, & B. Rimland (Eds.), *Modern therapies*. Englewood Cliffs, N.J.: Prentice-Hall, 1976.

Chapter 8

A Summing Up

Buford Stefflre and Herbert M. Burks, Jr.

Now that we have examined eight current counseling theories and the place of such formulations in counseling settings, we may be ready to make some observations regarding their similarities and differences. An unexpected similarity may lie in the extent to which they fail to qualify as "theories" by any rigorous definition of that term. They attempt to account for relatively few of the phenomena that are observed in the counseling relationship, and their explanations are characterized by little precision and certainty. Perhaps a more accurate designation of these statements would be "counseling approaches" or "counseling positions" or "points of view about counseling." However, the value of boggling at strained terminology is not great, so theories or not, let us proceed to a consideration of their usefulness, likenesses, and uniqueness. And, as we do so, it is but honest to acknowledge a frankly relativistic bias that militates against our ever actually finding the Holy Grail, while it continues to point out promising hiding places—a bias against the question "Which theory is best?" and for such questions as "Who will feel most comfortable using which theory?" and "Which clients and problems are most apt to be helped by which procedures?" The true believer will not be comforted by such a view, but true believers find their comfort in other ways.

The substantive elements that are expected in a theory of counseling, as specified in Chapter 1, will establish the framework for a summary comparison of the theories.

THE BASIC NATURE OF PEOPLE

Although few clear philosophical or theological beliefs about the nature of people are found in the theories, some plain implications emerge. Although unstated assumptions may be difficult to clarify, several differences are apparent.

One way of categorizing these differences is found in Ford and Urban's *Systems of Psychotherapy*, in which the authors refer to conceptions of the person as a "pilot" and conceptions of the person as a "robot" (1963, pp. 595–598).

The pilot conception sees people as being capable of determining their course and assuming responsibility for their voyage. The externals of wind, reefs, and currents are secondary to the subjective decision to select and make for a port of one's own choosing. The client-centered and reality therapy positions seem to embody this view most completely, although it is also shared largely by the trait-factor, rational-emotive, and gestalt positions. Transactional analysis might also be included here, in the sense that once any undesirable effects of early parental influences have been overcome, individuals are capable of charting a wise course for themselves.

Those who are said to view people as analogous to robots believe that people only appear to be self-directing, while in fact their behavior is determined by the nature of their mechanism and perhaps by the signals emanating from a power outside themselves. Focus is on the field of forces—events, situations, other people—that call into motion those responses that occur from among all those that are available theoretically but do not occur. Theorists who subscribe to the robot view of people attend to ways in which behavior becomes acquired, selected, and generalized. Proponents of this position include those who espouse the psychodynamic and behavioral views.

Unfortunately, this neat dichotomy is mussed by further examination. The self-directing individuals described by those of the pilot persuasion appear to choose a port but in reality sail to the only available harbor that is compatible with their individual charts of the world and with their conceptions of themselves as captains. They select the choice that seems most self-enhancing, growth-producing, or autonomous, as surely as a computer calculates the sum of squares on command. It is only from our external frame of reference that they look as if they were choosing, and indeed it may *look* the same to them, for they adopt our framework in describing themselves as actors. Beck (1963, pp. 66–70) has done an excellent job of considering choice as a pseudoconcept in counseling.

Conversely, the psychodynamic and behavioral adherents, althouth they are agreed that past and present actions are determined, seem to be working toward a situation in which greater perceived choice is possible. By equipping the individual with self-control techniques and lessons in psychological map reading, they imply that the individual will become less of a robot and more of a pilot.

Not surprisingly, none of the theories has been available to unravel one of humankind's oldest, most snarled Gordian knots—free will versus determinism. They explain behavior in robot terms, while they hope for future adventures in piloting.

Another dimension to be examined in determining the nature of people is their basic trustworthiness. The client-centered, gestalt, transactional analysis, and reality therapy theorists posit a fundamentally "reliable," "constructive," and "good" person. They say that when nature takes its course, good results are obtained, for human beings are to be trusted. A gyroscopic self-enhancing mechanism enables us to do the right thing for ourselves and for our fellows. An ethical phototropism is innate in all of us, and counseling is designed to remove the deterrents to the proper functioning of this characteristic.

The psychoanalytic schools, particularly the orthodox Freudian, are less sanguine about the basic nature of the person and have less difficulty in seeing the skull beneath the flesh. Evil is seen as not only something done by people but as something natural *to* them. Counseling, then, has the function of the proper housebreaking for the part of our nature that loves to romp. One goal becomes awareness, acceptance, and control of primitive drives, so that they serve both society and the self.

Later psychoanalytic thinkers, including those of the ego-analytic and more psychodynamic orientations, as well as those of the trait-factor, rational-emotive, and behavioral positions, seem to see people as having a wider repertoire of responses and as possessing much talent both for good and for evil. This more neutral view of people suggests that they have in common with the little girl who has a little curl right in the middle of her forehead, a tendency when they are good to be very, very good, and when they are bad to be horrid. Counseling may then release potentialities of all kinds, although since it is provided within a societally defined structure, it should tend to shape behavior in a way that permits and acknowledges the presence and rights of others.

HOW BEHAVIOR IS CHANGED

Counseling is a form of purposeful intervention into the lives of clients. The purpose of the intervention includes the changing of behavior—in the broadest sense. Such change may replace a vague uneasiness regarding choice of an academic major field with greater certainty regarding the decision. It may replace panic and anxiety about the purpose of life with greater focus and acceptance. The client as well as the counselor expects differences to result from counseling, although the client's overt desire for change may be unexpressed and minimal. As a result of being concerned with changing the ways in which the client behaves, the counselor presumably will act from some theoretical base that includes a point of view about how change is best accomplished.

The client-centered theorists suggest that behavior is changed by the restructuring of the phenomenal field that takes place when an individual is placed in a setting of maximum security and minimal threat. Under such conditions, clients can reexamine their views of themselves and their world and let the self-enhancing tendencies that are inherent in them be operative. Behavior is thus changed by creating a situation where it can change itself. The counselor does not act directly on the behavior in order to change it, but establishes a climate that is conducive to the self-actualizing and at the same time societally valued behavior that is the natural expression of the individual.

The gestalt and reality therapy views are somewhat similar to the client-centered school in this regard—that is, behavior change is brought about by providing a certain kind of atmosphere or relationship that mobilizes the inner resources of the individual. In gestalt therapy, the focus is upon removing obstacles that prevent client growth, so that individuals can freely and spontaneously use their innate tendency to form and destroy gestalts in their continuing contact with the environment. In reality therapy, the client is placed in a situation of deep and genuine involvement with another person, which then frees inner resources and enables the client to give up a fantasy world of irresponsibility, and face and cope with the world of reality and responsibility instead.

The trait-and-factor theorists suggest that behavior changes when new information is made available to the client. The emphasis, then, becomes one of providing facts about the individual (largely through test information and a consideration of past events) and facts about the world of work (largely through information about occupations and the style of life accompanying them). The notion that people behave rationally leads to concern for providing facts that they will take into account in guiding their behavior. Behavior is thus changed by information and thinking.

The strongest and best-known emphasis upon behavioral change through change in thinking is undoubtedly found in Ellis' rational-emotive approach. Here it is postulated that psychological disturbances are caused by the natural tendency of the human organism to engage in irrational thinking. The remedy for irrational behavior is to reorganize the perceptions of the individual so as to produce rational and logical thinking, which then leads to rational and logical behavior.

Another highly cognitive approach is found in transactional analysis. Here, behavior change is said to result from gaining insight into how one's personality operates, including how one interacts with others, and from an understanding of one's life decisions and their consequences. Thus acquainted with these facts and understandings, the individual is equipped to effect desirable changes in his or her own life.

Behavioral theorists have perhaps the clearest and most explicit plan for changing the behavior of clients. Since maladaptive behavior is learned, counseling is therefore concerned with unlearning or relearning. The learning paradigms that are utilized appear to be of four major kinds (Krumboltz, 1966b, pp. 13–20): (1) operant learning, in which behaviors that are reinforces or "rewarded" are strengthened, and those that are not reinforced are weakened and eventually extinguished; (2) imitative learning, in which individuals are exposed to models of more adaptive behavior; (3) cognitive learning, which is focused upon verbal instructions, decision making, role playing, the use of behavioral contracts, and the appropriate timing of cues; and (4) emotional or respondent learning, which focuses upon anxiety reduction through desensitization and other counterconditioning techniques.

Similarly, the psychoanalytic theorists are clearly committed to a reduction of anxiety in the belief that more flexible and discriminating behavior will result. Counseling is needed when much energy is being used in intrapsychic conflict that is caused by forces blocking the immediate—and often socially unwise—discharge of primitive forces. Verbalization in counseling leads to the substitutive discharge of controllable quantities of energy. Pent-up feelings are thus recognized, accepted, and canalized. Behavior is changed in that it becomes less feared, blind, and restricted. A clear commitment to change behavior is a hallmark of this theoretical position.

In varying degrees, these eight counseling approaches recognize that the counselor is a change agent. Some hope to induce change by providing the client with an appropriate atmosphere for change, some by providing factual information, some by changing habits of perception and thinking, some by specifying areas and direction of change explicitly, and some by sensitizing the client to the depths of his or her nature and thus inducing change. All would seem to be committed to furthering change, although the client-centered advocate finds it more difficult to accept openly the responsibility that accompanies this function.

GOALS OF COUNSELING

The general goals of counseling are sometimes phrased at a rather high level of abstraction. Client-centered: The client is more congruent, more open to experience. Psychodynamic: "Ideally, the number of cues to which the client may respond is multiplied. Restrictions on both perception and response are minimized and are subjected eventually to an altered and increased conscious control" (Snyder, 1963, p. 28). Gestalt: The client is moved from environmental support to self-support and from personality fragmentation to integration. Transactional analysis: The client becomes autonomous, a state characterized by awareness, spontaneity, and intimacy. Reality therapy: The client learns a more effective approach to life, which is characterized by assumption of personal responsibility and development of general cognitive coping skills. Rational-emotive: The client's irrational thinking is changed to rational thinking, with resultant changes in social behavior. Trait-and-factor: The client is more capable of self-understanding and self-management, and thus has reached a higher level of personal development in the quest for areté, or excellence.

Little disagreement is evident in these statements of general goals—all seek liberation from the forces of darkness and ignorance, so that rational, flexible, and satisfying behavior can result. The fact that the model of psychological health varies somewhat for different theorists, however, is suggested by Glad, who contrasts values that are related to the psychodynamic and client-centered views by suggesting that the former strives for an individual who is an "internally organized, emotionally controlled, parent-like person" and the latter for an "internally articulated, comfortable selfhood, prizing his own individuality, and democratically understanding the individuality of others" (1959, p. 62).

When these high-level abstractions are traced to specific referents, some contradictions and confusions may eventuate. That is, when we ask the question, "How can we tell whether the client is better off than before?" we get less unanimity regarding the answer. (This question, incidentally, is not the same as "How can we tell whether counseling helped?", which is an even more difficult query that will be discussed later.)

Behavioral theorists tend to help their clients state their own goals in highly personal and idiosyncratic fashion, subject to appropriate ethical and professional considerations. At the same time, it must be recognized that behavioral *criteria* for having been "helped" are often cited by adherents of other schools as well, and that from an ultimate philosophical view these indicators may not in every case be valid (even when used by behavioral counselors). For example, behavioral manifestations of having been helped might include such diverse outcomes as educational and vocational achievement (measured by such criteria as grade-point average, attendance, staying in school, money earned, promotions received, and so on); different and more pleasing behavior as viewed by friends, teachers, spouses, and employers; establishment of vocational goals seen as more "suitable" by judges; and absence of apparent symptoms that were present previously. The difficulty with such criteria is that for any one individual, any single criterion might be completely inappropriate and misleading. For example, educational achievement in the aggregate is desirable, but perhaps Mary is investing too much time in school and not enough in other activities. Pleasing others is often desirable, but Riesman, Denny, and Glazer's (1970) concept of the consequences of extreme other-directed behavior and Fromm's (1957) concern with the "market place" aspects of some nonproductive orientations would suggest that *not* pleasing others may sometimes be more healthy. A panel of judges might well have viewed Gauguin's decision to leave a fine job in banking for the vicissitudes of art as clearly "unsuitable." Perhaps for such reasons, "goals" in many of the counseling approaches tend to be stated in mystical, sonorous ambiguities, and research tends to turn to investigations of process rather than of outcomes. The consideration of the extent to which counseling goals are achieved is perhaps at a stage parallel to that of considerations being given to the extent to which teaching goals are achieved. Judgments may need to be suspended until we know more about the practitioners' characteristics and the practitioners' behavior (process). Estimation of effectiveness must be preceded by (a) descriptions of behavior, (b) judgments and consensus regarding which behaviors manifest effectiveness, and (c) studies of the relationship among characteristics, behavior, and accepted evaluative criteria (Ryans, 1963).

ROLE OF THE COUNSELOR

The counselor, regardless of the theoretical framework involved, may be met by expectations from the client that are similar to those faced by counselors of other and differing persuasions. Clients' expectations will vary with their sophistication and current needs, but will rarely if ever be fulfilled completely as presented originally to the counselor. The expectations themselves may change as clients enlarge their views of themselves and of the presenting problems; the counselor's uniqueness will preclude his or her fulfilling precisely the preconceived role expectations; finally, the counselor's greater professional knowledge will usually result in behavior that is unforeseen and unexpected by the client. In spite of the literally unique nature of the interaction between any one counselor and any one client, there are counselor role expectations that are common to the theoretical positions considered, although the patterns of role fulfillment will vary with the counselor, the client, and the hour on the face of the sociopsychological clock that measures their changing relationship. More clearly, what the counselor does is a function of

(a) the counselor's own personality, including knowledge, skills, and needs; (b) the client as perceived by the counselor; (c) the instant in the history of their relationship in which the counselor is acting; and (d) the counselor's notion of what *should* be done, which is a value related to the counselor's total theoretical position on counseling.

Tests

Although the client may approach counseling with the expectation that tests will be prominent in the experience, the types of tests given and the centrality of their use to the total experience will vary with the orientation of the counselor. Trait-and-factor theorists are most apt to make use of cognitive measures because of their greater emphasis on this aspect of problem solving. The use of "objective and verified data" to permit greater self-understanding and exploration is a hallmark of this position, in which measures of interests and aptitudes are particularly prominent. The adaptation of the client-centered method for school, college, and other nonclinical settings in which educational-vocational concerns are frequent makes room for the use of tests, and excluding the most orthodox doctrinaire, counselors taking this stand will give tests at least occasionally. Here, however, tests are apt to come late in counseling and are rarely used routinely. In the psychodynamic approach, tests are used largely as a phase of diagnosis rather than of solution and are more generally of a projective nature. Problem checklists or surveys and self-rating forms, while not tests in the usual sense of the word, are used by rational-emotive and behavioral adherents, largely as diagnostic measures and as indicators of progress as counseling proceeds. While the remaining theories—gestalt therapy, transactional analysis, and reality therapy—do not explicitly endorse the use of tests, neither is their use specifically excluded. In reality therapy in particular, where one of the counselor's functions is to help the client establish realistic short-term and long-term goals, tests of the trait-and-factor variety would appear to be a potentially useful adjunct to counseling.

Case Histories

Although perhaps varying in completeness and focus, case histories appear central to the conception of the trait-factor, psychodynamic, and behavioral views. Especially for the latter two, they would serve to provide information to enable counselors to decide whether their skills, orientation, and institutional responsibilities are such that they should undertake to counsel the individual who has appeared for counseling. The focus of the case history is likely to be personal adjustment, and perhaps it would cover such areas as family relationships, peers, attitudes toward authority, and emotional expressiveness and appropriateness. The trait-factor orientation would seem to call for more attention to educational-vocational successes, failures, and perceptions, although other aspects of life might well be included. The other theoretical formulations leave no explicit place for case-history taking, but they do raise the problem of which clients should be dealt with, and a solution to this problem would seem to rest in part upon information gleaned from a "case history," or at the very least from certain minimal data gathered from the referral source or through intake procedures. Otherwise, such formulations would appear to (a) make no diagnosis because it might interfere with a desired structure of the counseling relationship or (b) diagnose everyone who appears for counseling as someone who could benefit from the theoretical approach that is practiced by the counselor whom the client happens to see.

Values

The once widely held belief that the counselor's position concerning values should be eunuchoid was long ago shattered effectively for many by Gardner Murphy in his 1954 address to the convention of the American Personnel and Guidance Association, in which he said, "While no one knows enough to construct an adequate philosophy of life, nevertheless, if he who offers guidance is a whole person, with real roots in human culture, he cannot help conveying directly or indirectly to every client what he himself sees and feels, and the perspective in which his own life is lived." He went on to call for an emphasis in counselors on "sound, rich, generous, and wise personality" rather than on "tricks of the trade" (Murphy, 1955, p. 8).

Today, the usually held view is that the counselor's values not only are present and are held consciously, but they constitute an important part of the counselor's armamentarium. The debate has shifted from the question, "Should counselor's values be apparent to the client?" to the question, "Should counselors have in mind values that they will attempt to implant in the client?" The affirmative position is stressed by Williamson and Biggs in their chapter about trait-factor theory. Other positions that clearly endorse the open expression of the counselor's values as an aid to the therapeutic process are the rational-emotive and reality therapy approaches. The behavioral approaches have also acknowledged the influence of the counselor's values. Krumboltz (1966a, p. 154), for example, emphasizes that before agreeing to help a client work toward a particular goal, it should first be determined that the goal is compatible with the counselor's values (although not necessarily identical to them). Value issues are not discussed explicitly by the psychodynamic, gestalt, or transactional analysis schools, although in view of the heavily confrontive nature of these approaches, it would seem difficult for such counselors not to reveal some of their values.

A persuasive case against counselor neutrality toward values is made by Samler, who writes:

> One can list a set of troubles, the therapies of choice and their underlying orientation:
> For the demanding and infantile—assumption of responsibility;
> For the vocationally disoriented—assumption of a working role congruent with the picture the client will develop of himself;
> For the guilt ridden—tolerance for himself and life's reality;
> For the unloved and unloving—self acceptance and kindliness;
> For the achievement and power ridden—appreciation of the rich resources in human beings;
> For the highly controlling—reduction of anxiety and a more trusting and optimistic outlook (1960).

The negative position on the implanting of values has come to be associated with the client-centered counselor and is characterized by a belief that the client must freely accept or reject the moral and ethical values of the counselor, who would leave to such social institutions as the church, the family, and the school the teaching of values (Patterson, 1958; Arbuckle, 1970).

Because there is agreement that the counselor's intervention is a stimulus that affects the client and because the nature of the intervention must be a consequence of the counselor's value system, some rapproachement would seem possible. The apparent difference may lie in the client-centered counselor's lesser reliance on societally constructed signposts in finding viable values. That is, the value communicated may be a consequence and a meriting of personal standards to a greater extent than is true with other theories placing greater (although, of course, not exclusive) reliance on social consensus. If so, it follows that recognition must be given to the fact that personal responsibility, self-determination, and freedom to reject the counselor's values are themselves a value commitment, and the counselor's behavior may be designed to inculcate this position in the client. Strickland (1972) has presented a strategy, couched in client-centered terminology, for helping clients to deal with their values in the counseling situation. A four-step process of synthesizing is presented in which clients (1) become aware of their values and devise a plan for self-development; (2) put their plan into action, testing their values and opportunities; (3) receive feedback from their actions; and (4) reevaluate their resulting self-image and begin the synthesizing process again if necessary.

Finally, Gladstein (1972) suggests a set of guidelines that counselors can use to help resolve the values dilemma. First, it should be determined whether the work setting requires that the counselor be responsive primarily to society's needs. Second, the level of maturity of clients and the kinds of value-laden issues or problems that occur most frequently in that setting should be identified. Third, the counselor should examine carefully his or her assumptions about the basic nature of people. Answers to such questions should provide useful guidelines for counselor behavior.

Group Procedures

All the theoretical positions have some history of group counseling activity. The trait-and-factor position has been used in high school classes—variously labeled "occupations," "vocational problems," or "orientation"—that are designed to teach about aptitudes and occupations. Analytically oriented group therapy, behavioral counseling, and client-centered therapy provide models for group counseling, sometimes supplemented by individual sessions. In rational-emotive therapy, frequently the same client is seen both individually and in a group setting as an ongoing part of treatment. In the "newer approaches"—gestalt therapy, transactional analysis, and reality therapy—group procedures are the primary medium for treatment, although in gestalt therapy the counselor usually deals largely with one individual at a time, in the presence of other group members.

Conditioning plays a large part in the rationale for group counseling. Clients are enabled to act out new ways of behaving, and they achieve reinforcement from the other group members. They learn that it is possible to say things that they had suppressed previously, to think thoughts that they had rejected previously, and to perform in new ways, with support from group members and continued success in maintaining their regard. While obvious modifications are called for in moving from an individual to a group procedure, the theoretical framework would seem to hold and to provide clues for the counselor's behavior.

SUPPORTIVE EVIDENCE

In earlier chapters that were devoted to specific theories, the reader will have noted occasional references to supporting evidence. Some of the theories have produced more research than others. The client-centered, behavioral, trait-factor, and rational-emotive approaches appear to have generated more empirical support, while the psychodynamic and reality therapy positions have been somewhat less productive in this regard. Transactional analysis, while its postulates would appear to be readily testable, has produced very little formal research. Gestalt therapy, despite its strong appeal to many and the numerous case examples found in its literature, seems devoid of empirical supporting evidence. While counselors of all persuasions rely heavily in their daily work upon their own observations and upon the client's verbal report as indices of progress or success, there seems to be little evidence of any other kind for the effectiveness of the gestalt position.

It has been questioned, of course, whether counseling and psychotherapy— whatever the variety—have any desirable effects whatsoever. Some time ago, Eysenck (1961) concluded after a review of the literature on the effects of psychotherapy that, with the possible exception of treatments of the behavioral type, there was no evidence that people get better as a result of therapy. There is some fairly recent evidence, however, that questions such a gloomy conclusion. Luborsky, Singer, and Luborsky (1975), who examined data from 25 years of research on the outcomes of psychotherapy, conclude that most forms of psychotherapy have produced constructive changes in clients, and that these changes are usually greater than those that are seen among clients in control groups. In the same vein, Glass (1976), who used a complex methodology termed "meta-analysis" for integrating the findings of psychotherapy outcomes in nearly 400 studies involving psychodynamic, client-centered, behavior modification, and rational-emotive approaches, concludes that the average client improved substantially across therapies in comparison with control group clients. At the same time, he found no significant differences among the various theoretical orientations in terms of their relative effectiveness. A similar conclusion has been reached by Sloane, Staples, Cristol, Yorkston, and Whipple (1975), who found no differences in effectiveness between insight therapy and behavior therapy in reducing the presenting symptoms of clients, although clients in both approaches improved more than those assigned to a waiting period.

It may be more productive, therefore, to lay aside—at least temporarily— the question of whether counseling and psychotherapy, in the generic sense, can "help" clients, or whether this or that theoretical approach is uniformly, or even generally, better than another. As Gomes-Schwartz, Hadley, and Strupp (1978) have pointed out on the basis of their extensive review of the literature, the most important questions at present and in the coming years may well be concerned with what kinds of changes can be expected in clients, and under what conditions. "Conditions" would include such counselor characteristics as skills and techniques, as well as the attitudes and expectations of clients.

In order to answer such questions, changes in counseling research are needed. Problems of methodology and research design abound. Deficiencies in counseling research have been pointed out, and remedies proposed by a number of commentators—Patterson (1963), Whiteley (1967), Thoresen (1969), and Goldman (1976), to name a few. The perceptive analysis and recommendations by Patterson are still timely:

   1 Consideration must be given to the goals and objectives of counseling and guidance services and to the criteria relevant to the attainment of these goals and objectives developed and used in future studies.
   2 Attention must be given to specifying and to defining the nature of the treatment variable in order that studies may be replicated and in order that one may know to what variable what results may be attributed. Study of specific, defined methods or services in terms of specific criteria will lead to knowledge of what leads to what and will enable investigators to select methods or approaches that will lead to desired criteria or outcomes.
   3 An adequate test of the effects of counseling, especially when criteria of personality changes are used, must provide counseling services that are sufficiently extensive and intensive to provide realistic expectations for such changes. It is unreasonable to expect superficial one-interview counseling to have such effects.
   4 Any adequate test of the influences or effect of counseling must be based upon the use of counselors who are trained and experienced and who have competence in the methods or approaches they use.
   5 Although it is of interest to study the effects of counseling on unmotivated clients or on clients who do not apply or volunteer for counseling, the primary concern is with individuals who are interested in or desirous of receiving counseling. Studies using involuntary clients are not a test of the effects of counseling in a normal counseling situation.
   6 Long-term follow-up is necessary to ascertain the nature and persistence of effects. In some instances, there are delayed effects; in others, there may be superficial effects immediately following counseling which will not persist. Controlled experiments which meet these requirements are difficult and expensive to conduct, not only in terms of experimental design and controls, but also in terms of time, including the duration of the experiment and the follow-up. It would appear that, as in other areas of research, an adequate study requires more than the resources of a single investigator. The time is ripe for an extensive, long-term investigation with adequate financial support, in which existing knowledge may be applied to the conduct of meaningful research on the effects of counseling and guidance services (1963, p. 222).

Goldman (1976, pp. 543–551), a more recent critic, deplores what he considers to be the overreliance of counseling researchers upon research models that have been borrowed from the physical sciences. He sees an overemphasis upon precision and control, because the counseling process and its participants do not lend themselves to exact measurement. On a more positive note, Goldman cites seven promising developments and trends: (1) macroscopic or broad-scale study of the total behavior of persons, as opposed to "microscopic" examination of bits and pieces of behavior; (2) field-based as opposed to laboratory-based research; (3) use of the individual person as the unit of investigation, as in the intensive case study design; (4) the establishment of a contractual arrangement between the researcher and the subject, in order to minimize spurious experimenter effects and to encourage the open and informed collaboration of the subject; (5) greater attention to the evaluation of ongoing programs in field settings, so that counselors can do a better job of evaluating the effects of techniques used in their work; (6) regarding the investigator as an instrument of research— calibrating and certifying the researcher as a valid research instrument—and then placing greater trust in the researcher's observations and inferences; and (7) anticipating carefully the intended use of the research—designing the study with users in mind, involving them in the study as much as possible, and training them in the interpretation and use of the results of the study.

Krumboltz has posed the basic question to be answered by all counseling researchers: "What will counselors do differently if the results of this research come out one way rather than another?" (1967, p. 191). Obviously, counseling research should have relevance for counseling practice. Yet, as Stefflre (1963) has pointed out, if we did in the name of counseling only those things that research has proved to be worth doing, we would have a good deal of free time on our hands.

Present knowledge in counseling can be divided into three categories. There is a very small category of knowledge that we know to be true as a result of sound research evidence. There is an extremely large category of "knowledge" that we "know" from common sense or from scholastic revelation; such knowledge may be said to be a part of the "conventional wisdom." Finally, there is a category of knowledge, which is growing rapidly, that indicates what we do not know! Well-designed research in counseling typically results in transferring "knowledge" from the second category to the third one. The most common conclusion that is reached as a consequence of carefully designed research in counseling is the verdict "Not proved."

To be more specific with regard to our present situation, let us take a look at the research that deals with the value of counseling. In reviewing such research, Stefflre and Matheny, in the *Encyclopedia of Educational Research*, state that:

> The following observations appear justified: (1) evidence that counseling is clearly superior to the unspecified happenstances of life in the treatment of complex personality problems remains to be demonstrated; (2) counseling appears to bring about changes in the self concept, as measured by Q-sorts, but accompanying behavioral changes have frequently not been shown; (3) counseling has sometimes proved valuable in promoting satisfactory occupational selection and adjustment, but it remains to be shown that it is valuable in improving academic achievement; (4) many studies

have failed to obtain positive results either because their goals were too ambitious or because their treatments were too brief; and (5) variation among rates of improvement claimed by different theoretical orientations is probably related to the kind of client problems characteristically dealt with by a given orientation and the degree of specificity employed by the orientation in the establishment of goals (1969, p. 263).

CRUCIAL DETERMINANTS

The practical consequences of commitment to a given theoretical position continue to be somewhat unclear. Relevant studies are concerned with frankly psychotherapeutic activity, and may not be generalizable to counseling. In an important early study, Fiedler (1950) found that experienced psychoanalytic, client-centered, and Adlerian therapists tended to resemble one another in their behavior more than experienced therapists of any one of these orientations resembled inexperienced therapists of the same orientation.

Later factor-analytic studies, however, have tended to dispute Fiedler's conclusions. Sundland and Barker (1962) compared therapists of the Freudian, Sullivanian, and client-centered positions and found that differences among the therapists' responses were accounted for by their theoretical orientation rather than by their level of experience. McNair and Lorr (1964) postulated three essential dimensions of therapeutic practice—psychoanalytic, impersonal versus personal, and directive techniques. A factor analysis of the data that had been collected from an extensive sample of psychotherapists confirmed the presence of the three postulated dimensions. Pattern scores of therapists on the three factors were significantly related to their profession, to their sex, and to their amount of personal psychotherapy, but not to their level of experience. Finally, Wallach and Strupp (1964) made a comparison among orthodox Freudian, general psychoanalytic, Sullivanian, and client-centered therapists and found significant differences in terms of theoretical orientation for three of the four factors studied. No significant relationships were found between any of the factors and amount of experience.

Patterson (1973, p. 528) has attempted to reconcile the findings of these later studies with those of Fiedler's earlier research. He points out that the items used in the Fiedler study were concerned with the importance of the counseling relationship, and therefore that no differences among theoretical orientations should have been expected in response to those items. In Sundland and Barker's study, however, items upon which therapists agreed were deleted and only those items that were controversial were retained. Under those conditions, it is not surprising that differentiation on the basis of theoretical orientation occurred. He concludes, therefore, that while therapists of the different orientations surveyed do differ on many matters, they are of one mind on the importance of the relationship. Patterson further points out that behavioral practitioners were not sampled in any of these studies and speculates that if they had been included, they would probably have minimized the importance of the relationship. This hypothesis could, of course, be tested by further research that incorporates be-

haviorists along with those of other orientations. At least some behavioral practitioners have placed considerable emphasis upon the importance of the relationship, although they consider it a foundation upon which other procedures and
techniques are to be built, rather than as the essence of therapy itself (Krumboltz,
1966b, pp. 7–8).

Perhaps the present state of research on the relationship between theoretical
orientation and therapist behavior has been summed up most aptly by Gomes-
Schwartz, Hadley, and Strupp, who concluded in their review of the literature that:

> There is reasonable evidence to suggest that therapists of differing orientations behave
> in ways that are consistent with their theoretical training. However, it remains to be
> demonstrated that what the therapist does has an impact over and above the effects
> of a supportive relationship (which therapists of varying orientations may be capable
> of providing) (1978, p. 445).

COMMON ELEMENTS

At the risk of some violation of niceties within the eight schools of thought, let
us search for some common elements as a corrective against the possible mag-
nification of differences. This consideration does not constitute a synthesis but
rather a recognition that "counseling," of whatever style, is apt to use bricks that
are basic and solid regardless of the aesthetic principles advanced by the architect.
Ten facets of counseling that seem both crucial and common will determine the
structure of our examination of elements in common.

1 Flexibility

Although counseling procedures are seen most clearly in extremes approaching
caricature, they are apt to be used by any one counselor along several continua—
from active to passive, directive to compliant, cognitive to affective, and so on.
The hallmark of the experienced counselor seems to be the ability to fit one's
style to the unique character of the client and of the relationship at any one time.
All schools imply that some variation in style is advisable, although they differ
in their emphasis on this matter. No theory advocates fitting a client to a mold; all
presuppose reasonable flexibility in the application of theoretical principles.

2 Motivation

While it is not always made explicit, it would seem that the several theories are
agreed that clients who want counseling are more apt to profit from it than those
who do not. The unmotivated client may be dealt with, but the likelihood of success is felt to be minimal. The school, agency, or other institution that drags the
reluctant client to the counselor's door will find little optimism in the counselor's
assessment of his or her chances of being helpful. Motivation for counseling would
appear to be a necessary condition for behavior change and counseling "success."
Research that has not taken this crucial variable into account is open to much
criticism.

3 Relationship

From time to time, one theory or another tries to claim the concept of "relationship" as its personal discovery, and all are agreed that it is a most important element. Some might say it *is* counseling; all would agree that it plays a crucial role in counseling. The concept includes, but goes beyond, the notion of rapport to take in (a) improved interpersonal relationships as a goal of counseling, (b) practice in relating to another person during the interview, and (c) relationship as the base upon which the entire structure of counseling is built. To attempt to create a relationship is to give an earnest of caring; to establish a relationship is to make counseling possible; to continue a relationship is to permit growth and change.

4 Respect

Again, respect for the individuality, humanness, and wonderful complexity of the client is shared by all counselors. This respect for the other grows with self-respect and an appreciation of the command to love others as you love yourself. For the counselor to appreciate the client, it is first necessary to appreciate oneself so that out of this self-acceptance, out of this deep understanding of one's own virtues and weaknesses, and out of the recognition and control of one's own needs, come the skill, the wit, and the love to respect another in a way that makes counseling result in growth.

5 Communication

Whether through words or nonverbal cues, through symbolizations or plain speaking, through physical arrangements or limited time, the counselor and client must communicate, and all eight theories are concerned with this problem. The sensitivity and objectivity of the counselor will greatly determine the extent and accuracy of communication. If the counselor—with a "third ear"—can hear and understand the story of the client's personal world, if the counselor can help find a Rosetta stone to aid in the translation of the client's private language and symbols, and if the counselor can detect the presence and meaning of nuances of tone, word choice, and bodily gestures, then communication and counseling become possible. The greatest sensitivity we need as counselors, however, may be that reserved for our self-understanding. Why do we press testing onto the client—or alternately—blind ourselves to the service it may sometimes perform? Does our silence mean support, approval, or anxiety? Is our restraint in the face of client provocation the result of maturity shown by the control of impulses in the interests of work to be done, or is it the result of that narcissism, that higher smugness, which is expressed as an angelic air of patience and forbearance that has been called the vocational disease of counseling (Wyatt, 1948)?

Sensitivity to self and sensitivity to the client are necessary conditions for the kind of communication required in counseling.

6 Learning

Although the psychodynamic adherents may tend to be skittish about the use of the term, the concept of learning is present in all eight theoretical formulations.

Basically, clients learn more about themselves and their world and, therefore, perform better. The explanation of why they learn may vary from the client-centered, reality, and gestalt emphasis upon the climate for learning, to the trait-and-factor, rational-emotive, transactional analysis, and behavioral belief in the value of the structured lesson and plan. The fact that this learning has so often defied measurement would seem to be related to differences in the subjects being taught (for example, information or release), in teachers (counselors), in readiness (motivation and maturity), and in the tests (types of outcome) used to measure the results of teaching (counseling). However, all counselors face and answer, openly or covertly, the basic pedagogic question, "What do I want the client to learn?" (Sometimes, of course, it is expressed—"How do I want the client to be different after counseling?" or "What is the justification and purpose of my intervention into the client's life?")

7 Direction

Although it once served as a psychological litmus paper that was thought capable of differentiating types of counseling clearly, the concept of direction of the client by the counselor is now seen more frequently as an omnipresent aspect of all counseling. All but the client-centered group have clearly recognized and consciously used their capacity for direction. Client-centered counselors have, on the contrary, largely resisted the view that their presence or behavior directs the client. (The term "nondirective," as noted in a previous chapter, was originally used to label the point of view in which the client-centered roots are found.) The consideration of the counselor's responses as a stimulus in a conditioning sequence has resulted in an extensive literature that has long since demonstrated that such responses as "mmm-hmm" or "I see" do reinforce positively the making of affective statements (Krasner, 1958).

Concern now shifts from the presence or absence of direction to the extent, method, and purpose of direction. Some direction may be explicit and clear (trait-and-factor, behavioral, rational-emotive, transactional, reality, and perhaps gestalt), some subtle and tentative (psychodynamic), and some intuitive and largely unrecognized (client-centered), but most would agree that it is always present. Perhaps the struggle should shift to the arena of social direction. Perhaps we should ask—does the counselor direct the client's attention to societally established (external) or personally derived (internal) signposts? Answers to such a question result in much overlapping among the theories (for like most dichotomies, this one is unstable), but they direct the dialogue to a more meaningful level of disagreement.

8 Support

The presence, interest, and activity of the counselor are seen by theorists of all schools as supporting the client. The counselor gives the client support by acting out such messages as "You are deserving of my time and concern," "We can talk and by doing so can 'touch' and teach each other," and "You will be able to cope with the decisions, crises, and problems facing you." The openness and form of the support would be likely to vary with the personality of the counselor and with the perceived needs of the client, as well as with the moment of interaction, more than with the theoretical orientation of the counselor. By cultural definition, the counselor is one who provides support, but this may be done either unconsciously and incidentally or deliberately and directly.

9 Rewards

The counselor rewards clients for their presence and for some of their behavior. (For the argument that the counselor rewards all the client's behavior equally, or perhaps not at all, as suggested by some client-centered practitioners—see "Direction," number 7 above). Such consequences may go beyond support as discussed in the previous section, to the kind of conditioning mentioned previously. An aspect of reward that is sometimes overlooked, however, is the reward received by the counselor from the client (Stewart, Winborn, Johnson, Burks, & Engelkes, 1978, p. 245). If as counselors we do not understand the basis in our own need system for the rewards we feel, we may be in danger of exploiting the client out of insatiable psychic greed. If we refuse to recognize the limitations of our training and role and therefore undertake to counsel those whose needs are beyond our training, we have probably failed to be significantly cognizant of the nature of the rewards that have "hooked" us.

All eight theories have room in them for an explanation of the mutually rewarding nature of the interaction between the counselor and client, although the psychodynamic position is the most explicit about the genesis, dangers, and function of this reward. The superior status of the counselor and of the counseling relationship is so unmistakable that the client would have to be completely outside our culture not to be affected by it. This status is active in direction, support, and reward. It cannot be cast off—it can only be used consciously, neutralized partially, or denied blindly.

10 Purposes

The discussions of counseling goals show us many common elements among the approaches with regard to this dimension of counseling. All seek free, informed, responsible persons who are conscious of themselves—their strengths and weaknesses, their sickness and health—and are capable of viewing the world unblinking and unafraid; capable, too, of making decisions for themselves, in harmony with their unique natures and with at least minimal societal requirements.

CONCLUSION

Beginning counselors may need to remind themselves that, although theories are best separated by concentrating upon their differences, successful counseling is best accomplished by attending to their similarities. What these theories have in common needs to be learned and put into practice before fine doctrinal disputes distract us from the core activity, which is helping the client to find identity in a culture that, like the human condition itself, is both baffling and beautiful.

Theory is needed to help us conceptualize the interrelationship of data, to help us temper intuition and rigidity, and to help us examine the efficacy of our actions. Reasonable freedom from theory is also needed if we are to overcome the smugness of the "in" counselor, if we are to free the individual to add himself or herself to the counseling equation, and if we are to be capable of making that higher synthesis that results in better and more inclusive theories. The learning of theory may be likened to the learning of the descriptive rules of grammar. Only after theories are known, understood, examined, and evaluated may they be breached safely.

BIBLIOGRAPHY

Arbuckle, D. S. *Counseling: Philosophy, theory, and practice* (2nd ed.). Boston: Allyn & Bacon, 1970.

Beck, C. E. *Philosophical foundations of guidance.* Englewood Cliffs, N.J.: Prentice-Hall, 1963.

Eysenck, H. J. The effects of psychotherapy. In H. J. Eysenck (Ed.), *Handbook of abnormal psychology.* New York: Basic Books, 1961.

Fiedler, F. E. A comparison of therapeutic relationships in psychoanalytic, non-directive and Adlerian therapy. *Journal of Consulting Psychology*, 1950, *14*, 436–445.

Ford, D. H., & Urban, H. B. *Systems of psychotherapy: A comparative study.* New York: Wiley, 1963.

Fromm, E. Man is not a thing. *Saturday Review*, March 1957, 9–11.

Glad, D. D. *Operational values in psychotherapy: A conceptual framework of interpersonality.* New York: Oxford University Press, 1959.

Gladstein, G. A. Counselor role and client values. *Counseling and Values*, 1972, *16*, 187–191.

Glass, G. V. Primary, secondary, and meta-analysis of research. *Educational Researcher*, 1976, *5*(10), 3–8.

Goldman, L. A revolution in counseling research. *Journal of Counseling Psychology*, 1976, *23*, 543–552.

Gomes-Schwartz, B., Hadley, S. W., & Strupp, H. H. Individual psychotherapy and behavior therapy. *Annual Review of Psychology*, 1978, *29*, 435–471.

Jahoda, M. *Current concepts of positive mental health.* New York: Basic Books, 1958.

Krasner, L. Studies of the conditioning of verbal behavior. *Psychological Bulletin*, 1958, *55*, 148–170.

Krumboltz, J. D. Behavioral goals for counseling. *Journal of Counseling Psychology*, 1966, *13*, 153–159. (a)

Krumboltz, J. D. (Ed.) *Revolution in counseling: Implications of behavioral science.* Boston: Houghton Mifflin, 1966. (b)

Krumboltz, J. D. Future directions for counseling research. In J. M. Whiteley (Ed.), *Research in counseling: Evaluation and refocus.* Columbus, Ohio: Merrill, 1967.

Luborsky, L. B., Singer, B., & Luborsky, L. Comparative studies of psychotherapies: Is it true that "everyone has won and all must have prizes"? *Archives of General Psychiatry*, 1975, *32*, 995–1008.

McNair, D. M., & Lorr, M. An analysis of professed psychotherapeutic techniques. *Journal of Consulting Psychology*, 1964, *28*, 265–271.

Murphy, G. The cultural context of guidance. *Personnel and Guidance Journal*, 1955, *34*, 4–9.

Patterson, C. H. The place of values in counseling and psychotherapy. *Journal of Counseling Psychology*, 1958, *5*, 216–223.

Patterson, C. H. Program evaluation. *Review of Educational Research*, 1963, *33*, 214–224.

Patterson, C. H. *Theories of counseling and psychotherapy* (2nd ed.). New York: Harper & Row, 1973.

Riesman, D., Denney, R., & Glazer, N. *The lonely crowd: A study of the changing American character*. New Haven, Conn.: Yale University Press, 1970.

Ryans, D. G. Assessment of teacher behavior and instruction. *Review of Educational Research*, 1963, *33*, 415–441.

Samler, J. Change in values: A goal in counseling. *Journal of Counseling Psychology*, 1960, *7*, 32–39.

Sloane, R. B., Staples, F. R., Cristol, A. H., Yorkston, N. J., & Whipple, K. *Psychotherapy versus behavior therapy*. Cambridge, Mass.: Harvard University Press, 1975.

Snyder, B. R. Student stress. In T. F. Lunsford (Ed.), *The study of campus cultures*. Boulder, Colo.: Western Interstate Commission for Higher Education, 1963.

Stefflre, B. Research in guidance: Horizons for the future. *Theory into Practice*, 1963, *2*, 44–50.

Stefflre, B., & Matheny, K. Counseling theory. In R. L. Ebel (Ed.), *Encyclopedia of educational research* (4th ed.). New York: Macmillan, 1969.

Stewart, N. R., Winborn, B. B., Johnson, R. G., Burks, H. M., Jr., & Engelkes, J. R. *Systematic counseling*. Englewood Cliffs, N.J.: Prentice-Hall, 1978.

Strickland, B. A rationale and model for changing values in helping relationships. *Counseling and Values*, 1972, *16*, 202–208.

Sundland, D. M., & Barker, E. N. The orientations of psychotherapists. *Journal of Consulting Psychology*, 1962, *26*, 201–212.

Thoresen, C. E. Relevance and research in counseling. *Review of Educational Research*, 1969, *39*, 263–281.

Wallach, M. S., & Strupp, H. H. Dimensions of psychotherapists' activity. *Journal of Consulting Psychology*, 1964, *28*, 120–125.

Whiteley, J. M. (Ed.) *Research in counseling: Evaluation and refocus*. Columbus, Ohio: Merrill, 1967.

Wyatt, F. The self-experience of the psychotherapist. *Journal of Consulting Psychology*, 1948, *12*, 83–87.

Name Index

Subject Index

Abreaction, 194
Achievement of students in trait-factor
    counseling, 110–113
  over- and underachievement, 111–112
Achievement tests, 95
Actualizing tendency, 33, 36–38, 81
    (*See also* Self-actualization)
Adolescence, Freudian concept, 153
Adult (in transactional analysis), 276, 281–282,
    284, 287–289, 292
Adulthood, Freudian concept, 153–154
Allport-Vernon-Lindzey Study of Values, 118,
    119
Ambiguity, concept, 20
Ambivalence, 148
American Psychological Association, Division
    of Counseling Psychology, The Current
    Status of Counseling Psychology, 13, 16, 18,
    25
American Psychological Association,
    *Standards for Educational and
    Psychological Tests and Manuals,* 105,
    130
Analytically oriented counseling (*see*
    Psychoanalytic method)
Anxiety:
  in client-centered theory, 54
    defense against, 46–47
  in Freudian theory, 154–155, 169
    dreams, 163
  in rational-emotive therapy, 181
    systematic desensitization for, 239–242
Aptitude tests, 95, 98
Areté, concept, 101, 321
Army Alpha Test, 91, 95
Army Beta Test, 91, 95
Awareness in gestalt therapy, 269
  lack of, 265–266

Behavior:
  changing, counseling systems compared,
    319–321
  Freudian theory on, 137–138
  in trait-factor theory, 96–99
    covariance and clusters, 98
Behavior modification:
  goals in counseling, 49
  and rational-emotive therapy, 173, 178
  transactional analysis in, 294
Behavioral counseling, 220–253
  classical (respondent) conditioning, 225–226
  cognitive-behavioral techniques, 247–249
  cognitive methods, 173–174
  compared with other theories, 318, 320–336,
    332
  conceptual models, 225
  goals, 232–233, 235–236
  history of, 220–222
  learning concepts, 228–232
    discrimination, 231
    extinction, 231, 248
    generalization, 231
    individualized, 237–238
    punishment, 230
    reinforcement, 228–230, 248
    shaping, 232
    vicarious processes, 232
  major features, 223–224
    educational process, 223
    experimental methodology, 223
    individually tailored techniques, 223
    scientific methodology, 224
  modeling, 227, 228, 242–245, 248
  multiple learning, 237
  normality, concept, 224–225
  operant (instrumental) conditioning,
    226–227